— Sixth Edition —

Three Genres
The Writing of Poetry, Fiction, and Drama

STEPHEN MINOT
University of California, Riverside

PRENTICE HALL   Upper Saddle River, New Jersey   07458

Library of Congress Cataloging-in-Publication Data

Minot, Stephen.
  Three genres : the writing of poetry, fiction, and drama / Stephen
Minot.—6th ed.
    p.   cm.
  Includes biographical references and index.
  ISBN 0-13-491929-7
  1. Creative writing.   I. Title.
PN145.M5   1998
808'.02—dc21   92-20256
                                                              CIP

Acquisition editor: Maggie Barbieri
Editorial/production supervision
  and interior design: Shelly Kupperman
Buyer: Mary Ann Gloriande
Cover design: Bruce Kenselaar
Cover credit: "Titre Emmêler IV," monoprint "19¹/₂ × 26"
  by Pamela Moore, NY, NY.

The book was set 10/12 Palatino by Automated Composition Service, Inc.
The book was printed and bound by Courier-Westford, Inc.
The cover was printed by Phoenix.

Copyright acknowledgments appear on pages 399–402,
which constitute an extension of the copyright page.

Printed in the United States of America

10 9 8 7 6 5 4 3 2 1

ISBN 0-13-491929-7

To Ginny—
with continued gratitude
and affection

CONTENTS

PREFACE FOR STUDENTS

What Kind of Writer Are You?

People write poetry, fiction, and drama for many different reasons. Here are three of the most common:

1. Many find that the best way to learn about creative writing is to write it. Just as those who have played a particular sport become better spectators, and those who play an instrument listen to music with greater awareness and pleasure, those who have written poems, short stories, or plays read with a special understanding and appreciation. They see more in what they read, and as a result they enjoy reading more. Reading is a resource that stays with them for life.

2. For others, writing is in itself a rewarding avocation. A great majority of those in creative writing classes or adult workshops don't plan to make writing their primary vocation. They are like those who play a musical instrument seriously but without any intention of joining the Boston Symphony. They devote time to improving their skills, they take part in workshop groups, they may publish from time to time; but writing remains an avocation, not a vocation.

3. For a smaller group, writing has become a central commitment. It is not an easy route. Those who are college students may have to slight other courses. When they graduate, they will probably have to enter another field to earn enough to eat and pay the rent. In spite of these challenges, they identify themselves as *poet*, *writer*, or *dramatist*. To support this notion, they must allot a portion of each day to reading contemporary fiction, poetry, or drama in a close, professional way. They attend readings and conferences, but most important, they write regularly. In short, they are immersed in a particular genre—not just their own work but the best of what is being published as well.

Which group do you fall into? If you are just beginning, you may well be in a fourth category: those who are testing the field. They aren't sure just how important writing may become in their lives, but they know that they are not going to find out simply by wondering. They are determined not to become one of those wistfully passive adults who keep saying, "I've always wanted to write."

It may be that you will begin with high expectations and will discover after graduation that you are really a reader rather than a writer. But you will have lost nothing because you will have become a far more perceptive reader than you were before. Or perhaps you will begin with a commitment to one genre and find that your real talent and interest lie in another. Writers, unlike ballet dancers and atomic physicists, don't have to start early and stay on a single track. In writing, anything is possible at any stage and at any age. There is no way of predicting how much talent and commitment will develop until you make an initial effort.

What This Textbook Can't Do

Just reading this textbook won't make you a writer. It will serve as your guide, but it won't substitute for the effort of actually writing poetry, fiction, and drama. There is a fundamental difference between *content* texts such as those in history, philosophy, and political science and *process* texts such as those in the creative and performing arts. *Process* involves learning by doing. *Doing* in this case means writing.

Second, this textbook will not persuade you that every step of the way will be fun. Workshop sessions are often the most enjoyable classes on campus, but producing good writing takes effort. What this text can do is make that effort more rewarding, and it will certainly speed the process of development.

How to Get the Most from This Text

- In the poetry section, spend extra time on Chapter 2, "Read These Poems!" The rather strident title stresses how important this chapter is. It consists of 44 poems carefully selected to illustrate the rich variety of poetric approaches available to you. Almost every one will be used to illustrate poetic techniques in the chapters that follow. Don't just read this chapter, study the poems carefully in relatively short, concentrated sessions.

- There are five stories in the fiction section and three plays in the drama section. Allow extra time for them just as you did for the poems in Chapter 2. The analysis of literary concepts will seem abstract and confusing unless you can apply them to specific works. Review these selections frequently.

- Try to use the terms introduced in this text accurately and often. Some will be new to you, but when you start to use them in discussions, they will soon become familiar and helpful. They will help you to be precise in discussing literary works.

- If some section seems unclear or puzzling, get help. Talk it over with your teacher or someone else using the text. Or e-mail me at *s.minot@juno.com.*

- Mark up your book with legible, helpful marginal notes. Link the various concepts and approaches with works you have read. Underline passages that are important. Tests have shown that those who take reading notes improve their comprehension. They convert passive reading into active involvement.

All this will take you a little more time than it would simply to read a textbook from beginning to end. But creative writing is not a skill that can be mastered in ten easy steps. It is a slow process of growth—growth both in your understanding of what literature has to offer and in your ability to create new work with your own individual stamp.

Stephen Minot

PREFACE FOR TEACHERS

Why a New Edition?

A sixth edition? After the first five, what is there left to change? As a cynical friend asked, "Still can't get it right after 32 years?"

As a fellow teacher, I know how annoying a new edition can be. Those familiar marginal notes lost, those favorite works dropped for no good reason, old syllabi made obsolete. And from the writer's point of view, a new edition means two years of work, much of it tedious.

For all that, there are justifications. First, although excellent literature is timeless, students are not. Their needs and expectations change. A work that draws them into the world of literature one decade will strike students in the next educational "generation" as naive or pedestrian. Yes, we who are involved with literature do proselytize. We want to use works that will attract today's students and will still give them enough complexity to stretch their abilities.

Second, analysis and examples that seem highly effective in manuscript don't always fare as well as expected when tested in many classrooms. This text has now been adopted in all 50 states, in a great variety of institutions. There are good reasons for every change in each edition, but the ultimate test is in a multitude of classrooms. I depend on teacher response.

Third, while the text is new for each succeeding class of students, it becomes more than familiar for those of us who use it regularly. We as teachers need fresh examples, fresh approaches to the art of writing.

The Mechanics of a New Edition

Putting out a new edition is a two-year process, at best. The first step is to elicit feedback. Four formal critiques from teachers are commissioned by the publisher. These are anonymous and represent different types of schools in different sections of the country. In addition, I maintain a file of comments I have received. Opinions vary, of course, and sometimes contradict each other directly. The diagram of the relationship between similes, metaphors, and symbols, for example (page 64), has just as many enthusiasts as detractors! Ultimately I have to make a series of judgments.

The next stage is deciding on the poems, stories, and plays that will serve as illustrations. This means securing permissions. In many cases, even works that are retained have to be renegotiated. Some agents and certain publishers are unrealistic about what is a fair permission fee. Bargaining is a slow and frustrating process. It takes six months at best.

Then comes the actual writing. By revising about one-third of the text and replacing one-third of the examples, I try to strike a balance between change and continuity. At best, this takes another six months.

It takes almost a full year from the time the completed manuscript is delivered to the publisher to the time the actual book is available. My wife and I proofread the manuscript, the edited manuscript, and the page proofs in addition to the work of the in-house proofreaders. (Even after these nine professional proofreadings, every new edition contains at least two elusive typos!) This is all a long, time-consuming process, but we hope that it results in a text that meets the needs of both teachers and students.

What's New This Time?

1. *Stress on "Poems for Study":* The poems that are used as illustrations throughout the text now appear as Chapter 2 rather than at the end of the poetry section. My hope is that teachers will spend extra time focusing on these poems at the outset, establishing a base for the analysis that follows. My apologies for the strident tone of the title, "Read These Poems!" but I do want to impress on students that the poems themselves are of prime importance.

2. *More poems as illustrations:* There are nine more poems included in their entirety. I urge teachers to use supplementary anthologies, but adding illustrative material within the text allows me to offer a greater range of analysis.

3. *Expanded fiction section:* There is one more story in the fiction section and a new chapter entitled "Liberating the Imagination." These additions expand the analysis to include innovative and unrealistic fiction. They stress the fact that even new aproaches have structure and form.

4. *Expanded drama section:* The extra play in the drama section allows me to introduce three strikingly different tonal approaches: tragedy, comedy, and farce.

The Instructor's Manual will once again be available upon adoption of the text. It contains suggestions for syllabi as well as exercises for individual topics. I urge teachers to contact the publisher for a copy of this helpful resource which has been prepared especially for them.

Special Thanks

I owe sincere thanks to my production editor, Shelly Kupperman, for her most able assistance. Thanks also to those initially anonymous critics for your thoughtful suggestions: Joyce Dayton, Indian River Community College; Toni Libro, Rowan College of New Jersey; Gay Davidson-Zielske, University of Wisconsin-Whitewater; Betsy Watson, Davenport College; and Susan Hubbard, University of Central Florida. Finally, I owe an immeasurable debt to my wife, Virginia S. Minot, who has in the past three decades proofread 22 sets of typescripts, galleys, and page proofs for this text alone without so much as a sigh of protest.

Stephen Minot

1

WHAT MAKES A POEM A POEM?

Five distinguishing characteristics of poetry: use of the poetic line, heightened use of sound, poetic rhythms, images, and density. Simple versus sophisticated poetry. Using poetic conventions to achieve true originality.

Yes, but is it really a poem? This question keeps coming up whenever we discuss poetry—particularly contemporary work—but we rarely take the time to answer it. Defining poetry seems difficult because the **genre**[1] includes such an astonishing variety of forms and approaches—from lengthy Greek epics to three-line haikus, from complex metrical schemes to the apparent formlessness of some free verse. And the definitions offered by poets themselves tend to reflect their own work.

In spite of all this variation, however, there are certain basic characteristics shared by poetry of all eras. These not only help to distinguish poetry from prose, they suggest special assets which have drawn men and women to this genre in almost every culture since before there were written languages. As readers, we have come to expect these qualities unconsciously. When they are missing, we may sense the lack without knowing exactly what is wrong. As writers of poetry, we depend on them.

There are five fundamental qualities that distinguish **poetry** from **prose**: concern for the **line** as opposed to the sentence, greater attention to the *sound* of language, development of **rhythms**, a heightened use of **images**, and a tendency to create **density** by implying far more than is stated directly.

When we read a poem, we necessarily slow down. We do this partly because of the density. We're looking for all those implications and **overtones** that often don't exist in prose. We are also responding to the sound of language. Even if we are reading silently, we tend to hear the lines as if they were being read aloud. There's no "speed reading" with poetry.

---

1. Words in **boldface** are defined in the Glossary-Index.

Evaluating a poem is even more deliberate than reading. Anyone can say "I like it" or "I don't like it," but those judgments tend to be as subjective as one's preference for a particular ice cream. A good critic doesn't treat a poem like a dessert. Poets (and serious readers) examine what works and what doesn't, what is effective and what isn't. To do this, we have to take a close look at all five of those aspects: the use of the line, the sound and the rhythm, the use of images, and the density of suggestion.

When you start writing poetry, make sure that you are dealing with something you honestly feel or have actually experienced. Genuine emotions are the base of any good poem. But if you want to make full use of the genre, you will want to keep these five aspects in mind as you write. Return to them when you look over each new draft. Every poem, of course, will vary in the degree to which it makes use of these five elements, but they are at the heart of what makes poetry so different from prose. Because they are so important to both the creative process and to revision, each deserves a close look, both here and in subsequent chapters.

The Poetic Line

When you write **prose**, the length of the line is determined simply by the size of the paper you are using. If your work is published, the length of the line will be altered to fit the magazine column or book page. Prose writers don't mind because line length isn't a part of the art form.

With poetry, however, the length of the line is definitely a part of the art form. For a printer to change it would be as outrageous as revising the wording itself. This first characteristic, then, is embedded in the very definition of the genre.

The importance of the **poetic** line is more than just a matter of definition. The line is for most poets the basic unit of composition. When we write prose, we naturally think in terms of sentences; but when we turn to poetry, we usually move line by line. Sentences still exist, but their importance is muted.

Every poem differs in its formation, but most move from one visual image to the next. As we write, we are guided more by association than by a logical sequence, particularly in early drafts. Lines tend to migrate through successive drafts. The final version will have a structure of some sort, but what was once the first line may end up as the fifth or the last, and the original ending may now be buried in the middle.

This does not mean that lines always end with a period. Both the sentence structure and the idea or feeling expressed frequently continue smoothly into the next line in what is called **enjambment**, or **run-on lines**. But the poet tends to compose line by line nonetheless.

The importance of the line in poetry actually preceded the written word. Epics such as the *Iliad* and the *Odyssey* apparently were memorized and recited before they were written, and the rhythms of spoken lines were an essential aid to memorization. So was **rhyme**. This theory has been further supported by the discovery of lengthy Yugoslavian epics that even today have been memorized by individuals who can neither read nor write.

As soon as poetry was recorded on the page, there was less need for memory aids. But it has never lost its roots in the spoken language nor its reliance on the line. This is why most poets keep reading their work aloud as they compose so that they can hear as well as see the lines as they develop. This also accounts for the increasing popularity of poetry readings, in which an audience can respond to the auditory aspect of the genre.

In the case of metered verse, the length of the line is determined at an early stage. **Meter** is based on a recurring pattern of stressed and unstressed syllables in each line, so the length of the line is determined in advance by the poet's choice of a metrical scheme. Writing a metered poem does not mean giving up control; it merely means that the choice is made at the outset rather than line by line. Meter is a structuring of natural speech rhythms, just as formal dance steps are agreed-upon patterns drawn from improvised dancing.

Free verse, like free-style dancing, has no such overall or preset structure, so the length and nature of each line is determined as the poem develops. But, again as in free-style dancing, those variations can be extremely important. They can be used to control the pace of reading, to emphasize a key image, to establish rhythms, and sometimes even to give the printed poem as a whole a significant shape on the page.

Both metered and free-verse poems are organized by lines. For many poets, the patterning of lines becomes a kind of signature, an identifiable **style** by which his or her work becomes distinct from all others. In addition, a poet's control over the line provides control over white space—an element similar to what artists call negative space. White space consists of the areas where there are no printed words. It includes vertical space (margins) and horizontal space between lines. White space is important both in metered verse (as in the visual distinction between couplets and quatrains) and in free verse (as seen dramatically by E. E. Cummings' "Buffalo Bill's," which appears on page 32).

Control over the line is one of the special attributes of poetry. It is also an absolute distinction that differentiates all verse from all prose. The degree to which the line becomes a unit of thought in the creation of poetry is highly significant.

The remaining four characteristics of poetry are not as absolute. One can find poems that do not make use of them all. But they are the qualities that we associate with the genre and that give us the sense that a particular work is indeed a poem.

Heightened Use of Sound

When we think of how poetry makes use of the sound of language, we are apt to think of **rhyme**. This association is natural enough, since ending two lines with matching sounds is an unmistakable device. Jingles, nursery rhymes, and simple ballads almost always rhyme in an obvious way. But as we will see, rhyme can be muted to keep it from becoming obtrusive. In addition, there are two other ways to link words by sound: by matching the initial letter ("*green* as *grass*") or by selecting words in which internal sylla-bles echo each other ("*trees* and *leaves*"). The paired sounds, of course, must appear in words that are close enough together so that the reader can hear the linkage.

"Fern Hill" by Dylan Thomas is a good example of an unrhymed poem that nonetheless ripples with sound linkages. The poet is describing with dreamlike phrasing his memories of his childhood on a beautiful farm. Here are three of the 54 lines. I have circled several of the linkages in sound.

And once below a time I lordly had the trees and leaves

Trail with daisies and barley

Down the rivers of the windfall light.

The poem is printed in its entirety on page 24. You may wish to turn to it now and discover for yourself how intricate sound linkages can be, even in poetry that is not rhymed.

Prose can also appeal to the ear. We hear the effect of sound occasionally in oratory and sermons where repetition of initial sounds and repeated phrases create effects similar to those in the sample from "Fern Hill." Significant pauses sometimes provide an effect resembling that of a poem's white space on the page. But these techniques are rare in prose. The con-scious, regular use of the sound of language is a characteristic that is far more common in verse.

Poetic Rhythms

Rhythm is clearly an aspect of sound and can be thought of as the beat. It is that aspect of sound we can imitate with clapping hands.

Because words—especially in English—are made up of **stressed** and unstressed syllables, it is a fairly simple matter to create regular patterns of these stresses. Some of those systems have become regularized as metrical schemes. Here are two lines taken from Richard Wilbur's "The Pardon":

In my kind world the dead were out of range

And I could not forgive the sad or strange

There are five stressed syllables (ı) in each line and five unstressed (ᴜ). If we group them in pairs of unstressed and stressed syllables, the rhythm sounds like ta-*tum*, ta-*tum*, ta-*tum*, ta-*tum*, ta-*tum*. Traditional patterns like this are called meter, and I will return to metrics in Chapter 6. Although these lines are unusual in their regularity, I use them here simply as an example of how language can be infused with a regular rhythmical system without being made to sound artificial.

Although metrics dominated British and American poetry for some five hundred years, looser systems referred to as **free verse** have dominated the work of our own century. Now, since the 1980s, there has been a renewed interest in metrical schemes; this revival of metrics is generally referred to as the **new formalism**. Poets disagree, often vehemently, on whether or not this is a good development, but behind the debate is the fact that both approaches are ways of infusing language with rhythms not generally found in prose.

Nonmetrical rhythms are not unique to our own century. Samples of what we now call free verse can be found as far back as the Song of Songs, one of the books of the Old Testament.

Nonmetrical rhythms can be created in many ways. Some poets develop a recurring pattern based on the number of syllables in each line. The **haiku** is about the shortest form of this, with five syllables in the first line, seven in the second, and five in the third. "Fern Hill" by Dylan Thomas is a much more complex example, and I will return to both it and the haiku in Chapters 7 and 8.

Other poets arrange long and short lines on the page in such a way as to highlight certain phrases or even trip the reader. The poems by Denise Levertov and E. E. Cummings in Chapter 2 are good examples. I will be analyzing these techniques in greater detail in Chapter 9, "Unique Rhythms." I mention them here simply as an overview of the range of rhythmical techniques available to the poet.

The Use of Images

The fourth characteristic of poetry is its heightened use of **imagery**. We think of images as objects we can see, but actually the term includes any item that we can respond to with one of the five senses—sights, sounds, tastes, tactile sensations, and even smells. That may seem like a wide net, but think of all the **abstractions** it excludes—words like *love, hate, democracy, liberty, good, bad,* and *death.* Indeed, *life* itself is an abstraction.

Essays tend to be rooted in abstractions. Philosophical works, for example, often explore the nature of good, evil, or truth. They use abstractions to describe abstractions. Economic papers analyzing the gross national product, poverty, or profit margins do the same.

Many poems also deal with abstract themes, but they usually translate those broad concepts into objects we can see or respond to through one of the senses. The abstraction *desire,* for example, is too broad and general to have impact on a reader. We know what it means, but only intellectually. The poet Philip Appleman helps us to *feel* as aspect of desire by comparing it with the ocean's undertow. (The poem is on page 36.) *Fear* and *guilt* are also too abstract to have emotional impact by themselves, but Sharon Olds makes them concrete—almost literally—by describing a child's fantasy of being locked up in Alcatraz (poem on page 16).

Images can be used by themselves or to create **similes, metaphors**, and **symbols**. More about those later. The point here is that most poetry is rooted in objects we can see or respond to through the senses. Poetry is by nature sensate—a genre of the senses.

Density

The fifth and closely related characteristic is **density**. Fiction is loose and wordy by comparison with poetry. One reason we read poetry more slowly and often repeatedly is that it usually implies much more than the immediate, surface meaning. Both the statement and the emotions are frequently layered with **overtones**. In fact, the resistance some feel to reading a new poem comes from the realization that it will probably take more work than does a short story or an article. With practice, however—and it does take practice—this more densely packed genre offers the reader special pleasures which make it well worth the effort.

When we turn to writing poetry, we may have to spend hours, often spaced over several days, going through draft after draft to achieve this density. The process may seem slow, but the reward comes when we have the feeling that we have said more in a few lines than a prose writer could have said in pages.

The fact that poems are concentrated does not mean they necessarily have to be short. Long **epic** poems like the *Iliad* and *Beowulf* deal with the mythic and historical events that unify a culture. In spite of their length, however, they still have greater density than prose. One cannot read them at the same rapid pace as one does a novel.

We still produce "epics" today—works that deal with major historical events and help to define our culture—but they are more likely to take the form of novels or films. Perhaps as a result, poets have turned increasingly to personal experience and the subtleties of private emotions. Even when they are making blunt social or political statements, they frequently draw on their own lives, creating impact through language charged with overtones.

One way poetry achieves density is through words and phrases that are evocative. All words have a **denotative** meaning—their literal definition; but most have **connotative** meanings as well—their associations. *Waking*, for example, denotes literally the end of sleep, but it can also imply (or connote) awareness, as in "I suddenly woke to the idea that. . . ." *Sleep* has, in addition to its literal meaning, the connotation of death. So when Theodore Roethke begins "The Waking" (page 31) with the statement, "I wake to sleep," we recognize, at least on second reading, the connotations and understand that he is describing how he plunges abruptly into life's experiences knowing full well that he is mortal and will ultimately die. Notice, however, that it took 17 words to explain rather clumsily in prose what he communicated in four.

Poetry also achieves density through comparisons known as **similes** and **metaphors**, and through symbolic language—all of which will be discussed in Chapter 5. What is important here is the fact that what all these devices have in common is the capacity to make language suggest far more than its literal meaning.

As you start out to write poetry, the most fertile sources to consider will be your own feelings and experiences. What is important to you can be shared with others if you are truly honest. But poetry isn't simply a collection of feelings spilled out on the page like journal entries. Useful as journals are, their entries are no more than snapshots that some artists take to recall specific scenes. A poem, like a painting, is an artistic construction. No matter how personal the subject matter may be, a poem is a verbal and auditory art that makes special use of the line, the sound of words, the rhythms of language, images, and compression. These are not only the recurring characteristics of poetry, they are the special assets of the genre that poets keep working to develop. They form the core of the chapters that follow.

Simple versus Sophisticated Poetry

What is a *good* poem? This question invites a second: good for what? If a poem is intended for a mass market—as greeting cards are—it should have a positive message and be phrased in unvaried metrical lines with a regular rhyme scheme. Both the sentiments and phrasing should be familiar, not fresh or startling. To be "good," a mass-market poem should soothe, not probe.

Poems that are **literary**, however, are intended for readers who ask for an entirely different set of characteristics. These poems attempt to share personal experience and feelings honestly, to comment in a fresh manner on what it is to be human. They often probe deeply and can contain disturbing insights. The language is fresh and sometimes demanding. They may create unusual rhythms. Some such poems emphasize language itself, playing with words in complicated ways; others are more concerned with image and statement. Many assume that the reader has some previous familiarity with the genre and is willing to work a little.

There are problems with calling this kind of work literary. For one thing, the term seems a bit pretentious when applied to contemporary work. Besides, we then face the problem of defining *literary*. Our problems are compounded when we call it "good" poetry. This seems like a value judgment and implies that popular, mass-market poetry is "bad." It is as subjective as calling classical music "good" and popular music "bad." Too often, the terms lead to lengthy and pointless arguments.

The best solution is to borrow two terms from the language of science. To a biologist, simple forms of life are *simple* and complex forms are *sophisticated*. Thus, the bird is not better in any objective sense than the jellyfish, but it is far more sophisticated in that its potential as a living creature is greater.

In writing—as in nature—**simple** and **sophisticated** are not absolutes. They represent a scale with an infinite number of points. The clever, comic verse of poets like Ogden Nash and Dorothy Parker are certainly more sophisticated than most nursery rhymes, but less sophisticated than the poems of, say, Dylan Thomas. The works of an individual poet will also vary. The fact that someone is able to write highly sophisticated work that is dense in meaning and complex in treatment does not mean that he or she can't also write comic verse or light, satiric pieces as well.

Should all poetry be sophisticated? Of course not. Many people continue to enjoy fourteenth- and fifteenth-century Scottish ballads, metrical tales of adventure and passion, and millions have been delighted with nineteenth- and twentieth-century ballads by poets like Rudyard Kipling and Robert Service. Today we have the enormously popular work of Rod McKuen, and the verse of Hallmark cards have reached more readers than T. S. Eliot and Robert Frost combined. Writing popular but forgettable verse like that is an honest craft that requires practice. There are "how-to" books that help those who want to succeed at it, but this is not one of them.

Sophisticated writing—poetry, fiction, and drama—is the subject of this text. Such work is by definition complex, but it is not necessarily cluttered or obscure. There are technically complex poems in which the intricacies of meter or repeated refrains become a kind of game; but these may end up being less sophisticated as poetry than a three-line haiku that manages to convey a wide range of suggestion. Complexity of meaning is not always achieved by complex language or metrical schemes.

Joyce Kilmer's "Trees" has been used many times in battles over what is and what is not "good" poetry. Let's sidestep that argument and take an objective look at what makes it a good example of highly popular simple verse. Here are the first three of its six stanzas:

> I think that I shall never see
> A poem lovely as a tree.
>
> A tree whose hungry mouth is pressed
> Against the earth's sweet flowing breast;
>
> A tree that looks at God all day
> And lifts her leafy arms to pray; . . .

What can we say objectively about these six lines? First, they clearly come from a poem. The length of the lines has been set by the writer, and we can hear some kind of regular rhythm simply by reading it aloud. In addition, the intentional use of sound is unmistakable: the lines are grouped in pairs that end with the same sounds to form rhyming couplets.

We can also say objectively that it is relatively simple verse. As with nursery rhymes, there is great regularity to the rhythm and to the rhyme. Without knowing anything about meter, one can detect four distinct beats to each line, and every rhyme is an exact matching of sound landing on a stressed syllable. This regularity creates a singsong effect.

As for the element of suggestion, that too is on a fairly simple level. Since trees are generally regarded as beautiful, the poet is repeating a commonly held view, a **truism**, rather than presenting a fresh concept or experience. Seeing the tree as a praying figure is somewhat **hackneyed**. We can't say that the poem is "bad," since it has given pleasure to millions of readers. But we can say that both the poetic techniques and the assertion it makes are on a simple level.

By way of contrast, here in its entirety is a two-line poem by Ezra Pound:

In a Station of the Metro

The apparition of these faces in the crowd;
Petals on a wet, black bough.

If this were printed in a solid line like prose, we would probably assume that it was merely a fragment—perhaps from a journal—and skip over it quickly. But because it is presented with a title and in two lines, we are assured at the outset that this is a poem and that it is intended to be read with some care. As with "Trees," its very shape on the page has influenced the way we will read it.

How seriously should we take it? After a single reading it is clear that this is not a comic jingle, nor is it a conventional statement about the beauty of nature. Something more sophisticated is going on. Perhaps, though, it is just a descriptive poem. Saying "just" suggests that such poems are not as sophisticated as those that have some kind of contrast or conflicting emotion. If this poem were, as it seems at first, merely a quick verbal snapshot of faces in the Metro (the Paris subway), then it would be more sophisticated than a jingle but not the kind of poem we need to spend much time on.

But what is being suggested with that word "apparition"? These faces have appeared suddenly, almost like ghosts. In what way might they resemble "petals on a wet, black bough"? Faces seen in the windows of a dark subway car come to mind. The car has abruptly arrived at the station and the faces inside remind the poet of petals.

Are there any more overtones? Petals that have been torn from blossoms by a rainstorm and plastered on the limb of a branch are being swept along by events over which they have no control. Does this apply to the passengers? The wording of the poem suggests that it does. This is how they appeared to the poet.

It would be a mistake to push the poem beyond this. There is nothing here to suggest forces of evil against good; the poet isn't calling on the passengers to rebel. Nor are we told that this is beautiful or pitiful. It is more as if the poet has seized our arm and said, "Hey, look at that!"

Except for this: The poet has not only caught our attention the way one might in conversation; he has created the scene as well. The suddenness of the "apparition," the fragile quality of those petals torn loose by the rainstorm, and the impact of the subway car highlighted by those three stressed syllables at the end—"wet, black bough"—all these help us to share both the visual impression and his reaction to it.

There is no rhyme in this poem, but like the lines from "Fern Hill" quoted earlier, it has a number of linkages in sound. "Crowd" and "bough" echo the same vowel sound in what is known as a **slant rhyme**. The second line has two linked pairs: the *e* sound in "petals" and "wet" and that heavy *b* in "black" and "bough." Unlike most prose passages, these lines are linked together not only with meaning but with sound.

The essential difference between these two poems is that Kilmer makes a conventional or commonplace assertion about trees in general, while Pound gives us a unique insight drawn from a very specific scene. In addition, the two poems represent a difference in technique which often distinguishes simple from sophisticated work: Kilmer employs rigid metrical and rhyme schemes, while Pound mutes both the rhymes and the sound linkages so that they do not become obtrusive. Even with the sonnet, a metered and rhymed form I will turn to in Chapter 8, rhythm and sound can be kept in the background.

Simple verse has various functions. In the case of **ballads**, it entertains by presenting a simple story in a rhythmical manner. Greeting-card verse soothes by rephrasing conventional beliefs and sentiments. **Occasional verse**—poems written for occasions such as weddings or birthdays—is often comic. Who wants to be told that he or she is impossible to live with at 15 or getting cranky at 65?

Sophisticated poetry, the subject of this text, has more complex and subtle rewards: It gives us pleasure through fresh insights, genuine feelings, and the subtle use of form. When it speaks to us, we don't throw it away after the first reading. We savor it.

Conventions versus Individuality

Are there poetic rules? No. But that doesn't mean that anything goes. There are **conventions** that poets make use of in an infinite number of ways.

An artistic convention is any pattern or device that is used in a large number of works. As we have seen, the poet's control over line length is one of the conventions that differentiates poetry from prose. Beginning each line with a capital letter is a convention that some poets use and others do not. Heightened use of images to create metaphors and symbols is a looser convention.

The use of **meter**—patterns of stressed and unstressed syllables, discussed in Chapter 7—is a more precise convention, highly regarded by some poets such as Robert Frost and Richard Wilbur. Another convention unique to poetry is creating rhythmical patterns by means of line length and vertical spacing. This device is known as **typography** and is preferred by poets like E. E. Cummings and Denise Levertov. **Rhyme** is also a convention enjoyed by some and not by others. Traditional forms like the **sonnet, haiku,** and **villanelle**—described later—are all conventions worth considering.

Every art form has its conventions. Those familiar with popular music, for example, distinguish blues from bluegrass and rock from jazz. Fine artists distinguish realists from impressionists, surrealists, and minimalists. Within each category there are usually subdivisions. Familiarity with basic terms makes conversation about music or art more precise and enjoyable even for the casual listener. Those who compose music or who paint use these conventions to shape their own work and to develop their own individuality.

Without being familiar with poetic conventions, the would-be poet runs the risks of merely writing prose in short lines. Such work may be sincere, but so can be the efforts of a violinist who refuses to practice. On the other hand, allowing poetic conventions to stifle individuality and genuine feeling can make the work sterile. As we have seen, heavy-handed use of rhythm and a blatant rhyme scheme help to make Joyce Kilmer's "Trees" not only poetically simple but conventional in the worst sense.

As with any creative art, the first step is to explore and then practice the conventions of the genre. There is no freedom in ignorance. Only if you have actually written a sonnet or a typographically innovative free-verse poem are you really free to decide which approach is best for you.

Practicing poets base their decisions partly on personal preference and partly on the needs of a particular poem. They can do this only when they are at home with various techniques.

The following eleven chapters deal not only with the conventions of the craft but also with the ways in which you can mute those conventions and use them subtly. These chapters will also help you to learn directly from the limitless body of published poetry.

As you study the various options open to you and apply them to your own creative work, you will find yourself developing your own individual "voice" as a poet. This will reflect what is unique in you—your specific feelings and insights.

2

READ THESE POEMS!

Why poets read poetry. Why it is essential that you study these before read-ing more about poetry. How to read these poems. How to increase your pleasure. The poems themselves.

Musicians listen to music. Novelists read fiction. Poets read poetry. It's as simple as that. One problem is that many of those who would like to write poetry have listened to more music and read more stories than they have read or listened to poems.

The reason poets read poetry is that like any art form it cannot be cre-ated by following a series of rules or instructions. It's not a science or a com-puter program. The poet relies on having in memory a backlog of many works that give a sense of what is possible in the genre.

For some, there will be a real temptation to skip over this chapter and get to "the real stuff." Wrong! *This* is the real stuff, these poems. The chapters that follow will suggest ways to read the real stuff and ways to start creating your own. If you skip over this chapter, you will be like the absent-minded gar-dener who waters and fertilizes the plot but has forgotten to plant the seed.

It will take you about an hour to read these poems. I suggest that you break this into two half-hour sessions. Poetry is compressed. If you own this text, you will get much more from your reading if you jot down just a few very brief comments in the margin beside each poem. (If it is a borrowed copy, consider photocopying these pages.) Your notes don't have to be insightful. Almost every poem here will be discussed in some way in the chapters that follow. If you provide one phrase about the content and one about what you feel the theme is, this will help to record the work in your memory. You may want to review the poem when it is referred to in the ana-lytical chapters (page references will always be given), but even if you don't in every case, you will have the tremendous advantage of recalling at least in general terms the poem as a whole.

If you have not enjoyed much poetry in the past, relax. There is something here for everyone—some humor, some wit, and plenty of insight to make you think about your own life and experience. Some are by men and about an equal number by women. The poems include a wide range of types, both metered and free, and the poets represent a variety of ethnic and racial backgrounds. Of course there will be poems you don't like. Like people you meet at a party, they won't all be your type. But remember this: A poet can learn from every conscientiously composed work.

Read, enjoy, and take notes. The chapters that follow will help you to appreciate these poems fully and to start composing your own.

Design

ROBERT FROST

I found a dimpled spider, fat and white,
On a white heal-all, holding up a moth
Like a white piece of rigid satin cloth—
Assorted characters of death and blight
Mixed ready to begin the morning right,
Like the ingredients of a witches' broth—
A snow-drop spider, a flower like froth,
And dead wings carried like a paper kite.

What had that flower to do with being white,
The wayside blue and innocent heal-all?
What brought the kindred spider to that height,
Then steered the white moth thither in the night?
What but design of darkness to appall?—
If design govern in a thing so small.

As the Cold Deepens

ELIZABETH W. HOLDEN

She is eighty-six
and her friends are dying.
"They're dropping like flies," she grumbles
and I see black winged bodies crumbling
on window sills when we open our summer house.   5

Flies all over!
Brushing them onto the floor, sweeping
them up, we drop black mounds into the bag.
"What a mess!" my mother declares.

I think of flies   10
how they live in a weightless armor
tough, resistant like a finger nail.

My mother is almost weightless now,
her flesh shrinks back toward bone.
Braced in her metal walker   15
she haunts the halls, prowls
the margin of her day, indomitable
erect in this support
that fuses steel with self.

At noon the flies mass on the sills   20
flying up and down the pane
pressing for sun.
What buzzing agitates the air
as the swarm becomes a single drive
a scramble up, a dizzy spin.   25

It is hard to hold the light
which grows weaker every day.
The temperature is falling
The glass is cold.

Looking for Judas

ADRIAN C. LOUIS

Weathered gray, the wooden walls
of the old barn soak in the bright
sparkling blood of the five-point mule
deer I hang there in the moonlight.
Gutted, skinned, and shimmering in eternal   5
nakedness, the glint in its eyes could
be stolen from the dry hills of Jerusalem.
They say before the white man
brought us Jesus, we had honor.
They say when we killed the Deer People,   10
we told them their spirits
would live in our flesh.
We used bows of ash, no spotlights, no rifles,
and their holy blood became ours.
Or something like that.   15

Regret

JUDY KRONENFELD

It's 3:30 on a gray afternoon
late in November.
Winter is homicidal in the air,
a knife-blade at my cheek.
At the apartment door I reach   5
for the key-string on my neck
and know at once it's gone.
I frisk my school-books, my gym clothes,
my shoes, imagining luck
tricky as an acrobat's timing.   10
My memory interrogates the day
like a white light in an empty white room,
but won't surprise me with the key,
asleep in a forgotten pocket.
What I recall, like pictures of the dead,   15
is the knot,
only double-tied.

There is nothing to do but sit
in the dingy hall, lost in revery
over the key. It lay like a talisman   20
on my chest bone, where I am hollow now.
I would give anything for its good weight.
There is nothing to do but think
of past joy. Cannily
it slipped into the lock,   25
and was made for the lock;
beautifully the tumblers turned,
the bolt obeyed.

Alcatraz

SHARON OLDS

When I was a girl, I knew I was a man
because they might send me to Alcatraz
and only men went to Alcatraz.

Every time we drove to the city I'd
see it there, white as a white   5
shark in the shark-rich Bay, the bars like
milk-white ribs. I knew I had pushed my
parents too far, my inner badness had
spread like ink and taken me over, I could
not control my terrible thoughts,   10
terrible looks, and they had often said
they would send me there—maybe the very next
time I spilled my milk, *Ala
Cazam*, the iron doors would slam, I'd be
there where I belonged, a girl-faced man in the   15
prison no one had escaped from. I did not
fear the other prisoners,
I knew who they were, men like me who had
spilled their milk one time too many,
not been able to curb their thoughts—   20
what I feared was the horror of the circles: circle of
sky around the earth, circle of
land around the Bay, circle of
water around the island, circle of
sharks around the shore, circle of   25
outer walls, inner walls,
iron girders, steel bars,
circle of my cell around me, and there at the
center, the glass of milk and the guard's
eyes upon me as I reached out for it.   30

Turnabout

Linda Pastan

The old dog used to herd me through the street
As if the leash were for my benefit,
And when our walk was over he would sit
A friendly jailer, zealous, at my feet.
My children would pretend that they felt fine   5
When I was anxious at some hurt of theirs
As if they were the parents, for the tears
At their predicaments were often mine.

And now against the whiteness of the sheet
My mother, white faced, comforts with the story   10
of Brahms, the boy, who couldn't sleep for worry
Until a chord achieved its harmony,
So down the stairs he crept to play the C.
She means her death will make a circle complete.

Domestic Animals

LINDA PASTAN

The animals in this house
have dream claws and teeth
and shadow the rooms
at night, their furled tails dangerous.
In the morning, all sweet slobber   5
the dog may yawn, the cat
make cat sounds deep
in its furred throat.
And who would guess
how they wait for dark   10
when into the green
jungle of our sleep
they insinuate
themselves, releasing
their terrible hunger.   15

The Gift

CAROLE OLES

Thinking she was the gift
they began to package it early.
They waxed its smile
they lowered its eyes
they tuned its ears to the telephone   5
they curled its hair
they straightened its teeth
they taught it to bury its wishbone
they poured honey down its throat
they made it say yes yes and yes   10
they sat on its thumbs.

That box has my name on it,
said the man. *It's for me.*
And they were not surprised.

While they blew kisses and winked 15
he took it home. He put it on a table
where his friends could examine it
saying *dance* saying *faster*.
He plunged its tunnels
he burned his name deeper. 20
Later he put it on a platform
under the lights
saying *push* saying *harder*
saying *just what I wanted*
you've given me a son. 25

Anger Sweetened

MOLLY PEACOCK

What we don't forget is what we don't say.
I mourn the leaps of anger covered
by quizzical looks, grasshoppers covered
by coagulating chocolate. Each word,
like a leggy thing that would have sprung away, 5
we caught and candified so it would stay
spindly and alarmed, poised in our presence,
dead, but in the shape of its old essence.
We must eat them now. We must eat the words
we should have let go but preserved, thinking 10
to hide them. They were as small as insects blinking
in our hands, but now they are stiff and shirred
with sweet to twice their size, so what we gagged
will gag us now that we are so enraged.

Sonnet 29

WILLIAM SHAKESPEARE

When in disgrace with fortune and men's eyes,
I all alone beweep my outcast state,
And trouble deaf heaven with my bootless[1] cries,
And look upon my self and curse my fate,
Wishing me like to one more rich in hope, 5

---

[1]Useless.

Featured like him, like him with friends possessed,
Desiring this man's art, and that man's scope,
With what I most enjoy contented least,
Yet in these thoughts my self almost despising,
Haply I think on thee, and then my state,   10
Like to the lark at break of day arising
From sullen earth, sings hymns at heaven's gate,
    For thy sweet love remembered such wealth brings,
    That then I scorn to change my state with kings.

The Heroes

Louis Simpson

I dreamed of war-heroes, of wounded war-heroes
With just enough of their charms shot away
To make them more handsome. The women moved nearer
To touch their brave wounds and their hair streaked with gray.

I saw them in long ranks ascending the gang-planks;   5
The girls with the doughnuts were cheerful and gay.
They minded their manners and muttered their thanks;
The Chaplain advised them to watch and to pray.

They shipped these rapscallions, these sea-sick battalions
To a patriotic and picturesque spot;   10
They gave them new bibles and marksmen's medallions,
Compasses, maps, and committed the lot.

A fine dust has settled on all that scrap metal.
The heroes were packaged and sent home in parts
To pluck at a poppy and sew on a petal   15
And count the long night by the stroke of their hearts.

War

Robley Wilson

Sometimes I have wanted to go to war.
The stories are always good—Thermopylae
Was good, the Gallic campaigns were as good
As you could get against barbarians,
The Crusades were outright inspirational.   5

Everyone ought to go off to a war
Before he is too old to have the good
Of it. The people we call pacifist
Forget (or never learned) the power of it,
The sense of godliness killing provides.   10

Who would not want to be an angel, high
Over the enemy's cities with wings
Broad as the foreshadow of death? What boy
Cannot recall from his pitiless dreams
That carnage laid about him in his bed   15

Of adults and girls? War is for the young
And keeps them young; war is to make a man
Immortal; war is to subvert boredom
And all the dull authority of states.
Who favors war knows what liberty is.   20

Think about us. War would spare us the vice
Of guilt, the curse of inadequate love,
The remorse of aimlessness. War transforms;
It is a place to start from, props up pride,
Writes history. Out of war, art makes itself.   25

Sometimes I have wanted to go to war,
To turn flame in anyone's heart. Old names
Dazzle me: Alexander, Genghis Khan,
Caesar, Napoleon—will any man
Shrink from riding such fame to his grave?   30

Are you the one gone soft now over peace?
Nonsense. Woman has always profited
From men at war. Since time began, if you
Camp-followed any conqueror, you too
Could count a hundred lovers on the sand.   35

Ice River

DAVID BAKER

Only after a couple of months of hard
cold, by mid-January usually,
no sooner, is the river ready, shards
of ice dropping to it from the white trees.
Before this, even in the early snow,   5
a frost-crust on mud and weed, it runs slowly

on, and on past wherever I might stand
to watch it, finally, freeze. Now it has.
I walk out toward that blue light at the bend
in its banks, the cold end of day, out past   10
the shore and skid of frozen mud to where
the snow lies flat as a road: the river

itself. I have waited this long to be
alone and small. Here the only sound is that
dull chewing, boots on snow. Even the trees   15
along the banks loom close, bent, the wet
rock-face bearded with long ice. I have come
back as to some trackless past, and I'm numb

with cold. Nothing moves, or appears to. Yet
under this sheet—snow on ice, thin inches   20
of support—the river runs black and fast.
As I walk I feel its deep pulse in the clenched
sagging of my weight. Even now, the ice
cracks a little, and small shoots pass

from my steps, to the river-edge, like roots.   25
In a few months I may return to fish
or walk long on the green land. Still, this mute
day is ending now, no sun, only this:
wind pulling in the heavy trees, the faint
light of snow, the blood stopped cold in my feet.   30

Haiku

ETHERIDGE KNIGHT

1

Eastern guard tower
glints in sunset; convicts rest
like lizards on rocks.

4

To write a blues song
is to regiment riots
and pluck gems from graves.

5

A bare pecan tree
slips a pencil shadow down
a moonlit snow slope.

River Sound Remembered

W. S. MERWIN

That day the huge water drowned all voices until
It seemed a kind of silence unbroken
By anything: A time unto itself and still;

So that when I turned away from its roaring, down
The path over the gully, and there were   5
Dogs barking as always at the edge of town,

Car horns and the cries of children coming
As though for the first time through the fading light
Of the winter dusk, my ears still sang

Like shells with the swinging current, and   10
Its flood echoing in me held for long
About me the same silence, by whose sound

I could hear only the quiet under the day
With the land noises floating there far-off and still;
So that even in my mind now turning away   15

From having listened absently but for so long
It will be the seethe and drag of the river
That I will hear longer than any mortal song.

What the Mirror Said

LUCILLE CLIFTON

listen,
you a wonder,
you a city
of a woman.
you got a geography   5
of your own.
listen,
somebody need a map
to understand you.
somebody need directions   10
to move around you.

listen,
woman,
you not a noplace
anonymous   15
girl;
mister with his hands on you
he got his hands on
some
damn   20
body!

Fern Hill

DYLAN THOMAS

Now as I was young and easy under the apple boughs
About the lilting house and happy as the grass was green,
        The night above the dingle starry,
                Time let me hail and climb
        Golden in the heydays of his eyes,   5
And honoured among wagons I was prince of the apple towns
And once below a time I lordly had the trees and leaves
                Trail with daisies and barley
        Down the rivers of the windfall light.

And as I was green and carefree, famous among the barns   10
About the happy yard and singing as the farm was home,
        In the sun that is young once only,
                Time let me play and be
        Golden in the mercy of his means,
And green and golden I was huntsman and herdsman, the calves 15
Sang to my horn, the foxes on the hills barked clear and cold,
                And the sabbath rang slowly
        In the pebbles of the holy streams.

All the sun long it was running, it was lovely, the hay
Fields high as the house, the tunes from the chimneys, it was air 20
        And playing, lovely and watery
                And fire green as grass.
        And nightly under the simple stars
As I rode to sleep the owls were bearing the farm away,
All the moon long I heard, blessed among stables, the nightjars   25
        Flying with the ricks, and the horses
                Flashing into the dark.

And then to awake, and the farm, like a wanderer white
With the dew, come back, the cock on his shoulder: it was all
     Shining, it was Adam and maiden,   30
        The sky gathered again
     And the sun grew round that very day.
So it must have been after the birth of the simple light
In the first, spinning place, the spellbound horses walking warm
     Out of the whinnying green stable   35
        On to the fields of praise.

And honoured among foxes and pheasants by the gay house
Under the new made clouds and happy as the heart was long
     In the sun born over and over,
        I ran my heedless ways,   40
     My wishes raced through the house-high hay
And nothing I cared, at my sky blue trades, that time allows
In all his tuneful turning so few and such morning songs
     Before the children green and golden
        Follow him out of grace,   45

Nothing I cared, in the lamb white days, that time would take me
Up to the swallow thronged loft by the shadow of my hand,
     In the moon that is always rising,
        Nor that riding to sleep
     I should hear him fly with the high fields   50
And wake to the farm forever fled from the childless land.
Oh as I was young and easy in the mercy of his means,
        Time held me green and dying
     Though I sang in my chains like the sea.

This Winter Day

MAYA ANGELOU

The kitchen in its readiness
white green and orange things
leak their blood selves in the soup.

Ritual sacrifice that snaps
an odor at my nose and starts   5
my tongue to march
slipping in the liquid of its drip.

The day, silver striped
in rain, is balked against
my window and the soup.   10

Balances

NIKKI GIOVANNI

in life
one is always
balancing

like we juggle our mothers
against our fathers   5

or one teacher
against another

(only to balance our grade average)

3 grains salt
to one ounce truth   10

our sweet black essence
or the funky honkies down the street

and lately i've begun wondering
if you're trying to tell me something

we used to talk all night   15
and do things alone together

and i've begun

(as a reaction to a feeling)
to balance
the pleasure of loneliness   20
against the pain
of loving you

Rhymes for Old Age

CHASE TWICHELL

The wind's untiring saxophone
keens at the glass.
The lamp sheds a monochrome
of stainless steel and linens,
the nurse in her snowy dress   5
firm in her regimens.

The form in the bed
is a soul diminished
to a fledgling, fed
on the tentative balm of spring,   10
sketch for an angel, half-finished,
shoulder blades the stubs of wings.

Darkened with glaucoma,
the room floats on the retina.
The long vowel of *coma*   15
broods in the breath, part vapor.
What has become of the penetralia?
Eau de cologne sanctifies the diaper.

Flood and drag, the undertow.
One slips into it undressed,   20
as into first love, the vertigo
that shrinks to a keepsake of passion.
Sky's amethyst
lies with a sponge in the basin.

The Pardon

RICHARD WILBUR

My dog lay dead five days without a grave
In the thick of summer, hid in a clump of pine
And a jungle of grass and honeysuckle-vine.
I who had loved him while he kept alive

Went only close enough to where he was   5
To sniff the heavy honeysuckle-smell
Twined with another odour heavier still
And hear the flies' intolerable buzz.

Well, I was ten and very much afraid.
In my kind world the dead were out of range   10
And I could not forgive the sad or strange
In beast or man. My father took the spade

And buried him. Last night I saw the grass
Slowly divide (it was the same scene
But now it glowed a fierce and mortal green)   15
And saw the dog emerging. I confess

I felt afraid again, but still he came
In the carnal sun, clothed in a hymn of flies,
And death was breeding in his lively eyes.
I started in to cry and call his name,   20

Asking forgiveness of his tongueless head.
. . . I dreamt the past was never past redeeming:
But whether this was false or honest dreaming
I beg death's pardon now. And mourn the dead.

Even with Insects

Issa

Even with insects . . .
Some are hatched out musical . . .
Some, alas, tone-deaf

In a Station of the Metro

Ezra Pound

The apparition of these faces in the crowd;
Petals on a wet, black bough.

After Spring

Chora

After spring sunset
Mist rises from the river
Spreading like a flood

Night Song

LISEL MUELLER

Among rocks, I am the loose one,
among arrows, I am the heart,
among daughters, I am the recluse,
among sons, the one who dies young.

Among answers, I am the question,   5
between lovers, I am the sword,
among scars, I am the fresh wound,
among confetti, the black flag.

Among shoes, I am the one with the pebble,
among days, the one that never comes,   10
among the bones you find on the beach,
the one that sings was mine.

The Bay at West Falmouth

BARBARA HOWES

Serenity of mind poises
Like a gull swinging in air,
At ease, sculptured, held there
For a moment so long-drawn-out all time pauses.

The heart's serenity is like the gold   5
Geometry of sunlight: motion shafting
Down through green dimensions, rung below rung
Of incandescence, out of which grace unfolds.

Watching that wind schooling the bay, the helter-skelter
Of trees juggling air, waves signalling the sun   10
To signal light, brings peace; as our being open
To love does, near this serenity of water.

Merritt Parkway

DENISE LEVERTOV

As if it were
forever that they move, that we
   keep moving—
        Under a wan sky where
     as the lights went on a star   5
          pierced the haze & now
   follows steadily
        a constant
  above our six lanes
  the dreamlike continuum . . .   10

And the people—ourselves!
  the humans from inside the
  cars, apparent
  only at gasoline stops
           unsure,   15
    eyeing each other
        drink coffee hastily at the
    slot machines & hurry
 back to the cars
    vanish   20
   into them forever, to
   keep moving—

Houses now & then beyond the
sealed road, the trees / trees, bushes
passing by, passing   25
   the cars that
     keep moving ahead of
  us, past us, pressing behind us
         and
     over left, those that come   30
    toward us shining too brightly
moving relentlessly

  in six lanes, gliding
 north & south, speeding with
 a slurred sound—   35

On a Maine Beach

ROBLEY WILSON

Look, in these pools, how rocks are like worn change
Keeping the ocean's mint-mark; barnacles
Miser on them; societies of snails
Hunch on their rims and think small thoughts whose strange
Salt logics rust like a mainspring, small dreams   5
Pinwheeling to a point and going dumb,
Small equations whose euphemistic sum
Stands for mortality. A thousand times
Tides swallow up such pools, shellfish and stone
Show green and yellow shade in groves of weed;   10
Rocks shrink, barnacles drink, snails think they bleed
In their trapped world. Here, when the sea is gone,
We find old coins glowing under the sky,
Barnacles counting them, snails spending slow
Round lifetimes half-awake. Beach rhythms flow   15
In circles. Perfections teach us to die.

The Waking

THEODORE ROETHKE

I wake to sleep, and take my waking slow.
I feel my fate in what I cannot fear.
I learn by going where I have to go.

We think by feeling. What is there to know?
I hear my being dance from ear to ear.   5
I wake to sleep, and take my waking slow.

Of those so close beside me, which are you?
God bless the Ground! I shall walk softly there,
And learn by going where I have to go.

Light takes the Tree; but who can tell us how?   10
The lowly worm climbs up a winding stair;
I wake to sleep, and take my waking slow.

Great Nature has another thing to do
To you and me; so take the lively air,
And, lovely, learn by going where to go.   15

This shaking keeps me steady. I should know.
What falls away is always. And is near.
I wake to sleep, and take my waking slow.
I learn by going where I have to go.

"Buffalo Bill's"

E. E. CUMMINGS

Buffalo Bill's
defunct
      who used to
      ride a watersmooth-silver
                stallion   5

and break onetwothreefourfive pigeonsjustlikethat
                            Jesus
he was a handsome man
                and what i want to know is
how do you like your blueeyed boy   10
Mister Death

Bedtime

DENISE LEVERTOV

We are a meadow where the bees hum,
mind and body are almost one

as the fire snaps in the stove
and our eyes close,

and mouth to mouth, the covers   5
pulled over our shoulders,

we drowse as horses drowse afield,
in accord; though the fall cold

surrounds our warm bed, and though
by day we are singular and often lonely.   10

Morning Swim

MAXINE KUMIN

Into my empty head there come
a cotton beach, a dock wherefrom

I set out, oily and nude
through mist, in chilly solitude.

There was no line, no roof or floor   5
to tell the water from the air.

Night fog thick as terry cloth
closed me in its fuzzy growth.

I hung my bathrobe on two pegs.
I took the lake between my legs.   10

Invaded and invader, I
went overhand on that flat sky.

Fish twitched beneath me, quick and tame.
In their green zone they sang my name

and in the rhythm of the swim   15
I hummed a two-four-time slow hymn.

I hummed *Abide with Me*. The beat
rose in the fine thrash of my feet,

rose in the bubbles I put out
slantwise, trailing through my mouth.   20

My bones drank water; water fell
through all my doors. I was the well

that fed the lake that met my sea
in which I sang *Abide with Me*.

The Dalliance of the Eagles

Walt Whitman

Skirting the river road, (my forenoon walk, my rest,)
Skyward in air a sudden muffled sound, the dalliance of the eagles,
The rushing amorous contact high in space together,
The clinching interlocking claws, a living, fierce, gyrating wheel,
Four beating wings, two beaks, a swirling mass tight grappling,   5
In tumbling turning clustering loops, straight downward falling,
Till o'er the river pois'd, the twain yet one, a moment's lull,
A motionless still balance in the air, then parting, talons loosing,
Upward again on slow-firm pinions slanting, their separate diverse flight,
She hers, he his, pursuing.   10

Those Winter Sundays

ROBERT HAYDEN

Sundays too my father got up early
and put his clothes on in the blueblack cold,
then with cracked hands that ached
from labor in the weekday weather made
banked fires blaze. No one ever thanked him.   5

I'd wake and hear the cold splintering, breaking.
When the rooms were warm, he'd call,
and slowly I would rise and dress,
fearing the chronic angers of that house,

Speaking indifferently to him,   10
who had driven out the cold
and polished my good shoes as well.
What did I know, what did I know
of love's austere and lonely offices?

We Real Cool

GWENDOLYN BROOKS

The Pool Players.
Seven at the Golden Shovel.

We real cool. We
Left school. We

Lurk late. We   5
Strike straight. We

Sing sin. We
Thin gin. We

Jazz June. We
Die soon.   10

Names of Horses

DONALD HALL

All winter your brute shoulders strained against collars, padding
and steerhide over the ash hames, to haul
sledges of cordwood for drying through spring and summer,
for the Glenwood stove next winter, and for the simmering range.

In April you pulled cartloads of manure to spread on the fields,   5
dark manure of Holsteins, and knobs of your own clustered with oats.
All summer you mowed the grass in meadow and hayfield, the mowing machine
clacking beside you, while the sun walked high in the morning;

and after noon's heat, you pulled a clawed rake through the same acres,
gathering stacks, and dragged the wagon from stack to stack,   10
and the built hayrack back, uphill to the chaffy barn,
three loads of hay a day, hanging wide from the hayrack.

Sundays you trotted the two miles to church with the light load
of a leather quartertop buggy, and grazed in the sound of hymns.
Generation on generation, your neck rubbed the window sill   15
of the stall, smoothing the wood as the sea smooths glass.

When you were old and lame, when your shoulders hurt bending to graze,
one October the man who fed you and kept you, and harnessed you every morning,
led you through corn stubble to sandy ground above Eagle Pond,
and dug a hole beside you where you stood shuddering in your skin,   20

and lay the shotgun's muzzle in the boneless hollow behind your ear,
and fired the slug into your brain, and felled you into your grave,
shoveling sand to cover you, setting goldenrod upright above you,
where by next summer a dent in the ground made your monument.

For a hundred and fifty years, in the pasture of dead horses,   25
roots of pine trees pushed through the pale curves of your ribs,
yellow blossoms flourished above you in autumn, and in winter
frost heaved your bones in the ground—old toilers, soil makers:

O Roger, Mackerel, Riley, Ned, Nellie, Chester, Lady Ghost.

Lizards and Snakes

ANTHONY HECHT

On the summer road that ran by our front porch
    Lizards and snakes came out to sun.
It was hot as a stove out there, enough to scorch
    A buzzard's foot. Still, it was fun
To lie in the dust and spy on them. Near but remote,   5
    They snoozed in the carriage ruts, a smile
In the set of the jaw, a fierce pulse in the throat
Working away like Jack Doyle's after he'd run the mile.

Aunt Martha had an unfair prejudice
    Against them (as well as being cold   10
Toward bats.) She was pretty inflexible in this,
Being a spinster and all, and old.
So we used to slip them into her knitting box.
    In the evening she'd bring in things to mend
And a nice surprise would slide out from under the socks.   15
It broadened her life, as Joe said. Joe was my friend.

But we never did it again after the day
    Of the big wind when you could hear the trees
Creak like rockingchairs. She was looking away
    Off, and kept saying, "Sweet Jesus, please   20
Don't let him hear me. He's as like as twins.
    He can crack us like lice with his fingernail.
I can see him plain as a pikestaff. Look how he grins
And swings the scaly horror of his folded tail."

Desire

PHILIP APPLEMAN

1

The body
tugged like a tide, a pull
stronger than
the attraction of stars.

2

Moons   5
circling their planets,
planets
rounding their suns.

3

Nothing is what
we cannot imagine:
all that we know we know   10
moves in the muscles.

4

Undertow:
I reach for you,
oceans away.   15

Coast to Coast

Philip Appleman

The bird that shook the earth at J.F.K.
goes blind to milkweed, riverbanks, the wrecks
of elm trees full of liquor and decay—
and jars the earth again at L.A.X.

Once, on two-lane roads, our crazy drives   5
across the country tallied every mile
in graves or gardens: glimpses in our lives
to make the busy continent worthwhile.

Friendly, then, the smell of woods and fields,
the flash of finches and the scud of crows,   10
the rub of asphalt underneath our wheels
as tangible as sand between the toes.

From orchards out to prairies, then to cactus,
the rock and mud and clay were in our bones:
as birches turned to oak, then eucalyptus,   15
we learned our lover's body stone by stone.

Now, going home we're blind again, seven
miles above the earth on chartered wings:
in a pressurized and air-conditioned heaven
the open road's a song nobody sings.   20

Lust

Steven Bauer

Once in a liquor store, stopped
at the end of an aisle, debating
what goes with lamb, I saw him. His eyes,

darker than I remembered,
flashed like the broken neck   5
of a bottle swiped on rock.

The day he bloodied my eye
in the schoolyard,
he hoisted me up,

and hanging by my jacket   10
from the cyclone fence,
I jerked as if a thousand volts

inflamed my brain.
I'd imagined him leaving
the shambles of that afternoon   15

to find an invisible job
alone in an oversized city
and I felt blessed

brooding over wine.
I'd been wrong about his future.   20
He would always stick out: like a pier

stretching its neck into deep water,
or a handgun hidden in a pocket
mistaken for the stiff outline of lust.

A Secret Life

STEPHEN DUNN

Why you need to have one
is not much more mysterious than
why you don't say what you think
at the birth of an ugly baby.
Or, you've just made love   5
and feel you'd rather have been
in a dark booth where your partner
was nodding, whispering yes, yes,
you're brilliant. The secret life
begins early, is kept alive   10
by all that's unpopular
in you, all that you know
a Baptist, say, or some other
accountant would object to.
It becomes what you'd most protect   15
if the government said you can protect
one thing, all else is ours.
When you write late at night
it's like a small fire
in a clearing, it's what   20
radiates and what can hurt
if you get too close to it.
It's why your silence is a kind of truth.
Even when you speak to your best friend,
the one who'll never betray you,   25
you always leave out one thing;
a secret life is that important.

The Mapmaker's Daughter

ANITA ENDREZZE

the geography of love is terra infirma

it is a paper boat
navigated by mates
with stars in their eyes

cartographers of the fiery unknown   5

it is the woman's sure hand
at the helm of twilight, the salt
compass of her desire

the map of longing is at the edge
of two distant bodies   10

it is the rain that launches thirst
it is the palm leaf floating on waters
far from shore

the secret passage into the interior
is in my intemperate estuary   15

the sweet and languorous flowering
is in the caliber of your hands

the circular motion of our journeying
is the radius of sky and sea, deep
territories we name   20
after ourselves

3

WHERE POEMS COME FROM

Responding to what you see and hear. Reacting to friends and relations.
Probing inner feelings. The dynamics of ambivalence. Delight in language.
The Seven Deadly Sins of Poetry. Getting started.

Most poems spring either directly or indirectly from personal experience. Something happens that generates a new insight. Some people are convinced that their lives are dull and uneventful, but that's only because they haven't taken the time to be observant. One of the characteristics that poets share is that they observe what is going on around them and make note of their reactions. They are aware of the fact that their lives are unique and that each new experience may provide a new insight.

The first step to writing good poetry is learning how to be observant. You may have to downshift. In an age in which speed and efficiency are encouraged both in and out of school, we sometimes forget to look at the world around us. The best advice for a would-be poet comes from the signs that mark many railroad crossing: Stop, Look, and Listen.

Responding to What You See and Hear

Stop, for example, and look at the way flower petals have been plastered against a wet, black bough. That's what Ezra Pound did, remember? The poem is on page 28 if you need to review it. What made it a poem was not just the visual aspect, it was the connection he made between those petals and human faces in a subway station. He stopped, looked, and let his mind make a sudden leap, a connection.

It is similar in some ways to a vision Barbara Howes had while standing on the beach. This is the first of three stanzas:

Serenity of mind poises
Like a gull swinging in air.
At ease, sculptured, held there
For a moment so long-drawn-out all time pauses.

We can be fairly certain that she didn't start out planning to write a poem about serenity. Poets don't usually begin by reflecting on an abstraction. The stimulus for that poem was almost certainly the sight of a gull poised on an air current. How can we be so sure? The title, "The Bay at West Falmouth," refers to a specific place, not an abstraction.

Fortunately for us, she wasn't the sort to shout out the obvious, "Hey, isn't that pretty!" or to start fumbling for her camera. Instead she took the time to let that image, the gull, stimulate her imagination. To her it seemed like a sculpture, and like many sculptures, it seemed to make time pause.

In the next two stanzas (the whole poem is printed on page 29), she expands on that initial impression so that eventually the scene

...brings peace; as our being open
to love does, near this serenity of water.

Where did the poem come from? The gull. But it took a poet's imagination to let that vision suggest a sculpture, a pause in time, serenity, and eventually the concept of being "open to love."

This is not to suggest that the poem came to her in final form as she stood at the edge of that bay at West Falmouth. It's almost never that easy. She probably worked over successive drafts in the weeks that followed. Poems often evolve slowly, occasionally frustratingly, as one searches for the right phrasing. But our concern here is for the moment of conception. The gull for Barbara Howes provided that initial stimulus just as those faces in the Paris subway did for Ezra Pound.

Visual impressions rank high among poets, but the other four senses are also used frequently. Sounds that launch poems may take the form of a fragment of music, an adult crying, the breaking of glass. Tactile sensations range from a frosty glass of lemonade to a dentist's drill. While taste and smells are less often used, occasionally they can be intense stimuli.

Reacting to Friends and Relations

This second source of poetry is apt to be less sudden. It includes your relationship with all those you know well, past and present. Consider the full range: parents, stepparents, grandparents, siblings, aunts and uncles, teachers, employers, classmates, roommates, spouses, lovers, even dogs and cats. The relationships you have with these people (and animals) are rarely simple. Often they are charged. Greeting cards, of course, also deal with many of these categories, but with cartoon-like simplicity. Sophisticated poems deal with real or as-if-real people and reveal complex emotions that are often mixed. They probe what is unique in relationships.

Nikki Giovanni's "Balances" (page 26) might seem on first reading to have begun with the abstraction of the title. In the first two of nine irregular stanzas she presents the topic and gives a couple of examples:

> in life
> one is always
> balancing
>
> like we juggle our mothers
> against our fathers
>
> or one teacher
> against another

That, however, is only a preamble. At the end of the poem we find out what is really on her mind:

> and I've begun
>
> (as a reaction to a feeling)
> to balance
> the pleasure of loneliness
> against the pain
> of loving you

What started off appearing to be a generalized little commentary on how one balances relationships turns out to be a reconsideration of a very specific relationship. The poem describes how the speaker has to weigh loneliness against the pain involved in maintaining their life together. Although the true concern is withheld until the end of the poem, it was probably the starting point in her mind, the stimulus that started her writing.

Elizabeth Holden's "As the Cold Deepens" is also rooted in a personal relationship. The entire poem appears on page 14, but we are concerned here with the point of origin, the initial stimulus. In the first of six stanzas, the speaker introduces us to her mother:

> She is eighty-six
> and her friends are dying.
> "They're dropping like flies," she grumbles
> and I see black winged bodies crumbling
> on window sills when we open our summer house.

We know who the subject of the poem is, her age, and her mood. The opening is so direct that it sounds almost like prose.

But in the third and fourth stanzas we see that the mother's **cliché,** "dropping like flies," is going to be used in some important way:

> I think of flies
> how they live in a weightless armor
> tough, resistant like a finger nail.
>
> My mother is almost weightless now,
> her flesh shrinks back toward bone.

The starting point was clearly not "mothers" in the generic sense of greeting cards and sentimental verse, *nor was it even her mother alone.* The moment that poem sprang to life was when the poet saw the connection between this aging woman and the pathetic but "tough, resistant" flies that "live in a weightless armor" until they finally die and are swept up. Although the writing and revising may have taken weeks or months, the moment of insight was probably as quick as a vision.

Probing Inner Feelings

We think we know what we feel, but sometimes we startle ourselves. Those moments when we feel a jolt of surprise at our own reactions are worth a close look. Stay clear of conventional views. Leave them to Hallmark. Have the courage to explore your private feelings.

As Stephen Dunn points out, we all have secrets we choose not to reveal. Here is the first third of his poem "A Secret Life" (page 38):

> Why you need to have one
> is not much more mysterious than
> why you don't say what you think
> at the birth of an ugly baby.
> Or, you've just made love
> and feel you'd rather have been
> in a dark phone booth where your partner
> was nodding, whispering, yes, yes,
> you're brilliant....

Another such secret many of us share has to do with war. Officially we're opposed to it. The cliché is that it's hell. But whenever someone extends an invitation to fight, almost everyone accepts. Odd? Robley Wilson explores that very phenomenon in his poem "War," which was published in the *New Yorker.* The full text is on page 20, but here is the first of seven stanzas as a sampler:

Sometimes I have wanted to go to war.
The stories are always good—Thermopylae
Was good, the Gallic campaigns were as good
As you could get against barbarians,
The Crusades were outright inspirational.

Wilson is not speaking for General Patton. He is exploring a secret buried in many of us, a set of feelings we may well find just a bit embarrassing.

The Dynamics of Ambivalence

Ambivalence is a crucial concept in the writing of poetry and fiction as well. It comes from *ambi-*, meaning *both* (as in *ambidextrous*) and *valence*, from the same root as *value*. It describes a combining of two emotions—love and hate, fear and desire, courage and cowardice. In its true sense, it does not refer to alternating emotions but to that most common and often disturbing capacity to experience opposite emotions at the same time.

A simple poem usually reflects a single, simple emotion, often unadulterated love or unquestioning admiration. Joyce Kilmer, for example, expresses no reservations in "Trees." They are simply wonderful. Most sophisticated poems, on the other hand, contain at least two different emotions or attitudes that create what is referred to as poetic **tension.** Ezra Pound's petals on that wet, black bough are both beautiful and, as one thinks about their having been plastered there by a storm, subtly tragic.

Take another look at the Wilson poem "War." Does it support war or oppose it? That first line, "Sometimes I have wanted to go to war," has to be taken seriously. We know from all those war-related volumes in every bookstore that this is not an unusual feeling. But the poem also contains just enough **irony** (a literary form of sarcasm) to let us know that it is not pro war:

> ...What boy
> Cannot recall from his pitiless dreams
> That carnage laid about him in his bed
>
> Of adults and girls?

The desire for glory exists at the same time as the opposition to it—not alternating views but simultaneous.

When casting about for a subject that might generate a poem, consider your mixed feelings. And be honest about them! Few student poets make the mistake of attempting love poems that are simple expressions of unalloyed affection. They've heard enough of that in routine song lyrics. But tributes to older people like grandparents sometimes take on that same simple character in spite of good intentions. Watch out too for the inverse, the expression of unalloyed hostility. Parents are often the target, as are suburban values, drugs, and street violence. Such poems are more effective when there is a range or, as in "War," a mix of emotions. And that mix has greater impact if it takes the form of true ambivalence.

Delight in Language

Although many poems spring from what the poet has seen and felt and from relationships with others, another important factor is sheer love of language.

All writers have to be aware of how they use words, but poets often take a special pleasure in fresh and ingenious phrasing. Because poems are read more deliberately than prose, poets can push language into new configurations.

E. E. Cummings is a good example. Here is "Buffalo Bill's," a poetic tribute to the skill and grace of a great performer from the past:

> Buffalo Bill's
> defunct
> 　　　who used to
> 　　　ride a watersmooth-silver
> 　　　　　　　　　stallion
> and break onetwothreefourfive pigeonsjustlikethat
> 　　　　　　　　　　　　Jesus
> he was a handsome man
> 　　　　　　and what i want to know is
> how do you like your blueeyed boy
> Mister Death

The historical Buffalo Bill was a showman, so it is most appropriate that the poet use some showy tricks himself: running words together to create a ripple effect and personifying death in a way that is both colloquial in style and serious in theme. What a waste, the poem seems to ask, to have a man of such dazzling ability lost to the stillness of death.

Or take the word play in almost any section of Dylan Thomas' "Fern Hill" (page 24). Here is just a sample:

> All the sun long it was running, it was lovely, the hay
> Fields high as the house, the tunes from the chimneys, it was air
> 　　　And playing, lovely and watery
> 　　　· 　And fire green as grass.

Logical? It's not the logic of prose. But the images bounce off each other to give a sense of delight and wonder. Roughly translated: "All day long the sun shone and I raced about; life was lovely as I played among haystacks tall as houses; I was lively as fire and supple as a green sprout." The "tunes from the chimneys" refer to squeaking metal chimney pots. As for the "fire green as grass," I'll return to his symbolic use of "green" later. For now, just savor the whimsy and high spirits.

Perhaps no one has ever suggested that you can actually have fun with language. If so, here is an exercise that will start you thinking about language in a nonintellectual way—that is, in a poetic way. Buy a journal, a separate notebook for poetic "sketching," and carefully draw at the top of a fresh page these two shapes:

If each shape had a name, which one would be Kepick and which Oona? Write the name you have selected under each figure and then record these choices: If they are a couple, which is the man? If one is a brand of gasoline and the other a type of oil, which is which?

Suppose one is a melon and the other a lemon? And now listen to them: one is a drum and the other a violin. Two easy? One is a saxophone and the other a trumpet; one is the wind and the other a dog's bark. It is an odd and significant fact that nineteen out of twenty people will give identical answers. This is the "language" of association, of **connotation,** which is the special concern of the poet both consciously and subconsciously.

Thinking of them once again as a couple, give each of them four more nonsense names. Now try a few lines of very free verse describing Oona and Kepick, using their other names as adjectives or verbs. (Surely you think of Oona looking feenly in the shane, but what happens when Kepick kacks his bip and zabots all the lovely leems?)

There is no end to this. It won't lead directly to sophisticated poetry, but it does help to link language with music. The two should not be confused, but poems often have as much to do with sound, rhythm, and overtones as they do with making a pronouncement.

The Seven Deadly Sins of Poetry

Poems that don't succeed often fall into one of seven basic types. They keep recurring in creative writing classes. You will save yourself hours of futile revision time and will improve the quality of any workshop course you may take if you can learn to avoid them.

• *The Impenetrable-Haze Poem.* The conscientious reader struggles from line to line without detecting any direction or coherence. Individual images may seem to make sense, but nothing hangs together. The work as a whole does not suggest a theme that any two people can agree on.

Why is obscurity so tempting for beginning poets? For some, all those years of analyzing good but complex poems have convinced them that filling the page with indecipherable phrases is sophisticated. In other cases, obscurity is simply a form of shyness. The writer is reluctant to reveal genuine feelings or experiences and hides behind fuzzy language.

More often, however, the would-be poet simply doesn't have a clear concept and is trying to fake it. A frequent defense: "It means whatever you want it to mean." That's another way of saying it doesn't mean anything.

When you read the poems in Chapter 2, you may have puzzled over some lines, but in general you understood what the poet was suggesting. Would you have enjoyed a poem that remained impenetrable even after conscientious effort? If not, why impose that frustration on your reader? Complexity is often necessary, but obscurity is a poetic sin.

• *Life-and-Truth-in-a-Nutshell.* When a poem tries to define truth, beauty, love, or evil in the abstract, it usually sounds like a little essay in short lines. A truth (as in "War") is a manageable subject. *An example* of beauty (like the gull in the Barbara Howes poem) is fine. Your best approach is to start with the specific and *imply* the abstract.

• *Oh-Poor-Me! I-Bleed-I-Die!* Sadly, young poets seem most tempted by this misuse of poetry. In some cases it may reflect genuine despondency, and those feelings deserve a sensitive response. But a poem that is based on unrelenting self-pity is more suitable in a psychiatrist's office than in a writing class. Almost all poets have gone through deep periods of depression or, as Robert Frost put it, "have been...acquainted with the night." But a mature writer knows that for a poem to be effective as a literary work it must be presented with some restraint, subtlety, and a sense of balance.

• *The Metronome Poem.* Every poem should have some type of rhythmical effect, but unvaried meter tends to dominate the work. It becomes obtrusive. We're used to a hand-clapping beat in nursery rhymes, greating-card verse, and marching bands, but the subtleties of sophisticated poetry are drowned out by an unvaried drumbeat just as they are by a too-blatant rhyme scheme. Later we will look at specific ways to mute rhythm and rhyme as well.

• *Hark, the Antique-Language Poem.* Lo, yonder bovine ruminates 'twixt bosky dell and halcyon copse. No, it never gets this bad. But watch out for those time-honored yet dated contractions such as *o'er* and *oft* as substitutes for *over* and *often*. They are particularly tempting when one first tries metered verse. Sometimes they're sprinkeled in like chocolate jimmies to make a work seem profound. Resist the urge. Every age has its own linguistic flavor, and like it or not, you're writing for the twenty-first century.

• *The Violin-and-Tears Poem:* Genuine feelings are the stuff of good poetry, but when the reader's emotions are manipulated to evoke tears, the poem is no longer sincere. Honest sentiment focuses on the specfic and is true to the poet's feelings. **Sentimentality** supercharges those feelings simply to produce a surge of emotion.

• *The Generic Poem: One Size Fits All.* Even if you are not sentimental, you run a risk when writing about mothers in general, grandparents as a group, working people, the very rich, all men, all women, or any group as a class. When you deal with a group generically—even if favorably—you are apt to make sweeping generalizations. A specific relative, however, or a particular migrant worker, your former employer, a certain friend, or a particular experience all have potential. Once again, start with the specific and imply the general.

Don't let these warnings inhibit you. If you review the first few lines of the poems in Chapter 2, you will see that your options are almost limitless. Just make sure that the subject matter you are working with is specific and familiar to you personally and that your treatment of it is honest.

Five Ways to Generate a New Poem

Don't stare at a fresh sheet of paper, hoping it will give you a topic. It won't say a word. Your new poem has to come out of you. Here are five ways to locate the material that is already within you. It's all there, waiting to be given words.

First, get in the poetic mode by reviewing samples of verse. If you have been keeping a journal, look it over. See if any of the fragments bring new thoughts and feelings to mind. If you haven't been keeping a journal, use a collection of poems such as those in Chapter 2. Read for stimulation, not close analysis. Let the poems wash over you. Often what was important to the poet will bring to mind events or feelings that are important to you.

Second, draw on your five senses. List very briefly those objects you saw today that you will remember ten years from now. What is it about them that makes them memorable? Try the same for last summer. Reach back for visual impressions from your childhood.

Now turn to sound. Music may come to mind first, but don't forget the voice or laugh of a particular person; the sounds of mechanical objects like a car, truck, or old refrigerator; or natural sounds like wind or rain. Describe these with fresh language—no babbling brooks or howling gales.

Try the same for memorable sensations of touch, taste, and smell. If memories flood back, make lists. If they come slowly, describe them in greater detail.

Third, recall some of the most vivid experiences you have had in the past year. Why do they stick in your mind? Can you remember and describe specific details that no one else would have noticed?

Do the same for the dramatic events of your childhood. Did they change your attitude? Did they help you to see things in a different light?

Now ask yourself some tough questions about your own life. Have you ever been truly frightened? Would what frightened you then frighten you now? Were you every deeply ashamed? As you look back, was that shame justified? Did you learn anything from it? Have you ever had a moment of elation that turned to disappointment or even depression?

Fourth, consider your friends and relations. Are there in any of them contradictions that are worth exploring? Have you ever had to act the parent to a parent or older person? What did it feel like? Is there anyone you once hated whom you now understand or perhaps even like? Whose death would really hurt you? Why that person and not others? When dealing with your relationships with others, look closely to see if there is some type of ambivalence worth developing. It may not be as dramatic as love mixed with hatred; it may be a mix of admiration and resentment, respect and disapproval, pleasure and displeasure.

Finally, as soon as you select a topic that might serve as the kernel of a poem, start writing. Get phrases down even before you are sure. Then lines. At this stage, don't worry about the order. Postpone that until later in the process. Lines that come to you early may end up at the end of a developed poem. Phrases you originally put down in a cluster may eventually be separated. Stay loose. Don't rush it. Keep trying different versions. Let the developing poem speak to you as it takes shape.

Keep in mind that most of your writing and your training as a student has been in prose. As I have pointed out, prose is wordy compared with poetry and makes little use of the sound of language or rhythmical effects. As you work on a new poem, compress your language and keep reading it out loud to hear the sound of what you are writing. At first you will have to compose somewhat intuitively. In later chapters, however, we will be examining techniques of rhythm and the sound of words that will give you a broader range of options from which to choose. For now it is enough to remember that poetry is not just communication; it is an art form in which sound, shape, and implication are all a part of the communication.

4

RIGHT PHRASE /
WRONG PHRASE

A poet's preoccupation with phrasing. The search for fresh phrasing. Finding the right noun. Probing for strong verbs. The power of compression. Marking up each draft.

When you write nonfiction prose such as an essay, your main concern is for theme and organization. To a large degree, phrasing takes care of itself. Poets, however, focus on phrasing from the outset. They become preoccupied with the question of whether each word and word cluster is the best possible choice.

At first you may tend to settle too easily for an early draft. This tendency is understandable since you don't know what kinds of questions to ask about your own work. The previous chapter dealt with selecting a promising topic; this chapter focuses on the writing itself. It poses four questions you will want to ask yourself over and over, line by line, phrase by phrase: Is the language fresh? Is that exactly the right noun? Is that verb strong enough? Can I compress that phrase? When these questions become automatic, you will find yourself littering your early drafts with enough questions, comments, and alternative phrasing to propel you into still another draft.

Keeping It Fresh

Every phrase in a poem is like a fish at the supermarket: If isn't fresh, it will spoil everything else. The most odoriferous type of bad phrasing is the **cliché.**

We have all been warned against clichés since grade school. Yet they remain a temptation—particularly when we are tired and careless. It is important to understand what a cliché is and why it is so damaging to any kind of writing, especially a poem.

The cliché, as George Orwell points out in his essay "Politics and the English Language," is actually a dying metaphor—that is, an expression that was once fresh enough to create a clear picture in the reader's mind but has now lost its vitality through constant use. The normal function of both metaphors and similes (discussed in greater detail in the next chapter) is to clarify an abstract word (*serenity*, for example) by linking it with a concrete one (like *gull*). But when comparisons like this are used over and over, they lose all visual impact. Thus, "sharp as a tack" has become dull; "free as a bird" no longer takes flight; "clean as a whistle" sets readers wondering whether they are to picture one of those bright, shiny referee's whistles or the sound of someone whistling. And as Orwell points out, "to toe the line" (literally to place one's toe on a line) has strayed so far from the original metaphor that it is now often seen in print as "to *tow* the line."

When a metaphor or simile finally "dies," it often becomes a part of the language as a single word that no longer appeals to a visual comparison. For example, to be baited like a badger has created a new verb, to *badger*, but most of us have forgotten that the badger was originally the victim, not the tormentor. The meaning is the same as to *hound* someone into doing something, but the original image was just the opposite. We accept these new verbs, *badger* and *hound*, without seeing them as metaphors. The same applies to *cliché* itself and to *stereotype*, both of which were originally printer's terms for metal plates of print. They are now useful nouns. There's no harm in these **dead metaphors.** What does the damage to poetry are those phrases that are both wordy and too familiar to provide a mental picture. They are excess baggage.

There are three different ways of dealing with clichés that appear in a first draft. First, one can work hard to find a fresh simile or metaphor that will force the reader to see (hear, taste, and so on) the object being used in the comparison. One can drop the comparison completely and deal with the subject directly. Finally, one can twist the cliché around so that it is reborn in some slightly altered form. This technique is often seen in comic verse, but it can be highly effective in serious poetry as well.

For example, if you discover that you have allowed "blood red" to slide into your verse, you can avoid this ancient cliché with such alternatives as "balloon red," "hot red," or "shouting red," depending on the overtones you wish to establish. If none of these will do, go back to just "red."

A good way to improve your skill in dealing with clichés is to apply the above techniques to the clichés "mother nature," "strong as an ox," "wise as an owl," and "where there's smoke, there's fire."

Hackneyed language is a broader term; it includes phrases that have simply been overused. They may not be true clichés, but they have been seen in print too often.

Certain subjects tend to generate hackneyed language. Take, for example, sunsets. The "dying day" is a true cliché, but perfectly respectable words like *golden, resplendent, magnificent,* and even *richly scarlet* all become hackneyed when used to describe a sunset. It is not the word itself that should be avoided—one cannot make lists; it is the particular combination that is limp from overuse.

In the same way, smiles are too often "radiant," "infectious," or "glowing." Trees tend to have "arms" and frequently "reach heavenward." The seasons are particularly dangerous: Spring is "young" or "youthful," suggesting virginity, vitality, or both; summer is "full blown"; and by autumn many poets slide into a "September Song" with only slight variations of the popular lyrics. Winter, of course, leads the poet to sterility and death, terms that too often describe the quality of the poem as well.

Our judgment of what is hackneyed depends somewhat on the age in which we live. What was fresh and vivid in an earlier period may have become shopworn for us. Protesting "But Pope used it" does not make a metaphor acceptable for our own use. Standards of fresh language, however, are far less tied to period than many believe. It is difficult to find lines in, say, Shakespeare's sonnets that would even today be considered hackneyed. Conversely, many of the conventions he attacked as stale and useless have continued in popular use and reappear like tenacious weeds in mass-market poetry.

In "Sonnet 130," for example, he protests that

> My mistress' eyes are nothing like the sun;
> Coral is far more red than her lips' red....
> And in some perfumes is there more delight
> Than in the breath that from my mistress reeks.

The poem is directed not so much at his mistress as at those poets of his day who were content to root their work in conventions that were even then thoroughly stale. Yet more than 300 years later poetry is produced (more often by the greeting-card industry than by students) in which eyes sparkle like the sun, lips are either ruby or coral red, and breath is either honeyed or perfumed.

Remember that your task as a poet is to find fresh insights. If you are dealing with seasons, don't announce that spring is a time for growth. We know that. There are other aspects of spring, however, that are worth considering. Here is what T. S. Eliot saw in that season and described in the opening of "The Waste Land":

> April is the cruellest month, breeding
> Lilacs out of the dead land, mixing
> Memory and desire....
> Winter kept us warm, covering
> Earth in forgetful snow, feeding
> A little life with dried tubers

Not only is he telling us that in some ways winter is "kinder" by keeping the ground covered, he is suggesting that sometimes memory and desire awaken aspects of ourselves which we would rather forget. Both are reversals of the simple sentiments we see so often in simple verse.

Archaic diction is, of course, another type of diction that is no longer fresh. As we saw in the last chapter, it creates an antique flavor admired by some in furniture but rarely in verse.

Finding the Right Noun

Adjectives modify nouns. They have their function, but too often they are used to modify a noun that isn't quite right. Here is a list of nouns that are modified because they don't exactly describe what the poet has in mind. On the right is a single noun that means essentially the same and would probably have more impact:

a large stream	a river
almost a hurricane	a gale
a small lake	a pond
a loud voice	a shout
extreme fear	terror
excessively thrifty	a miser

There is no need to avoid adjectives at all costs. They are like fine tuning. But in some first drafts fully half of the modifiers could be removed. Look at each one critically.

Finding the right noun also requires that you be absolutely sure about the meaning. This is no problem with most **concrete** nouns—words you can respond to with the five senses. Less familiar abstract nouns, however, may pose problems. We all have words in our passive vocabulary that we understand well enough when we are reading but we have not yet used in speech or writing. Look these up. You may be surprised at the precise meaning.

Those with computers may wish to add an electronic dictionary. These, unlike the spell checks, provide full definitions without leaving the document you are working on. The Random House Electronic Dictionary has the particular advantage of including derivations. In any case, take the time to check the range of meanings for any word you are not sure about.

Don't hesitate to make your nouns describe specific people, places, or objects. W. S. Merwin, for example, when writing "River Sound Remembered" (page 23), doesn't try to comment on all rivers. He starts out "That day the huge water drowned all voices…." He's referring to a particular time and by implication a particular river. As we saw earlier, Barbara Howes didn't write a tribute to gulls generally. She chose a specific scene and identified it in the title, "The Bay at West Falmouth" (page 29).

While Steven Bauer uses an abstraction in his title "Lust" (page 37), there is nothing abstract about his opening:

> Once in a liquor store, stopped
> at the end of an aisle, debating
> what goes with lamb, I saw him....

Precise and direct. We know exactly where we are. The same is true of Judy Kronenfeld's "Regret" (page 16), in which the title is also abstract but the opening sets a scene with vivid nouns:

> It's 3:30 on a gray afternoon
> late in November.
> Winter is homicidal in the air,
> a knife-blade at my cheek.

It's afternoon, November, winter—all common nouns setting the scene. Now look at the temperature: not "cold" in the abstract but "a knife-blade at my cheek." Nothing fuzzy or vague about that!

Probing for Strong Verbs

Verbs generally describe some type of action, and "probe" is what you may have to do to find the right one. It's far stronger than "find." You may have to work to unearth a verb with impact.

What is a strong verb? One that the reader will respond to. Every verb has to be selected in context, so you can't make up lists of "good" and "bad" verbs, but here are some examples from some of the poems included in this volume:

In Kronenfeld's "Regret" (page 16) the narrator doesn't just "look for" her lost house key, she "frisks" her school-books, gym clothes, and even her shoes. Notice how an unusual verb is used in tandem with precise nouns to generate the narrator's sense of alarm.

Elizabeth Holden is equally selective in her choice of verbs in "As the Cold Deepens" (page 14). The flies at the window that become such a strong symbol in that poem don't just "gather," they "mass on the sills." Later they "scramble up" the window in one last flurry before dying.

There are also good examples of strong verbs in Robley Wilson's "War" (page 20). In the last two stanzas "deeply admire" is rejected in favor of "dazzle me." The narrator asks if any man would hestitate to seek fame, but his far more dramatic phrasing is "...will any man / Shrink from riding such fame to his grave?" As for women, he points out how they tend to admire war heroes, but "admire" is too bland for his intent. The narrator's brutal accusation is that they have through history "camp-followed any conqueror."

The Power of Compression

As I pointed out in the first chapter, density is one of the characteristics that distinguishes poetry from prose. Most poems suggest more through implication than would an essay of the same length. As a result, poems not only have to be read more deliberately than prose, they require more time to compose.

The first step to effective compression is cutting unnecessary modifiers. We have already seen how adjectives can often be eliminated by selecting a better noun. The same applies for adverbs—words that modify verbs. Make sure they are essential.

Next take a look at each phrase to make sure it is necessary. If in doubt, read the passage without the phrase. Is the revised version just as good or even better?

Then look at wordy phrases that might be compressed by being presented in the form of a simile or metaphor. These closely related techniques, which are forms of comparison, can dramatize an abstraction by turning it into something we can see or feel. Since they will be described and illustrated in the next chapter, I will merely mention them here as invaluable methods of achieving compression.

Important as compression is, early drafts sometimes err in the opposite direction: They skim over the surface. This tendency is particularly common when the subject is personal and you feel ambivalent about revealing too much about yourself. In such cases, examining each phrase will help you to see the work as an artistic effort, not just a confession. This process of analyzing your poem as a literary work, turning yourself into an objective reader, may open up new veins that are well worth exploring.

Marking Up Each Draft

At first the major effort in writing poetry seems to be finding the right subject matter. But as you gain experience, you will find yourself spending much more time on the revision process. This is because the more you study poetry, the more concerned you become with the language itself. Finding just the right word, the most effective phrasing, becomes almost a compulsion.

Even with experience, you will have to guard against Clean-Copy-Rapture. There it is, neatly typed or computer printed on white paper seductively looking like the work of an established poet in an anthology. A voice within you murmurs, "Don't touch it."

Resist! This is the moment to get professional. Grab a pen (preferably red) or pencil and mark up that draft. Question vague words, cross out weak or inaccurate phrasing. Be your own tough critic. Suggest new words, alternative phrases.

To encourage this process, here are some lines that cry out for revision. Each has marginal comments of the sort a conscientious but kindly critic might offer. Although the revised lines are borrowed directly from poems in this volume, the unsuccessful versions are invented and should not be blamed on the poet.

EXAMPLE 1

Too impersonal

(Children) do not think of (death) or dying.

A solution from Richard Wilbur's "The Pardon":

In my kind world the dead were out of range

EXAMPLE 2

Not the true subject of poem   *Watch out for these abstractions.*

(The mind) is never sure of (truth) and so

(It) turns to (feelings) for what we think we know   *whose feelings?*

A solution from Theodore Roethke's "The Waking":

We think by feeling. What is there to know?

EXAMPLE 3

Be more specific   *avoid sentimentality*

(For many years) the (poor dead horse) lay in his grave,

while weeds and trees grew to cover (the spot)   *Focus on the horse*

A solution from Donald Hall's "Names of Horses":

For a hundred and fifty years, in the pasture of dead horses,
roots of pine trees pushed through the pale curves of your ribs

EXAMPLE 4

Sentimental

In (childlike joy) I played in wagons and orchards   *Seems formal for*
                                                        a kid's view
        Pretending to be the (king of my realm)

A solution from Dylan Thomas' "Fern Hill":

   And honoured among wagons I was prince of the apple towns

EXAMPLE 5

                              dull—too
How about   I (search my memory) *prosaic*
a metaphor?   *hackneyed*
          in (cold desperation) (but in vain,)

A solution from Judy Kronenfeld's "Regret":

   My memory interrogates the day
   Like a white light in an empty room,

How long should you keep revising? Until you are utterly sick of it. Then set it aside and try again the next morning.

Sophisticated poetry stimulates the reader in some way—intellectually, spiritually, or emotionally. To achieve this goal, you have to work until the language is truly fresh and every line works to achieve the goal you have in mind.

5

THE IMPACT OF IMAGES

The image defined and contrasted with abstractions. Images used as figures of speech. The image as symbol. Building image clusters. Playing with images in your journal. Shifting to serious work.

We think of an image in poetry as any visual detail, but as I pointed out earlier, the term also includes sounds, textures felt, odors, and occasionally even tastes. Images are also referred to as concrete details, though it is a little difficult to think of the delicate scent of a rose as "concrete."

At the opposite end of the spectrum are abstract words. They are concepts the mind must grasp intellectually. *War, peace, love, democracy,* and even the word *abstraction* are abstract.

There is nothing reprehensible about **abstractions.** Civilization (itself an abstraction) depends on them. Mathematics, for example, contains an entire language of abstractions called *numbers.* Philosophers spend their lives dealing with abstractions such as truth, knowledge, and ethics.

Poets also deal with abstractions. In this very volume we have poems titled "Balances," "Lust," "Desire," and "Regret." But one of the special attributes of poetry is its ability to translate those chilly abstract concepts into the language of the five senses. We see "balances" dramatized through the relationship between former friends or lovers; we are introduced to an aspect of "lust" in the form of a schoolyard bully grown into a brutish adult. "Desire" is communicated through the feel of the ocean's undertow. As for "regret," we feel it as we identify with a schoolgirl who has lost her house key on a cold November afternoon.

If you are in doubt about whether a word is abstract or **concrete,** ask yourself whether it refers to something you can see, hear, taste, smell, or feel. How much does truth weigh? What are the dimensions of death? Try to calculate the square footage of happiness.

Although abstractions are in many ways the opposite of images, there is no sharp line between them. They represent points on a continuum. *Serenity*, for example, is an abstraction that, like all abstractions, cannot be seen or heard. You can't weigh it or put it in a cage. *Bird* is more concrete, but it is still rather general. It includes everything from a sparrow to an ostrich. *A gull* is more specific, and "a gull swinging in air, / At ease, sculptured, held there..." is a fully developed image. We not only see the bird, we see it in motion. As you probably remember from previous references, this image is taken from Barbara Howes' poem "The Bay at West Falmouth" (page 29).

Here are some other examples showing the continuum between highly abstract words or concepts and images that a poet might use:

Reliability is an abstraction.

A workhorse is one way to suggest that abstraction.

Ned, a specific workhorse is a far more concrete image.

Chance is an abstraction.

Seeing a *white spider on a white flower* is an example.

Seeing a *white spider on a white flower holding a white moth* is a once-in-a-lifetime chance occurrence that is so unusual as to raise questions about whether there is some design in the natural world.

Poverty is an abstraction.

A graph showing the increase of poverty worldwide helps us to see a pattern in lines.

An unemployed mother of five gives a face to statistics.

Images as Figures of Speech

To this point, I have been describing images used simply as descriptive details—things seen, heard, felt, smelled, and tasted. Images also serve as the concrete element in almost any **figure of speech.**

Figurative language most commonly takes the form of the **simile** and the **metaphor.** These are both comparisons, the simile linking the two elements explicitly with *like* or *as* and the metaphor implying a relationship. Here are four similes from three different poems in Chapter 2. I have already quoted from the first two poems several times without having to explain similes or metaphors. That I was able to do this shows how familiar we as readers are with figurative language. Only as writers do we have to analyze just how they work. The marginal comments are the type you might find helpful when studying poems—assuming you own the book or magazine they are in.

1. From Barbara Howes' "The Bay at West Falmouth":

> Serenity of mind poises
>
> (Like a gull) swinging in air   *simile*

2. From Robley Wilson's "On a Maine Beach":

> ...rocks are (like worn change)   *simile*

3. From Linda Pastan's "Domestic Animals":

> ...into (the green   *metaphor*
>
> jungle) of our sleep

4. From Chase Twichell's "Rhymes for Old Age":

> *a wailing*   The (wind's untiring saxophone)   *metaphor*
> *lament*   (keens at the glass.)   ———— *2nd metaphor*

It should be clear from these examples that similes are not simple comparisons. When we compare, for example, a starling with a grackle, we imply that *in most respects* the two objects are similar. But when Barbara Howes describes serenity as being like a gull, she certainly does not want us to picture the emotion as having a sharp bill or a raucous cry. Serenity is like a gull *only in certain respects*—in this case, the way it seems to float effortlessly in the air. As with most similes, the area of similarity is far narrower than the area of differences. Its impact depends on how sharply it can make the reader see a new relationship.

A metaphor is often described as a simile that doesn't use *like* or *as*, but the real difference is much deeper than that. Similes are a special kind of comparison, but they are nonetheless phrased like comparisons. A metaphor, on the other hand, is a statement that is literally untrue. We understand its meaning only by implication.

It doesn't make literal sense, for example, to refer to a house as "lilting." Lilting is normally applied to melodies, not objects. You won't get far telling a builder to construct a lilting house. Yet this is the word Dylan Thomas uses in the second line of "Fern Hill" (see page 24), and we understand his meaning through the context of the poem.

To analyze how a metaphor works, convert it to a simile. The result may be awkward, but it is a good technique to use with your own work as well as with published poems. In the case of Thomas' metaphor, the conversion comes out something like this: "A house as cheerful and merry as a lilting tune."

Notice how compressed the metaphor is compared with the corresponding simile. This is a case where a metaphor is far more than just a simile with *as* left out. Its compression makes it a kind of shorthand that provides greater impact. More than that, it's a true transformation. Because it is literally untrue, it seizes the reader's attention in ways a simile rarely can.

There are two more terms that are extremely helpful in analyzing any figure of speech—including those in your own work. The critic I. A. Richards has suggested **tenor** to describe the poet's actual subject of concern (often an abstraction) and **vehicle** as the image associated with it. Take, for example, the simile in this line from "Fern Hill": "Happy as the grass was green." The tenor or true subject here is "happy," and "green grass" is the vehicle—with overtones of spring growth, vividness, intensity.

One advantage of being familiar with these terms is that they can help you identify and get rid of **mixed metaphors.** A mixed metaphor is one with two contradictory vehicles. Here is an invented example with marginal comments:

> The wind's untiring (saxophone)   *mixed metaphor*
>
> (hammers) at the glass

The wind, the tenor, here is described as being *like* the sound of a saxophone—an effective metaphor. The second metaphor is intended to suggest that the wind is also like a hammer pounding at the glass—not as fresh, but usable. Joined together, however, they are "mixed" badly since saxophones are rarely used as hammers.

Here is the harmonious and effective version we saw in Chase Twichell's "Rhymes for Old Age":

> The wind's untiring saxophone
> keens at the glass.

This version also uses a double metaphor (that is, two vehicles applied to one tenor), but the vehicles are harmonious. A saxophone often produces a wailing sound, and the verb *to keen* means to wail for the dead. The two tenors work together, and that wail is appropriate to the theme of the poem, which is a lament for a woman close to death.

The term **figurative language** is used primarily to describe similes and metaphors. Most other figures of speech are specialized forms of the metaphor and are of more value to critics analyzing literature than to writers in the process of composition. Three, however, concern us here. They are techniques you may wish to use.

Hyperbole is usually defined as extreme exaggeration, but in most cases it is a metaphorical exaggeration as well. Shakespeare, for example, in "Sonnet 3," writes, "Thou doest beguile the world," meaning that his love charms everyone. In "Sonnet 9," in a darker mood, he writes, "The world will wail thee." More recently, Lucille Clifton in "What the Mirror Said" has her narrator look at her reflection and cry, "listen, / you a wonder / you a city / of a woman." This cheerful bit of self-affirmation is not only an exaggeration, it is a metaphor. Converting it back to a simile, we end up with something like, "You're so complex and interesting, you're like an entire city."

Even the **pun** can be seen as a form of metaphor when one is able to separate the tenor from the vehicle. In Dylan Thomas' "A Refusal to Mourn..." he uses a play on "grave":

> I shall not murder
> The mankind of her going with a grave truth....

The tenor here is "a...truth," and he has, in effect, added "*as if* spoken at the graveside." He uses essentially the same device in "Do Not Go Gentle Into That Good Night" with the line, "Grave men, near death, who see with blinding sight...." Once again, we have only to convert the pun to a simile in order to see it as a part of a metaphorical construction.

Unfortunately, the pun is in low repute in the twentieth century and is apt to be greeted with groans. But as Dylan Thomas has shown, it can be used seriously if you select your phrasing with care and restraint. Subtle puns can also be used effectively in humorous poems.

Synecdoche, the third of these helpful terms, is a figure of speech in which a part is used for the whole. When we say "bread for the starving" we're not just appealing to baking companies. Bread represents food in general. Sometimes an individual is used for a group. When we say "the plight of the blue-collar worker" it's understood that we are referring to a whole class, not just an individual wearing a work shirt.

These examples are taken from common speech; poetic use of synecdoche is fresher and as a result has more impact. Compare the prosaic phrase "All day long" with Dylan Thomas' version, "All the sun long." The sun is only one aspect of the day, but by allowing it to stand for the day he is able to catch the overtones of summer warmth and, in this context, childhood.

Synecdoche occasionally reverses the process, using the general to represent the specific, although this device is far less common in poetry. In the phrase "deceit won the election," the abstraction defines the individual. Notice that here too the figure of speech can be translated into a simile: "The candidate, as if the embodiment of deceit, won the election."

Figures of speech are important in poetry because they help to increase the degree of compression. That is, they allow you to suggest more without being wordy. Be careful, however, not to "dress up" a poem by using figurative language merely for adornment. Sometimes straightforward language is more appropriate. A fine example of this is Donald Hall's "Names of Horses" (page 34). There are almost no figures of speech in that 29-line poem, yet it generates true strength and resonance. The decision on when and how much to use figurative language should be based on the poem itself and on your own inclination.

Image as Symbol

Symbols also add density of meaning to a poem, but the way they function is the opposite of figures of speech. As we have seen, a figure of speech introduces an image simply for comparison. A **symbol,** on the other hand, uses an image that exists as a part of the poem and adds to it a greater range of meaning. If that strikes you as confusing in the abstract, consider these examples.

First, here is a simile with italics added: "Alone and in a pensive mood, his life seemed *like a frozen river.*" We can convert the phrase to a metaphor: "His life *was a frozen river.*" We're not tempted to take that literally. It's clear that the river has been used figuratively. It was introduced merely to dramatize his mood, help us to see it and feel it in our imaginations.

In contrast, David Baker in "Ice River" (page 21) describes a real river in winter:

> ... Nothing moves, or appears to. Yet
> under this sheet—snow on ice, thin inches
> of support—the river runs black and fast.
> As I walk I feel its deep pulse in the clenched
> sagging of my weight....

Out of context, that might seem like a simple description, but as we study the poem in its entirety, we see that the river suggest his life, frozen over on the surface yet still running "black and fast" beneath the surface. How can we be sure of his symbolic intent? Mainly by a succession of hints he has provided such as that "deep pulse in the clenched / sagging of my weight" and the lines suggesting that "In a few months" he may return to walk along the banks.

In distinguishing metaphor from symbol, ask this simple question:

Should I take this vehicle literally? If not, it is a figure of speech. If it is literally there (like the river), it may have symbolic meaning.

You may not want to be this analytical in your first draft. That's a time to be intuitive. Let yourself go. But when you come to revising, these distinctions will help you to determine just what has been successful and what needs further work. And if you use these terms accurately in a workshop, your criticism will be far more helpful.

For some, diagrams are anathema. If you are one of them, skip over the schematic drawing below. But others find the pictorial approach more helpful than any description in words.

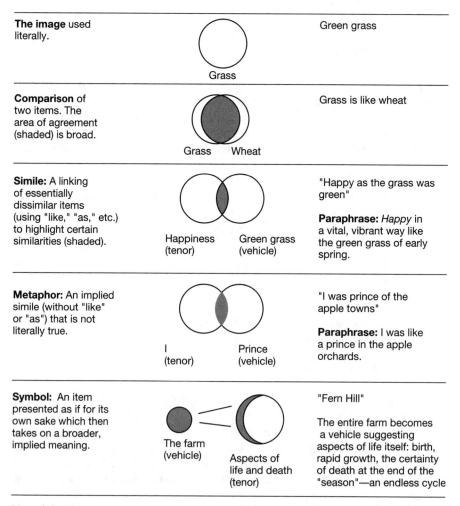

The image used literally.	Grass	Green grass
Comparison of two items. The area of agreement (shaded) is broad.	Grass Wheat	Grass is like wheat
Simile: A linking of essentially dissimilar items (using "like," "as," etc.) to highlight certain similarities (shaded).	Happiness (tenor) Green grass (vehicle)	"Happy as the grass was green" **Paraphrase:** *Happy* in a vital, vibrant way like the green grass of early spring.
Metaphor: An implied simile (without "like" or "as") that is not literally true.	I (tenor) Prince (vehicle)	"I was prince of the apple towns" **Paraphrase:** I was like a prince in the apple orchards.
Symbol: An item presented as if for its own sake which then takes on a broader, implied meaning.	The farm (vehicle) Aspects of life and death (tenor)	"Fern Hill" The entire farm becomes a vehicle suggesting aspects of life itself: birth, rapid growth, the certainty of death at the end of the "season"—an endless cycle

Use of the image in comparisons, similes, metaphors, and symbols.

Remember that the *tenor* is the principal subject and the *vehicle* is the word or phrase used to convey the subject to the reader. I have cited examples from "Fern Hill," but the diagram will be more helpful if you select an image in another poem and in a similar manner analyze the figurative techniques the poet has relied on to express it.

The term **public symbol** refers to symbols that are widely recognized and are almost a part of the language. Madison Avenue, for example, suggests commercial values; the flag represents the country; the cross stands for the Christian church. These are so common that they can be used in cartoons.

Because public symbols are hackneyed from overuse, poets usually construct their own **private symbols.** Devised for a particular poem, a private or unique symbol has to be introduced in such a way that its meaning is made clear through the context of the poem.

Often the symbolic suggestion in a poem will come relatively late in the creative process. Suppose you are working on a poem that contrasts the way a house looked in its early construction and its appearance five years later nestled into the neighborhood with lawns and plantings. This transformation of an ugly work site with its piles of lumber and concrete blocks into a finished home may be enough for a successful poem. Now suppose that after the fourth draft you see a parallel between that process and, say, the formation of a painting in the mind of the artist. This symbolic suggestion may add a new dimension to the poem, give it more **resonance.** Or it may not. It's up to you to weigh carefully whether developing that symbol will offer these benefits or whether it will simply clutter up a poem that was strong enough without an additional layer of suggestion.

Important as symbols often are, don't feel that they are essential. Donald Hall's "Names of Horses" (page 34) is a moving tribute to farm horses who served patiently and willingly over the years, and it may remind the reader of loyal servants, but the central image is never developed into a symbol. It's a mistake to tack a symbol on to a poem that has power and strength without it.

Examine your subject carefully and determine what it has meant to you. Try to get beyond the simple observation that you liked it or hated it. If at that point, a symbol comes to mind, let it develop naturally. Revise the poem so that you can share the symbolic suggestion with your readers, being careful in the process not to make it so obvious that it becomes obtrusive. When symbols are shaped this way, they will be an organic part of the poem.

Building Image Clusters

Regardless of whether images are used figuratively, symbolically, or simply as enriching details, they are often more effective if presented in clusters. That is, a group of images that have the same source (a farm, a beach) or are linked visually gain a certain strength as compared with those that are used once and then dropped. When you read a new poem, look for such **image clusters** or groups of related details even before you are entirely clear about the theme. If you own the book, it is well worth the time to circle these clusters and identify them. If you do not, photocopy the poem and mark the copy. This kind of visual analysis not only is helpful in the process of understanding new work, it will help you to adopt the same techniques in your own writing.

Here is a copy of "On a Maine Beach" by Robley Wilson annotated with marginal notes indicating image clusters. An unmarked copy appears on page 31, and you may wish to review that first.

money images   Look, in these pools, how rocks are like worn change

Keeping the ocean's mint-mark; barnacles

Miser on them; societies of snails

circle images   Hunch on their rims and think small thoughts whose strange

Salt logics rust like a mainspring, small dreams

Pinwheeling to a point and going dumb,

Small equations whose euphemistic sum

cycles of the tide   Stands for mortality. A thousand times

Tides swallow up such pools, shellfish and stone

Show green and yellow shade in groves of weed;

Rocks shrink, barnacles drink, snails think they bleed

In their trapped world. Here, when the sea is gone,

We find old coins glowing under the sky,

Barnacles counting them, snails spending slow   *a return*

circles and cycles   Round lifetimes half-awake. Beach rhythms flow   *to money images*

In circles. Perfections teach us to die.

The first of these image clusters is coins. The second has to do with circles and spirals. As the last line suggests, watching these cycles of living and dying within the rock pool helps us to see our own mortality in perspective.

In this way, the life and death of the reader is included in the dominant image cluster of circles and cycles.

Playing Games with Images

When you first start working with similes and metaphors and their components, tenors and vehicles, the subject is apt to seem rather forbidding. It's hard to imagine playing games with them. But remember that although writing poetry is ultimately a serious and complex art, practicing in your own journal can be just plain fun—as well as valuable.

Here for a start is a list of sentences, that deal with abstractions or abstract qualities. The first is enhanced with a simile. See if you can do the same with the other four. Use images that are fresh and effective. Be careful to avoid clichés like "bright as a penny."

1. Her spirits rose *like a rocket.*
2. He felt fear like…
3. She was as bright as…
4. The desert was as desolate as…
5. A sad old dog like…

Now look over your list of similes and see if you can convert them to metaphors. In some cases you can simply delete *like* or *as,* but often you will have to recast the sentence. It doesn't make sense, for example, to say, "Her spirits rose a rocket." But you could revise it as "Her spirits rocketed."

Now reverse the process. Here is a list of six *images.* Three of them are visual, one olfactory, one auditory, and one tactile. The first has been used to create a metaphor. See if you can create similes or metaphors using each of the other five.

1. As a linebacker, he was a *charging bull.*
2. A tree bending in the wind
3. Broken glass
4. The smell of incense on a summer night
5. A child's shriek
6. The feel of rough concrete

Having trouble? Consider people, animals, songs, your mood on certain occasions. Recall moments when you were particularly contented, discontented, anguished, anxious, or joyful.

Games like these are for poets what finger exercises are for pianists. They are warming-up exercises, to use another metaphor. You are thinking in images, the language of poetry. Remember that as you develop personal feelings and experiences, you will probably detect ambivalent feelings. Your old home, your high school, your best friend in the eighth grade, your first love, a parent, your sister or brother, a hated uncle. How can you best communicate the unique quality of your feelings? What kinds of metaphors can you find that will help your reader share your feelings?

From Games to Serious Work

Poets never stop playing with language. But there is a difference between random experimentation in a journal and the concentrated effort required for a poem you take seriously. Journal writing is for your own benefit, but a poem you ask others to read is on another level. Presumably it has been carefully revised. It is your best work.

In general, the more poetry you read, the more time you will spend revising your own work. I will have more to say about this at the end of the poetry section, but for now consider this: A textbook like this can suggest what to look for in a poem, but it cannot substitute for careful reading of specific examples. This chapter has focused on various types of images and the ways in which they can serve to create similes, metaphors, and symbols. Before you go on to the next chapter, take some time to review the poems in Chapter 2 and perhaps others from an anthology. Circle the images you consider effective and determine for yourself whether they are used directly or as vehicles for similes or metaphors. Link image clusters. Identify those that have symbolic overtones. No good poem is ever spoiled by analysis.

Then apply the same objective view to your own work. Have you made the best possible use of images? No matter how penetrating or insightful your theme may be, your poem will depend on the effectiveness of your images.

6

THE SOUND OF WORDS

*The oral tradition in poetry. Nonrhyming devices of sound including allit-
eration, assonance, consonance, and onomatopoeia. True rhyme; its use in
rhyme schemes. Achieving subtlety in sound. Sound as meaning. Training
your ear.*

Poetry was recited aloud long before it was written down to be read from the
page. We are fortunate today to have such an enormous body of work available in print, but the genre has never lost its roots in the oral tradition. The
growing popularity of readings and recordings and the introduction of
poetry videocassettes are good indications of how poetry, far more than
prose, continues to appeal to the ear.

There are two approaches to developing the musical aspect of poetry,
and while there is no sharp division between them, it is helpful to consider
them separately. One makes use of **rhyme schemes**—traditional patterns of
regularly recurring rhyme endings. The other, generally known as **free
verse,** relies instead on more irregular patterns. It also shifts the emphasis
from word endings to similarities of sound at the beginning of words and
within words.

When we consider the sound of language, we are apt to think of rhyme
schemes first because this particular device dominated the genre for so many
centuries. Also some of the major poets of our own century have preferred
rhymed to unrhymed verse. Anthony Hecht, Louis Simpson, Richard
Wilbur, and Maxine Kumin are good examples. They are all represented in
Chapter 2.

The term **new formalists** (also called *neo-formalists*) refers to contemporary poets who are making innovative use of traditional verse forms.
Although few poets like to be classified in this or any way, the term is useful
in describing an interest that has risen sharply in the past ten years.

It is important to remember, however, that varieties of free verse still
dominate the poetry scene, as they have for most of this century. Although

these do not draw on systems of regularly recurring rhyme endings, they can and often do make "music" with words. Sometimes the techniques are so subtle that the casual reader is aware only that the poem "sounds nice." For those who write, however, it is important to examine these devices closely in order to make good use of them.

Nonrhyming Devices of Sound

Nonrhyming sound techniques are found both in rhymed and unrhymed poems. Because they are the least technical, they are a good introduction to sound in language. They also serve as a reminder that there is less difference between traditional, metered work and free verse than many people think.

Significantly, these devices can be found in prose and oratory as well. The following passage, for example, is actually prose in spite of its **lyrical** or "musical" quality. It comes from Dylan Thomas' "August Bank Holiday" and describes a summer day at the beach not through plot but, in the manner of poetry, through a succession of vivid images. The first paragraph is typical. I have made annotations to point out some of the linking sounds.

> August Bank Holiday.—A tune on an ice-cream cornet. A
> slap of sea and a tickle of sand. A fanfare of sunshades opening.
> A wince and whinny of bathers dancing into deceptive water. A
> tuck of dresses. A rolling of trousers. A compromise of
> paddlers. A sunburn of girls and a lark of boys. A silent
> hullabaloo of balloons.

What makes this prose passage sound "poetic"? Primarily it is all those linkages of sounds—vowels, consonants, and combination clusters—some occurring at the beginning of words and others within words. Notice also how some words themselves echo an action or evoke an object or sensation.

Anyone interested in poetry should be familiar with the following four techniques for using sounds.

• **Alliteration** is the repetition of consonants, particularly at the beginning of words. There are three groups of these in the Thomas paragraph:

> slap—sea—sand
> wince—whinny (a similarity, not an identity of sound)
> dancing—deceptive

• **Assonance** is the repetition of similar vowel sounds regardless of where they are located in the word. Some good examples in the passage are:

> *wi*nce—whi*nn*y
> sunb*ur*n—g*ir*ls (similarlity of sound, not spelling)
> Hullaba*loo*—ball*oo*ns

• **Consonance** is the repetition of consonantal sounds. Whereas *alliteration* is used to describe similarity in initial sounds, *consonance* usually refers to sounds within the words. Often the two are used in conjunction. There are three sets of consonance in this passage:

> wi*nce*—whi*nn*y
> gir*ls*—*l*ark
> si*l*ent—hu*ll*aba*l*oo—ba*ll*oons

• **Onomatopoeia** is often defined as a word that sounds like the object or action it describes, but actually most onomatopoetic words suggest a sound only to those who already know what the meaning is. That is, we are not dealing with language that mimics life directly; it is usually just an echo. There are three good examples in Thomas' paragraph:

> slap of sea (the sound of a wave on the beach)
> whinny (an approximation of a horse's cry)
> hullabaloo (derived from "hullo" and "hello" with an
> echo of "babble")

Analyses like these tend to remain abstract and theoretical until one tries the technique in actual composition. Stop now and think of a scene, a friend, or a piece of music that comes to you with the soft, gentle contours you associated with the Oona figure in Chapter 3. Now try a paragraph of descriptive prose in which you make use of as many sound devices as possible. Remember that this is prose, so there is no need to worry about rhythm or a regular rhyme scheme. It might help to circle the linkages in sound. The point of this exercise is merely to help you find and use sound clusters.

Now, by way of contrast, think of a place, a person, or a piece of music that more closely resembles the sharp characteristics of the Kepick figure. Again, work out one or two prose paragraphs. This exercise is to poetry what preliminary sketches are to a finished painting.

The Sound of Rhyme

A rhyme scheme is one device that is the exclusive property of poets. Prose may contain scattered rhymes, but only when the writer controls the length of the line is a rhyme scheme or system possible.

True rhyme can be defined in three short sentences: (1) It is an *identity in* *sound in accented syllables.* (2) The identity begins with the *accented vowel and continues to the end.* (3) The sounds preceding the accented vowel must be *unlike.*

Here are three examples of true rhymes:

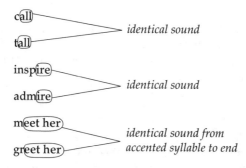

In the three-sentence definition above, I have italicized the key concepts that seem to give the most trouble. First, we are describing true rhyme as opposed to the slant rhymes or off rhymes that will be discussed shortly. True rhyme is not a general similarity in sound like assonance and consonance, it is an actual identity. Thus "ru*n*" and "co*me*" are not true rhymes, because of the subtle difference in sound; nor are "see*n*" and "crea*m*." These are called **slant rhymes.**

Second, rhyme is a matter of sound, not spelling. "Girl" and "furl" rhyme, but "to read" and "having read" obviously do not. The latter are called **eye rhymes.** It is often necessary to repeat the final syllable aloud several times before being sure whether the thyme is true or not—as do composers when testing the relationship between chords.

Next, there is the matter of continuing identity, which must begin with the accented vowel and run through to the end of each word. This is a problem only with two-syllable rhymes (known as **feminine rhymes**). In "running," for example, the accented vowel is *u* and the only words that rhyme with it end with *unning*, like "sunning." The word "jumping" has the *u* sound, but the *mp* keeps it from rhyming with "running."

Finally, the sound that comes before that accented vowel must differ from its rhyming partner. Thus, "night" and "fight" rhyme since the accented vowel (*i*) is preceded by *n* in one case and *f* in the other. But "night" and "knight" do not; such pairs are technically known as *identities.*

Since rhyme is based on the sound of syllables and has nothing to do with the division of words, the same principles apply when more than one word is involved in each rhyming end. "Bind me" and "find me" rhyme (the accented vowel is *i* in each case, and the rhyming sound is *ind me*), but neither rhymes with "kindly" because of the *l.*

Rules like these seem artificial when you first meet them; but like the rules of any new game, they become second nature once you get used to working with them.

If you have the mechanics of rhyme clearly in mind, study the table on pg. 74. To test yourself, cover the explanations and judge whether the pair of related words on the left is a true rhyme or not, and what makes it so.

For a less mechanical examination of rhyme, take a close look at the first stanza of Anthony Hecht's poem "Lizards and Snakes" (page 35). Although the rhyme scheme is perfectly regular, it is not obtrusive. In fact, casual readers often miss it altogether. This is so partly because Hecht has chosen a deceptively informal, almost conversational tone. In addition, his rhymes occur on alternate lines—a pattern referred to as *abab*. Here is the first stanza with the rhyme endings marked:

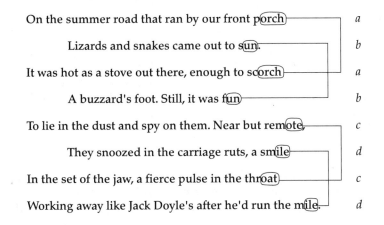

On the summer road that ran by our front porch	*a*
Lizards and snakes came out to sun.	*b*
It was hot as a stove out there, enough to scorch	*a*
A buzzard's foot. Still, it was fun	*b*
To lie in the dust and spy on them. Near but remote,	*c*
They snoozed in the carriage ruts, a smile	*d*
In the set of the jaw, a fierce pulse in the throat	*c*
Working away like Jack Doyle's after he'd run the mile.	*d*

Notice that every rhyme in this stanza is true. In fact, in the entire poem there are only two slant rhymes. (If you look for them, be sure to identify the accented syllable.) Jack Doyle, by the way, was a famous runner whose specialty, the mile, is a convenient rhyme with "smile."

Poems that make use of a regular rhyme scheme are almost always metered. We will turn to metrics in the next chapter. A rhyme *scheme* implies a regular and recurring pattern. The basic unit of a rhyme scheme is the **stanza.** Sometimes the end of a stanza is indicated with an extra space and sometimes not. In either case, each stanza begins where the cycle of the rhyme pattern starts again.

Stanzas in poetry are a little like paragraphs in prose. But in metered poetry, each stanza usually has the same number of lines. I will return to stanza patterns and how they relate to meter in Chapter 8; our concern here is systems of sound.

The rhyming **couplet** is the shortest possible stanza; it consists of two rhymed lines. Pairs of rhymed lines are designated as *aa, bb, cc.* This pattern

RELATED WORDS	ACCENTED VOWEL SOUND	ACTUAL RELATIONSHIP AND EXPLANATION
1. night/fight	*i*	True rhyme (meets all three requirements)
2. night/knight	*i*	An identity (preceding consonant sounds are identical)
3. ocean/motion	*o*	True rhyme (*cean* and *tion* sound the same); also known as *double* or *feminine rhyme* (two syllables)
4. warring/wearing	*or* and *air*	Consonance or slant rhyme (accented vowel sounds do not match)
5. track to me back to me	*a*	True rhyme (a triple rhyme)
6. dies/remedies	*i* and *em*	Eye rhyme (*dies* is similar only in spelling)
7. then you see us; when you flee us	*e*	Quadruple rhyme—true rhyme (rare and usually appears forced—often comic)

was popular in the eighteenth century, but it is used less often today, partly because the paired rhymed endings are apt to be so obvious. Unless skillfully done, they have all the auditory subtlety of a suitcase dragged down a long flight of stairs.

Maxine Kumin's "Morning Swim" (page 32) is proof that couplets don't have to sound that way, however. Here are the opening two stanzas that set the scene:

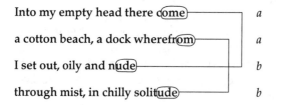

You can see from this excerpt that poetic stanzas often have more to do with units of sound than with the units of meaning we are used to in prose.

Triplets (also known as **tercets**) are more popular than couplets, partly because it is easier to complete an idea in three lines than in two, but also because the rhyme can be made far less pronounced by connecting every other line. Rather than having the *aa, bb, cc* of couplets, you can work with the muted pattern of *aba, cdc, efe*. As you can see, this pattern gives you one "free" line—one for which you don't have to find a rhyme.

If, however, you are feeling ambitious, you can also use the triplet in a pattern that links each stanza with the next by rhyming the center lines this way: *aba, bcb, cdc,* and so on. It is a somewhat demanding form in English because the language doesn't have as many rhyme endings as does Italian or Spanish, but using what is known as **terza rima** puts you in good company. Dante invented it, and Robert Browning, W. H. Auden, and T. S. Eliot all used it.

Quatrains, stanzas of four lines, give an even wider range of rhyming options. Patterns of *abab* and *abba* are the most common. Or you can leave the third line unrhymed to make a less demanding rhyme scheme of *abcb*.

Richard Wilbur uses quatrains in "The Pardon" (page 27), and he rhymes every line in a system that is essentially *abba*. I say "essentially" since he occasionally uses slant rhymes, to which I will turn shortly. The third stanza uses true rhymes consistently and is the clearest example of the pattern used throughout:

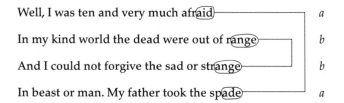

As we have seen, Anthony Hecht uses the rhyme scheme *abab* in "Lizards and Snakes." The stanzas appear to be eight lines long, but if you examine them closely you will see that the rhyme scheme starts fresh every four lines. These quatrains are visually run together.

Longer stanzas and more complex rhyme schemes were popular in earlier centuries and are well worth careful study. But the trend today is toward relatively simple systems. The poems in Chapter 2 provide a wide range of options.

Achieving Subtlety in Sound

When the sound of language becomes obvious and draws attention to itself, it dominates the entire poem—even the theme. This is no problem with nursery rhymes where rhyme and rhythm are half the fun, mass-appeal poems like Kilmer's "Trees," and **occasional verse**—light pieces written for special occasions like anniversaries or birthdays. Comic verse also uses blatant rhymes, often as part of the comedy. But if you are working with a serious and complex set of themes, obtrusive rhymes can reduce all your efforts to a jingle. Even a free-verse poem can be made to sound trivial if you use techniques like alliteration without restraint. The most common problem, however, is the singsong effect in rhyming poetry.

One way to mute rhyme is to use **enjambment** or run-on lines occasionally. An enjambed line is one in which the grammatical construction or the meaning continues to the next line. It is distinguished from the **end-stopped lines,** which usually end with a period or a semicolon. Rhyme is less noticeable when the reader is drawn without a pause to the next line.

As I pointed out earlier, maintaining subtlety of sound in rhyming couplets is a real challenge. One of the best examples of the use of enjambment to accomplish this is Maxine Kumin's "Morning Swim." In this poem there are twelve stanzas rhyming *aa, bb, cc,* and so on. Ten of the twelve stanzas are enjambed. Some are fully enjambed, like this one:

> Invaded and invader, I   *No pause here*
> went overhand on that flat sky.

There is no way you can stop or even pause at the end of that first line. Other lines are partially enjambed, like this couplet:

> that fed the lake that met my sea || *slight pause*
> in which I sang *Abide with Me.*

You could stop at "sea" without being confused, but the sentence does continue into the second line.

Only two of the twelve stanzas are truly end-stopped. Here is one:

> Fish twitched beneath me, quick and tame. || *Full pause*
>
> In their green zone they sang my name

End-stopped lines usually conclude with a period or a semicolon, but not always. The deciding factor is whether the reader must continue to the next line to make grammatical sense.

Although you may have missed this on first reading, Kumin's use of capital letters is a second method of muting the rhyme. A majority of metered poems (and many free-verse poems as well) begin each new line with a capital letter. These emphasize the rhythm of the line as opposed to the rhythm of the sentence. Kumin, however, has punctuated this poem like prose, using capital letters only at the beginning of sentences. You can see the same technique in Denise Levertov's poem "Bedtime" (page 32), which is written in much looser rhyming couplets and punctuated as one long sentence.

This device may seem too minor to make a difference, but it does affect our reading. It causes us to pay less attention to the rhythm of the line—and the impact of the rhyme endings—and more to the sentence itself.

A more radical method of muting rhyme is simply to separate the rhyming lines. As I have already pointed out, triplets, quatrains, and longer stanza forms allow you to alternate the rhyme endings, as in *abab, cdcd*. More radical still, you can leave a line regularly unrhymed—triplets with *aba, cdc* or quatrains with *abcd, efgf*.

A fourth method of muting the sound relationships is to use a few **slant rhymes** instead of true rhymes. Slant rhymes (also called **off rhymes**) are similar but not identical in sound, as in *account* and *about*. Often they are simply a form of assonance placed at the end of two lines.

Slant rhymes are frequently used in combination with other muting techniques to keep the rhyme from taking over like a drumbeat. Here, for example, is a drumbeat revision of the second stanza of Richard Wilbur's "The Pardon." Remember, this is *not* how Wilbur wrote it.

> I went in close to where the poor dog was.
> I heard the flies' intolerable buzz.
> The air was heavy with honeysuckle-smell.
> It was twined with another whose source I could not tell.

Notice that every line ends with a true rhyme and that the scheme has been converted to *aa, bb* as it were two couplets. More important, each line is end-stopped, with the rhyme landing heavily at the end: *was—buzz, smell—tell*.

Here is the actual stanza as written by Richard Wilbur:

> Went only close enough to where he was
> To sniff the heavy honeysuckle-smell
> Twined with another odour heavier still
> And hear the flies' intolerable buzz.

You can hear the difference even from a casual reading of these two versions, but you have to look more closely to see how it is achieved. The rhyme is there, but *smell* and *still* are slant rhymes. In addition, the scheme is, like the rest of the poem, *abba*. No line in this stanza is a complete sentence ending with a period, so there is no tendency to place a heavy emphasis on the rhyming words.

Wilbur uses slant rhymes sparingly—only three pairs out of twelve—and he distributes them through the poem. If you find that your slant rhymes are bunched toward the end, it probably means you were tired and quit too soon!

Robley Wilson's "On a Maine Beach" (page 31) makes such extensive and consistent use of slant rhymes that you may have assumed on first reading that it was free verse. As with some recurring phrases in music, the effect of the rhymes is almost subliminal. But the pattern is unmistakable if you look closely.

To see the rhyme scheme, it helps to divide the poem into four groups of four lines each. These "stanzas" are for analysis only. Here is a list of the last words in each line, with marginal identifications:

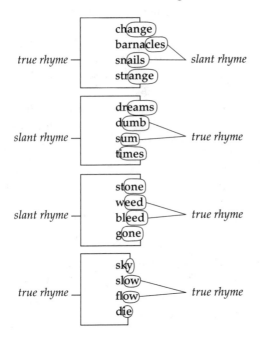

The rhyme scheme is hidden partially by the fact that the poet has not used stanza divisions. And even after we divide the lines for the purpose of analysis, the true rhyme endings are separated by two apparently nonrhyming lines. The last "stanza," however, is made up of true rhymes in a pattern of *abba*, and when we look closely at the other lines we see that the scheme is completed with slant rhymes.

In addition to this somewhat hidden rhyme scheme, Wilson has used alliteration (initial sounds), assonance (vowel sounds) and consonance (consonantal sounds) on almost every line. There are three pairs of these nonrhyming devices in the first two lines:

Look, in these pools, how rocks are like worn change

Keeping the ocean's mint-marks;...

And later he uses **internal rhyme,** rhyming words within the line.

Rocks shrink barnacles drink snails think they bleed

Many poets avoid rhyme altogether, but this does not mean that they necessarily ignore the sound of language. Dylan Thomas in "Fern Hill" (page 24), for example, relies almost entirely on alliteration, assonance, and consonance in much the same way he did in the prose passage quoted at the beginning of this chapter. The only trace of a rhyme is seen (if you look hard) linking the third and the eighth lines in all but one stanza. These are slant rhymes, and the gap is far too great to hear on first reading, but when they are added to the heavy use of other sound devices, they contribute to what we sense as the "musical tone" of the poem as a whole.

The number of sound connections in this poem is astonishing. Almost every line contains two or more words that are linked by sound. Yet the connections are muted enough so that we sense the general effect long before we see the mechanics of how Thomas achieves it.

Some contemporary poets rely more heavily on images than on the sound of language. Donald Hall's "Names of Horses" (page 34), for example, not only is unrhymed but contains very few examples of assonance or consonance. The effect he achieves comes through a succession of highly visual, fresh, and memorable images. Nevertheless a significant number of poets continue to draw on the auditory aspect of the genre in one form or another.

Sound as Meaning

When working with rhyme, guard against the tendency to treat it like a mechanical game, filling in the appropriate blanks. Sound devices are most effective when they become a part of the meaning. The best rhymes are those that draw together two images and produce a heightened or expanded meaning. In Maxine Kumin's "Morning Swim," for example, one of the most effective rhyming couplets links the act of swimming with that of singing a hymn of praise:

> and in the rhythm of the swim
> I hummed a two-four-time slow hymn

This is more than a casual link. The rhythmical pattern of four stresses in each line echo the musical "two-four-time" of the hymn the narrator is singing, and the two types of rhythm are joined by the rhyme of the two key words, "swim" and "hymn." Sound and sense are fused.

Assonance, the similarity of vowel sounds, is less noticeable than rhyme because it is often buried within the line; but it can also be used to link key images. Robley Wilson's "rocks like worn change" is essentially a visual association, but the similarity of those round *o* sounds helps to fuse the vehicle ("rocks") and tenor ("worn change").

Dylan Thomas, in "Fern Hill," uses both assonance and **consonance** (similarity of consonantal sounds) in the auditory metaphor "the *sabbath* r*a*ng *s*lowly." The *s* sounds and the repeated *a* sounds and the pacing of those three stressed words all add to the illusion of church bells ringing. In the same poem his vision of fields marked with "r*i*vers of the w*i*ndfa*ll* *l*ight" is almost more auditory than it is visual as those *i, i, l, l* sounds ripple through the reader's mind. And what finer way is there to bid farewell to childhood than through an image fused by alliteration in "the *f*arm *f*orever *f*led from the childless land"?

Walt Whitman's poem "The Dalliance of the Eagles" (page 33) is also unrhymed and also studded with assonance and consonance. Take a close look at the four central lines that describe the fierce contact between the two eagles in flight:

> The rushing amorous contact high in space together,
> The clinching interlocking claws, a living, fierce, gyrating wheel,
> Four beating wings, two beaks, a swirling mass tight grappling,
> In tumbling turning clustering loops, straight downward falling,

Not one rhyme ending here, but look at the way those high-voltage verbs are linked by *ing:* "rushing, clinching, interlocking, living, gyrating, beating, swirling, grappling, tumbling, turning, clustering, falling." All these packed into four lines! More subtle, there is the suggestion of a revolving motion in the *u* sounds as they begin to fall in "t*u*mbling t*u*rning cl*u*stering loops." In addition, listen to the clash in the hard *c* sounds in "*c*linching interlo*ck*ing *c*laws," as well as the *b* sounds in "*b*eating wings, two *b*eaks."

Walt Whitman, like Edgar Allen Poe and Vachel Lindsay, often painted in bold strokes. Some find this kind of verbal gymnastics lacking in subtlety, while others find it exhilarating. Regardless of preferences, the Whitman poem is an excellent example of how sound itself has overtones or associations that help to establish meaning in poetry. If you recall the word games you played with those abstract forms named Kepick and Oona back in Chapter 3, you will understand how the sound itself of "clinching interlocking claws" communicates a different set of signals than does the sound of, say, Dylan Thomas' "rivers of the windfall light."

Training Your Ear

It is hard to imagine a musical composer who doesn't spend a good deal of time listening to music. Yet some beginning poets are reluctant to read too much published poetry for fear of being influenced. Actually there is no danger of becoming imitative if one reads a wide variety of works. Only by reading—preferably aloud—can one begin to appreciate the ways in which poetry is written for the ear.

So far in this chapter we have examined a variety of ways in which one can utilize the sound of language in poetry. But passively reading about these techniques is like studying a book on how to play the trumpet. The learning process doesn't really start until you begin working on your own. Now that you know what to look and listen for in poetry, turn to the Robley Wilson's "On a Maine Beach" on page 31. First read it through without stopping—preferably aloud. Then go through it again, carefully marking as many of the rhyme endings and the nonrhyming sound devices as you can find. Now read the poem aloud once again for pleasure. This sequence of reading, analyzing, and then reading again is a good way to alternate an overall sense of the poem with close analytical study.

Next, turn to Chase Twichell's "Rhymes for Old Age" on page 26. It is similar to the Wilson poem in that it has a rhyme scheme highly muted with slant rhymes. In fact, there are only two pure rhymes. Although some of the connections are difficult to hear, the basic pattern for each stanza is *aba cbc*. Look closely and sound out the linked words. You can teach yourself how to identify the sound in poetry if you use the same sequence with this poem as with the Wilson poem: Read for pleasure, analyze carefully, and read again.

In training your ear to hear the sound of language, be careful not to stress rhyme at the expense of other devices. Alliteration, assonance, consonance, and onomatopoeia are equally important. For many poets like Walt Whitman, Dylan Thomas, and E. E. Cummings, they are even more important.

Another method of training your ear is to listen to recordings of poets reading their own work. Most libraries have collections of tapes and videocassettes. Dylan Thomas' readings are particularly effective. Consider buying tapes for your own personal use. Repeated listening is valuable as well as pleasurable.

Listening to a good reading is entertaining, but if you want to develop your own abilities as a poet, don't be a passive listener. Whenever possible, listen with a copy of the poem in front of you. Make marginal comments and then play the tape again. You will actually hear more as you become increasingly familiar with the work.

Finally, practice sound combinations in your poetry journal. Don't limit yourself to those lines that might develop into finished poems. Let yourself go. Experiment with assonance, with alliterative runs, with light verse in rhyme. Try a few imitations of poets with pronounced styles.

Sound in poetry is partly a matter of knowing what you are doing—technique. But it is also a matter of hearing what you are writing—a sensitivity to spoken language. Good poetry requires both.

7

TRADITIONAL RHYTHMS

Rhythm as a part of daily life. Rhythm of stressed words. Syllabics—counting syllables. From syllabics to meter. Metrical doodling. Keeping meter subtle. The appeal of meter.

Rhythmical patterns are a part of our daily life. We generate them in children's games, commercial jingles, and all forms of music. This phenomenon is more than just custom. There is considerable evidence that many rhythms are buried deep in the human psyche. Our emotions, for example, are influenced by phases of the moon, patterns of light and dark, and sleep cycles. At a faster pace we sense the drumbeat of our hearts, and within each ebb and flow of blood the brain records a crucial rat-a-tat of electric beats night and day.

It is not surprising that people in almost every culture feel the need to create verbal rhythms. The schoolyard chants young people throughout the world learn to enjoy are taught to them not by teachers but by older children, generation after generation. Rhythmical music and dance are a part of almost every culture. They are activities that cross lines of class, age, and ethnic background. Rhythm is more than just a pleasure, it is a human need.

The rhythms of poetry, then, are not mere adornment. They are not frills to be added. The rhythms of poetry are echoes of the rhythms of life.

If you look again at the previous three sentences, you will see two overlapping prose rhythms repeated: *not…not; rhythms…rhythms…rhythms.* This is a simple pattern compared with what one finds in poetry, and it is easily missed here. But it contains the prime element found in every rhythmical system: a pattern of repetitions. It also illustrates how rhythmical patterns can become a part of the meaning—in this case by emphasizing two key words as effectively as if I had added, "and this is really important."

Poetry is not music, but it is a first cousin. We can sing poems or read song lyrics as if they were poetry. And it seems natural to use the word **verse** to designate both poetry in general and lyrics to be sung. Most important, it's hard to imagine either without some sense of rhythm.

There are two different approaches to creating rhythm in poetry. Although they are not absolutely separate, they provide a helpful way of looking at the subject.

Traditional rhythms, the subject of this chapter, are patterns that have been shared by poets over a period of centuries. They are familiar to those who enjoy reading poetry. Although each poet uses a traditional pattern in a slightly different way, part of the pleasure for the reader is the interplay between the basic pattern and the variation developed in a specific work.

Unique rhythms, on the other hand, refers to patterns that are devised exclusively for a particular poem. They are unique to that work. Although they are associated with what in our own century has been called **free verse,** unique rhythms go back to Biblical verse. Creating unique rhythms is the subject of the next chapter.

Rhythm of Stressed Words

The simplest traditional rhythm in use today is based on the fact that when we speak we naturally place greater emphasis on some words than on others. We may not be consciously aware of doing this, but it is a part of how we use the language. Take, for example, this straightforward sentence:

> I went to town to buy some bread.

Written on the page, it looks like eight one-syllable words of even weight. But imagine how that same sentence might sound to someone who doesn't understand English.

> i-WENT t'TOWN t'BUY s'mBREAD

The stressed words have muscled out the unstressed. This is why you can study a foreign language from textbooks for years and still be baffled when you first hear it spoken. But the frustrations of a language student become an asset for the poet. It is easy enough to construct lines in which there are, say, four stressed words—especially in English, which has always relied heavily on stress. In fact, this is exactly the system used in *Beowulf,* the Old English epic.

Here is a passage (translated into modern English) in which Beowulf, the hero, pursues a sea monster (the "brine-wolf") to her underwater lair. Read the selection a couple of times and underline the stressed words.

> Then bore this brine-wolf, when bottom she touched,
> the lord of rings to the lair she haunted,
> whiles vainly he strove, though his valor held,

> weapon to wield against wondrous monster
> that sore beset him; sea-beasts many
> tried with fierce tusks to tear his mail

It is obvious that poets in this tradition never counted syllables. They were concerned only with having two stresses, a pause known as a **caesura,** and two more stresses in each line. They concentrated on this simple beat, and in *Beowulf* it is so clear that one can pound on the table while the song is chanted or sung—which is probably just what the ancients did in the mead hall over a thousand years ago.

Such poems also make heavy use of **alliteration**—similar initial sounds. You can hear it in the *b* sounds of "*b*ore this *b*rine-wolf, when *b*ottom she touched" and "*w*eapon to *w*ield against *w*ondrous monster." For this reason, *Beowulf* and many poems of this sort are referred to as **alliterative verse.**

The version above is a translation of a manuscript that dates from the eighth century, so one might think that its rhythmical systems would be of interest only to scholars. But poets can and do recycle anything that seems appropriate. In the 1970s the poet and playwright George Keithley wrote a book-length account of the ill-fated Donner party, a group of pioneers most of whom perished trying to cross the Sierra Nevada range in the 1840s. Like *Beowulf*, this is a dramatic story dealing with heroic effort, violence, and death. He adapted the same system of stresses, often using two in each line or, as in the following example, two pairs of stressed words. Here is a brief sample from *The Donner Party*, one of the few book-length **narrative poems** to become a Book of the Month Club selection, an opera, and a play.

> The tongues of our flames licked at the dark.
> In time, our talking floated up like smoke
> and mingled with the chatter of the leaves.
> But the night unnerved us even as we spoke.

Syllabics: The Counting of Syllables

Rhythm that relies on stressed words in each line lends itself to long narrative poems—especially those with echoes of the spoken language. But its weakness is that it is not very subtle. Another approach is to count syllables rather than stressed words.

Syllabic verse establishes a pattern based not on stresses but on the number of syllables in each line. In some cases, every line has the same number of syllables. In others, line length varies, but the first stanza sets the pattern: the number of syllables in the first line of each stanza is the same; the number in each second line matches the other second lines, and so forth.

Syllabic poems are usually unrhymed, and no effort is made to have a consistent number of stresses in a line. The pattern may not be immediately apparent when the poem is read aloud. But it does constitute a rhythmical system since the structure is apparent on the page, and that in turn cues a reader who is reading it aloud.

The **haiku** is a good example of syllabics. This is a short Japanese form with a long and distinguished history. It has come to us in English as an unrhymed and unmetered poem in which the first line has five syllables, the second has seven, and the third has five. There are also traditions regarding the content, but I will return to those in the next chapter. Our concern here is simply with the syllabic aspect of the form.

Syllabics can also take highly complex forms in longer works. Dylan Thomas' six-stanza poem "Fern Hill" (page 24) is a fine example. Clearly this poem is not metered. The lines are far too varied in length to fit any traditional stanza pattern. But you can read the poem many times (as I did) without realizing that it is meticulously composed in stanzas that repeat the same pattern of syllables line by line.

To be specific, the first line of every stanza has fourteen syllables and so do all the second lines. The third line of every stanza has nine syllables, the fourth line regularly has six syllables, and the fifth line always has nine. Up to this point the system is absolutely regular.

The sixth line has fourteen syllables in every stanza except the first (which has fifteen); the seventh line also has fourteen in every stanza but—you guessed it—the last (which again has fifteen). The eighth lines are either seven or nine syllables, and the final lines are either nine or six. Even Thomas' variations take on a certain order.

This is an astonishingly complex system. Why on earth should he bother when a majority of his readers will enjoy the poem as if it were an essentially formless work? There are three possible answers, all speculative. First, one might argue that his hidden structure beneath apparent formlessness echoes the portion of the theme that deals with the rhythms of life: "young and easy" in youth, yet mortal and already heading toward aging and eventual death—as sure as the tides, another rhythm. Thus, the line "I sang in my chains like the sea" reflects the rhythmical patterns of the poem itself, the "chains" being the limits set by line length.

A second and less academic explanation is his obvious delight in working with form for its own sake. Thomas, like many other poets, enjoyed working with ingenious systems.

Finally—and most significantly—hidden form has its effect even on readers who have not analyzed the system precisely. There is a certain sense of control in these stanzas that one senses even without counting syllables. This is probably the best reason for considering some type of rhythmical system even in an apparently free work.

From Syllabics to Meter

Syllabic poetry has been the norm in Japan for centuries and has traditionally been popular in France and Italy as well. It has never, however, been as
widely adopted by British and American poets. This is so partly because in
English we stress certain syllables and glide over others. For example, we
pronounce *animal* with a heavy accent on the first syllable, but the French
pronounce *l'animal* with equal stress on each syllable. These natural stresses
in English are like a rhythmical system waiting for development. All one
has to do is go one step beyond syllabics and establish identifiable patterns
of stressed and unstressed syllables. Doing this produces a rhythmical system that is far more subtle than merely counting the stressed words in the
tradition of *Beowulf* and is much more readily discerned by the ear than any
system of syllabics. As a result, it has become the basis of all **meter** in
English.

Historically, meter came to English verse when the French language was
imposed on the Anglo-Saxons after the Norman invasion. It has been in use
ever since, although it has gone through considerable refinement over the
centuries. Remember that meter is basically a way of structuring the natural
rhythms of the spoken language. It is similar in this respect to the way an
established dance step creates rhythms from the motions we go through in
daily living. The poet selects a metrical system that reflects the mood and
tone of the poem being developed and then adds to it his or her own style
and variations.

Before we turn to the terminology of meter, here is a quick review of the
various ways one can create rhythm. The examples are reworked fragments
taken from different lines of Richard Wilbur's poem "The Pardon." These are
for illustration only. The correct version appears on page 27.

1. *Prose.* Here is a simple prose sentence about a boy whose dog has died:

    I started to cry and call his name.

2. *Rhythm of stress* (also called *alliterative verse*). The stressed words are in italics:

    I *started* to *cry* and *call* his *name*.
    I *felt afraid* and *tried* to *run*.

Not until you add a second line can you begin to create a true rhythmical system. Even then a reader can't be completely sure until there are more lines that
continue to maintain the pattern.

If you as writer were going to continue with rhythm of stress, you would
want to make sure that a good number of lines have a *caesura*, a pause between
the first and second pairs of stresses. In addition, you would want to consider

more samples of alliteration like "cry...call," since that traditionally is a part of the form.

3. *Syllabics*. Here we shift from counting stressed *words* in the line to counting *syllables*. In this case I have added enough words to each line so that they both have ten syllables:

> I started in to cry and call his name
> But now it glowed a fierce and mortal green.

If you were going to continue with syllabics, you would have two choices. You could either make sure that all the lines had exactly ten syllables, or you could create stanzas with lines of unequal length as Dylan Thomas did in "Fern Hill," adjusting the number of syllables in each line to match the number in the corresponding line of the other stanzas. If this still seems confusing, review the analysis of "Fern Hill" earlier in this chapter.

4. *Meter*. To create a metrical system, you create patterns of unstressed syllables (marked ᴗ) and stressed syllables (marked ı) If we read these same lines out loud, we hear a pattern like this:

> ᴗ ı | ᴗ ı | ᴗ ı | ᴗ ı | ᴗ ı
> I start|ed in | to cry | and call | his name
>
> ᴗ ı | ᴗ ı | ᴗ ı | ᴗ ı | ᴗ ı
> But now | it glowed | a fierce | and mor|tal green.

The rhythm of these metrical lines can be described as *ta-TUM, ta-TUM*. With a little revision work, we can reverse that pattern so that it sound like *TUM-ta, TUM-ta*:

> ı ᴗ | ı ᴗ | ı ᴗ | ı ᴗ | ı ᴗ
> Shocked and | stunned I | wept a |loud and | called his
>
> ı ᴗ | ı ᴗ | ı ᴗ | ı ᴗ | ı ᴗ
> name but | now it | glowed a | fierce and | mortal
>
> ı ᴗ
> green and . . . .

This conversion, which departs still further from the Wilbur poem, changes the tone by starting each line with a heavy beat. This shows how much depends on how we begin a line of metered verse. The pattern you start with is frequently (though not always) the scheme used throughout the line. Controlling the rhythm this way is one of the advantages poets have over writers of prose.

Since it gets cumbersome to talk about how *ta-TUM* differs from *TUM-ta* and *ta-ta-TUM*, it's worth a few moments to learn some standard terminology. I will include here only those terms that are essential for discussing metered poetry. If you don't use terms accurately, discussions tend to fall back on vague statements of preference.

First, each traditional unit of stressed and unstressed syllables is called a **foot.** The foot with the pattern *ta-TUM* is an **iamb.** The **iambic foot** is by far the most popular in English.

One reason for its popularity is that so many two-syllable words fall naturally into this pattern: ex*cept*, al*low*, dis*rupt*, a*dore*, and the like. In addition, there is a natural tendency for sentences to begin with an unstressed syllable—often with words like *a, the, but, he, she, I.* There are three other types of feet that are also used as the basis for metered poems, and two that serve as useful substitutions.

The **trochee (trochaic foot)** is the reverse pattern we formed above by beginning the line with a stressed syllable: "Shocked and stunned I wept aloud...."

Although trochees can be used as the basic foot for an entire poem, they are more often used as substitutions for an iambic foot in an iambic poem. As we will see, this shift can give a special emphasis to a word or phrase, particularly if it is placed at the beginning of a line.

The **anapest** consists of three syllables—two unstressed followed by one stressed: *ta-ta-TUM.* It has a lively, cheerful beat, as in this anonymous couplet:

$$\text{With a swoop} \mid \text{and a glide} \mid \text{the swift} \mid \text{in delight,}$$
$$\text{Arous} \mid \text{es our en} \mid \text{vy, our long} \mid \text{ing for flight.}$$

Each line here has three anapests and one iamb. Notice how naturally the two iambic substitutions blend in and mute what might have been a singsong effect. Conversely, anapests serve well as substitutions in a basically iambic poem. The anapest is not used as the basic meter in many poems, but it has real potential for work that is light and **lyrical.**

One striking exception is Louis Simpson's poem "The Heroes," a bitter anti-war poem in which anapests are used to create the illusion of a merry tone. The entire poem appears on page 20, but here are two lines describing the aftermath of a war in which the jaunty rhythm heightens the ferocity of the satire:

$$\text{A fine dust} \mid \text{has set} \mid \text{tled on all} \mid \text{that scrap met} \mid \text{al.}$$
$$\text{The he} \mid \text{roes were pack} \mid \text{aged and sent} \mid \text{home in parts}$$

The **dactyl** is the reverse of the anapest: *TUM-ta-ta,* is in "*heav*ier," "*follow*ing," and "*talk* to me." It's a weighty foot.

Almost every metered poem in English uses one of these four feet as a basic pattern, and more than half take the iambic pattern. There are, however, two more feet that are useful when you **scan** a poem—that is, analyze it metrically. You will find yourself using them as substitutions as well.

FOOT	ADJECTIVE	STRESS PATTERN	EXAMPLES
iamb	iambic	*ta-TUM*	except; the deer
trochee	trochaic	*TUM-ta*	asking; lost it
anapest	anapestic	*ta-ta-TUM*	understand; in delight
dactyl	dactylic	*TUM-ta-ta*	heavily; talk to me
spondee	spondaic	*TUM-TUM*	heartbreak; faithful
pyrrhic	pyrrhic	*ta-ta*	in the; on a

The **spondee** is two heavy stresses, as in the word "spondee" itself, and in "heartbreak." The **pyrrhic** is two equally unstressed syllables, as in "in the" or "and the."

As a review, the table above shows the six metrical feet, with the stress pattern and examples of each.

In addition to the types of feet, there is the matter of how many feet are used in each line. In most cases, line length is kept consistent. One of the most popular lengths in English is five feet—**pentameter,** a word that comes from the Greek *penta* for "five," as in *pentagon.*

Iambic pentameter has been a favorite metrical scheme from Shakespeare to Robert Frost and Richard Wilbur. Most poets, however, soften the effect of their meter with variations. The pentameter fragments echoing Richard Wilbur's "The Pardon" earlier in this chapter were reworked here to create artificially unvaried meter just for illustration. Good examples of iambic pentameter in this text are "The Waking" by Theodore Roethke (page 31) and "Design" by Robert Frost (page 14). Unrhymed iambic pentameter is called *blank verse.*

The four-footed line, **tetrameter,** is a close second. **Trimeter** is also used widely. Lines that are longer than pentameter and shorter than trimeter are used far less frequently, but for the purpose of clarity, here is a list:

Two feet to each line (rare and usually comic)	*dimeter*	
Three feet to each line (fairly common)	*trimeter*	⎫
Four feet (sometimes combined with trimeter)	*tetrameter*	most common
Five feet (most common in English)	*pentameter*	⎭
Six feet (less used in this century)	*hexameter*	
Seven feet (rare)	*heptameter*	
Eight feet (a heavy, very rare line)	*octometer*	

Don't let these traditional terms, collectively known as **scansion,** put you off. They are intended for your use both in reading metered verse and in composing. At this point, it would be helpful to try writing three lines of iambic tetrameter. Take some simple topic as if you were about to write a haiku and follow the iambic pattern: *ta-TUM, ta-TUM, ta-TUM.* Don't worry about rhyme and don't feel you have to be profound. This exercise is just to help you feel the rhythm.

Now try shifting your lines so that they are trochaic; *TUM-ta, TUM-ta,* and so on. Once you get the line started, the rest should follow somewhat more easily.

Next, shift the topic to something lighter and try a few lines of anapests: *ta-ta-TUM, ta-ta-TUM.* For example: "In a leap and a bound, the gazelle in delight welcomes spring!"

Iambs and anapests end on a stressed syllable, creating what is called **rising** (or *ascending*) **meter.** Trochees and dactyls end on unstressed syllables and therefore are called **falling** (or *descending*) **meters.** This distinction becomes important when one begins to use substitutions for variety and special effects.

Keeping Meter Subtle

Until now, I have been working only with skeletal outlines. They may appear to be as far from the actual creation of lyrical poetry as the study of notes and clefs appears to be from musical composition. But the process of absorption is similar in both cases. What appears at first to be a set of arbitrary rules eventually becomes—even for those who may then depart from them—an internalized influence.

When you first begin working with meter, there is a natural tendency to make it as perfect and obvious as possible. The result is apt to be like the effect of the dancer who is still counting out each step. As soon as possible, try to mute your meter—not by careless construction but by adopting the methods of poets you admire.

There are four ways of keeping your metrical rhythm from taking over a poem, and often you will find three or even all four of them used in a single work.

1. The most commonly used method is to make sure that at least some of your words bridge two metrical feet. Here is a line of iambic tetrameter in which this is not done. Every foot is made up of two separate one-syllable words:

From woods | to fields | and then | to bone-|dry lands,

Here, in contrast, is a looser treatment, in which every foot breaks up a word. It is taken from Philip Appleman's "Coast to Coast" (page 37).

From or | chards out | to prair | ies, then | to cac | tus,

There is nothing technically wrong with the first version, but the second avoids the regularity and monotony of a too blatant metrical line. Appleman has also allowed an extra unstressed beat at the end, a fairly common practice.

2. A second method of muting meter is to use **enjambment,** also known as the **run-on-line.** An enjambed line, described briefly in the previous chapter, is one in which both the grammatical construction and the sense are continued into the next line. It is opposed to the **end-stopped line,** which is followed by a natural pause—usually with a comma or a period. Some end-stopped lines are more abrupt than others, of course, and the more pronounced such a pause is, the more it will emphasize the meter.

Enjambment helps to soften the impact of meter just as it mutes rhyme endings. At the conclusion of Wilson's "On a Maine Beach" (page 31), for example, the run-on line appropriately echoes the "beach rhythms" he is describing:

> Round lifetimes half-awake. Beach rhythms flow
> In circles. Perfections teach us to die.

3. Another technique of softening the impact of meter is rare, but well illustrated in Anthony Hecht's "Lizards and Snakes" (page 35). Instead of writing consistently in lines of pentameter or tetrameter, he alternates between these two. The first line has five feet and the next has four. A few of his lines even have six feet.

This is a risky approach, since the reader is apt, at least unconsciously, to expect greater regularity. One reason it seems natural here is that the poet has consciously adopted an informal, conversational tone.

4. The most frequently used method is called **substitution.** The poet occasionally substitutes a different foot from the one that has been adopted for the poem as a whole.

We have already looked at Richard Wilbur's "The Pardon" for examples of how to mute the sound of rhyme. It is also a good illustration of how to keep iambic pentameter meter from becoming monotonous. Here, for instance, is how he uses a trochaic substitution with the phrase "twined with."

To sniff | the heav | y hon | eysuck | le-smell |

Twined with | anoth | er o | dour heav | ier still |

The substitution not only offers variation, it also highlights the metaphor that links the way smells mix and the way vines twist about each other. The substitution, then, is not arbitrary—not simply a matter of the poet getting tired. It adds to the emotional impact of the line.

Later in the same poem there is a line that has two substitutions, the first an anapest and the second a trochee. I have left it unmarked so that you can scan it yourself.

> In the carnal sun, clothed in a hymn of flies

How much substitution can a poem absorb? Anthony Hecht's "Lizards and Snakes" comes close to the limit. The poem is essentially iambic, but here is a line in which three of the five feet are non-iambic substitutions. Can you scan it and spot the variations?

> In the set of the jaw, a fierce pulse in the throat

The most logical way to scan this is to read the opening six words as two anapests. The other substitution is the trochee in "pulse in."

With so many variations, why do we call the poem iambic? Because *most* of the lines are largely iambic, with no more than one or occasionally two substitutions. When we come to a line like the one just quoted, we retain the memory of that iambic beat and assume that the poem will return to it, as indeed it does. If the poem contained a great many lines with so few iambs, we would begin to conclude that it was unmetered.

The Appeal of Meter

Metered verse dominated British and American poetry for some 500 years. During our own century, varieties of free verse with its unique systems of rhythm became a firm part of our tradition. As I mentioned in the last chapter, the 1980s and 1990s have produced a renewal of interest in metrical systems under the general heading of **new formalism.** Although it is not a dominant movement, it has many enthusiastic adherents.

When one is introduced to meter, it may seem mechnical and limiting. There are new terms to master, just as there are when one is learning the grammar of a foreign language. But poets who prefer to work metrically don't usually start out by selecting a meter as if it were a mold into which one could pour words. Instead, they are more likely to let a poem begin intuitively and see what kind of line develops. If you have been reading metered poetry, your initial lines may suggest a metrical pattern that seems natural and appropriate for your material.

Once we get beyond the introductory stage in metrics, it becomes clear that what we speak of as an iambic pentameter or a trochaic trimeter line is an abstract concept to work with rather than an accurate description of the completed poem. Poet and reader keep that metrical beat in mind, but the pleasure comes in the interplay between that pattern and the variations that the poem presents.

Those who listen to jazz know what it is to improvise around the melody, alternately straying from it and returning to it. Stray too far and too often, and the memory of the melody is lost; stick too close, and you run the risk of monotony. In the same way, those who enjoy working with meter find pleasure in variety without losing contact with the traditional rhythm.

There are two other benefits to writing in meter that its proponents often mention. One is that using a metrical pattern frequently leads to finding words and phrases that one didn't think of at first. That is, the meter (and the rhyme too, if it is used) often pushes the poet into exploring possibilities that might not have been tried with a less structured system.

Second, many poets like the opportunity of emphasizing or highlighting a word or phrase through the natural stress of a metrical foot or, stronger still, through substitution. We have seen how using the heavy initial beat of a trochaic foot in a bascially iambic poem can add emphasis, and how the lilting quality of an anapest can give a lift to a line that is otherwise consistently iambic or trochaic. This technique provides a delicate control of language not possible when one is writing prose.

The choice of whether to work with meter or not is a personal one, but like so many aspects of the arts, it is not a true choice until one has tried both possibilities. Many prefer the looser structure of free verse, but there will always be poets for whom meter is a valuable asset.

8

FIXED FORMS

Why fixed forms? The haiku, a nonmetrical fixed form. Rhyming couplets: uses and risks. Triplets, rhyming and not. Quatrains and the ballad tradition. Sonnets, English and Italian. The villanelle.

For some, the very thought of a **fixed form** in poetry is an anathema. Why should there be limits? Oddly, no one asks that question about sports. As Robert Frost pointed out, tennis with the net down is no fun. And the net is only a part of the game. The entire court is divided into precise rectangles, and the players agree to use those areas in prescribed ways, following a specific sequence of activities. The same is true of football, baseball, or any other organized sport. Every card game has its rules as well, and we don't look kindly on the man who starts playing poker with a deck of 53 cards.

The satisfaction we get from any sport usually begins by watching others play. From them we learn "the rules of the game." We come to admire the skill and ingenuity of individual players. Then we see how well we can perform within those same limits.

The various poetic forms that have been devised over the centuries provide for many the same kind of pleasure. As in an any sophisticated game, there is an infinite range for personal expression. Part of the pleasure comes from comparing our efforts with the work of those who have adopted the same set of guidelines. As we do this, we enter a fellowship of thousands.

The Haiku

We think of fixed forms as being metered and rhymed. But the **haiku**, one of the oldest of fixed forms, is neither. As we saw in the last chapter, it is a sophisticated form of syllabics.

To review quickly, in English the haiku traditionally consists of three lines with five syllables in the first, seven in the second, and five in the third.

Unlike most fixed forms, the convention also includes certain aspects of the content as well. Haiku almost always contain images from nature, and they also either state or imply a season. Third, most suggest a striking similarity or even an identity between two seemingly different objects. Here is a haiku from Chapter 2. Written by the Japanese poet Chora, it makes use of all three characteristics.

> After spring sunset
> Mist rises from the river
> Spreading like a flood.

As you can see, the syllable count in this translation follows the 5–7–5 pattern exactly. The poem also identifies the season, spring, and compares the gentle movement of spreading mist to that of a potentially dangerous flood.

Centuries later Etheridge Knight, an African-American, taught himself to write haiku in prison and composed many that make full use of the same tradition both in structure and in content. Here is a sample from Chapter 2:

> A bare pecan tree
> slips a pencil shadow down
> a moonlit snow slope.

In this winter scene a moonlight shadow is seen as a pencil line on a white sheet of paper. Though separated by centuries and distinctly different cultural traditions, these two poets share a type of vision through this fixed form.

Knight, in commenting on his development as a poet, described his indebtedness to the haiku. He found that the requirements of the form helped him to give up abstractions and search instead for simple but striking images. Other examples of his haiku can be seen on page 22.

Rhyming Couplets: Uses and Risks

The great asset of rhyming **couplets** is that each pair of lines becomes a tight little unit linked by sound and often by content as well. In the seventeenth and eighteenth centuries, poets like Alexander Pope (1688–1744) and Oliver Goldsmith (1728–1774) used them to deal with subjects we would now handle in prose as essays.

At that time, the couplets were often end-stopped (concluded with a comma or a period). Occasionally they were complete on their own in what is called an **epigram**, a brief and pithy saying. For example, in speaking of how a nation can become prey to "hastening ills," Goldsmith wrote:

> Ill fares the land, to hastening ills a prey,
> Where wealth accumulates, and men decay.

The great liability of couplets, as I pointed out earlier, is monotony. In unskilled hands, it becomes a boring beat and an obtrusive rhyme. As a result, the couplet has fallen on hard times, often reduced to jingles, greeting cards, and occasional verse (lines composed for occasions, like anniversaries and retirements). Even if you are working with a serious, sophisticated topic, your efforts may seem trivial by association with these simple versions.

If one is on guard against these risks, however, the form lends itself to highly sophisticated contemporary verse. It is particularly effective with **narrative poems**—those that tell a story.

The couplets that comprise Maxine Kumin's "Morning Swim" (page 32) are an excellent example. The story line is simple: the narrator's early-morning dip becomes a spiritual experience. As we have seen, both the rhyme and the meter (iambic tetrameter) are muted through the use of enjambment, run-on lines. Our attention is held not with a rousing plot but with the thematic suggestion—the subtle but moving link between the rhythm of the lines, her swimming strokes, and the hymn that she begins to hum.

Triplets, Rhyming and Not

Triplets, also called **tercets**, are occasionally used in unrhymed and unmetered verse to provide a visual structure and to control the pace of reading. Steven Bauer's "Lust" (page 37) is a good example. Since it is written in perfectly regular triplets, one might think at first glance that the poem must be metered and rhymed. It isn't. Instead of serving as a metrical base, the stanza divisions provide a looser rhythm that acts as counterpoint to the rhythm of the sentences. In this way, the stanza divisions muffle the effect of the sentence structure. There are six complete sentences in this poem, and if no stanza divisions had been used, these sentences would dominate the way we read the poem just as they would in prose. By dividing the poem into eight stanzas each of which breaks up a sentence, Bauer encourages us to move at a slower pace, responding with greater deliberation.

Here, for example, is how he emphasizes a brutal simile, placing the tenor (the subject) at the end of one stanza and the vehicle (the figurative image) in the next stanza, forcing us to give it weight rather than skimming over it as we might a sentence in prose:

> His eyes,
>
> darker than I remembered,
> flashed like the broken neck
> of a bottle swiped on rock.

More traditionally, triplets are the base of a metrical system, usually iambic tetrameter (four feet to the line) or iambic pentameter (five feet to the line). The rhyme scheme is occasionally, *aaa*, but a pleasing and less obtrusive rhyme is *aba*. Separating the rhymed lines with one that is not softens the effect.

The **terza rima** is a beautiful extension of the triplet and lends itself best to longer poems. The middle line of each triplet is made to rhyme with the first and last lines of the next triplet in this manner:

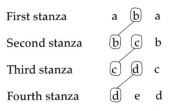

First stanza	a b a
Second stanza	b c b
Third stanza	c d c
Fourth stanza	d e d

In this way each stanza is subtly linked with the next, but the sound linkages are never obtrusive.

Quatrains and the Ballad Tradition

The four-line stanza, or **quatrain,** is probably the most popular of all fixed verse forms. One advantage is that it allows for such a variety of possible rhyme schemes. High on the list is *abab*, nonobtrusive yet never fully lost. Less noticeable (and less demanding as well) is *abcb*, which leaves the third line unrhymed. Occasionally quatrains are left unrhymed and even unmetered as Bauer did with triplets in "Lust."

Perhaps because quatrains are ideal for memorization, the four-line stanza has become the traditional form for ballads. The term **ballad** refers to works that are intended to be sung, recited, or read, but what they have in common is a lively story line and in most cases a four-line stanza. Ballads in English are often iambic tetrameter, although the five-footed pentameter is also popular. The rhyme scheme varies in the ways described above: either *abab* or the looser *abcb*.

Ballad meter is a variation in which the length of the lines alternate regularly between iambic tetrameter and iambic trimeter. Normally the rhyme scheme is *abcb*.

The term *folk ballad* refers most often to those thousands of Scottish and English works in ballad meter that were composed and sung by untrained, often illiterate balladeers from the fourteenth to the sixteenth centuries. That tradition of relatively simple narrative poems dealing with love, war, and the supernatural is alive today in the form of popular folk songs. In fact, the word *ballad* is applied equally to poetry and song.

Literary ballads are merely a refinement of this same tradition. "The Rime of the Ancient Mariner" by Samuel Taylor Coleridge is one of the best known. Although he allowed himself occasional variations in traditional ballad meter, here is a dramatic stanza that contains only one rather inconspicuous substitution.

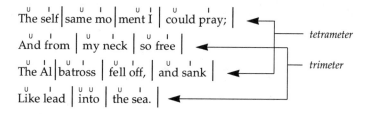

In this volume, Anthony Hecht's "Lizards and Snakes" (page 35) adapts the ballad form to tell a story that is more complex than it appears on first reading. His stanzas are visually eight lines long, but if you draw a line after each fourth line and look at the rhyme scheme, you will see that it is really composed in quatrains like most ballads. He has increased the traditional line length by alternating iambic pentameter with iambic tetrameter. His rhyme scheme is *abab* throughout.

Hecht's variations on the basic ballad form show that there is nothing sacred about literary tradition. But notice that once he establishes his version of the ballad, he stays with it. A poem that begins with a traditional form and then deteriorates toward the end suggests that perhaps the poet was working late at night to meet an early morning deadline.

Sonnets, English and Italian

While the balland lends itself to story telling, the **sonnet's** precise length is best suited for a single, well-defined thought or set of feelings. There are two basic versions, English (also called **Elizabethan**) and Italian (also called **Petrarchan**). They are both 14 lines long and both are traditionally written in iambic pentameter—five feet to the line. Where they differ is mainly in the rhyme scheme.

The English sonnet, made famous by Shakespeare, can be thought of as three quatrains and a final rhyming couplet: *abab, cdcd, efef, gg*. The first eight lines are referred to as the **octave** and the last six as the **sestet**. Often there is some shift of mood at the beginning of the sestet, providing poetic tension. In these cases, the unity of the poem is established with the resolution in the final rhyming couplet.

If you have been reading sonnets, you can identify the form in advance just from the basic 14-line shape. Occasionally Elizabethan sonnets are printed as an unbroken block, but more often they are printed as an octave and a sestet. That concluding couplet is a distinguishing characteristic both in rhyme and, usually, in the subject matter as well.

The second basic type, the **Italian sonnet,** is also based on 14 lines of iambic pentameter, but it is usually arranged as two quatrains and two triplets: *abba, abba, cde, cde.* You can differentiate it from the Elizabethan sonnet immediately from the fact that it has no concluding couplet.

Sonnets are printed in various ways, but here is a schematic representation of the spacing and rhyme scheme often adopted:

ENGLISH SONNET   ITALIAN SONNET

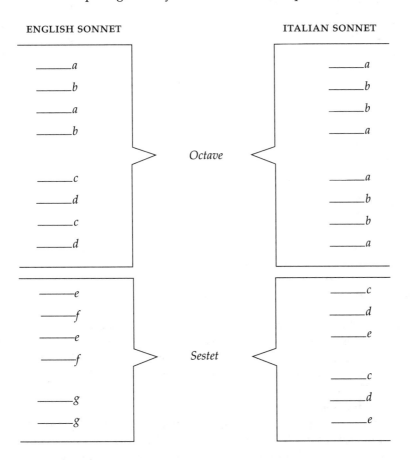

Robert Frost in his sonnet "Design" (page 14) follows the Italian form faithfully with one exception: He ends the poem with a rhyming couplet as if it were an English sonnet.

The Villanelle

The **villanelle** may seem intimidating when you first see it described, but once you see the pattern and compare it with the two examples in this text, it becomes quite manageable. Its repetitions have a haunting quality that can be highly effective.

As with dance steps and football plays, diagrams are more helpful than words. Remember that the whole poem is in iambic pentameter and has only three rhymes, *a*, *b*, and *c*.

THE VILLANELLE

1.	First refrain	*a*
2.	——————	*b*
3.	Second refrain	*a*
4.	——————	*a*
5.	——————	*b*
6.	First refrain	*a*
7.	——————	*a*
8.	——————	*b*
9.	Second refrain	*a*
10.	——————	*a*
11.	——————	*b*
12.	First refrain	*a*
13.	——————	*a*
14.	——————	*b*
15.	Second refrain	*a*
16.	——————	*a*
17.	——————	*b*
18.	First refrain	*a*
19.	Second refrain	*a*

"The Waking" by Theodore Roethke (page 31) is a villanelle. The opening phrase, "I wake to sleep," is central. It suggests that life is a gradual waking followed by death, an eternal sleep. He goes on to say that with this in mind he will prolong this waking process as long as he can: ". . . take my waking slow." This key concept is, because of the villanelle form, repeated in the even-numbered stanzas: second, fourth, and sixth.

The other key concept is that one gains experience simply by moving through life toward inevitable death: "I learn by going where I have to go." This is repeated in the odd-numbered stanzas, three and five, as well as in the final stanza.

If you look at how these two key concepts are used, you will see how the seeming complexity of the form allows a poet to highlight certain themes. Form and content work together.

Here are the first two stanzas with annotations showing the meter and the two refrains that are repeated alternately in the other stanzas:

I wake | to sleep, | and take | my wak|ing slow. | *first refrain (repeated at end of even-numbered stanzas)*

I feel | my fate | in what | I can|not fear. |

I learn | by go|ing where | I have | to go. | *second refrain (repeated at end of odd-numbered stanzas)*

We think | by feel|ing. What | is there | to know? |

I hear | my be|ing dance | from ear | to ear. |

I wake | to sleep, | and take | my wak|ing slow. |

If you look carefully at the whole poem, you will notice that Roethke takes certain minor liberties with the form. Some of the rhymes, for example, are slant rhymes, and one of the refrains is subtly altered (without giving up the pentameter). But he is essentially faithful to the form, and if you enjoy this kind of challenge you will want to match his fidelity.

For some, fixed forms provide a framework within which they can find a full range of personal expression. Many poets have described how the requirements of a particular form will lead them to consider words or phrases that wouldn't have come to mind otherwise.

For others, the requirements seem too restrictive. They would rather devise unique rhythms for each poem in ways we will consider in the next chapter. Remember, however, that there is no sharp division between the two approaches. Traditional forms can be altered to fit the needs of a particular poem, and even the most intuitive free-verse poem may benefit from techniques we associate with metered verse. The more poetry you read, the more you will understand how wide your options are.

9

UNIQUE RHYTHMS

Freedom from meter: assets and liabilities. Visual patterns: typography and white space. Auditory patterns: the oral tradition. The line versus syntax: the uses of sentence structure. The border with prose. Developing your own rhythms.

The term **unique rhythms** describes rhythms that are devised to meet the needs of an individual poem. Since they do not rely on the formal patterns we have been calling traditional rhythms, they are unique to each work.

In our own century, unique rhythms are associated with **free verse**. Free verse abandons meter for other rhythmical devices, and it drops regular rhyme in favor of looser sound systems such as assonance and consonance. But poetry that makes use of unique rhythms was popular centuries before the term *free verse* was coined. The irregular patterns of unique rhythms are rooted in a variety of ancient sources, both written and oral.

Freedom from Meter: Assets and Liabilities

When working with unique rhythms, you are free to devise your own systems. There is no consistent pattern to serve as a guide. In early drafts, the writing may be highly intuitive.

There are advantages and disadvantages to this type of writing. On the one hand, it will seem as if anything is possible—a heady sensation. On the other hand, you're on your own! It's up to you to devise your own rhythmical patterns and sound linkages. If you don't, you're writing prose in short lines. Without traditional guidelines, it is more difficult to determine what is really effective and what doesn't work. It's harder to be sure at what point the poem has reached its full potential.

Although unique rhythms are more difficult to categorize than formal rhythms, there are two broad traditions from which you can draw. The first is **typography**, the arrangement of print on the page. Since this is primarily a visual aspect, it includes the white space around the poem: the margins, the extra space between lines, and the occasional use of extra spacing between words. The second tradition, older still, is *auditory*. This includes everything an audience can detect by ear.

We will examine these two aspects separately for the purpose of analysis, but in actual practice they are closely interrelated. The spacing of words on the page influences the way one reads a poem aloud. Readers respond to these cues both consciously and unconsciously. And on the other side, the oral effect you as poet want to achieve will influence the way you arrange your lines. You "hear" a poem as you write.

Visual Patterns: Typography and White Space

Typography is simply the arrangement of words on the page. Writers of prose, as I pointed out in the first chapter, have almost no control over the arrangement of their words. Since line length is left up to the printer, sentence follows sentence like a series of freight cars. The only typographical option left is the space that indicates a new paragraph. Poets, on the other hand, have full control over the placement of every word and even every syllable.

Some poets take full advantage of this option, spreading their lines out with many spaces. Other poets mold their free verse into fairly uniform units that look very much like metered stanzas. The choice depends partly on the poet's general style and partly on the demands of an individual poem.

Here, for example, is the opening stanza of Denise Levertov's "Merritt Parkway." The entire poem appears on page 30, but this portion is enough to remind you how she adopts an extremely loose typography to suggest the flow of traffic on a busy freeway:

      As if it were
   forever that they move, that we
      keep moving—
         Under a wan sky where
      as the lights went on a star
         pierced the haze & now
    follows steadily
        a constant
   above our six lanes
   the dreamlike continuum . . .

It would be an exaggeration to say that a reader could identify the subject simply through the arrangement of words on the page, but because we know what is being described from the outset, the shape of the lines becomes a part of the total meaning. Anyone who has driven on an interstate can feel the flow of traffic, almost unbroken and undulating as we shift lanes.

The form Levertov creates is unique in that it matches no other poem. Not only is there no meter or rhyme, there is no repetition of line length. Unlike Dylan Thomas' "Fern Hill" (page 24), the lines of each stanza do not match in length the corresponding lines of the other stanzas. Unless you look closely, you won't even notice that there are actually five stanzas. They vary in length, and because of the indentations, we hardly notice the extra space that separates one stanza from the rest. They are as unobtrusive and arbitrary as the gaps that occur in a line of traffic.

Compare these long, undulating lines with the short, unadorned lines of free verse in Philip Appleman's "Desire." Here are the first two of four stanzas from the poem which appears on page 36 in its entirety:

1
The body
tugged like a tide, a pull
stronger than
the attraction of stars.

2
Moons
circling their planets
planets
rounding their suns.

Here the effect is dramatically different from the flowing quality of the Levertov poem. Most notable is the fact that the lines are extremely short. Some have only one word. This alone prompts you to read the poem word by word.

In addition, Appleman has made every effort to isolate each stanza and give it an identity: Each is numbered, each begins with a noun (a tenor) that is then followed by amplification—a simile in the first stanza and a simple comparison in the second. These four-line stanzas (and the concluding three-line stanza) have the compression and simplicity of haiku even though they do not follow that syllabic form.

Why the difference between these two poems? In some cases, a poet's decision about how to shape a free-verse work is intuitive, but in this case we can see a direct relationship between the subject matter and the form. "Merritt Parkway" describes a specific east-coast freeway with its steady flow of traffic. It focuses on what it feels like to be gliding along in that "dreamlike continuum." Those long and varied lines can be described with the same phrase the poet uses to end the poem: "a slurred sound."

"Desire," on the other hand, is a delicate description of longing. The speaker is comparing his or her desire for someone who is, in the last stanza, "oceans away." The poem moves from image to image, and the brevity of each line and each stanza urges us to read deliberately as if walking on stepping stones.

White space refers to the margins of the poem, the blank space between words, and the extra space between lines which designates the division between stanzas. The concept is similar to what painters refer to as *negative space*—the patterns made by the areas between the objects on the canvas. Poets and painters share the ability to create significance literally from nothing.

White space in the form of extra spaces in the line itself is sometimes called **horizontal rhythm**. Think of it as gaps on the horizon. In "Merritt Parkway" these gaps have the effect of moving the line left or right. Some of these indentations seem arbitrary, like the motion of cars shifting lanes, but others highlight a particular word. In the first stanza, printed above, "a constant" is isolated to the right. It emphasizes the fixed nature of the star above the moving cars. In the next stanza (see page 30) the word "unsure" is isolated to the right in exactly the same way. This stanza focuses on us, "the humans from inside the / cars." In this way the fixed position of the star is set off against the fluid, uncertain state of those driving.

In the same way, when extra spaces are left between lines, the result is **vertical rhythm**. Traditional stanza forms, of course, often make use of vertical rhythms by leaving an extra space between each stanza. But when a writer is working with unique rhythms as Levertov is in "Merritt Parkway," those spaces become irregular and in many cases closely tied to the meaning. They are **nonrecurrent stanzas**.

One note of caution, however: Simple, obvious use of typography can be just as damaging to a free-verse poem as simple, singsong use of meter and rhyme can be to traditional work. Because typographical arrangements are so blatant, so immediately apparent, they have to be used with considerable subtlety. Every writing class has been subjected to some version of this:

> And on that happy afternoon we
>   all
>   fell
>   down
>   laughing.

What do you have to do to achieve real freshness and ingenuity in typography? E. E. Cummings' poem "Buffalo Bill's" (page 32) is an example of a relatively extreme use of both vertical and horizontal spacing. Take, for example, these three lines:

> and break onetwothreefourfive pigeonsjustlikethat
>
>   Jesus
>
> he was a handsome man

Those run-together phrases are a sample of compressed horizontal spacing. Cummings actually speeds up your reading with that technique. This may not occur on your first reading, of course, since it takes time to figure out lines that are printed without spaces. But once you are used to the poem, these lines seem to ripple by as if they were moving:

Notice too how the word "Jesus" is suspended on the right with white space above and below. At first it seems to be an exclamation of admiration about his shooting ability. In prose it would be followed with an exclamation mark. But as you continue to read, it leaps forward as if tied to "he was a handsome man." Like an optical illusion, it flips back and forth, serving both functions, tricky as Buffalo Bill himself. Of course, something similar might be tried in metered verse, but the effect in free verse can be made far more pronounced by the use of all that white space.

Notice, incidentally, that Cummings uses a form of syllables in addition to typography. His run-together phrase "onetwothreefourfive" has exactly the same number of syllables as "pigeonsjustlikethat"—linking the number of his rapid-fire shots and the series of clay pigeons on a skeet range. This is a good example of the fact that when working with the unique rhythms of free verse, you can combine several techniques.

When we analyze poems like "Merritt Parkway" and "Buffalo Bill's," it should become apparent that much of what appeared on first reading to be arbitrary placement is in fact carefully planned to create an effect. Levertov's horizontal and vertical rhythms create our sense of cars moving on the highway, and Cummings controls the speed of our reading with precision and plays tricks with our expectations.

Don't expect to find a rational explanation for every typographical element. As with the brush strokes of a painter, many decisions that go into making a poem are intuitive. If it were not for this aspect, typographical rhythms would tend to seem contrived, even forced. This is why it is important to keep working on different versions of the same poem, writing out each and reading them aloud. Trust your ear as much as your mind.

One extreme form of typography is the **shaped poem**, which molds the shape of the work into the object it is describing. This form was particularly popular in the seventeenth century and is well illustrated by Herbert's "The Altar" and "Easter Wings," as well as by Herrick's "The Pillar of Flame," each of which resembles the object suggested in its title. More recently, contemporaries like Allen Ginsberg have published poems in the shape of atomic clouds and, with the aid of punctuation, rockets.

For unknown reasons, what has for centuries been called *shaped poetry* was renamed **concrete poetry** in the early 1960s and hailed as a new technique. It quickly became a fad, often reduced to mere tricks. As a poem begins to rely more and more on its shape, it generally makes less and less use of the sound of language, rhythms, or metaphor. Even the theme becomes simplified. Highly obtrusive visual effects tend to overpower all other aspects. One can, for example, repeat the word *death* all over the page in such a way as to resemble a skull. It takes time and a certain mindless patience to do this, but the result is more like a cartoon than a poem. In general, the more extreme experiments in shaped poetry are remembered more for their curiosity value than for their literary worth.

Even nonpictorial use of typography has its drawbacks if used excessively. If you flip through any anthology, or the poems in Chapter 2 of this volume, you will see that the technique is employed by less than a third of the poems. It is difficult to match the thematic complexity of E. E. Cummings and all too easy to become captivated by mere trickiness. It is an interesting approach, but if you try it, make sure the poem has thematic depth as well.

Auditory Patterns: The Oral Tradition

Poetry, much more than prose, draws on the oral tradition. As I pointed out earlier, epic poems were recited long before they were written, and even today in many parts of the world they are memorized for oral delivery.

In our own culture memorization is less valued, but the continuing popularity of poetry readings and recordings demonstrates how much we enjoy hearing a poem as well as seeing it on the page. It's no accident that we use the word *verse* equally for works to be recited and those to be sung.

Anaphora is probably the most conspicuous auditory device in poetry. It is the repetition of a word or words at the beginning of two or more lines or sentences. The effect is often strengthened by using a similar type of sentence such as a series of questions or pronouncements. This creates what is sometimes called **syntactical rhythms**. It is an auditory device that is frequently heard in oratory as well. The high point of Martin Luther King's "I have a dream" speech, for example, is an excellent example.

Here is a sample of anaphora in poetry combined with syntactical rhythm. It is taken from Walt Whitman's "Passage to India." The anaphoral word is *who* and the syntactical rhythm is created by a series of short questions.

> Ah who shall soothe these feverish children?
> Who justify these restless explorations?
> Who speak the secret of impassive earth?
> Who bind it to us? what is this separate Nature so unnatural?
> What is this earth to our affections? . . .

In prose we generally try to avoid redundancies, yet here is a string of them. They seem appropriate in poetry mainly because rhythm is a part of the genre and this particular type of rhythm has long been associated with the oral tradition.

Allen Ginsberg wrote "Howl!" in 1959, 104 years after Whitman first published "Leaves of Grass," and his indebtedness is clear. Here Ginsberg describes "the best minds of my generation":

> who bared their brains to Heaven under the El and saw
>   Mohammedan angels staggering on tenement roofs
>   illuminated,
> who passed through universities with radiant cool eyes
>   hallucinating Arkansas and Blake-light tragedy among the
>   scholars of war,
> who were expelled from the academies for crazy & publishing
>   obscene odes on the windows of the skull,
> who cowered in unshaven rooms in underwear, burning their
>   money in wastebaskets and listening to the Terror through
>   the wall, . . .

Ginsberg is clearly influenced by Whitman, but both of them drew on a still earlier source, the Bible. Although the version Whitman knew was in English (the King James translation), and Ginsberg's version was in the original Hebrew, both men were strongly influenced by the rhythmical patterns found there. Compare, for example, the selections quoted from these two poets with this passage from Job 38:34–37:

> Canst thou lift up thy voice to the clouds,
>   that abundance of waters may cover thee?
> Canst thou send lightnings, that they may go
>   and say unto thee, Here we are?
> Who hath put wisdom in the inward parts?
>   or who hath given understanding to the heart?
> Who can number the clouds in wisdom?
>   or who can pour out the bottles of heaven?

Here too, it is the entire syntactical unit that is repeated to achieve the rhythm. The anaphoral words are merely cues that signal the repeated form. For further examples, read over the rest of the Book of Job and review the Psalms. Then go back and study the complex system of syntactical rhythms in Genesis. Doing this makes one far more open to the rhythms not only of Whitman and Ginsberg but of Ferlinghetti, Gregory Corso, John Ashbery, Amiri Baraka, and many others writing today.

Anaphora combined with a recurring sentence structure doesn't have to be thundering to succeed. The technique as used by Lisel Mueller in "Night Song" (page 28) is gentle yet effective. It borrows from a centuries-old form called the *riddle poem*, though it is far more subtle in theme than most of them. Here is the first stanza:

> Among rocks, I am the loose one,
> among arrows, I am the heart,
> among daughters, I am the recluse,
> among sons, the one who dies young.

The simplicity of the form is deceptive. If you read the poem over as a whole, you will see how the speaker finally becomes a symbol of poets everywhere. "Among the bones you find on the beach," she concludes, "the one that sings was mine."

Both Mueller's poem and the earlier examples by the way, demonstrate the close relationship between syntactical rhythms and typography. If we wrote out "Night Song" or the selection from Job in lines of prose, the resulting **prose rhythm** would be unmistakable, just as it is in certain types of traditional oratory:

> Among rocks, I am the loose one; among arrows, I am the heart,
> among daughters, I am the recluse; among sons, the one who
> dies young.

Prose rhythms can be highly effective, but because poets control the arrangement on the page, they can place each repeated phrase at the start of a new line. In this way, typography emphasizes the syntactical rhythms already there. This is one of the advantages poets have over writers of prose.

In the examples we have been considering, anaphora is unmistakable because it is followed by a pronounced similarity of sentence structure. But often it is used alone.

Lucille Clifton's poem "What the Mirror Said" (page 23) appears to be light, spontaneous, and conversational. But if you look at it carefully, you will see that in the first half it is structured through three anaphoral words: "listen," "you," and "somebody":

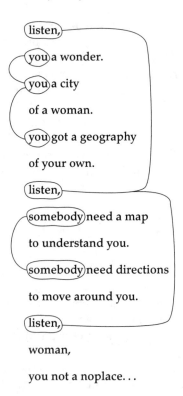

listen,

you a wonder.

you a city

of a woman.

you got a geography

of your own.

listen,

somebody need a map

to understand you.

somebody need directions

to move around you.

listen,

woman,

you not a noplace...

This rhythmical use of anaphora is not repeated toward the end of the poem, but Clifton does continue to use the one-word line to create a rhythm as emphatic as thumping one's hand on the table.

The Line versus Syntax: The Uses of Sentence Structure

When you read prose, you respond to the punctuation of the sentence even if you can't tell a compound sentence from a compound fracture. You pause at commas, come to a full stop at periods, and take a deep breath at the end of paragraphs.

When you read poetry, you tend to respond the same way to the ends of lines. When schoolchildren recite poetry, they sometimes have to be reminded not to pause unnecessarily at the conclusion of each line. As adults reading to ourselves, we unconsciously pause even when the context suggests that we should keep going.

When you write poetry, you have at your disposal both of these rhythmical devices—sentence structure and line length. Occasionally you will find a poem that emphasizes syntax to the point of ending each line with a period or a comma. Theodore Roethke's villanelle "The Waking" (page 31) is such a poem. Out of 19 lines, all but one are end-stopped, concluding with a period, a comma, or a question mark. The syntactical rhythm—that generated by the sentence structure—matches a almost perfectly the line length and in this case the meter as well. This matching, however, is rare. Most poems mute the metrical line through emjambment and other techniques described in Chapter 7. By having the sentence run on into the next line, the two rhythmical systems, line and syntax, are slightly blurred to keep the reader from adopting a singsong rendition.

At the other extreme, a few poems avoid all punctuation, relying exclusively on the line for rhythmical effect. This is a technique that lends itself to relatively short poems with short, syntactically simple lines. Haiku, for example, rarely use punctuation.

Nikki Giovani's "Balances" (page 26) is one of the few longer poems in this volume that uses no punctuation at all. Notice how in these first five lines the lack of punctuation keeps the poem uncluttered. The effect is almost like someone walking step by step along a tightrope.

> in life
> one is always
> balancing
>
> like we juggle our mothers
> against our fathers

The great majority of poems use punctuation along with line length, the two working in subtle harmony or in some cases as counterpoint to each other. Steven Bauer's "Lust," which I analyzed in Chapter 8 (page 96), is an excellent example of this contrapuntal rhythm, the syntax played against the regularity of triplets.

Both metered and unmetered poetry, of course, give you the option of whether to highlight the syntactical rhythms with punctuation. The temptation to do without any punctuation seems great when you first plunge into the heady freedom of free verse. Remember, however, that syntax, sentence structure, still exists simply through the context, whether you use punctuation or not. Most established poets find it helpful to use punctuation deliberately, since it provides one more rhythmical system.

The Border with Prose

Between free-verse poetry and prose there is a misty, unmarked border. Some poets, for example, place little emphasis on the deliberate rhythmical systems we have been discussing, preferring instead to think in terms of

breath units. On a literal level, that phrase suggests that a line is broken where the reader of the poem would naturally take a breath when reciting aloud. But different poets seem to have remarkably different lung capacities. In addition, the notion is complicated in poems that are presented through a **persona**, an implied speaker who may have cadences of his or her own.

In point of fact, lungs have less to do with poetic composition than does the poet's own sense of rhythm. It was not emphysema that caused Philip Appleman to describe his sense of longing and desire with these concluding lines:

> Undertow:
> I reach for you,
> oceans away.

Nor was it deep-breathing exercises that led Donald Hall to adopt lines like these in "Names of Horses" (page 35):

> For a hundred and fifty years, in the pasture of dead horses,
> roots of pine trees pushed through the pale curves of your ribs,

Both of these poets made deliberate choices, each selecting a line length he felt would create the tone he wanted to achieve.

The hazy border between poetry and prose is called **prose poetry**. This apparent contradiction in terms is a hybrid form written in lines that look essentially like a prose paragraph. Although the writer maintains control over the line length, lines are usually similar in length. Some of these works have less rhythm and fewer sound linkages and figurative language than the prose of, say, Dylan Thomas in "August Bank Holiday" quoted in Chapter 6. Some feel that this form serves no function except to slow the reader down, but its defenders point to examples that achieve a compression of statement and contain echoes of speech rhythms.

Developing Your Own Rhythms

When you begin composing a new poem, let the first few lines speak to you. Often they will suggest the kinds of rhythms that are appropriate for that particular poem. Your emotional involvement with the material, your personal preferences, and the nature of the subject matter will all influence what develops. And because so many factors are involved, the result will be unique.

As the poem develops, consider some of the techniques we have examined in this chapter: manipulation of words on the page, horizontal and vertical rhythms, the use of white space, the oral tradition of anaphora and syntactical repetitions, and the use of punctuation as an additional rhythmical system. Remember that although we have analyzed them separately, they are all interrelated. Because of these interconnections, strive to keep your rhythms subtle. Try not to overwork any one device so heavily that the technique becomes obtrusive. Experiment with a number of different approaches and trust your feelings.

With this in mind, here is an exercise that will help you keep your options open. First, read the three prose sentences quoted in the next paragraph. Forget that they have been taken from a poem you have studied. Imagine that this is simply a prose passage that happens to be highly charged with visual and auditory images:

"The wind's untiring saxophone keens at the glass. The lamp sheds a monochrome of stainless steel and linens, the nurse in her snowy dress firm in her regimens. The form in the bed is a soul diminished to a fledgling, fed on the tentative balm of spring, sketch for an angel, half-finished, shoulder blades the stubs of wings."

After you have become familiar with the passage (you may want to look up a couple of words), convert it to two quite different poems using the same wording but breaking the lines in different ways. Consider both horizontal and vertical rhythms, stressing different words by your choices. You may not be able to improve on the original version that is printed on page 26, but you will come to understand how fluid this approach to rhythmical language is. You may also discover how deeply the rhythmical patterns affect the tone and even the statement of a poem.

Another helpful exercise is to take a descriptive prose passage from an article about nature or travel. This time, don't limit yourself to the wording of the original. Find your own language to add freshness and intensity to the passage and then, as before, devise two different rhythmical approaches. This is the kind of "sketching" that will make your poetry journal an effective part of your development.

In addition to exercises like these in your journal, spend some time each day examining the rhythms of published poetry. Since most poetry contains rhythmical patterns of some sort, every anthology and literary quarterly can serve as a source for study. By combining practice work in your journal and extensive, careful reading, you will soon acquire a facility in poetic rhythms.

10

A SENSE OF ORDER

Order: the arrangement of a poem's content. Contrasts and comparisons. Shifts in attitude. Overt themes. The narrative sequence. Image clusters. Repetition and refrains.

In previous chapters we examined both fixed and flexible forms. They provide a variety of shapes. They are like containers. We now turn to the content.

If a poem rambles or lacks a sense of order, it will probably fail no matter how carefully you have worked on the form. Although it is quite possible to begin a poem with little thought about the structure of the content, don't ignore it entirely. Creating a sense of order is an integral part of the creative process.

The best time to examine this aspect is after you have completed one or two drafts. At this point, stop and take a close, analytical look at what holds that poem together. Why have you placed a particular line before another? Would a different order be more effective? If there are stanzas, are they in the best possible order? The poem probably has some type of structure which you have adopted without much thought. Now is the time to see if you have used the most effective sequence.

There are many different ways of structuring a poem. This chapter will deal with six that have been used frequently over the years. Obviously not all of your work will fit one of these categories, but examining them closely will give you the option of adopting them or devising some system of your own.

Contrasts and Comparisons

As a basic organizing strategy, the use of contrasts and comparisons is one of the most popular. In some cases the contrast may be directly stated, but in others it may be so subtle that it remains almost subliminal.

Philip Appleman's "Coast to Coast" (page 37) is a fine example of a contrast that dominates the entire poem. It's introduced at the end of the second stanza. In the first stanza the poet describes how when we travel by jet we are oblivious to the scene below. As he puts it, we are "blind to milkweed, riverbanks, the wrecks / of elm trees" below us. In the second stanza he describes crossing the country by car "on two-lane roads" from which one can see all those things that "make the busy continent worthwhile."

In the next two stanzas he gives us a series of highly visual, auditory, and tactile images depicting the kind of details we can respond to when driving:

> . . . the smell of woods and fields,
> the flash of finches and the scud of crows,
> the rub of asphalt underneath our wheels
> as tangible as sand between the toes.

The final stanza returns to jet travel: "Now, going home we're blind again."

Not only is this a contrast in modes of travel, it is also a contrast in the speaker's preference. Clearly he misses the sights, sounds, and even the feel of auto travel. He regrets the fact that fewer and fewer people are singing the song of the "open road."

Linda Pastan works with an entirely different type of contrast in "Domestic Animals" (page 18). During the day the friendly dog is "all sweet slobber" and the cat purrs with its deep "furred throat." But at night they have "dream claws and teeth" as they recall their origins. This contrast takes on broader implications with the phrase "the green / jungle of our sleep." The word *our* suggests that we too have our primal roots and perhaps a lingering "terrible hunger."

A third example is seen in a poem we have examined earlier for its use of syllabics: "Fern Hill" by Dylan Thomas (page 24). A careless reader might assume that the poem is simply a nostalgic set of memories of when the narrator was "young and easy under the apple boughs." Unlike the two poems mentioned above, it doesn't reveal the significant contrast until the last of six fairly lengthy stanzas. It is there that he wakes "to the farm forever fled from the childless land," leaving the narrator singing in his "chains like the sea." The boy in him still longs for those carefree days, but his adult self is aware that life is limited by mortality just as the restless sea is limited by the shoreline. Essentially, then, the poem is youthful innocence contrasted with adult realism, though most of the lines are devoted to the former.

Because comparisons, as opposed to contrasts, are made up of similar elements, you might think they would be less effective. But they often serve well. Any poem that is dominated by what is called a *controlling simile* or *dominant metaphor* is essentially a poem of comparison. Remember, though, that the comparison isn't a basic organizational element unless it dominates the poem as a whole. Some of the best examples are in haiku, where traditionally some type of comparison is fundamental. Etheridge Knight, for example, compares convicts at the end of a work day to lizards in this brief but haunting picture:

> Eastern guard tower
> glints in sunset; convicts rest
> like lizards on rocks.

For a longer, more complex example of a comparison poem, review Barbara Howes' "The Bay at West Falmouth" (page 29). It starts off with a simile in the first two of twelve lines, and this comparison is a controlling image for the length of the poem:

> Serenity of mind poises
> Like a gull swinging in air,

Everything in that poem depends on and amplifies that initial comparison.

Shifts in Attitude

Poems based on some basic shift in attitude are closely related to those with contrasts. They focus, however, on inner perceptions and feelings rather than on external objects and events. One of the more famous of these is Shakespeare's Sonnet 29, often referred to by its opening phrase, "When in Disgrace with Fortune" (page 19).

The entire octave—the first eight lines—is downbeat. The speaker describes feeling like an outcast; he is one who has cursed his fate, envying others. But in the sestet, just about at the point when we think he is indulging in excessive self-pity, the poem shifts with the word "yet."

> Yet in these thoughts my self almost despising,
> Haply I think on thee, and then my state,
> Like to the lark at break of day arising
> From sullen earth, sings hymns at heaven's gate,

The poem is a good example of how sonnets frequently adopt a new tone at the end of the octave. What concerns us here, though, is the fact that the basic structure of the poem is a dramatic shift in attitude.

Adrian Louis' "Looking for Judas" (page 15) has a shift that is, sadly, just the reverse. The narrator, a Native American, has just gutted and skinned a deer and starts dreaming about how in the old days his people had honor. In those days they would tell the deer that in killing them their spirits "would live in our flesh" and "their holy blood became ours."

If the poem ended with that line, the tone would be one of romantic hope for a rebirth of pride. But the last line crushes that optimism with a kind of verbal shrug:

> Or something like that.

What might have been a slightly sentimental poem becomes harshly realistic, with the myths of the past relegated to fading memories. The structure of the whole poem is based on that contrast in attitude.

Overt Themes

Some poems are organized around a dominant theme clearly stated either at the beginning of the end of the poem. I hesitate to list this approach at all because it is fraught with danger. In fact, it is the cause of countless student failures and the distress of creative writing teachers everywhere. The perceptive reader, however, will discover two such poems in Chapter 2, so it seems prudent to discuss why they succeed and why so many imitators fail.

Stephen Dunn's "A Secret Life" (page 38) is one. We know exactly what the theme of this poem is going to be from the title and the opening four lines:

> Why you need to have one
> is not much more mysterious than
> why you don't say what you think
> at the birth of an ugly baby.

There it is: an overt statement of his theme. And he sticks with it through 27 lines. The other poem is "War" by Robley Wilson (page 20). Like Dunn, Wilson starts out with a direct assertion: "Sometimes I have wanted to go to war." The poem goes on to argue that most of us—both men and women—have a secret love of war.

Why is this a risky way to organize a poem? Because too often beginning poets try to write editorials in verse. The result often repeats some **truism,** a widely accepted belief like the assertion that there shouldn't be so many poor people in a rich nation, we shouldn't be cutting down the rain forests, battered women need greater protection, it's terrible to be wasting food when so many are hungry. These are all good causes, but they won't be helped with bad verse. Nor will writing classes. Poems organized around topics like these are unsuccessful mainly because they say nothing new, but on a deeper level they fail because they confuse poetry with editorials. An editorial presents an argument in straight, logical prose. Its function is to inform or convince. A poem, on the other hand, is a literary art form that gives pleasure through its use of language and only secondarily describes some feeling or presents an insight.

So why are these two works successful as poems in spite of being blatantly organized around a thematic statement just like an editorial? First, neither of them is based on a truism. In fact, they both take a strikingly unorthodox position. It is widely believed these days is that we should communicate all our feelings. We are constantly told that total honesty is the key to happy relationships. Dunn runs counter to this notion by suggesting that secrets have their place. In fact, he argues that "your silence is a kind of truth."

As for war, everyone claims to be against it. The truism is that war is hell. Wilson doesn't support war, but he runs counter to popular belief by suggesting that in spite of what we say, we all have a secret admiration for the glories of war.

Equally important, both poems are fundamentally unlike editorials because they use language in an artful manner which itself gives pleasure. That is, they are not just logical arguments; they are verbal works of art. Dunn starts off with two witty examples of the kind of secrets we actually keep. He goes on to develop ingenious metaphors. He describes what we write in our private journals late at night as being

> . . . like a small fire
> in a clearing, it's what
> radiates and what can hurt
> if you get too close to it.

In the same way, Wilson doesn't present his case in logical steps like an editorial or magazine article. The poem is supercharged with ironies, playing our fascination with war against our awareness of how terrible it really is:

> Everyone ought to go off to a war
> Before he is too old to have the good
> Of it.

We wince, but also enjoy the way he describes the "benefits" of war, using words like *immortality* in connection with what we know is generally a slaughter of young people:

> . . . War is for the young
> And keeps them young; war is to make a man
> Immortal;

The examples of wry wit, irony, and word play are not mere adornments added to a logical argument; they are a part of the art form itself.

How does this apply to one who is just starting to write poetry? Generally speaking, you will be on solid ground if you avoid sweeping social statements altogether and focus on your own personal experience and your own feelings. Scenes, events, and personal relationships from your own life may well suggest broader concerns, but if these are rooted in what you personally know about and genuinely feel, they will maintain a sense of authenticity. No matter what you choose as a subject, however, remember that if it isn't more artful than prose in short lines, it isn't really a poem.

The Narrative Sequence

A **narrative** is a story, a sequence of events. It is as natural a structure for poetry as it is for prose. Although prose has come to be the preferred genre for lengthy fiction, poetry still draws on narrative as an organizing principle in shorter work.

Anthony Hecht's "Lizards and Snakes" (page 35) is a good example. As I pointed out in the chapter on fixed forms, he has adapted the literary ballad by using a slightly longer line and running his quatrains together to form eight-line stanzas. What concerns us here, however, is the way the story line is used as a basic method of organization.

At first the narrator describes how he and his friend Joe used to study lizards and snakes that came out to sun on hot days. He reports that they used to slip lizards into his Aunt Martha's knitting box so that they would leap out and frighten her. But in the final stanza there is a high wind and they overhear her as she sees a vision of the devil, an image that is close to the lizards they used to catch. They never played the trick again.

It is a relatively simple anecdote that starts with playful humor and ends with a more serious note. The reference to "carriage ruts" places the event back when belief in a literal devil was more common. The theme deals with the fact that what seems funny at one stage in your life changes as you grow up, but it is the story line that holds the poem together.

The narrative line in some poems is so underplayed that you hardly think of the work as telling a story, but the mere hint of a sequence of actions can provide an organizational structure. "The Pardon" by Richard Wilbur (page 27) is a good example. It begins with the summer day on which the persona, a boy of ten, finds the body of his dog. It continues through the burial. Then it jumps forward to when he had a nightmare about the experience. On waking, he begs "death's pardon." This is a highly sophisticated poem with a complex theme about reactions to death, yet it is organized and unified with a relatively simple story line.

In the same way, the story line in Maxine Kumin's "Morning Swim" (page 32) is minimal. The narrator simply goes swimming in the early morning and has a spiritual experience. That's barely a plot in fictional terms, but it is enough to unify the poem. It is a good reminder that a narrative sequence can be slight and still provide a structure for a poem.

On the other hand, narratives can become so complex that you don't really think of the poem as telling a story at all. Donald Hall's "Names of Horses" (page 34) is such a case. Turn to it now and review it carefully. See if you can on your own sort out three different narrative sequences that are woven together in that poem.

The first of these sequences is based on seasons of the year. It starts out "All winter" and moves in the second stanza to "April," turns to summer with "noon's heat" and finally to the fall with "one October" in the fifth stanza. This use of seasons is clear and fairly common as a device. But there is a second and longer sequence that is based on the stages of a single horse's life. The first four stanzas focus on the mature years when the horse can do heavy work; the fifth stanza starts when he is "old and lame" and is taken out to be shot, and the seventh stanza deals with the horse after death, when the roots of trees "pushed through the pale curves of your ribs."

The third cycle is the longest and most subtle. Far lengthier than the seasons of a single year, longer even than the story of one horse's life and death, it is that succession of horses moving through the same cycle "generation on generation." This generational sequence is the underlying narrative thread and the primary concern of the poem. We know that from the last line, a moving tribute to the long series of horses over the years: "O Roger, Mackerel, Riley, Ned, Nellie, Chester, Lady Ghost."

Just as a complex sound like a sustained note on a cello can be analyzed precisely as having sound waves of high, medium, and low frequency working together to produce a single note with rich overtones, so a poem can combine narratives of differing length to produce a single, unified effect. This is what we mean when we say that a poem has **resonance**.

Image Clusters

An **image**, as described in Chapter 5, is literally any detail that can be perceived with one of the five senses. In the early drafts of writing a poem, it is natural enough to use a series of similar images. If we write about tide pools, then snails and barnacles naturally come to mind; and if our subject is life on a farm, then barns, cows, and fields will doubtless play a part just as they would if the topic came up in conversation. To turn these chance similarities into a *system* of related images known as **image clusters** may take further revisions.

Philip Appleman's four-stanza poem "Desire" (page 36) is a clear example of how related images can be made to unify a poem. The first stanza focuses on "tide"; the second, on "moons," the cause of tides; and the final stanza highlights "undertow." Although his topic is the abstract sense of longing which could be presented through a wide variety of images, he unifies the poem by selecting images that all relate to sea currents.

This tactic is somewhat similar to the one used in Robley Wilson's "On a Maine Beach" (page 31). As I pointed out in Chapter 5, each section (it has no stanza breaks) is organized around groups of closely related images. If you turn back to page 66, you can review the linkages among "worn change," "mint-mark," "miser," "rims," "mainspring," "pinwheeling," "coins," "round lifetimes," "beach rhythms," and "circles." What we were examining there as image clusters linking certain lines actually form in a broader sense a unifying principle for the poem as a whole. The entire poem is subtly bound together not only by subject matter—rock pools—but also by a harmony of images, all forms of circles.

One of the richest and most sustained image clusters appears in Anita Endreszze's "The Mapmaker's Daughter" (page 39). It is a poem about love, a risky subject because of all the simple and sentimental attempts on this topic. But her slightly surreal, sensual treatment is absolutely fresh. The "mapmaker" of the title is the one who will navigate "the geography of love" of the first line. While we normally live on *terra firma*, solid ground, the state of love is, she reminds us, "terra infirma."

We navigate this uncertain area in "a paper boat." A woman is at the helm, armed with "the map of longing." There is "rain that launches thirst" and "secret passages" and ultimately the couple discover "deep / territories we name / after ourselves." The scene is misty and dreamlike, but we are able to follow it thanks to Endrezze's "compass of . . . desire"—and her beautifully harmonious series of closely related images.

Repetitions and Refrains

When we write prose, we do our best to avoid repetitions. Repeated words are referred to as redundancies, and repetition of longer units are condemned as bad organization. Poets, however, love repetition. The genre is like music in that repetitions are often used for rhythm or for emphasis. When used regularly through the length of a poem, they can serve as the organizational structure for the work as a whole.

The most blatant form of the **refrain** is the chorus, a repeated line or group of lines. It has long been a popular way to unify ballads. Whether sung, recited, or read silently, these repeated sections—often quatrains—help to hold a wandering narrative together.

As you remember, the one-line refrain is also an integral part of the villanelle. Each of the five tercets has one of two refrains, and the concluding quatrain has both. Even if you don't spot this recurring pattern of a villanelle on first reading, it unmistakably unifies the poem.

We have already examined the ways anaphora, the repetition of initial words or phrases, can serve as a rhythmical device. If it is used more or less consistently through the length of a poem, it can also serve as a basic organizational device.

In Lisel Mueller's "Night Song" (page 28) the repetitions we examined in the chapter on unique rhythms also serve as a basic organizational device. Starting with "Among rocks, I am the loose one," she repeats "among" at the beginning of ten of the twelve lines. Furthermore, the second half of seven lines start with "I am." This is an organizational technique we associate with poetry for children, but her subject, the qualities of a poet, is highly sophisticated.

Although this device is rare, a poem can also be unified by the repetition of the final word in a majority of lines. Gwendolyn Brooks' "We Real Cool" (page 34) follows this pattern. It may be the only poem in existence in which seven out of eight lines end with "We," with the grammatical sentence concluded on the next line.

These are only some of the many ways of creating a sense of order in a poem. There are poems, particularly longer ones, that will be structured in other ways. Remember too that many poems combine two or more techniques. "Fern Hill" not only is organized by a basic contrast between carefree youth and an adult awareness of mortality, but also is faintly narrative. It moves from childhood to adulthood in the concluding stanza. Carole Oles' poem "The Gift" (page 18) is not only a grim narrative, it is also a bitter contrast: the status of men as opposed to that of women.

To what degree should a poem be given a sense of order? That's up to you and the nature of each poem. It's important, however, to look over your rough draft and see what kind of organization has occurred naturally. Then decide whether it should be sharpened and, if so, what is the best approach.

11

VARIETIES OF TONE

How meaning depends on tone. The wide range of tones. The uses of irony. The cutting edge of satire. Creating tension through tone. You and your persona are not the same. Keeping the tone honest.

"I want that."

This looks like a clear, unambiguous statement. How could we mistake its meaning? Easily. In fact, we can't even respond until we identify the speaker and the tone of voice. Here are three different situations, each with its own tone. Notice how the meaning changes even though the words do not:

1. A stranger on a dark street says this, holding a gun.
2. A friend says this with a laugh as you both gaze longingly at an elegant BMW.
3. A woman says this with a sarcastic sneer about an unexpected tax bill.

The literal statement, the **denotation**, is the same in each case. But the implied meaning, the **connotation**, in each case is entirely different. The first is a threat, the second is a joke, and the third means exactly the opposite of the literal statement. Clearly, tone in everyday speech is not just an adornment to language; it is a fundamental aspect of meaning.

The same is true in poetry. **Tone** reveals your attitude toward your subject and in some cases the attitude of the **persona** or implied speaker of the poem as well. Although many poems are written in a neutral style, others rely so heavily on a certain tone that it becomes an essential part of the meaning.

The Wide Range of Tones

When we refer to the tone of a poem, we use such words as *cheerful, reflective, somber, wry,* and *angry.* Keep in mind, however, that there are really as many different shadings of tone as there are different tones of voice and that there are no sharp divisions between them. Like the names of colors, they are convenient segments of a spectrum.

Oddly, you may not even know what your attitude toward your subject is when you start a new poem. You can be drawn toward an occurrence, an experience, a relationship, a setting, without knowing why. It may take one or two drafts of a poem before you realize that what attracts you to the material is a sense of love or perhaps anger or a feeling of nostalgia. The very act of translating experience into lines of verse occasionally opens up veins of emotions you hadn't expected—some stratum of love for someone you thought you hated, a hidden fear of a situation you thought you enjoyed, anxiety in an area where you thought you were secure. In such cases, developing a poem with honesty may take considerable courage.

A *cheerful* or *comic tone* is too often avoided on the grounds that the writer won't be taken seriously. There is an unfortunate confusion in the English language between *serious* as a furrow-browed emotion and *serious* meaning complex or insightful. It is quite possible for a poem to be cheerful, even comic, and still offer genuine feelings and significant insights that are worth thoughtful consideration.

Lucille Clifton's "What the Mirror Said" (page 23), for example, is comic in tone. The speaker looks in the mirror and compares herself to a whole country. She is so complex that someone would have to have a map to understand her. We smile. It's a comic use of **hyperbole**. But we also respond to the deeper implications. This is clearly a woman's statement, and the as-if-spoken cadences suggest that she is black. The poem is an assertion of self-worth on both counts. The true theme of the poem is rooted in two major social issues: black pride and female self-esteem.

Sharon Olds' "Alcatraz" (page 16) also has a comic tone, but in this case you have to read the ending carefully before you understand the serious theme that lies under the surface. It starts off with a memory from childhood:

> When I was a girl, I knew I was a man
> because they might send me to Alcatraz
> and only men went to Alcatraz.

It goes on to describe her memories of the island prison "in the shark-rich Bay" and the other men who had "spilled their milk one time too many." Up to this point, her fears seem so groundless as to be comic. But the tone changes two-thirds of the way through:

> what I feared was the horror of the circles: circle of
> sky around the earth, circle of
> land around the Bay, circle of
> water around the island, circle of
> sharks around the shore . . .

It continues right down to the guard's eyes upon her as she reaches out for her glass of milk. The guard, of course, is a parent, and what started as a comic recollection turns into a dark picture of a childhood sense of guilt.

A *reflective tone* is a broad and inclusive category. In many cases, the poet has seen something that he or she wishes to share with readers. "Look, in these pools, how rocks are like worn change," Wilson says at the opening of "On a Maine Beach" (page 31). He goes on to describe the scene and also to draw an analogy from it. In the same way, Maya Angelou draws the reader into her kitchen in "This Winter Day" (page 25) and points out how the vegetables she is cutting up "leak their blood selves in the soup." At the end of the poem she tells us that making soup is a kind of bulwark against the rain outside.

The subject matter of Walt Whitman's "The Dalliance of the Eagles" (page 33) is more dramatic, but essentially he, like Wilson and Angelou, is pointing out something and saying, "Look!" They are all reflective in that they are urging us to look more closely at the world about us.

Somber tones often dominate student poems. Remember, though, that listening to a whiner isn't much fun; reading complaints in verse can be just as bad. But it is possible to be somber without being depressingly negative or indulging in self-pity.

In "As the Cold Deepens" by Elizabeth Holden (page 14) the subject is the narrator's mother, who at 86 is acutely aware that her friends are "dropping like flies." On the one hand, the poem never dips into the sentimental notion that life at that stage is "golden," and on the other, it doesn't indulge in self-pity or conventional lamentations about the inevitability of death. Instead, it focuses on the metaphor of flies that at the end of the season move "up and down the pane / pressing for sun." The sense of impending loss is never ignored or smoothed over, but the way the poem uses that metaphor suggests that this is a part of an inevitable cycle. Rather than reiterating what we already know, the poem helps us to see the situation in richer terms.

Chase Twichell's poem "Rhymes for Old Age" (page 26) is another good example of a poem in which the tone is somber without being depressing. The subject is an old woman who is close to death. Twichell stays clear of sentimentality by using starkly clinical details; on the other hand she avoids cold detachment by showing a deep compassion for the subject of her poem. Establishing just the right tone in a poem requires careful adjustment.

A *wry tone* is an excellent way to avoid self-pity. Theodore Roethke in "The Waking" (page 31) is talking about the brutal fact that we are mortal. If he had started with "We're hopeless, born only to die," many readers would quickly move on to another poem; only teachers and parents are obliged to finish reading unpromising verse. The tone of that opening line seems to promise unrelenting, self-pitying despair. Instead, Roethke begins with "I wake to sleep, and take my waking slow." The tone of the metaphor is light, almost whimsical, and his determination to make the most of life while it lasts provides a wry acceptance of our mortality. This does not mean that he is cheapening a serious subject by trying to make a joke out of it. These lines toward the end indicate how serious he is:

> This shaking keeps me steady. I should know.
> What falls away is always. And is near.

But even recognizing the eternal quality of death ("What falls away is always") and his advancing age ("And is near"), he still ends with the notion that he will be learning, growing, until the very end.

Anger and *protest* have long been expressed in poetry. Some of the strongest examples come from the Hebrew prophets. They tended to stand outside the mainstream of their own cultures and were highly critical of the societies of their day. Their language was blunt and direct. Take this brief example from Isaiah 3:24–25:

> And it shall come to pass, that instead of sweet smell
>   there shall be stink; and instead of a girdle, a rent;
> And instead of well set hair, baldness; and instead of
>   a stomacher, a girding of a sackcloth;
> And burning instead of beauty.
> Thy men shall fall by the sword,
>   and thy mighty in the war.

African-Americans have often struck the same note of protest. Clarence Major speaks for many black poets with this statement from the introduction to his anthology. *The New Black Poetry:*

> Our poetry is shaped by our experience in the world, both deeply personal and social . . . . We constantly mean our poems to reshape the world; in this sense all excellent art is social.

Another approach to expressing anger and outrage in poetry is through satire, a technique we will examine shortly.

The Uses of Irony

All forms of **irony** are based on a reversal of some sort. **Verbal irony** (also called *conscious* irony) is the type often used in daily conversation. On its simplest level it takes the form of saying the opposite of what we mean, such as responding to a hurricane with the statement, "Great day for a picnic." We know the speaker isn't crazy because we are so used to this kind of irony in daily speech. When it takes this form, we refer to it as **sarcasm**.

In poetry, however, irony is usually subtler and may be not at all sarcastic. It is often achieved by bringing together elements we normally consider incongruous. There are several examples in these lines from Richard Wilbur's "The Pardon" (page 27). The scene, you will remember, is the one in which the persona dreams he sees the ghost of his dog. In the following quotation, I have indicated with arrows how the overtones of certain words are pitted against those of other words in the same line.

I felt afaid again, but still he came

In the carnal sun, clothed in a hymn of flies,

And death was breeding in his lively eyes.

It is ironic to have a hymn associated with a "carnal sun" and a swarm of flies. It is equally ironic to think of death as "breeding." And there is a grim irony in those "lively eyes" of a dog that died some time ago.

There is another sample of irony in Chase Twichell's "Rhymes for Old Age" that you may have spotted in earlier readings of that poem. She describes the process of dying this way:

> One slips into it undressed,
> as into first love . . .

When an ironic contrast is phrased in a way that makes it sound like a complete contradiction, it is called a **paradox**. John Donne, for example, in his sonnet "Death Be Not Proud," ends with these lines:

> One short sleep past, we wake eternally,
> And death shall be no more; Death, thou shalt die.

On one level it is illogical to say that death shall die, but as a description of eternal life, it makes sense metaphorically.

All these examples are contained in specific phrases. There are also broader ironic contrasts that are in some cases at the very heart of a poem as a whole. As we have already seen, "Fern Hill" appears to describe unending youth and apparent immortality; yet all that time he was actually "green and dying."

This type of irony is called *verbal* because it is formed with words, not from events in life; it is also called *conscious* irony because the writer is intentionally linking the incongruous items. There are two other uses of the word *irony* which, though not directly connected with poetry, should be mentioned here to avoid confusion.

Cosmic irony refers to reversals of expectation. The Olympic swimmer who drowns in the bathtub, the fire chief who becomes an arsonist, the drought-stricken farmers who finally receive rain only to be flooded. The other type is **dramatic irony,** in which characters on the stage speak lines that the audience knows have an entirely different significance. In *Oedipus Rex*, for example, a messenger says "I bring good news" and the well-read audience shudders, knowing that disaster is at hand. More about that in the drama section of this volume.

The Cutting Edge of Satire

Satire criticizes or ridicules through some form of exaggeration. In mild satire the exaggeration may be only a matter of selecting some characteristics and neglecting others; the tone may be a gentle kidding. At the other extreme, satire may be wildly exaggerated and the tone vitriolic.

Satire and irony can be used independently from each other. All the examples of irony above are nonsatiric, and the first example of satire below does not use irony. But ridicule is particularly effective when it is presented "with a straight face." That is, the cutting edge of satire is sharpest when the poet gives the illusion of presenting an unbiased view. It is the tension between the poet's apparent honesty and the actual intent that makes satire almost invariably ironic. In fact, when satire is presented without irony, the result often appears rather crude. Such is the case with Kingsley Amis' "A Tribute to the Founder." In this first of four stanzas, the intent to ridicule is clear, but because the material is presented directly rather than ironically the attack lacks subtlety:

> By bluster, graft, and doing people down
> Sam Baines got rich, but mellowing at last,
> Felt that by giving something to the town
> He might undo the evils of his past.

There is, of course, irony in the title, since "tribute" is not intended literally. But the first line destroys all chance of sustaining subtlety. As soon as we see the words "bluster, graft, and doing people down," we know exactly where the poet stands, which is no sin in itself unless one asks more of poetry than one does of a good newspaper editorial.

William Jay Smith describes essentially the same sort of individual in his poem "American Primitive," and he also is satiric. But notice how different the effect is when irony is sustained:

> Look at him there in his stovepipe hat,
> His high-top shoes, and his handsome collar;
> Only my Daddy could look like that,
> And I love my Daddy like he loves his Dollar.

The lines flow like the ripple that runs silently down the length of a bull-whip; and with his final word comes the "snap," which is sharp enough to make the most sophisticated reader jump. This is still fairly light verse, but the satire, sharpened with irony, draws blood. The tension here lies in the contrast between the *apparent* tone of sentimental tribute and the *actual* tone of cutting protest.

Louis Simpson's "The Heroes" (page 20) develops a similar tension between apparent mindless good cheer and his actual intent, a savage attack on war and the notion of wartime heroes:

> I dreamed of war-heroes, of wounded war-heroes
> With just enough of their charms shot away
> To make them more handsome. . . .

Simpson maintains that ironic stance right through the poem. In addition, he uses a lilting meter enlivened with anapests which make even the rhythm seem lighthearted. Listen to the cadence of the third stanza:

> They shipped these rapscallions, these sea-sick battalions
> to a patriotic and picturesque spot;
> They gave them new bibles and marksmen's medallions,
> Compasses, maps, and committed the lot.

There is nothing heroic about a bunch of seasick troops, and there is nothing picturesque about a war zone, so we know the poet is speaking ironically. His intent is to ridicule the notion of heroes, and his tone is sharp rather than gentle.

Robley Wilson's "War" (page 20) also has samples of irony and satire in it. There is an ironic double meaning in the line I quoted earlier, "War is for the young / And keeps them young." Those who die young are, tragically, remembered just that way. But the poem is not consistently satiric the way Simpson's poem is. Wilson satirizes the "benefits" of war, but when he suggests that many of us have a more-or-less secret admiration of war—at least from a distance—he is not being ironic.

The sharpest and most bitter example of satire in this volume is Carole Oles' "The Gift" (page 18). Unlike Simpson, Oles does not reveal her ironic tone at the opening. In fact, the first few lines may seem almost sweet:

> Thinking she was the gift
> they began to package it early.

But it doesn't take long before you realize that their gift is not *for* the girl, it is the girl herself! Referring to this poor female as *it* gives you an idea of how she is being raised as a product. After they have straightened her teeth and curled her hair and taught her to speak in honeyed tones, she is given to a man who puts her on exhibit as a trophy. Her ultimate function is to provide him with a son. As you read that poem in its entirety, notice how the ferocity of the satire keeps building right through to the final line.

Satire on television and in magazines such as *Mad* and *National Lampoon* tends to be relatively simple. Like cartoons, it is designed as one-shot entertainment. Satire in sophisticated poetry, however, usually has more intricacies, more nuances. It draws us back for repeated readings.

Creating Tension Through Tone

If you study a sophisticated poem carefully, you will almost always find some sort of contrast, mixed emotion, or apparent contradiction in tone. These are the cross-currents that help to keep a poem from becoming static. They are ways of creating poetic **tension**.

Contrasts in attitude are common and fairly easy to identify. We have already touched on a few: Brooks' easygoing use of street language contrasted with the jolting prophecy at the end of "We Real Cool"; Hecht's merry anecdote played against the darkly dramatic image of the devil in "Lizards and Snakes"; Dylan Thomas' dreamlike description of an apparently ideal childhood played against a dark recognition of mortality in the last stanza of "Fern Hill."

Ambivalence—conflicting emotions about a person, place, or thing—was introduced in Chapter 3. It is an important concept because poems without mixed feelings are apt to be simple, like greeting-card verse. Ambivalence in tone is a reflection of the mixed feelings you may have about a character, a place, an occupation, or an institution.

Robley Wilson's "War" is a good example of high ambivalence. On the one hand the speaker is acutely aware of the brutality and senselessness of war, all of which he makes clear in ironic terms as described above. But at the same time, he is quite honest when he says he finds himself admiring war—the heroes like Alexander, Caesar, and Napoleon, and the stories of famous battles that add zest to history. Judging from the combat section in any bookstore, this is an ambivalence shared by many.

You and Your Persona

When we discuss a poem, we never know for sure whether the speaker in the poem represents the poet or an imagined character. For this reason, it is best to refer to "the **persona**," "the speaker," or "the narrator."

As a poet, however, you have a choice as to whether you wish to place yourself in your poem, using *I* to introduce yourself and your feelings, or whether you wish to present your poem through a character who is someone else. This distinction is referred to as **distance**, a term that we will return to in the section on fiction.

Since contemporary poetry is often personal, it is frequently set in the first person. This trend is reflected in many of the poems you read in Chapter 2. Theodore Roethke's "The Waking," Dylan Thomas' "Fern Hill," and Judy Kronenfeld's "Regret" all use "I" and have the illusion of personal experience. They may actually be fictionalized, so we refer to the speaker in each case as the persona, but the feeling we have is that the speaker and the poet are one.

Some poems increase the distance by having the persona or narrator recall an episode from the past. The narrator in Richard Wilbur's "The Pardon" describes the day he discovered the body of his dog. The insight and the language at the end of that poem is clearly that of an adult looking back. The same is true of the narrator's view of his childhood in "Fern Hill." Here too the conclusion—" . . . I sang in my chains like the sea"—is one that seems unmistakably that of an adult who is well aware of his own mortality.

In some poems the first person, *I*, does not appear at all. Chase Twichell's view of the old and dying woman in "Rhymes for Old Age" does not identify the viewer, nor does Donald Hall's "Names of Horses." It seems natural, however, to refer to an *implied* persona when discussing the tone, since in each case the sense of compassion comes through almost as if someone were talking.

In some cases, the poet is even further removed from the persona, criticizing the character through his or her own words. We have already seen how Gwendolyn Brooks uses "we" in "We Real Cool" to describe a character who is one of the pool players at the Golden Shovel. The narrator reveals himself (we assume "he" perhaps unfairly) and his future without quite realizing how much he is saying. The poet criticizes his way of life through his own words.

Keeping the Tone Honest

Tone is not your first concern when you begin a new poem. You don't select a tone in advance any more than you rationally decide the mood of the day when you wake up in the morning. Tone develops as the poem develops. It takes shape through successive drafts.

At some point in the revision process, however, you should take a close look at the tone you have adopted. There are two levels on which your tone may need further adjustment. On the deepest level is the matter of honesty.

When examining the tone of a poem you are working on, be sure to ask this crucial question: Is this what I *really* feel? Does the poem, for example, merely echo conventional sentiments (mothers and nature are wonderful; war and poverty are terrible), or does it honestly explore the complexity of what you feel?

More subtly, have you been softening the implications of your poem through psychic modesty? That is, have you been reluctant to reveal your private feelings? If so, the poem will probably lack a sense of power and authenticity. You would do better to present your feelings through a persona so as to mask your own involvement while still being true to the subject matter.

Modesty isn't always the problem. Exaggerating a personal agony or a painful experience can sometimes result in **sentimentality**. Intentional sentimentality is a form of dishonesty because it cheapens genuine feelings. It is contaminated with details selected primarily for their capacity to stimulate the tear ducts. It's a trick rather than a sharing of true emotions. But what about *unintentional* sentimentality? That is far more common. Occasionally you may honestly feel that you are the most miserable, most misunderstood person on earth or, on a happier note, that the person you love really is perfect. Remember, though, that if the poem sounds sentimental to others, its effect will be spoiled. Perhaps a wry, slightly distanced tone would help to provide perspective and hold your readers.

In the same way, if you overdramatize a conflict or protest, going beyond your real feelings, your poem may lose some of its dramatic impact and may come across as **melodrama**. When readers have the feeling that emotions like rage or indignation have been pushed artificially for their own sake, they will not take the poem seriously. Consider some form of irony. As a general rule, the most appropriate tone to adopt is an honest reflection of how you feel about your subject.

When you are sure that you have come to terms with your feelings on that deepest level, it is appropriate to examine your tone on a more craftsmanlike level: How successful have I been in communicating my tone to my readers? Never mind explaining to your friends, "But what I *really* felt was. . . ." Remember that a poem must reach readers on its own without your explanations. And readers are entirely dependent on the signals embedded in the work itself. The overtones of every word and phrase contribute to the overall effect. A soft word or phrase can weaken the impact of a protest poem; a harsh detail can send an unwanted jolt through a gently contemplative poem. As we have seen, tonal tensions are often effective, but make sure they are intentional and appropriate.

Ask yourself too whether the poem's tonal signals all repeat the same note. Poems that do this can lose effectiveness, just like a musical piece that strikes the same chord too often. This problem is relatively easy to correct if you can find a way to lighten the tone in some way. A note of humor can often provide a sense of balance. Or you may be able to reveal some type of ambivalence.

If you remember that the tone of your poem is an essential part of the meaning, you will understand why the revision process is not complete until you have established just the right tone.

12

FOUR ESSENTIALS FOR GROWTH

Why development in creative skills takes time. Read regularly and critically. Write regularly. Explore new approaches. Find or establish support groups.

Mechanical skills can be learned quickly. Artistic skills take time. Those are basic facts. For those who have become dependent on instant gratification, this slow process can be frustrating.

Oddly, there is a parallel between growth as a writer and development in a sport. Neither can be mastered just by reading a textbook. Both require steady and regular practice over a period of time. And in both you need the guidance and encouragement of support groups. Here are the essentials for poets.

Read Regularly and Critically

In Chapter 2 I pointed out that poets read the work of other poets. Serious poets read poetry seriously, that is, critically. This does not mean that they are necessarily critical in the negative sense—wonder, admiration, and sheer envy all have their place; but it does mean that they read analytically.

Is there a risk that you will become imitative? Not if you read widely. And consider the alternative: If you do not read other poets, you will end up imitating yourself, a sterile route. Besides, occasional imitation of poetry you admire is an effective form of study. Though imitations should remain in your journal, the process will bring you close to the model. When you return to your own original work, you will draw on what you have learned.

When students tell me that they are "very serious" about poetry, I don't ask how much they have written; I ask what was the last volume of poetry they read through to the end and what poetry journal they subscribe to. This isn't intended as a put-down. It is merely based on what I have observed: developing poets are readers even when they are not taking courses.

How do you find out what to read? If you are in school, take literature courses as well as writing seminars. Don't shun poetry from earlier periods. It all has a bearing on your own work. If you are not taking classes, buy anthologies and read poetry journals. Find out which poets speak to you. Then order collections of their work. Expensive? No more so than records and tapes of music or a dinner for two.

Reading critically requires more concentration than passive reading. It means applying what you have drawn from this and other analytical texts to what you are reading. It means marking up your own copy or photocopies of work printed in library books. It means commenting on these poems in your journal—not just likes and dislikes, but analytical aspects.

In short, when you read poetry critically, you adopt poets as your teachers. You will enjoy the works of some more than others, but you will learn from them all if you respond as a fellow poet.

And don't forget the auditory aspect. If you are near a library, try to attend poetry readings there as often as possible. An increasing number of bookstores and coffee shops offer readings and book-signing events at which you can meet and talk with the poet. Even if you live miles from the nearest library and commute to a mindless job in a cultural desert, there is a solution for you: Buy an inexpensive portable cassette player, record two new poems each evening, reading aloud from a collection, and then play them as you drive to work.

Write Regularly

Poets write regularly. Even when they have full-time jobs, they write regularly. Even when they have children or financial problems or are splitting up with their partners, they write. I have met poets who get up at 5:00 A.M. to write before going to work, and others who reserve the late hours of the night for composition. But they write. Regularly.

True, a busy schedule does not allow for long blocks of time. But one of the blessings of poetry is that it doesn't necessarily require lengthy work sessions. Unlike a novelist, a poet can often recapture the mood of an unfinished poem in minutes and make good use of a spare half hour a day. Thirty minutes a day may be frustratingly brief, but for most it is more productive than having a whole day for work once a week. Poems are relatively short, intense works, and they can take root in the chinks that remain in a tight schedule.

For most poets, even writing fragments on a regular basis is ultimately more fruitful than waiting for a summer vacation. Fragments have a way of generating work that can be developed. Waiting for ideal working time generates nothing.

Explore New Approaches

The third essential for growth is exploration. True exploration doesn't mean browsing. It means actually trying different approaches. Writing in imitation is one excellent technique. You learn what has gone into a poem when you try to emulate it in your own words. Such efforts are not generally for submission, however. (If you do submit such a work, credit should be given.) They are for your own growth and development.

The familiar is always safe. And if you have been rewarded for a particular subject matter or style, it will be tempting to imitate your own work. But if you do, your work may become increasingly sterile.

If you need to consider different subjects, look over this list and review the works suggested. They may help you explore different areas.

City living: Levertov (page 30); Brooks (page 34)

Life in the country: Thomas (page 24); Hayden (page 34); Merwin (page 23)

War: Wilson (page 20); Simpson (page 20)

Aging: Twichell (page 26); Holden (page 14); Pastan (page 17)

Animals: Pastan (page 18); Hall (page 34); Whitman (page 33); Wilbur (page 27)

Childhood: Kronenfeld (page 16); Olds (page 16); Bauer (page 37); Thomas (page 24)

The status of women: Oles (page 18); Clifton (page 23)

Love: Endrezze (page 39); Appleman (page 36); Giovanni (page 26)

Rivers: Baker (page 21); Merwin (page 23); Chora (page 28)

Or perhaps you need to try different rhythmical patterns. If you feel at home with traditional forms, try something in the style of E. E. Cummings (page 32) or Denise Levertov (page 30). On the other hand, if you have been writing nothing but free verse, try an Elizabethan sonnet following Shakespeare's model on page 19 or Robert Frost on page 14. If you feel venturesome, try villanelle in the style of Theodore Roethke's "The Waking" (page 31). Yes, it takes effort—particularly if the work hasn't been assigned as a class assignment. But what kind of artistic growth doesn't require effort?

The Importance of Support Groups

The clichéd image of the writer living alone in a garret may seem ideal if your life is harried with many conflicting responsibilities, but it's not the way writers generally develop. Yes, you need time to read and to write, but you also need people who know what you are trying to do and will react in helpful ways.

For many, the answer is creative writing classes. The best of them are not in the form of lectures, they are workshop support groups. The instructor will share his or her experience and will keep the sessions focused on writing, but much of the benefit comes from the reactions of the seminar as a whole. This group response becomes increasingly valuable in advanced classes because your peers will be increasingly perceptive. Don't make the mistake of defending every line you write. Listen carefully. Some comments will be of no benefit, but if you become defensive you will wall yourself off from comments that may be very insightful and helpful.

What comes after graduation? For many, it's life in the wilderness. You may discover that the kindly but vacuous responses of parents and lovers are, no matter how sweet, no more nourishing than cotton candy. Even good friends often don't know what questions to ask or how to advise. As a result, they tend to respond subjectively. "I like it. Sort of," one may say, playing it safe. Another reads the same poem and shrugs. "It doesn't do much for me," she says. A third complains, "Why don't you write about something cheerful?" Reactions like these will tell you more about the speaker than about your poem.

You may have the feeling that there is no one who shares your interests. Rest assured that there are tens of thousands of people who read and write poetry. Anyone who has judged a national poetry contest can tell you that the number of poets in this country is astonishing. The problem is not numbers, it is distribution. They are scattered across a very large country.

If you are serious about developing as a poet, you will have to make an effort to find or create a support group. One person who knows what you are doing is better than none. Two are better than one. Seven is ideal. Groups of twenty or more tend to become adulterated with people who would rather chat than work.

There are two great dangers to watch out for in any support group. The first is excessive assertiveness on the part of one or more members. Honesty is good, but harsh or insensitive comments either will turn the sessions into ego battles or will inhibit an open sharing of views. The other danger is the tendency to let the discussion turn into a bull session. Whenever the group strays off to personal preferences, personal experiences, or what they have read recently, the poem under discussion is no longer the subject. Someone in the group has to be navigator, keeping the discussion on course.

The kind of criticism that will be the most help to you as a practicing poet will be highly specific. It will focus on phrasing, on imagery, on rhythm. What you as writer need to find out is precisely what came through to the reader. In the process you may learn what didn't come through as well.

A helpful critic might say something like this: "Your three opening images are really dramatic and got me into the poem, but I lost track of them later." Or "Perhaps you could develop this stanza." Or "It seems heavier than the subject justifies."

You may be tempted to use the well-worn defense, "That's the way I intended it." But resist that impulse! Make a note of the suggestion and decide later whether to act on it. Some comments may be quirky or based on personal preferences, but pay particular attention to those views that are shared by several members of the group.

Your growth will depend on your reading, your commitment to writing, your willingness to explore new approaches, and your openness to criticism. These are the essentials. A good textbook should help you to get started, but it won't do the work for you. Growth in this or any creative art requires sustained effort.

Part Two

The Writing of Fiction

13

FACTS, FALSEHOODS, AND FICTION

Factual writing, lying, and fiction: some important distinctions. Fusing fact and fancy. Simple versus sophisticated fiction. The forms of fiction. Three motives for writing fiction: personal, commercial, and literary.

We start telling stories almost as soon as we can put sentences together. Whenever we talk about characters doing something, we are narrating a story.

At first, we may make no sharp distinction between what is make-believe and what really happened. But as we get older, we learn that this can get us into trouble. That's when we discover that fiction is one way to make things up without being called a liar.

That's an important lesson to remember because it reminds us that there are two significantly different types of stories. The first is *factual*. Factual writing that deals with characters and a plot is a type of a story, but we usually describe it with more precise terms like biography, autobiography, journalism, social history, and the like. When we work with these forms, we are committed to reporting the events as they occurred. We may offer opinions or even present an argument, but first we have to get the facts right.

The other way of telling a story is called *imaginative* or **creative writing.** Fiction, narrative poetry, and drama are all *creative* in the sense that we are creating some or all of it from our own imaginations. Our first loyalty is not to aspects of the real world but to the artistic object we are creating. Characters, places, and episodes from life are simply raw material to be artfully recycled. Familiar places can be divided, mixed, and altered. Even our best friends can be transformed by age, sex, or temperament. The sole commitment of fiction writers is to the creation of an artistic work, be it a story or a novel.

Fusing Fact and Fancy

Fiction, then, tells an untrue story in prose. It is "untrue" in the sense that it is at least partly made up. It is an artistic creation in that it stands on its own no matter how much it may make use of characters, events, and settings from life. As writers, we are free to take on a different **persona,** speaking in the first person from the point of view of someone utterly unlike us. We are free to assume the existence of unicorns or subterranean civilizations on the moon. A story or novel cannot be criticized for being "untrue"; it is judged on whether it *seems* true.

One of the best ways to achieve this sense of authenticity is to draw heavily on the world you know best—your own life. Some beginning writers feel that their lives have been too ordinary, but everyone has had complex relationships with parents or foster parents, everyone has had to deal with people their own age, everyone has had defeats, successes, and learning experiences. And every experience is unique.

This does not mean that *unrevised* experience makes good fiction. Our lives are a jumble of unconnected events and repetitious activities. There is nothing as dull as a step-by-step account of what has happened to you over the length of an average day. Even a specific event almost always needs extensive revision before it becomes a successful story. Usually there are many unrelated details that need cutting. Sometimes the event was too mild or, conversely, too melodramatic for fiction. So we begin cutting this and adding that. Our goal is not a factual record of events as they occurred but an artistic creation with its own sense of unity and significance. To some degree we do this without thinking when we tell a friend about something that happened to us. A husband's version of a trip abroad will differ in tone and selection of detail from his wife's, no matter how dedicated each is to "the truth." With fiction we are liberated from real-life facts, but we are obligated to make "a good story."

Suppose, for example, you want to base a story on an intense argument between a man and a woman you overheard in a restaurant. You may decide to use much of their exact phrasing (pure fact) but make them brother and sister (invention) and put them in your uncle's house (factual memory), tell the story from the point of view of a six-year-old girl (invention) during a terrible rainstorm (factual memory). If you do this right, no one will be able to separate what was drawn from life and what was created from your imagination. The two have become fused into a single, credible story.

Simple versus Sophisticated Fiction

As soon as we talk about the *merit* or *worth* of an artistic work, we enter the slippery area of what is *good* and what is *bad*. It is so difficult to defend the worth of a story that some people duck the issue entirely by saying, "I only know what I like." Personal preference, of course, is everyone's privilege. Some like gentle stories, some want heavy drama; some prefer stories about women, others like to read about men. Arguing seriously about our preferences is as pointless as debating whether dogs are better than cats.

There is, however, one distinction about which we can reach a measure of agreement: Some stories, like some poems and plays, are relatively **simple** while others are significantly more **sophisicated**. This is a notion that is enormously helpful for writers and underlies all of the analysis in this book.

Essentially, sophisticated works "do" more in the sense that they suggest more, imply a greater range of possibilities, develop more subtle shadings of meaning than simple works do. This text is concerned with sophisticated writing, but that focus does not imply that such work is "better." It is simply "other" in the sense that the biologically simple crayfish is different from the far more sophisticated porpoise.

The span between the simplest fiction and relatively sophisticated fiction is enormous. Compare a comic strip about adolescents, such as *Archie, Gil Thorpe,* or even the slightly more daring *Luann,* with a novel about adolescents like John Knowles' *A Separate Peace* or J. D. Salinger's *Catcher in the Rye.* They are similar in that they are both samples of fiction, that is, they both tell untrue stories in prose. Further, they both have plot, characters, setting, and themes. Also they share certain basic fictional techniques: dialogue, thoughts, action, description, and exposition. They even draw on the same age bracket—that highly charged transition period between childhood and adulthood. And before we brand comics as "bad," remember that many intelligent adults read them with pleasure each morning. Conversely, while a majority believe that *Catcher in the Rye* is an excellent example of literary fiction, a few find it immoral and therefore "bad."

So what *is* the difference? To start with, Archie as a fictional character is *simple*; so are the stories in which he appears. The episodes (the plots) are highly repetitive and limited in scope. Imagine Archie dealing with such issues as teen pregnancy or drugs! Holden Caulfield, on the other hand, is a sophisticated character in that he is shown dealing with fairly complex moral issues and inner doubts. He struggles with the complexities that are often associated with that period in life. The pleasure many feel in reading the comic strip *Archie* is an escape from the challenges of daily living, and we all need periods of retreat. In contrast, the enjoyment we feel from reading *Catcher in the Rye* comes from a greater understanding of the world about us. In short, each type of fiction, serves a different need.

It is important here to distinguish this literary use of *sophisticated* from its popular use, which merely describes a type of socially suave individual. Literary sophistication describes the complexity, depth, and range of insight suggested not only by a fictional character but by the entire work in which that character appears. Mark Twain's Huck Finn, for example, is certainly unsophisticated as an individual, but the subtlety and insightfulness with

which the author presents him and the entire novel are literarily sophisticated.

As with poetry, there are an infinite number of gradations between the
simplest forms of fiction and the most sophisticated. Juveniles—stories and
novels written for adolescents—are far more intricate in characterization and
theme than comic strips. Gothic novels, for all their repetition of plots, have
a certain sophistication of vocabulary, but they are not intended to be as subtle or insightful as literary novels. In fact, a standard, mass-market gothic
novel manuscript may well be turned down by a publisher if it departs too
far from the familiar and relatively simple pattern. In the case of murder
mysteries, most of the sophistication takes the form of ingenious plots, but
thematically they tend to be fairly simple. They are for most enthusiasts "a
quick read."

Every magazine has a certain range in terms of fictional sophistication.
Larger-circulation publications such as *McCalls* and *Redbook*, for example,
offer relatively simple fiction. For sophisticated short stories, one must turn
to the literary journals and quarterlies like *Story* and *The North American
Review*, or to the "qualities" like *The Atlantic* and *The New Yorker*. (A longer
list appears in Appendix B.) These publications usually vary their offerings
from relatively accessible pieces to works that, like sophisticated poetry, may
require some effort on the part of the reader.

As a writer, how high should you aim? It would be a mistake to start out
by attempting an extremely complex plot and an intricate theme. If you have
one or two interesting characters and a single, insightful event, you can write
a story that is fresh and rewarding.

As you gain experience you will want to examine what makes some
works more sophisticated than others. Take a close look at the basic elements
of the story: plot, characters, setting, and theme.

Plot, whether simple or sophisticated, consists of a sequence of actions.
Simple fiction, however, not only reduces the complexity of plot, but usually
avoids originality as well. Simple plots tend to be based on well-used **conventions** known in the magazine field as **formulas.** The pleasure some people derive from, say, husband-tempted-by-widow-next-door-but-finally-
returns-to-wife is not the stimulation of fresh experience and insight but,
rather, the tranquilizer of familiarity and repetition.

Sophistication of plot does not necessarily mean complexity. What one
aims for is a situation and a sequence of actions that are fresh and provide
new insights. The determining factor is not how many twists and turns the
plot may take but how much is revealed about the characters and the theme
of the story.

Characterization, the creation of fictitious characters, is also significantly different in simple and sophisticated works. In simple fiction, the
characters may do a lot (the restlessness of a James Bond), but you never get

to know him or her the way you might come to understand someone in life. What you see is a repetition of the same traits. In sophisticated fiction, you often see a range of different aspects just as you do in someone you know well.

Setting in simple fiction often relies on geographic clichés that are repeated over and over. Students in New York are described as living in Greenwich Village even though that area has not been a low-rent bargain for over 40 years; businessmen have their offices on Madison Avenue; San Francisco scenes are "in the shadow of the Golden Gate"; Paris stories have vistas looking out on the Eiffel Tower. "Originality" frequently takes the form of the exotic—a ski resort high in the Andes, a spy headquarters 400 feet below the Houses of Parliament, a royal palace constructed entirely in glowing Lucite on the planet Octo. Exotic settings like these may *seem* original at first, but they are usually slightly disguised versions of other relatively simple stories.

Sophisticated fiction, on the other hand, tends to avoid both the hackneyed and the bizarre. The setting is used as a way of increasing credibility and placing the reader in the center of the story—regardless of whether it is based on an actual place or upon the dreamscape of the author.

Theme is another aspect of fiction that varies with the degree of sophistication. Simple themes suggest truisms that make no more impact on us than the background music in a restaurant. So-called detective magazines and their television counterparts reiterate endlessly, "Crime doesn't pay, but it's exciting to try." Many of television's situation comedies suggest repeatedly that "Nice girls eventually end up with nice boys, but only after being hurt." The fact that we know nice young women who have ended up with terrible husbands and fine young men who never married at all doesn't seem to weaken the popularity of this simple thematic concern.

Sophisticated fiction tends to have thematic concerns that suggest mixed feelings. Often these take the form of ambivalence, a blending of love and hate for the same person at the same time. Further complexity is sometimes achieved with irony, a reversal of one's normal expectations.

Whenever you read fiction, you evaluate the level of sophistication on the basis of elements like these, either consciously or unconsciously. And when you write, they are concerns that will hold your attention at every stage.

In addition to the content of a story, you will want to examine the way the material is presented. For purposes of analysis, it is helpful to see every sentence in a story as presented in one of five different ways or **narrative modes**: *dialogue, thought, action, description,* or *exposition.*

Dialogue and *thought* are two effective ways of suggesting character, and often they are used in tandem so that one sees a contrast between the inner and the outer person. In simple fiction, however, they are often sterotyped—predictable lines for predictable characters.

Action is the dominant mode for simple fiction—particularly for adventure stories. But as we will see in the examples in this text, sophisticated fiction makes significant use of action too. The difference is that as the story begins to gain a greater range of suggestion, the action necessarily must take on a more subtle role of implication. In other words, action shifts from being an end in itself to being a means of suggestion.

Description is a mode that beginning writers sometimes underestimate. Gothic novels often use description to create a sense of mystery and awe— moors, fog, howling dogs, half-deserted castles. Crime stories often pack in sordid details in the name of realism. Sophisticated fiction generally avoids descriptive passages that fit a well-known pattern or draw attention to themselves. Instead, such passages serve to augment some aspect of the theme.

Exposition is perhaps the most dangerous of the five narrative modes. It refers to those explanatory passages that give background information or commentary directly. "They lived in Chicago," or "He was more generous than they were" are expository statements if they are not presented through dialogue. In simple fiction, exposition is used to point up the theme as one progresses through the story and, often, to sum it up directly at the end. "Down deep," we are told periodically, "old Karl had a warm spot in his heart." And in case we missed it, we are given the clincher at the end: "Though his parting words were gruff, there was an undertone of kindness in the old prospector's voice. It was clear that he still knew the meaning of love."

Those who are used to sophisticated fiction grimace at this because it is a familiar convention. It is also close to the technique of the essay. A sophisticated story may use just as much exposition, but it will rarely label the theme in that way. This is not because authors want to be evasive, but because the success of literarily sophisticated fiction depends in part on the degree to which readers have the feeling that they themselves have discovered the thematic suggestions in a story. The process is similar to the way we make judgments about people and situations in actual life. We listen to what people say and watch what they do, and then we come to conclusions. In fiction, of course, the dialogue and action are carefully selected by the author, but when we read, we like the illusion of discovering significances on our own.

The Forms of Fiction

Fiction is commonly thought of as falling into four precise categories: the short-short story, the story, the novella, and the novel. These terms are handy, but they are far from precise. There is no sharp line between one length and the next.

Short-short stories are usually defined as being between 500 and 2,000 words. Since a double-spaced manuscript (see Appendix A for details) comes to about 250 words a page, a short-short is from two to six pages. Many have appeared over the years as "four-minute stories" in the *North American Review*. Contests for short-shorts such as the one periodically run by *Story* are normally limited to 1,500 words, or about six pages. For contests, be sure to determine your word count accurately.

At this length, most have no more than one or two characters presented in one or two scenes in a short overall time span. There is a temptation to indulge in trick endings, but with restraint you can generate real insight into character, feeling, and human relations.

Short stories generally run from 2,000 words (8 pages) to 6,000 words (24 pages). Some are longer, but these become increasingly difficult to place, since the greater length will force a magazine editor to reduce the total number of works in an issue. The great advantage of this length over the short-short is that it allows one to deal with more characters, have a more intricate plot, and make greater use of setting; but it is still a relatively tight art form.

Novellas generally run between 50 and 150 typed pages, halfway between a story and a novel. From time to time magazines will include one or will devote a special issue to several, but novellas are more often seen in published collections along with short stories by the same author.

Novels are more than just stories that have been expanded beyond 250 pages—or at least they should be. The length allows an author to do interesting things with the plot and to develop subplots. One can introduce many more characters than in a story or novella, and some of them can change and develop over the course of time. The theme of such a work can be broader and more intricate than in the shorter form.

When you start writing, the short-short story form is a good one to work with. In developing your creative abilities, it is important to try a number of different approaches—first person, third person, light tone, serious tone, close to experience, far removed from experience. You can achieve new skills and find your own voice better through a series of short-short stories than by locking yourself into a longer work too soon.

Three Motives for Writing Fiction

Whenever you become involved in creative work, it is worth asking yourself just what aspect of the activity is motivating you. Doing this may help you to determine in what direction you want to move right from the start.

There are many reasons for writing fiction, but they tend to fall into three broad groups. Since each involves a different approach and different goals, it is important to examine them separately.

First, there is the *private motive*. This is expressed in writing that is mainly for personal pleasure. It is intended for an audience of one—yourself. Often it takes the form of journal entries. Spontaneous and usually unrevised, journal writing requires no special training. Entries may be valuable for recording or clarifying your own feelings or as a way of sketching out possible scenes in fiction, or they may be just good fun as a release, but they shouldn't be passed off as finished work.

The second is the *commercial motive*. In its pure form, **commercial fiction** writing is the opposite of private writing since it is motivated largely by outer rather than inner demands. It is writing for others. Commercial writers usually define their work as a craft rather than an art, and their primary goal is monetary reward. They produce entertainment. Many spend more of their time writing nonfiction than they do fiction since the demand is greater.

The fiction produced by commercial writers tends to follow certain familiar conventions—the love story, high adventure, war, crime—because there is a large market for that kind of writing. As with businesspeople, their goal is to supply what the market wants. Although there is a tendency for literarily minded individuals to look down on commercial writing, it is an honest profession that fills a need.

The third is the *literary motive*. Although it generates most of the fiction one reads in school and college, it is perhaps the most misunderstood. Writers in this area are like painters, sculptors, and composers who value the quality of the work they produce. Having an audience is obviously important, and being paid for one's efforts seems only fair; but making money is not the principal drive. Because of this they do not generally tailor their work to meet the whims of the public, nor do they cater to commercial markets. They measure their efforts against what they consider to be the best fiction they have read.

Because literary writers require readers who have relatively sophisticated taste and experience, they must often (though not always) be content with a relatively small audience. Their novels may not be best-sellers, and their short stories frequently appear in "little magazines" that have small circulations and cannot pay their contributors lavishly. Many have to do something else for their major source of income. But they have a special satisfaction in knowing that they are reaching readers who will spend time with their work and will react to it with some sensitivity. In addition, they are working in one of the few areas where they do not have to compromise. For many, this is very important.

The literary motive is sometimes difficult for nonwriters to understand. It helps, though, to compare the literary writer with the opera singer who knows that rock singers earn ten times as much. Opera continues not because its performers like being paid less but because this is what they do best and enjoy most.

The emphasis in most creative writing courses is on sophisticated rather than simple work. The same is true of this text. This does not mean, of course, that personal entries in a journal are without value. Nor does it mean that commercial writing, which by definition is aimed at a wide audience, is to be scorned. What it does mean is that because sophisticated or literary writing requires careful study and a lot of practice, many people find writing courses and a text like this helpful. Selecting the kind of writing you want to do depends entirely on what motivates you.

Every writer—like every artist in the broadest sense—is driven by a combination of all three motives. Those who are concerned primarily with sophisticated writing, however, share a respect for literature as something of value in itself. With this as a base, there is no end of possibilities for fresh creativity.

14

THE SOURCES
OF FICTION

The search for fresh material. The stockpile of used plots. The "seven deadly sins" of fiction. The authenticity of personal experience: family relationships, male–female relationships, moments of growth and discovery. Transformation: necessary alterations of events, characters, and setting.

Sophisticated fiction depends on fresh material. When we draw on our own lives honestly, we can be sure that we are being original. Each person's life experience is unique. But as I pointed out in the previous chapter, creative writing is almost always a blend of what we know well and what we have invented.

Where does the new material come from? Ideally, it springs from our imagination. Unfortunately, however, our memories are cluttered with stockpiles of old plots, characters, and settings half-recalled from what we have read and, increasingly, what we have seen on television and in the movies. Like old toxic dumps, this material is often buried and hard to identify. It is all too easy to use bits and pieces unintentionally. When facing a writing deadline, you may even be tempted to use one intentionally. But if you do so, you may contaminate the rest of your work.

Familiar plot patterns and **stock characters** are **clichés** on a big scale. When commercial writers of fiction and scriptwriters adopt these conventions purposely, it is politely called **formula writing.** Like fast food, formula writing serves a wide market and often earns top dollars, but it usually sacrifices subtlety and insight. When these conventions filter their way down to the work of beginning writers, they are the tattered remains of material that wasn't fresh even in the hands of professionals. As soon as readers recognize one of these familiar patterns, they are apt to slip into the glazed half-attention with which they often watch a standard television drama or listen to background music at a restaurant.

The "Seven Deadly Sins" of Fiction

The popularity of particular stock plots and character types shift form year to year, but here are seven that are especially prevalent today. I list them here not to discourage invention but save you from spending valuable time on a story idea that may well be doomed from the start.

• **The High-Tech Melodrama.** A **melodrama** is any piece of fiction or drama that is overloaded with dramatic suspense. Unlike true drama, it is overdone. Television's relentless drive for more viewers tempts many scriptwriters to step over the line between drama and melodrama.

Everyone has a slightly different view of just where that line should be drawn, but regardless of labels, so-called suspense thrillers tend to have certain standard ingredients. Whether the protagonist is a solo detective, a cop, or a vice squad member, the props usually include both guns and late-model cars, and the plot turns out to be, at the mildest, some version of search-and-capture. More often, it's search-and-destroy. The high-speed chase is repeated as regularly as was the shootout in westerns of the 1950s. Replacing the magnum with a laser and moving the chase to another galaxy may be a challenge for the special-effects department, but the plot is remarkably similar, and the characters seem to speak the same lines.

It is not guns and uniforms by themselves that present the problem. If you have gone hunting, served on a police force, or been in the military, you should explore those experiences and find ways of sharing them with your readers. But serious problems arise when you start to borrow material from scriptwriters who themselves are borrowing from earlier scripts. Watch out for characters—male and female—who always maintain their cool in times of stress and reveal nothing of themselves. Guard against that too-easy dichotomy between the good and the bad. Keep asking yourself: Where did I get this stuff? Is it used property?

• **The Adolescent Tragedy.** The adolescent period is an excellent one for sophisticated fiction as long as you keep your material genuine and fresh in detail. But there are three pitfalls: lack of perspective, sentimentality, and melodrama.

Lack of perspective occurs when the experience is too fresh. In such cases, you find yourself *in* the story rather than *above* it. You cannot control it. This may well be your problem if you find yourself calling your fictional characters by the names of their nonfictional counterparts. Another sign is finding yourself reluctant to change the plot because "that's not the way it happened."

To avoid this lack of objectivity, make sure that enough time has elapsed between the event and your attempt to convert it into fiction. The more emotional the experience, the more time will be required to gain some measure of detachment.

Sentimentality may stem from secondary sources like magazines and television or may just as easily come from the simple desire to move the reader. The difference between the sentimental story and one that is genuinely moving is a matter of sophistication. When a story is simple and rigged to short-circuit the emotions of the reader, we say it is sentimental. These are the stories in which the lonely, misunderstood little boy, the plain little girl with glasses, the blind girl, or the son of alcoholics is placed in some pitiable situation—any cold street corner will do, but a bombed-out village is better—simply to evoke tears.

But what if you really were the plain little girl with glasses or the son of alcoholics? The fact that the background is from life is never an excuse for fiction that *seems* like a sentimentalized treatment. Your job will be to find those unusual details or to explore ambivalences that will break the mold and convince the reader that this is a genuine experience.

Melodrama is tonally the opposite. In musical terms, sentiment is played with plaintive violins, while melodrama pounds on the drums. Here is one sample in essence: Good kid is drawn into gang membership, is soon forced to test his loyalty and manhood, dies. How can this be melodramatic when it happens every day on the street? Because it has been worked over too often; because we can spot the ending from reading the first paragraph; because it sounds like another high-school film on family values. Those things will kill the story more quickly than the protagonist. Again, what if it almost happened to you? Find some corner of the experience that only you know about. Avoid the big, familiar pattern. Show us an aspect we never thought about before.

• **The Twilight Zone Rerun.** Like the fiction of Edgar Allan Poe, the scripts of the television program "The Twilight Zone" are characterized by the strange and the bizarre. They usually depend on a gimmick. A **gimmick** is a tricky idea worked into fiction or a script, one that surprises and entertains. In one episode, for example, a nearsighted book lover who is the sole survivor of World War III discovers an undamaged library for his uninterrupted use. As he reaches for a treasured book, he—you guessed it—drops and breaks his glasses. Entertaining, yes, but it is *simple* entertainment. The trick becomes more important than the development of character or subtlety of theme. Like the anecdote or well-told joke, it depends on a punch line. Once read, there is little reason for going back to it.

• **Vampires Resurrected.** Count (and Countess) Dracula have in their golden years managed to upstage werewolves, though just barely. The resurrection seems to have originated not in Transylvania but in Hollywood. It was once good dream stuff, but the convention has been repeated so often that it has sunk to the level of comic strips and Halloween masks. Even professional scriptwriters, experts in recycling, are reduced to treating it as self-satire. There is little likelihood that a beginning writer can in eight pages breathe life into either the once-proud count or his recently liberated countess.

• **The Yuppie Gone Wrong.** This is one of the most common patterns in college writing courses. The protagonist is a young, upwardly mobile individual who has put career and love of material objects ahead of personal relationships and spiritual values. He drives a Porsche, has a Jacuzzi, lives in Silicon Valley or some mythical place with the same climate. In the end, he pays for his sins and succumbs to drink, drugs, or a bullet—sometimes all three.

These are morality tales with their roots in the Faust legend—medieval tales (and later operatic works) portraying a hero who sells his soul to the devil in exchange for knowledge and possessions.

It would be nice to think that such plots were inspired by the Faust tradition or by more recent works like Theodore Dreiser's *An American Tragedy* or stories like F. Scott Fitzgerald's "Winter Dreams," both of which build convincing characters with some of these same characteristics. But it seems more likely that the source is television.

In keeping with the times, the yuppie plot is occasionally refashioned with a young woman as unhappy protagonist. But if the original concept was hackneyed, the revised version will be no better. The problem with these stories is not that such characters don't exist but that the fictional version is based on an imitation which in turn is based on an imitation.

But suppose you knew a hard-driving individual who really did own a Porsche and tragically did commit suicide? It still will be a risky incident for fiction. Suicide is generally too big and complex a subject to handle convincingly in a short-short story. You may have to substitute some subtler indication of a character's sense of defeat and despair. As for the other details, sometimes you have to revise life's events to keep them from echoing the conventions of simple fiction.

• **The Temptations of Ernest Goodwriter.** The protagonist walks up and down the beach, planning a great novel. He resists the invitations of fun-loving but superficial friends and spurns an offer to join a major advertising firm. In the end, he returns to his typewriter and his high literary principles.

Or perhaps he is in New York and will not change a word of a novel he has already written. Or he is in Los Angeles and is torn between writing a great novel and being paid a fortune to write hack scripts.

These are admirable morality tales, but morality tales make poor fiction. They are unconvincing because the characters have been replaced with abstract ideas: good pitted against bad with no complexity or insight into the way people really live. In some cases the hero is so wooden you can't help hoping he or she will "go Hollywood," make a fortune, and live happily ever after.

• **My Weird Dream.** Recording your own dreams can be interesting, even significant. They are good material for a journal. But listening to someone else's interminable and incomprehensible dream is a punishment few of us deserve. In most cases, the dream story is far more fun to write than to read.

It does have a long history—though not one most contemporary readers are familiar with. In the 1920s it was called **automatic writing.** Writers simply typed whatever came into their heads for three hours and called the final fifteen pages a "story." Occasionally these "stories" were published, but no one has republished them—for good reason.

There was another flurry of interest in the late 1960s, when this kind of writing was defended as "literary tripping," a hallucinogenic voyage on paper. Again, the writing was more fun than the reading.

This technique of aimless composition is not to be confused with **stream-of-consciousness** writing. The latter, made famous by James Joyce, is designed to give the illusion of entering the mind of a fictional character. It is used as a part of story, usually as the thoughts of a character we have already come to know through more conventional writing. As such, it is a literary device with a purpose. Recording a dream for its own sake may be of personal value to you, but the result belongs in your journal.

These, then, are seven of the most common causes for failure in short stories. You will be able to spot others. It is important to look closely at your plans for a new story, because time spent on shopworn material is time wasted.

These warnings may seem rather negative. You may even feel intimidated by them. Don't be. Remember that creativity is essentially a positive process and that if you draw on the many fruitful sources for fiction, your work is bound to be fresh and original.

The Authenticity of Personal Experience

You know your own life better than anyone else does. When you write about your own experiences, your family, your friends, your neighborhood, your own feelings, you have inside information. If you select fresh details, you can draw your reader into the world you create.

Sometimes beginning writers avoid using their own experiences because they feel that their lives are too uneventful. But short fiction does not require high drama. Your life is filled with problem solving, minor achievements, betrayals, reversals, and discoveries. You know more about the details than anyone else. And the people you grew up with—friends and relatives—have revealed themselves in interesting ways from time to time. If you learn how to draw on material like this and how to reshape it, you will have discovered how to use one of the basic ingredients of fiction.

A standard legal disclaimer states that "any similarity to actual persons or places is purely coincidental," but no one who writes fiction takes that seriously. A more honest statement would be that similarities to persons and places are frequent, intentional, and occasionally brazen, but generally fragmentary, inconsistent, and disguised with fanciful invention.

Using personal experience selectively and honestly is your best safeguard against work that is unconvincing. This is particularly true for those who are just beginning to write fiction. As you gain experience, you will learn how to keep one foot in the circle of familiarity while reaching out with the other. Memories of a summer job on a construction crew, for example, might allow you to explore what it would be like to be foreman or, pushed further, a civil engineer in conflict with the foreman. Some of the more demanding moments of baby-sitting might serve as the basis for a story dealing with the life of a single parent. At the outset, it is wise to stay relatively close to the original experience.

Finding a good incident with which to work may come easily, but often it will not. Even experienced writers have dry periods. Since "waiting for inspiration" is just a romantic way of describing procrastination, it is important to learn how to look for material in a constructive way. Here are some areas that are worth exploring.

Family relationships are natural subjects for fiction. Everyone has had either parents or foster parents; everyone has experienced in some proportion that mixture of love and resentment that is a natural part of that relationship. And that instable balance is normally in constant flux. In very general terms, it is apt to be a progression from idealization through disillusionment to a new acceptance, usually based on a fairly realistic evaluation. But this is a vast oversimplification, and stories based on a simple treatment of the theme "The day I discovered my father was no saint" are apt to turn out thin and unconvincing. The writer has to probe deeper in order to discover and dramatize those unique shifts in attitude. Often it is some *specific* characteristic of, say, the father, altered in some slight but significant way, that lends itself to good fiction.

In addition to child–parent relationships, there are a variety of other intrafamily attitudes that also shift significantly: brother and sister, two sisters and a maiden aunt, two brothers and their cousin, a daughter dealing with a stepfather, the reactions of three brothers to their uncle. Relationships like these keep shifting in real life, and the shifts are remembered because something was done (action) or said (dialogue) or thought in such a way as to dramatize the change. To some degree you can use such relationships directly, but often you will have to transform experience into something related but different—a process I will explain shortly.

Relationships between girls and boys and between men and women are used repeatedly in fiction, and there are hackneyed situations that you should avoid. But in most cases you can find a safe path by asking these two essential questions: What *really* happened? And what was there about the action, the thoughts, the outcome that was truly unique? Of course there are those situations that at first glance seem too close to clichés to be credible or interesting. Occasionally lovers really do patch up quarrels while standing on the shore of Lake Placid under a full moon in June. But not often. You may have to douse the moon, change the name of the lake, and give the characters some uneasiness about that reconciliation if the story is to take on a sense of authenticity.

Some of the best relationships to examine are those with individuals who are much younger or older. The greater the gap in age, the more difficult it may be to enter the mind of the other individual. But you can always write the story from the point of view of the character who is about your own age.

A different way of stimulating your memory is to recall moments of intensity. Often these involve some kind of discovery about yourself or another person. As you examine the event (a good use for a journal), you may not really understand why the experience has remained so vivid in your memory. But you can be sure that if it is still clear there must have been some special meaning in it for you.

Such a memory may be fragmentary. Settings like a particular shopping plaza, a playing field or vacant lot where you used to play, a view from a car window, or a kitchen seen only once often stand out with extraordinary sharpness. They have remained for a reason.

Characters (not to be confused with "characters" who are held to be "unforgettable" by the *Reader's Digest*) may remain in your mind only from an overheard conversation or a quick glimpse: a subway attendant, a store clerk, a hitchhiker, an auto mechanic. And incidents do not even have to be directly connected to the observer. It may be an argument overheard in a supermarket; the smashing of a window; an automobile accident; or the playful flirtation of a girl and three boys on a beach, in a park, or at a parking lot.

One of the first things to do with such a memory fragment is to recall every possible detail: the visual minutiae, the sounds, and the intricacies of your own feelings. From these you may discover why that particular experience remained in your memory while so many others drifted beyond recall. The final story may or may not include you as a character, and it will probably be far removed from the facts of the original episode, but it will have the advantage of being rooted in a genuine and personally significant experience.

The following chart may help you to explore the complex relationships you have with those about you. Only you know which of these categories apply to you, so circle the ones that do. Then take notes on those relation-

great aunts and great uncles	grandmother and grandfather	friends of grandparents
aunts and uncles adult friends of your parents	parents or stepparents	an employer a teacher a stranger met briefly
brothers and sisters half siblings cousins	YOU	your best friend irritating friend rival or enemy
nieces and nephews	younger sibling or your own child	the kid next door

Which of these relationships
  improved in some interesting or dramatic way?
  was shattered by events?
  led to a surprising discovery about:
    yourself, the other person, a third person?
  changed your attitude in:
    a positive and growing way?
    a negative way creating bitterness or resentment?
  affected your development for the better or worse?

ships that have potential. Use the names of actual people for now. (This is for your private use.) Later, as you begin to shape a story, be sure to change to fictional names. That is when you begin altering, revising, and the all-important process of inventing.

Transformation: An Essential First Step

Personal experience is important as a stimulus and a resource, but it is not fiction. Some published stories may seem like camcorder re-creations from the author's life, but they aren't. All that raw material necessarily went through a process of transformation.

Transformation refers to basic alterations of events, characters, viewpoint, or setting—occasionally all four. It is so fundamental and so primary that it is sometimes referred to as process of **metamorphosis,** a complete change in structure and appearance.

Unconscious transformation may well have altered your memories even before you have begun to plan a story. Without being aware of doing so, we block certain events and highlight others. We alter chronological sequences, forget that certain characters were present, shift scenes. For evidence of this phenomenon, listen to two people describe the same vacation trip. In a more serious vein, read the sworn testimony of different witnesses to the same crime.

Some of these transformations may be outright lying, but much is unconscious. We restructure memory to protect our own egos, maintain modesty, get a laugh, clarify or dramatize an incident. Indeed, in conversation we are often *expected* to alter events. "Come on," we say to a rambling storyteller, "get to the point."

Unconscious transformation of memory can occasionally work against you. You may be censoring an experience by making a fictional character kinder, wiser or more moral than the model on which she was based. That kind of unconscious transformation can sanitize experiences, making them too bland for fiction or too vague to reveal subtle contrasts in character.

We all tend to be shy when we contemplate writing about our friends and relatives. We are apt to have feelings about them we don't want to advertise. Even if we feel very close to a parent, friend, or lover, we also see aspects in him or her that are less than perfect. Indeed, there may even be aspects of ourselves that are less than perfect. Most of us an recall a number of incidents we would never reveal to a friend, much less to total strangers. How can we put these on paper for everyone to read?

More serious, unconscious censorship may prevent you from getting started at all. What is described as *writer's block* is frequently a reluctance to deal with what is still too close and personal.

The solution to all these problems is *conscious transformation.* Don't confuse this with *revision*, a more subtle process that doesn't start until you have completed the first draft. Transforming is the first step in converting those bits and pieces floating around in your memory into a coherent narrative known as fiction. The reason it is important early in the process is that it is your primary method of objectifying your subject matter. Unless you have some degree of objectivity, you will be hopelessly bound to the events and to the characters in your memory. Unless you feel free to shape your material, you will not be writing fiction.

To begin, change the names of your characters. Let them take on fictional identities of their own. If doing that isn't enough, change the appearance of one or two. If your model is fat, make him thin; if his wife is tall in reality, make her short in the fiction.

Sometimes even more transformations are needed. You may have to break the mold set by the experience itself. Very personal episodes are often easier to handle in the third person ("he" or "she") than in the first. Consider telling the story through the eyes of a character not based on yourself. Painful childhood memories, for example, are sometimes made manageable by visualizing the story through the eyes of a parent.

Changing the setting often helps. Moving the story to another locale gives you a fresh vision. And it is easier to change the sex of a character than one might think. The transformation often suggests new personality traits while freeing you from the real-life model.

How much transformation is necessary? There are two warning signs that are clear indications that more is still needed. First, if you find yourself referring to your **protagonist** as "I" and to your other characters by the names of their actual models, then you are still thinking of the piece as factual writing. Second, if you catch yourself saying, "I can't have them do that; it just didn't happen that way," you're in trouble. There is no clearer indication that your first loyalty is still to the events as they occurred. You have not yet begun to write fiction, an artistic creation in its own right.

Transformation, then, is almost always necessary for you to establish control over the material and start thinking about it in fictional terms. But in addition, transformation has purely literary functions. You will find that it is indispensable in the process of developing a clear and logical plot line. It will also help you to decide just what thematic elements you want to stress.

Daily life consists of a great clutter of experience, much of it routine. If you reported everything that happened to you during a 24-hour period, you would on most days end up with 100 pages of utterly boring material. This does not mean that your life is boring, but it does mean that we all spend a good deal of time doing routine things. Significant and interesting developments do occur from time to time, but they are almost always embedded in unrelated events. Weigh carefully whether you should include what you had for breakfast on the day you discovered that your kid brother had been arrested.

Bits and pieces (including characters) from a personal experience that are left in a story for no good reason are essentially junk details. They are confusing and occasionally misleading because readers assume that everything in a realistic story is relevant. The sequence of events may also be confusing to readers. You may have to drop characters, shift or consolidate scenes, invent action and dialogue not because that's the way the event occurred but because that's what the story demands.

In addition, a single episode may suggest several different themes. Which one do you want to develop? Suppose, for example, you and your parents and your 15-year-old sister go for a picnic in the country on a hot August day, only to have the car break down in the city's most depressed neighborhood. The incident has the feel of a short story, but what aspect will serve as the thematic center? Here are just a few of many possibilities:

1. A story about a father who discovers that his wife, whom he always thought of as rather immature, has hidden strengths in a time of crisis. This approach might require deleting the children altogether and reducing the ages of the couple by ten years.
2. A story about a mother and her adolescent daughter: Perhaps rather than getting rid of the father and the son, you could have them spend their time trying

to repair the car and then set off to locate a garage. In this version mother and daughter might get into a dispute, resolve it, and find their relationship altered as a result.

3. A story about a rebellious son: He is scornful about his father's mechanical ignorance and his mother's managerial manner and sets off on a 50-mile trek home with no money in his pocket. Or should he do this with his sister? Should he (or they) succeed? Should this be an initiation experience? Or should they fail, a lesson in humility?

Each of these possible stories is rooted in the same experience, but each has been transformed before being committed to paper in order to place the focus on a different character and highlight a different thematic concern.

There may be times, of course, when such basic restructuring will make you feel that the entire story is crumbling before your very eyes. Too much choice can be a problem. In that case, try to reestablish what it was that drew you to the incident in the first place. That is, rediscover the personal connection.

In spite of that risk, basic transformation of an experience will help you to gain control over your material, and it will also open up different fictional possibilities. When you consider the extraordinary variety of experience stored in your mind and add to that the infinite number of variations you can devise for each, you can see how each new story is unique. This is the true meaning of *creative* writing.

15

A STORY

by Stephen Minot

Sausage and Beer

I kept quiet for most of the trip. It was too cold for talk. The car was getting old and the heater hadn't worked for as long as I could remember. My father said he couldn't afford to get it repaired, but he bought us a camping blanket which was supposed to be just as good. I knew from experience, though, that no matter how carefully I tucked it around me the cold would seep through the door cracks and, starting with a dull ache in my ankles, would work up my legs. There was nothing to do but sit still and wonder what Uncle Theodore would be like.

"Is it very far?" I asked at last. My words puffed vapor.

"We're about halfway now," he said.

That was all. Not enough, of course, but I hadn't expected much more. My father kept to his own world, and he didn't invite children to share it. Nor did he impose himself on us. My twin sister and I were allowed to live our own lives, and our parents led theirs, and there was a mutual respect for the border. In fact, when we were younger Tina and I had assumed that we would eventually marry each other, and while those plans were soon revised, the family continued to exist as two distinct couples.

But this particular January day was different because Tina hadn't been invited—nor had Mother. I was twelve that winter, and I believe it was the first time I had ever gone anywhere alone with my father.

The whole business of visiting Uncle Theodore had come up in the most unconvincingly offhand manner.

"Thought I'd visit your Uncle Theodore," he had said that day after Sunday dinner. "Wondered if you'd like to meet him."

He spoke with his eyes on a crack in the ceiling as if the idea had just popped into his head, but that didn't fool me. It was quite obvious that he had waited until both Tina and my mother were in the kitchen washing the dishes, that he had rehearsed it, and that I wasn't really being given a choice.

"Is Tina going?" I asked.

"No, she isn't feeling well."

I knew what that meant. But I also knew that my father was just using it as an excuse. So I got my coat.

The name Uncle Theodore had a familiar ring, but it was just a name. And I had learned early that you just do not ask about relatives who don't come up in adult conversation naturally. At least, you didn't in my family. You can never tell—like my Uncle Harry. He was another one of my father's brothers. My parents never said anything about Uncle Harry, but some of my best friends at school told me he'd taken a big nail, a spike really, and driven it into his heart with a ball peen hammer. I didn't believe it, so they took me to the library and we found the article on the front page of the *Herald* for the previous Saturday, so it must have been true.

But no one at school told me about Uncle Theodore because they didn't know he existed. Even I hadn't any real proof until that day. I knew that my father had a brother named Theodore in the same way I knew the earth was round without anyone ever taking me to the library to prove it. But then, there were many brothers I had never met—like Freddie, who had joined a Theosophist colony somewhere in California and wore robes like a priest, and Uncle Herb, who was once in jail for leading a strike in New York.

We were well out in the New England countryside now, passing dark, snow-patched farm fields and scrubby woodlands where saplings choked and stunted each other. I tried to visualize this Uncle Theodore as a farmer: blue overalls, straw hat, chewing a long stem of alfalfa, and misquoting the Bible. But it was a highly unsatisfactory picture. Next I tried to conjure up a mystic living in—didn't St. Francis live in a cave? But it wasn't the sort of question I could ask my father. All I had to go on was what he had told me, which was nothing. And I knew without thinking that he didn't want me to ask him directly.

After a while I indulged in my old trick of fixing my eyes on the white lines down the middle of the road: dash-dash-dash, steady, dash-dash again. If you do that long enough, it will lull you nicely and pass the time. It had just begun to take effect when I felt the car slow down and turn abruptly. Two great gates flashed by, and we were inside a kind of walled city.

Prison, I thought. That's it. That's why they kept him quiet. A murderer, maybe. "My Uncle Theodore," I rehearsed silently, "he's the cop killer."

The place went on forever, row after row of identical buildings, four stories, brick, slate roofs, narrow windows with wire mesh. There wasn't a bright color anywhere. The brick had aged to gray, and so had the snow patches along the road. We passed a group of three old men lethargically shoveling ice and crusted snow into a truck.

"This is a kind of hospital," my father said flatly as we drove between the staring brick fronts. I had to take my father's word for it, but the place still had the feel of a prison.

"It's big," I said.

"It's enormous," he said, and then turned his whole attention to studying the numbers over each door. There was something in his tone that suggested the he didn't like the place either, and that did a lot to sustain me.

Uncle Theodore's building was 13-M, but aside from the number, it resembled the others. The door had been painted a dark green for many years, and the layers of paint over chipped and blistered paint gave it a mottled look. We had to wait quite a while before someone responded to the push bell.

A man let us in, not a nurse. And the man was clearly no doctor either. He wore a gray shirt which was clean but unpressed, and dark-green work pants with a huge ring of keys hanging from his belt.

"Hello there, Mr. Bates," he said in a round Irish voice to match his round face. "You brought the boy?"

"I brought the boy." My father's voice was reedy by comparison. "How's Ted?"

"Same as when you called. A little gloomy, maybe, but calm. Those boils have just about gone."

"Good," my father said.

"Funny about those boils. I don't remember a year but what he's had trouble. Funny."

My father agreed it was funny, and then we went into the visiting room to await Uncle Theodore.

The room was large, and it seemed even larger for the lack of furniture. There were benches around all four walls, and in the middle there was a long table flanked with two more benches. The rest was space. And through that space old men shuffled, younger men wheeled carts of linen, a woman visitor walked slowly up and down with her restless husband—or brother, or uncle. Or was *she* the patient? I couldn't decide which might be the face of madness, his troubled and shifting eyes or her deadened look. Beyond, a bleak couple counseled an ancient patient. I strained to hear, wanting to know the language of the place, but I could only make out mumbles.

The smell was oddly familiar. I cast about; this was no home smell. And then I remembered trips with my mother to a place called the Refuge, where the lucky brought old clothes, old furniture, old magazines, and old kitchenware to be bought by the unlucky. My training in Christian charity was to bring my chipped and dented toys and dump them into a great bin, where they were pored over by dead-faced mothers and children.

"Smells like the Refuge," I said very softly, not wanting to hurt anyone's feelings. My father nodded with an almost smile.

We went over to the corner where the benches met, though there was space to sit almost anywhere. And there we waited.

A couple of times I glanced cautiously at my father's face, hoping for some sort of guide. He could have been waiting for a train or listening to a sermon, and I felt a surge of respect. He had a long face with a nose so straight it looked as if it had been leveled with a rule. I guess he would have been handsome if he hadn't seemed so sad or tired much of the time. He worked for a paint wholesaler which had big, dusty offices in a commercial section of Dorchester. When I was younger I used to think the dirt of that place had rubbed off on him permanently.

I began to study the patients with the hope of preparing myself for Uncle Theodore. The old man beside us was stretched out on the bench full length, feet toward us, one arm over his eyes, as if he were lying on the beach, the other resting over his crotch. He had a kind of squeak to his snore. Another patient was persistently scratching his back on the dark-varnished door frame. Anywhere else this would have seemed perfectly normal.

Then my father stood up, and when I did too, I could see that what must be Uncle Theodore was being led in by a pock-marked attendant. They stopped some distance from us and the attendant pointed us out to Uncle Theodore. Then he set him free with a little nudge as if they were playing pin-the-tail-on-the-donkey.

Surprisingly, Uncle Theodore was heavy. I don't mean fat, because he wasn't solid. He was a great, sagging man. His jowls hung loose, his shoulders were massive but rounded like a dome, his hands were attached like brass weights on the ends of swinging pendulums. He wore a clean white shirt open at the neck and blue serge suit pants hung on suspenders which had been patched with a length of twine. It looked as if his pants had once been five sizes too large and that somehow, with the infinite patience of the infirm, he had managed to stretch the lower half of his stomach to fill them.

I would have assumed that he was far older than my father from his stance and his shuffling walk (he wore scuffs, which he slid across the floor without once lifting them), but his face was a baby pink, which made him look adolescent.

"Hello, Ted," my father said, "How have you been?"

Uncle Theodore just said "Hello," without a touch of enthusiasm, or even gratitude for our coming to see him. We stood there, the three of us, for an awkward moment.

Then: "I brought the boy."

"Who?"

"My boy, Will."

Uncle Theodore looked down at me with red-rimmed, blue eyes. Then he looked at my father, puzzled. "But *you're* Will."

"Right, but we've named our boy William too. Tried to call him Billy, but he insists on Will. Very confusing."

Uncle Theodore smiled for the first time. The smile made everything much easier; I relaxed. He was going to be like any other relative on a Sunday afternoon visit.

"Well, now," he said in an almost jovial manner, "there's one on me. I'd forgotten we even *had* a boy."

My face tingled the way it does when you open the furnace door. Somehow he had joined himself with my father as a married couple, and done it with a smile. No instruction could have prepared me for this quiet sound of madness.

But my father had, it seemed, learned how to handle it. He simply asked Uncle Theodore if he had enjoyed the magazines he had brought last time. We subscribed to *Life*, the news magazine, and apparently my father had been bringing him back copies from time to time. It worked, shifting the subject like that, because Uncle Theodore promptly forgot about who had produced what child and told us about how all his copies of *Life* had been stolen. He even pointed out the thief.

"The little one with the hook nose there," he said with irritation but no rage. "Stuffs them in his pants to make him look bigger. He's a problem, he is."

"I'll send you more," my father said. "Perhaps the attendant will keep them for you."

"Hennessy? He's a good one. Plays checkers like a pro."

"I'll bet he has a hard time beating you."

"Hasn't yet. Not once."

"I'm not surprised. You were always the winner." I winced, but neither of them seemed to think this was a strange thing to say. My father turned to me: "We used to play in the attic where it was quiet."

This jolted me. It hadn't occurred to me that the two of them had spent a childhood together. I even let some of their conversation slip by thinking of how they had grown up in the same old rambling house before my sister and I were born, had perhaps planned their future while sitting up there in that attic room the way my sister and I had, actually had gone to school together, and then at some point. . .But when? And how would it have happened? It was as impossible for me to look back and imagine that as it must have been for them as kids to look forward, to see what was in store for them.

"So they started banging on their plates," Uncle Theodore was saying, "and shouting for more heat. Those metal plates sure make a racket, I can tell you."

"That's no way to get heat," Father said, sounding paternal.

"Guess not. They put Schwartz and Cooper in the pit. That's what Hennessy said. And there's a bunch of them that's gone to different levels. They send them down when they act like that, you know. The doctors, they take a vote and send the troublemakers down." And then this voice lowered. Instinctively we both bent toward him for some confidence." And I've found out—that one of these nights they're going to shut down the heat *all the way. Freeze us!*"

There was a touch of panic in this which coursed through me. I could feel just how it would be, this great room black as midnight, the whine of wind outside, and then all those hissing radiators turning silent, and the aching cold seeping through the door cracks—

"Nonsense," my father said quietly, and I knew at once that it was nonsense. "They wouldn't do that. Hennessy's a friend of mine. I'll speak to him before I go."

"You do that," Uncle Theodore said with genuine gratitude, putting his hand on my father's knee. "You do that for us. I don't believe there would be a soul of us"—he swept his hand about expansively—"not a soul of us alive if it weren't for your influence."

My father nodded and then turned the conversation to milder topics. He talked about how the sills were rotting under the house, how a neighborhood gang had broken two windows one night, how Imperial Paint, where my father worked, had laid off a number of workers. My father wasn't usually so gloomy, but I got the feeling that he was somehow embarrassed at being on the outside, was trying to make his life appear less enviable. But Uncle Theodore didn't seem very concerned one way or the other. He was much more bothered about how a man named Altman was losing his eyesight because of the steam heat and how stern and unfair Hennessy was. At one point he move back in time to describe a fishing trip by canoe through the Rangeley Lakes. It was like opening a great window, flooding the place with light and color and the smells of summer.

"Nothing finer," he said, his eyes half shut," than frying those trout at the end of the day with the water so still you'd think you could walk on it."

He was interrupted by the sleeper on the bench beside us, who woke, stood, and stared down at us. Uncle Theodore told him to "Go blow," and when he had gone so were the Rangeley Lakes.

"Rangeley?" he asked, when my father tried to open that window again by suggestion. "He must be one of our cousins. Can't keep'em straight."

And we were back to Mr. Altman's deafness and how seriously it hindered him and how the doctors paid no attention.

It was with relief that I smelled sauerkraut. That plus attendants gliding through with carts of food in dented steel containers seemed to suggest supper, and supper promised that the end was near.

"About suppertime," my father said after a particularly long silence.

Uncle Theodore took in a long, deep breath. He held it for a moment. Then he let it go with the slowest, saddest sigh I have ever heard.

"About suppertime," he said at the end of it.

There were mumbled farewells and nods of agreement. We were thanked for copies of *Life* which we hadn't brought; he was told he was looking fine, just fine.

We were only inches from escape when Uncle Theodore suddenly discovered me again.

"Tell me son," he said, bending down with a smile which on anyone else would have been friendly," what d'you think of your Uncle Ted?"

I was overwhelmed. I stood there looking up at him, waiting for my father to save me. But he said nothing.

"It's been very nice meeting you," I said to the frozen pink smile, dredging the phrase up from my sparse catechism of social responses, assuming that what would do for maiden aunts would do for Uncle Theodore.

But it did not. He laughed. It was a loud and bitter laugh, derisive, and perfectly sane. He had seen my statement for the lie it was, had caught sight of himself, of all of us.

"Well," he said when the laugh withered, "say hi to Dad for me. Tell him to drop by."

Father said he would—though my grandfather had died before I was born. As we left, I felt oddly grateful that the moment of sanity had been so brief.

It was dark when we got back to the car, and it was just beginning to snow. I nestled into the seat and pulled the blanket around me.

We had been on the road about a half hour and were approaching our neighborhood by an odd route. My father finally broke the silence. "I could do with a drink."

This was a jolt because my parents never had liquor in the house. I knew about bars but had never been in one. I wondered if perhaps drinking was something men did—a kind of ritual.

"Sure," I said, trying to sound offhand." It's fine with me."

"You like sausage?" he asked.

"I love sausage." Actually I'd never tasted it. My mother said you couldn't tell what they put it it.

"A little sausage and a cool beer is what we need." And after a pause, "It's a place I go from time to time. Been there since God knows when. Ted and I had some good times there back then. But . . ." He took a deep breath and then let it out slowly. "It might be best if you told your mother we went to a Howard Johnson for a hamburger, O.K.?"

"Sure, Dad."

We were on city streets I had never seen before. He finally parked in what looked like a dark, threatening neighborhood and headed for a place with neon signs in the window. I had to trot to keep up. As soon as we entered, we were plunged into a warm, humming, soothing, smoky world. The sound of music blended with voices and laughter. There was a bar to our right, marble tables ahead, booths beyond. My father nodded at a waiter he seemed to know and said hi to a group at a table; then he headed toward the booths with a sure step.

We hadn't got halfway before a fat man in a double-breasted suit came steaming up to us, furious.

"Whatcha doing," he said even before he reached us," corruptin' the youth?"

I held my breath. But when the big man reached my father they broke out in easy laughter.

"So this is the boy?" he said. "Will, Junior—right?" We nodded. "Well, there's a good part of you in the boy, I can see that—it's in the eyes. Now, there's a girl too, isn't there? Younger?"

"She's my twin," I said. "Not identical."

The men laughed. Then the fat one said, "Jesus, twins sure run in your family, don't they!"

This surprised me. I knew of no other twins except some cousins from Maine. I looked up at my father, puzzled.

"Me and Ted," he said to me. "We're twins. Nonidentical."

We were ushered to a booth, and the fat man hovered over us, waiting for the order.

"Got sausage tonight?" my father asked.

"Sure. American or some nice hot Italian?"

"Italian."

"Drinks?"

"Well—" My father turned to me. "I guess you rate beer," he said. And then, to the fat man, "Two beers."

The man relayed the order to a passing waiter. Then he asked my father, "Been out to see Ted?"

"You guessed it."

"I figured." He paused, his smile gone. "You too?" he asked me.

"Yes," I said. "It was my first time."

"Oh," he said, with a series of silent nods which assured me that somehow he knew exactly what my afternoon had been like. "Ted was quite a boy. A great tackle. A pleasure to watch him. But no dope either. Used to win meals here playing chess. Never saw him lose. Why, he sat right over there."

He pointed out to the corner booth, which had a round table. All three of us looked; a waiter with a tray full of dirty glasses stopped, turned, and also looked at the empty booth as if an apparition had just been sighted.

"And you know why he's locked up?"

"No," I whispered, appalled at the question.

"It's just the number he drew. Simple as that. Your Dad, me, you—any of us could draw the wrong number tomorrow. There's something to think about."

I nodded. All three of us nodded. Then the waiter brought a tray with the order, and the fat man left us with a quick, benedictory smile. We ate and drank quietly, lost in a kind of communion.

16

THE MAKING OF A STORY

A Case History

Difficulty in tracing the development of published stories. Origins of "Sausage and Beer." Transformations: evasion and discovery. Revision, an unending process. The melding of memory and invention.

One of the best ways of learning how to write effective stories is to examine published work. In most cases, however, what we study is limited to the final, published version. We have to guess about where the material came from and what kind of transformations and revisions went into the work before it appeared in print.

Many writers are reluctant to discuss those long hours of effort, because they like to maintain the illusion of the story as a complete and seamless work. Revealing all the uncertainty, frustration, rethinking, and revision that goes into most stories makes the process seem less like an inspired burst of talent and more like what it is, a lengthy and often demanding effort.

The following case history of "Sausage and Beer" is not conjecture. It's a record that only an author can provide about his own work. The many stages this story went through are not unusual. If you are taking a workshop course in writing, you may not have time for this much reworking, but one of the ironies of fiction writing is that the more proficient you get, the less satisfied you become with early drafts.

Origins of "Sausage and Beer"

The story began with a determination to write something closer to my own life. Childhood trips to a mental hospital to visit my uncle were vivid in my memory. Those were the days before drug therapy. Large numbers of the insane were housed and fed, though the treatment was no more sophisticated than it had been in the asylums of the previous century.

The subject matter seemed promising partly because my feelings were an odd mix of fascination, revulsion, and fear. A combination of emotions has more potential for fiction than a single response. In addition, the setting appealed to me—at least as a writer. It was dramatically different from the routine home in a nondescript neighborhood. Odd and strange, the setting was something I could share with readers who had never been there.

Another purely factual element that drew me was the language of the insane. I don't think I could have invented that if I hadn't listened not only to my uncle on numerous occasions but also to other inmates. It was far from gibberish (although there was some of that too), but it was not consistently rational either. What I found particularly interesting was the way the mind can move from calm logic to delusion without missing a beat.

My selection of that particular experience suggests a general pattern in fiction writing. Looking for story ideas rarely involves ideas at all. It never occurred to me to explore the plight of the insane or how children deal with reticent fathers or the role pure chance plays in one's life. What started the story was not an abstract concept but an experience with a set of somewhat contradictory feelings and a vivid, relatively unusual setting.

It's like 'mining for charged material,' a simile worth keeping in mind: The process is like prospecting for uranium with a geiger counter. Listen for the hot spots and then start digging.

Transformations: Evasion and Discovery

These, then, were the factual memories that initiated the creative impulse. They were the memories I wanted to write about. But right from the start the developing story was being shaped by what I did *not* want to write about as well.

Those visits to the asylum were made with my mother, not my father. The patient was her brother, not my father's. That might have made an interesting story, but for me it was too close to some highly charged emotions. Fifteen years later I wrote a story about an adolescent and his mother called "Home," but at the time "Sausage and Beer" was written, the subject was too radioactive to handle.

Shifting an actual mother–son relationship to a fictional father–son relationship was an easy jump at first. It took the pressure off. But even that proved to be uncomfortable. So my real-life father, a short, overweight, outspoken man, became a tall, gaunt reticent fictional father. Where did he come from? A distant relative of my father's generation I barely remembered.

Major transformations of that sort can have consequences no writer can predict. What I had planned was a fairly simple initiation story: Boy faces the reality of insanity and ends up more mature. But I was still in the planning stage when I found myself with a father I never had. This guy was distant but approachable, basically kind, even vulnerable. What a delicious discovery it was to allow my protagonist to have a moment of sharing and understanding with his father, a bonding I never experienced in life.

The next question was what to do with the fictional Uncle Theodore. In reality he was lean and gaunt, physical characteristics I had already assigned to the fictional father. In spite of the fact that they were twins, I wanted to differentiate them. So Theodore ended up "a great, sagging man" whose stomach "had managed to stretch" until it filled his too-large pants. His hands were "attached like brass weights on the ends of swinging pendulums." Where did all that come from? I once saw a man in the lobby of a seedy hotel who looked just like this. I saw him only once and never spoke to him, but he got tucked away like those unsorted photos you shove into shoe boxes and store in the attic.

The bar scene at the end of the story comes from another shoe box. My real father never would have taken me to a bar, partly because he found children an annoyance and partly because he died when I was ten. The bar came to mind because I wanted to highlight the bonding that resulted from fictional father and son having shared this ordeal. A clap on the shoulder in the parking lot just wasn't enough. The bar had a slightly illicit overtone that had the right feel to it.

At the time, I thought I was inventing the place, but as I look back I now realize that it was an echo of an actual experience. On my thirteenth birthday I put at the head of my list of birthday wishes a trip to a real nightclub. Since I was then fatherless, a much older half brother volunteered. It was an act of kindness on his part, a low-key version of the bonding that went on in the story.

As I suggested in Chapter 14, transformation of details in the initial stages of planning can lead anywhere. In this case, by choosing to delete certain factual aspects, I inadvertently opened up new veins with real potential.

Revision, an Unending Process

The transformations described above occurred before I started writing. If they hadn't, I would have wasted a great deal of time producing fundamentally different versions. By the time I started typing, I had a fairly clear notion of where to go with the story. And once the first draft was completed, the revision process began.

Those who are new to fiction writing sometimes think of "revision" as consisting of one-word changes. As you begin to acquire a more demanding sense of what is necessary, however, you will find yourself adding or deleting whole paragraphs—sometimes pages. Revising usually takes far more time than writing the original draft.

Much of the bar scene, for example, was added in successive drafts. As I remember it, there was an early version in which the father merely suggested that they have a drink together. That was intended to suggest the newly formed bond between them. But that version didn't seem strong enough. The bar and the bartender began to take shape. The bartender's pronouncement on the role of chance in our lives ("It's just the number he drew") came very late and suggests a secondary theme that never occurred to me when I started the story.

A far more significant revision was made after the story had been accepted for publication by the *Atlantic*. Conscientious editors used to take the time to make helpful suggestions which, if the story had been accepted, could be acted upon or ignored. (Sadly, this is becoming less common.) What I submitted was about the sixth draft and to my mind perfect. One always has that illusion. That version had about two additional pages at the beginning about the narrator and his sister, Tina. My purpose was to highlight the twin pattern, linking the bond between the two younger people and that between the father and his brother Theodore. In each case, a warm and somewhat naive relationship is broken by the harshness of reality: The boy can never marry his sister, and the father can never reclaim the easy friendship he had with his twin brother.

The editor's point, however, was that so much emphasis on the sister early in the story would suggest to the reader that she would become a significant part of the plot. But she never appears again. That essentially needless material created a false lead. Stories make implied promises, and this promise was unfulfilled. Besides, all that background material made the opening sluggish. The story didn't really start until father and son were on the road. It was one of those suggestions that is so good it makes a writer feel stupid for not having seen it. So the story now begins with "I kept quiet for most of the trip."

Cutting blocks of material can be a painful act at any stage of your career. One way to ease the agony is to set the pages aside if you are typing or to establish a "LostGems" file if you are working on a computer. In two weeks you will wonder why you saved it.

Since stories are printed on paper, not etched on tablets, they can be revised at any stage. F. Scott Fitzgerald, for example, wrote a second version of his novel *Tender Is the Night* long after the first version was published. I hope I never feel obliged to do that, but revisions on this story continued years after its original publication. An author has a chance to revise every time a story is reprinted in an anthology, collection, or textbook, and many take advantage of that opportunity.

The first printed version of the story was set back in the late '20s, previous to my own memory. I did this so I could make that bar a speakeasy, one of those illegal nightclubs that flourished during Prohibition. To establish the historical setting, I identified the car in the third sentence as a 1929 Dodge and reinforced the historical period with a reference to a "bearskin robe," which many cars had before there were heaters, and a hand-operated windshield wiper toward the end of the story.

The advantage of this historical setting was that the illicit aspect of the speakeasy intensified the bond between father and son and dramatized that aspect of the story that suggests a coming of age. Speakeasies were common but illegal. Those who have retained the second edition of this text can compare that original version with the present one.

The disadvantage was that the story became a period piece. Fixing the date that far back seemed to suggest some thematic significance when in fact all I wanted was to use the overtones of the speakeasy, a minor detail. Besides, the number of readers who would even identify the bar as a speakeasy from my subtle hints and could respond to the overtones were approaching zero.

So I made another revision. I deleted the historical period simply by removing the date, the bearskin rug, and the manual windshield wiper. With those three minor changes I wiped out 40 years of history!

The Melding of Memory and Invention

Every story has a different ratio of memory to invention. Many, however, have a pattern similar to that in "Sausage and Beer": A specific memory serves as the starting point, and an increasing number of radically transformed memories and purely invented aspects are added as the work evolves through successive drafts. Here is a rough breakdown of this particular story:

MEMORY

Visits to the mental hospital (consolidated into an initial trip)
The narrator and his feelings
The setting, both outside and inside the hospital

TRANSFORMED MEMORY

The father's appearance (based on a distant relative)
Uncle Theodore's appearance (based on a stranger)
Uncle Theodore's dialogue (a composite of his and others')
The bar (borrowed from a later experience)
The twin sister, Tina (based on an older sister)

PURE INVENTION

The father's withdrawn personality
The mother
The twin motif
The hospital attendant
The bartender
The father–son bonding

As you can see, ascertaining whether a story was "based on experience" is about as difficult as determining whether an automobile is "American made."

The writer's ultimate concern is whether the final result has been melded into a single, convincing piece. Make sure the pieces fit together with a natural harmony. Here are three areas that call for special attention:

1. Merged episodes should follow one another logically. (Guard against inexplicable or confusing transitions.)
2. A borrowed setting must be internally consistent. (Don't let a lunch scene accidentally become a dinner or a city scene acquire suburban details.)
3. Transformed characters should be consistent. (Watch out for physical contradictions or inappropriate remnants of someone else's personality.)

You have to keep going over your work from start to finish, seeing it as a whole. Try to imagine yourself as someone else reading it for the first time. In addition, if it is at all possible, have someone else give you some honest critical responses. Remember that no matter how many pieces go into your story, the finished version must be a seamless work of art.

17

A STORY

by Deborah Joy Corey

Three Hearts

The morning after the big snowstorm Mama is real sick. Her hair has twisted itself into tight knots like spikes all over her head and she is so weak that her words are puffy and low. We are all up, listening to the radio that sits on top of the fridge to see if there will be any school. Bucky and I sit at the wooden table that wobbles on the crooked floor and wait with our elbows pressed like seams into the plastic tablecloth. Mama is lying on the kitchen couch, wrapped in a red robe, rolling her head from side to side, sighing.

Her eyes are like faded jeans and she sounds scared, so I go over and stand by her head. I take one of Daddy's newspapers from under the couch and fan her a bit. The newspaper leaves black on my finger and I rub it onto my soft corduroys. Mama has *nerves* and when my other brother, Eddie, drinks they get worse. She says that nothing could make her more weak than the fact that she has a fifteen-year-old child with a drinking problem.

Eddie has an angry streak like steel running through his heart. He quit school last year and now he sleeps all morning and stays out all night. He drinks with a man called Cake who lives on welfare and drives a big car. Mama and Daddy can't manage Eddie. They tried to make him go back to school, but whenever they brought it up his temper would roll, and he would slam himself at the walls. I remember Mama telling Daddy that maybe Eddie shouldn't go to school, that maybe his whole problem was that the teacher picked on him. But Daddy told her right up quick that Eddie had drinking in his blood just like Daddy's whole family did. Daddy used to drink on weekends. He'd go to the Legion every Friday night after supper and sometimes not come home until Sunday. The last time I saw my Daddy drunk, his lip was broken wide open and purple.

"Who did that to you?" Mama said.

"My old man." Daddy made the words sound like they were the last ones left in him. They echoed like a bobcat snarl.

Mama wrinkled here forehead. "Why?"

One of Daddy's eyes went wet. "Because he was drunk, too."

Mama blames herself for everything. When I smile at Mama, she always says, "Poor girl, she's got her Mother's crooked teeth," but I always say, "Mama, I grew these teeth, not you."

"I'm so warm," Mama says, and I think of calling Daddy at the County Garage to see what to do with her, but I figure he's sure to be out plowing the roads with all this snow. Mama is sicker than usual because Eddie didn't come home and she sat up all night waiting for him. In the night I could hear the rocking chair in Eddie's room moving back and forth like a song and I knew Mama had her face wrapped in her cool hands. I stroke Mama's hair and she says to the air: "You wonder if he's dead or alive."

The radio is playing "O happy day, when Jesus washed, my sins away," and I wonder how they get all those singers in the radio station so early in the morning. Bucky is still waiting at the table.

"I wish they'd say school's cancelled," he says.

"It is," I guess, and stand on the chair and press my face against the top part of the window so I can see out over the snow. In the shiny glass I can see my ghost looking back at me and I blow steam on the window and make three little hearts that Mama will complain about later. Big cutout flakes are still coming down and the veranda is a lake of snow, swirling up and around the railing and window in waves. I think of my feet sinking deep into the new snow—O happy day—and then I think of Eddie frozen in a snowbank.

"Upper Valley Elementary," Bucky yells. "We're closed. No school." He jumps up from the table and does a little circle. "Mama, where are my snow pants? Mama?"

He rubs Mama's face like he is polishing an apple and a smile sneaks out from under her half-moon lips.

When Eddie comes home, Bucky and I are in the hallway putting bread bags over our wool socks so our feet won't get wet. He comes through the door all dressed in black and loose and he looks like a puppet. A cigarette is burning at the side of his mouth and he steps over us as if we are stones.

"Eddie," Mama sits up. "Where have you been? I'm sick from waiting. What do you do all night?"

Eddie doesn't answer Mama. He gives her one of those stares that Daddy says could freeze hell and Mama stands up in front of him.

"Eddie," she begs and he uses his long blue hand to push Mama back down on the couch. Mama chokes back her air and cries like a baby that's got its feelings hurt. Eddie throws his cigarette in the sink and goes up the back stairs to his room and I know he is drunk by the way he smells. I twist a hole through the bread bag and listen for Mama to stop being sad. Bucky is all ready to go. Mama wipes at her face and pulls herself up. She ties her robe tight like a package and takes her pills from her pocket. She shakes them and reads the label.

"I need some sleep," she says to the bottle. Mama comes into the hallway and steps over the water spots that Eddie left. Her feet are pink and crusty. "Will you be warm enough?" She ties a green scarf around my neck and looks down at my face.

"Stop painting your lips with Mercurochrome," she says and she rubs my lips until they burn. "Double up on your mittens, Bucky."

Mama leans on the doorframe and watches us march out the door. "Have fun," she says, "your Mama's going to lie down."

The snow is white and heavy flour. Bucky pushes the wooden storm door closed behind us and we fall on our knees, piling the snow up at the door like we want to bury it.

"Now Mama can rest," Bucky says and he packs the cracks with lots of snow.

I love Bucky's face. It is pointed and always looks to smile like a dolphin's, and even though he is thirteen months younger than me, he seems older. We wade out to the yard and the snow is so deep and heavy that we just stop for a long time and look at things. The white cover is perfect except for Eddie's footprints in from the road. The tiny wind smells brand new and the telephone wires have so much snow on them that they are almost invisible. The snowflakes try to get in our eyes and we squint at one another.

"Catch it on your tongue," Bucky says. We tilt our heads back and stretch our tongues on our chins. Bucky's tongue is watermelon color.

We pull our scarves up over our noses and my breath is warm and wet on the wool. I look back at the house and in the fuzzy snow it looks like a big blank face. The windows are as dark as molasses and nothing moves in them. I think of Eddie hidden in a stack of pillows with his mouth open, while the wind whispers around his window. I think how Daddy will pull him out of bed when he comes home. "I told you to look for work today," he'll say, and Eddie will squirm out of Daddy's hands like he always does.

"Let's make angels," Bucky says.

We look at the yard which is as smooth as a statue and we begin to drop down on our backs and slide our arms like we are trying to fly. We make so many angels that there is no untouched snow left and I tell Bucky if the birds were out, they'd think it was an angel graveyard. We wade around the house and look at all the high drifts. There is a huge drift in front of the shed that is connected to our house so we go around where there is a wooden ladder and climb up on the shed's roof. The roof is slippery, but we know if we fall we will just land in the soft snow and laugh. We slide down the roof into the drift and the snow comes up to our hips. Bucky almost can't get out of the snow and he pretends he is in white quicksand. He waves his arms and screams: "Help, I'm drownin', help me."

"Kick your knees," I say half-mad, and he pushes himself free, tee-hee-ing.

We're lined up on the roof like pigeons when we hear the snowplow coming. We push off together and land just in time to see Daddy going by. He honks and we rush out of the snow so we can run and see him. Swish, swish, swish, our legs are fat and noisy in our snow pants. When we get there, there is nothing but a swirl of white dust and the low growl of Daddy's machine going over the far side of the dirt road. After, everything is soft and still.

We scuff our boots through the snow and blank out five whole angels. There's a big bank of snow by the road and we make foot holes and climb up to the top. The snow is all packed hard and the top is as flat as a stage. As soon as I get up, Bucky pushes me off. That's what Eddie used to do when he played with us, that's exactly what he did. I slide down over the bank and land on my back.

"I'm the king of the castle and you're the dirty rascal," he sings and I don't move. I let the snow whip around my face and I stay perfectly still until the ends of my fingers go stiff.

"Sis," Bucky says, "Sissy, get up. C'mon, let's play. Come back up."

He climbs down beside me. "You're not dead," he says and kicks a pile of snow in my face.

Bucky starts to build a tunnel in the side of the bank. We dig and round it out like an igloo. It's real warm on the inside and when we are finished Bucky leans back against the hard wall and sucks the snow from his mitten.

"Bucky, don't eat snow, it's got worms in it."

"It does not." He wipes his nose with the back of his jacket sleeve.

"Mama says it does," I say.

"It's not snow, it's blubber," he says and just the thought of it makes me laugh.

"Get some icicles," he says.

The icicles are always my job. Bucky says Eskimo women do all the stuff like that. "Anything they can do without their husband's help, they do. They're brave," he told me once.

I climb up on the railing along the veranda and grab one big icicle to knock the rest down. The icicles tick off as I move across the railing and they fall like darts in the snow. I dig them out and carry them back as if they are kindling. We use the tips of the icicles to draw on the walls of the igloo. I always draw a trailer park because that is where I would like to live when I grow up, but Bucky does different things. Today, he draws Eddie with a huge set of drums. Eddie likes the Beatles. He combs his black hair down over his forehead and seals it with Dippity-Do so he looks like Ringo.

Sometimes when Bucky and I come home from school, Eddie is sitting in Daddy's brown recliner beating the arms of the chair with two wooden spoons. His timing is even and his blue eyes are storm clouds when he plays. "Get away from me," he always says.

We get tired and pile the icicles in the middle for firewood then lie on our backs and study the white walls. We never make any rules, but both Bucky and I know that whenever we build an igloo, he's the husband and I'm the wife. After a while, he leans over and kisses my cheek with his wet lips and then lies back down. We both close our eyes.

When our pretend night is over, Bucky sits up, rubbing himself all over because he is freezing. "Get up," he says. "We need more firewood."

My head is still empty from my rest when I poke it out of the tunnel. The air is thick and cold and the flakes have turned into small white dots. I run through the snow to the veranda and climb up to get the icicles. In the distance, I can hear Daddy's plow. I turn and brace my feet holding two big sticks of ice in my hands like swords. I wave them crossways when I see Daddy coming. I think of the people on *Gilligan's Island* waving to airplanes. Snow flies up from the road and Daddy gives a big toot when he goes by and it looks like the plow is empty, like it is driving itself.

I carry the firewood back to the tunnel and I start to feel dizzy when I can't find the igloo's hole. I carry the icicles along the bank thinking maybe I've lost my place and slowly the whiteness is all I can see. I dump the ice and start to crawl through the heavy snow on my knees, and I say, "Bucky, Bucky."

I look back along the bank for a piece of Bucky and I dig at a dark spot hoping it is his mitten, but it's just dirt or a shadow. I stop and listen for him and the weather squeezes in around me. When I get to the veranda, I don't remember running there. The door is piled high with snow and I pull at the handle but the door won't move. I brush the snow back from it with both hands. I get it open just a tiny crack, but I still can't get inside. I jerk the handle back and forth and bang the door hard. "Eddie, Eddie," I holler after each bang.

I get so tired from banging that the ghost in me takes over and I begin to dream. I am dreaming while my body bangs the door. I am all grown up with breasts like Mama and I am standing in front of the house screaming for Eddie to wake up. His window is black and empty. I'm screaming "Eddie, help me. Bucky's suffocating. Eddie, help." I scream until my voice leaves me.

I dream that I climb up the side of the house toward the window. Splinters peel off the house and stick to my fingers until the tips turn purple and begin to bleed. The blood makes the wooden siding slippery and I start to slip back down to the ground. I leave long thin red strips like scratches on the house.

I am staring down, rubbing my frozen fingers together like I have just discovered them when Mama opens the door. Her face is foggy and I tell her fast what has happened.

"Go," she yells, pushing me out into the yard. "Show me."

I point at the flat side of the bank where I think the hole is and I'm scared that I am wrong and that Jesus won't wash my sins away. Mama's red robe works its way open in the front and her flowered nightie looks strange in the snow. I watch the soles of her feet right below me that are staring up with all their cracks and dryness and something about the way they twist and cuddle looks like two baby pigs. I wonder if they feel cold or if Mama has forgotten everything but Bucky. She is breathing with the wind.

"What happened?" She turns her eyes to me for the shortest second and I don't know what to say.

I remember how the plow shook the windowpanes in our house when it rumbled by. It reminded me of thunder.

"What happened?" she says again.

"The plow," I say, "The plow came by," and then I wished I'd blamed myself. That's what Mama would have done.

She has both arms in the snow and she is talking to herself like she is praying, like the bank is her altar. I look back at the house and wonder why Eddie hasn't heard us. Why he hasn't come to help? I am almost ready to let my tears out when Mama reaches way in with her head and all.

"Oh, my land," she says, her words just a whisper.

She pushes her shoulders in and she gets ahold of something and pulls two or three times. I can tell she is getting tired and I am afraid she will give up. She reaches one more time and hauls Bucky out by the arm. His body is limp and one double mitten falls to the white ground. He's flat on his back. Mama stares at his face which looks tired and sleepy and she shakes him.

"Bucky, Bucky, Bucky," she says quick, like his name is a rhyme. She puts her ear on his mouth and listens. She opens her thin lips and puts them on his in a circle. Specks of snow fall down and land on her hair. Bucky opens one eye and squints at the flakes.

"Bucky," Mama says soft and pushes her face against his cheeks, first one side, then the other. She holds his head on both sides. Bucky reaches his hand up and Mama pulls him to her chest and he snuggles into her flowered nightie. Mama's lips are shaking and her eyes are watery blue.

"It's all my fault," she says. She lifts Bucky up on his feet and keeps her hands under his arms. His face is red and full and I touch his bare fingers that hang in the wind like leaves.

"Come, baby," Mama says.

Bucky walks on his own, but Mama holds him tight. Mama's robe flies in the wind behind them and the way it swirls and prances makes me think she is dancing.

I fall back and let my bottom make a snug chair in the snow. I am jerky on the inside and my stomach feels small and hard. I thought Bucky would be dead and that his face would be caved in from the heavy snow. I pick up his mitten and try to forget the melted look that I thought he would have when Mama pulled him out. I take the mitten apart. The inside one is blue. The outside one is an old mitten of Eddie's and it is grey and full of holes. Each hole has a string of wool in it and I pull on the yarn to make the hole bigger, but the hole puckers together in a kiss. I fix every hole his way and the mitten rumples itself into a little ball.

I look at the house. Orange light comes from the kitchen and shadows move past the window in slow motion. I bet Mama is rubbing Bucky's chest with Vicks VapoRub. I think of his round chest that juts out in the middle and my throat goes all full and tight. I listen and everything is big and quiet and I wonder if Daddy will come home soon. I stuff Eddie's grey mitten inside of Bucky's and waddle myself free from the snow.

18

VIEWPOINT

Who's Seeing This?

Viewpoint: the one who sees the action. The single means of perception. Multiple viewpoints. Testing alternative viewpoints. First or third person? The focus. Reviewing your options.

Contemporary short stories are generally presented through the eyes of a single character. This is the character whose mind you enter. What this character sees and hears, you as reader see and hear. This character is known as the **viewpoint** or the **means of perception.**

Limiting the means of perception to a single character is not a rule—there are no absolute rules in fiction, only effective and ineffective tactics—but it is a dominant pattern in this century, particularly for short fiction as opposed to novels. There are variations which I will describe shortly, but they are rare.

This apparent restriction bothers some beginning writers because it seems limiting. Actually it is a powerful device for creating the illusion of reality with all its doubts and anticipations. Understanding viewpoint is an essential first step to understanding the difference between factual writing and fiction.

The Single Means of Perception

Limiting the means of perception to a single character means that you as writer can only hint about what is going on in the mind of other characters or the events in the next room. And you can't comment on what will happen next. If this limitation seems restrictive, remember that unless you are psychic, these are the restrictions you live with in daily life. Your reader shares the experience, including the uncertainties of the character who is the means of perception.

Take, for example, this simple fictional sentence: "The boy looked at his grandfather, wondering if the old man had understood." Here the means of perception is the boy. We know what he is wondering and so we are "in his head." We don't know what the grandfather is thinking, and if the story continues in this vein we, like the boy, will not find out until the old man speaks or reveals his thoughts through his actions.

Means of perception is synonymous with **point of view** and *viewpoint*. I will use them interchangeably. Keep in mind, however, that these alternate terms are also used loosely to refer to attitude, as in the phrase "from the British point of view." It doesn't matter which term you use as long as you remember that when applied to fiction it is a precise literary concept—and an important one.

Stories written in the **first person** are almost always limited to a single means of perception. The "I" who begins the story will, in almost every case, be our only source of information. Shifting to another narrator is possible, but it breaks the mood so severely that it is rarely done. What many beginning writers don't realize, however, is that most **third-person** stories are limited to a single means of perception as well. Once the means of perception has been established—usually at the outset of a story—it is normally maintained right through to the end. In our example of the boy and his grandfather, for example, readers tend to assume that the story will be presented through the eyes of the boy, that we will know his thoughts and not enter the mind of other characters. It would be unusual to have the next line read, "Actually Grandfather did agree, but he knew that he could never tell the boy." This jumps from the boy's mind to that of the grandfather. To some degree, the reader stands outside the story with this version. This sense of detachment is increased if the author steps in with an observation neither character could make at the time, such as "Little did either of them realize that later that day they would both take a trip to the hospital." That's called **author's intrusion.**

Author's intrusion was popular in the eighteenth and nineteenth centuries but is rare today, especially in short fiction. You will, however, find an unusual and effective example in the opening paragraph of "Obst Vw," the story that appears as Chapter 23.

The primary advantage of limiting the means of perception to a single character without commentary from the author is that it effectively draws the reader into the story. It increases the natural tendency to identify with a fictional character—a feeling that should not be confused with sympathy, respect, or even approval. It creates the illusion of being someone else for a short period of time.

Another advantage, closely related, is that it allows the author to withhold information. **Suspense** is one of the pleasures of reading fiction, and suspense is achieved by not knowing what is about to happen. When our view of events is limited to that of a single character, we share his or her desire to find out what comes next.

In "Sausage and Beer," for example, the boy's puzzlement about who Uncle Theodore is and what he will be like becomes the reader's puzzlement as well. There is no rule against beginning that story with a clear, explanatory introduction, but it would undoubtedly reduce the reader's sense of curiosity. Here is a blunt yet informative version of the opening:

> When I was twelve my father invited me to visit my Uncle Theodore, a patient in a large mental hospital. They were twins, but their lives had taken dramatically different routes.

If, after an introduction like that, I had then gone on with the boy's speculations about whether the uncle was a farmer, a solitary mystic, or possibly a murderer in prison, it might have sounded patronizing. Because the reader already knows whose the uncle really is, the tone becomes a bit condescending, as if we are smiling at him rather than sharing the experience with him.

The same applies to the boy's reaction of alarm when the man in the bar shouts "'Whatcha doing...corruptin' the youth?'" It is only a small moment of reader anxiety, but compare the effect with this heavy-handed bit of factual explanation:

> I was alarmed when the headwaiter came out and, pretending to be angry, said....

Deliberate withholding of information through a single means of perception is just as important in "Three Hearts." That story, like "Sausage and Beer," was written in the first person, but suppose it had been cast in the third person and Corey had unwisely begun with a heavy-handed use of author's intrusion like this:

> Sissy's mother looked frail and spent much of her time on the couch, groggy with tranquilizers, but before the day was out she would prove that deep within her lay maternal strengths strong enough to save her son Bucky from almost certain death.

You know that's a terrible opening, but why? Because the author has stepped in and not only predicted the plot but analyzed the theme rather than letting the story unfold through action and dialogue.

As we write, we are **omniscient,** that is, all-knowing. Because we usually limit what we reveal, what I have been calling a single means of perception is often referred to as *limited omniscience*. But the term is a bit misleading in regard to short stories particularly. The tendency is to rely entirely on the step-by-step discoveries of the implied **narrator.** In such cases, the author's knowledge of what will happen is intentionally withheld.

Multiple Viewpoints

There *are* exceptions to the single-means-of-perception approach. The most common is using the third person with occasional author's intrusion. Exposition that simply saves time without violating the viewpoint is not true author's intrusion. "His sister had joined the police force three years earlier," for example, provides information which, if it is something the protagonist knows, merely saves time. True author's intrusion provides information the implied narrator doesn't know: "He never suspected that for three years she had secretly been a CIA agent."

One reason author's intrusion was much more popular in the eighteenth and nineteenth centuries was that fiction often had the flavor of stories told out loud. It was not at all unusual to have detailed commentary on character ("He was a dour gentleman with a military man's high regard for order") or generalized commentary ("Such behavior is rarely rewarded these days"). This approach has become less popular today because the trend is away from the impression of listening to a narrated story and toward the illusion of entering a story directly—possibly an influence of film as a competing genre. But the voice of the author is still being used, particularly in novels by authors such as John Fowles, Margaret Drabble, and Milan Kundera. Because author's intrusion has been out of fashion for so long, it now appears fresh and innovative when employed skillfully.

The other variation on single means of perception is entering the mind of more than one character. This style is fairly common in novels, although often a single means of perception is sustained for the length of a scene or a chapter. The disadvantage of this technique in short stories is that every time the viewpoint shifts, the reader has to establish a new sense of identification. This brief lapse is a millisecond version of what happens with a scene change in a play. If a story does it frequently, the reader begins to lose the sense of being *in* the story, viewing it instead as an outside observer.

One frequently anthologized example of multiple viewpoints is "The Short Happy Life of Francis Macomber" by Ernest Hemingway. The story is unusual in that not only does the point of view shift from character to character, but at one point it even enters the mind of a wounded lion. Another highly popular experiment is Shirley Jackson's "The Lottery." She does not enter the minds of her characters at all, maintaining a journalist's objective style. The situation is so terrible that presenting it in a cool, detached manner keeps the story from spilling over into melodrama.

These are, however, exceptions from the general pattern. They are well worth studying, but they make risky models for those who are beginning. The single means of perception helps an author to draw the reader into the work and care about it.

Testing Alternative Viewpoints

When you start a new story, there is a tendency to stay with the viewpoint that first occurred to you. Nine times out of ten, that will be the right route. Still you can't be sure whether you're missing an even more effective approach unless you visualize your material with alternative viewpoints. Even if you stay with your original conception, the very act of imagining the material through different viewpoints often generates new insights.

What, for example, would happen to "Sausage and Beer"? In considering these transformations in viewpoint, resist the inclination to dwell on why they would be less effective. The real question is how, for better or for worse, such a change would affect the story.

First, imagine that story told from the father's point of view. Almost necessarily the story would highlight his attitude toward his son and probably toward children in general. Perhaps he entered into parenthood late and finds it difficult to relate to children. What impelled him to bring his son along for this visit and not his daughter? What might he recall about his own childhood growing up with Theodore? What kind of a relationship does he have with his wife? What does *she* think of Theodore? These questions are not even touched on directly in the published version, but they would all be important in a story told from his point of view.

How about the story with Theodore as the mean of perception? Fiction from the point of view of an insane patient is surprisingly popular with beginning writers, but too often such stories take the form of an apparently mild-mannered murderer. The pattern is so popular and so unvarying it might be nominated as the eighth "deadly sin" of fiction! In reality, the Hollywood version of the smiling, gentle creature who was driven to terrible acts by a single, identifiable trauma is a cliché. Using an insane character in fiction is risky unless you have listened a good deal to mental patients or have been one.

In spite of all these risks, however, it might be possible to present that story through the eyes of someone whose mind slides without warning from one decade to another and whose perceptions are frequently distorted by anxiety and by free-floating, erratic, but genuine fears. Imagining myself in Theodore's world helped me to present him sympathetically even though I did not write the story from his point of view.

"Three Hearts" offers even more possibilities, since there are more characters who could be given a central position. The mother comes to mind as a natural choice. One would lose most of the children's game play in the igloo, but some of that material might be revealed through some other game she might overhear indoors. Less would be seen of Sissy and her brother Bucky, but more might be developed about the father and the agonizing task of raising Eddie. A version like that would probably be more explicit about the past since the mother would be able to recall more of it than Sissy. The mother's memories might be interestingly blurred because of her medication.

A story told through Bucky's eyes would be similar to the published version, though the climactic scene would be far more dreamlike and necessarily less focused on the mother. Writing the story through Eddie's eyes, on the other hand, would be entirely different. His view of his parents would be distorted with resentment and possibly suppressed guilt. Such a story would hardly mention Sissy and Bucky, but it might make much more of "a man called Cake who lives on welfare and drives a big car," a character mentioned only once in the published version.

Clearly there are advantages and disadvantages to each approach, and even though you may have no intention of transforming your story, considering the alternatives early in your planning will provide fresh insights into your characters and the thematic potential of the story.

First or Third Person?

It does make a difference whether you cast a story in the first person, using *I*, or present it in the third person, referring to your protagonist as *he* or *she*. But the difference is more subtle than you might imagine. Oddly, it is sometimes difficult to remember whether a story you read the day before used the first or third person.

Here to test you are two versions of each of the two stories you have read so far. Can you spot which approach was used in the actual story?

A. He kept quiet for most of the trip. It was too cold to talk. The car was getting old and the heater hadn't worked for as long as he could remember. His father said he couldn't afford to get it repaired....

B. I kept quiet for most of the trip. It was too cold for talk. The car was getting old and the heater hadn't worked for as long as I could remember. My father said he couldn't afford to get it repaired....

A. The morning after the big snowstorm, her mother is real sick....They are all lined up, listening to the radio that sits on top of the fridge to see if there will be any school.

B. The morning after the big snowstorm Mama is real sick....We are all lined up, listening to the radio that sits on top of the fridge to see if there will be any school.

Both stories could have been written either way. Even if you identified the second as being the author's choice in each case, recasting these stories in the third person would not have been a major transformation. Shifting person from first to third or back to first is far less radical than changing the means of perception.

Still, it is worth reading the first page of a new story in both ways. Your initial choice may be the right one, but there are advantages to each that are worth considering.

One good reason for using the first person is that you may want to maintain the naiveté or innocence of a young protagonist. "Sausage and Beer" deals with a young boy who is going through a new and strange experience. Using the first person was a natural way to suggest a **narrator** and to share his feelings with the reader without commentary. "Three Hearts" deals with a girl who faces an emergency. It is different in that through her experience we learn something significant about the mother, but again, maintaining the naive voice of a child narrator is easier in the first person.

A closely related advantage of the first person is that you can adopt the tone of a story being narrated out loud. Such stories occasionally identify a listener, but more often they do not. The illusion is usually created by word choice and phrasing. Very few authors indulge in phonetic spellings like "goin'" for "going" and " 'em" for "them," because spelling changes easily become obtrusive. But you can suggest a regional or foreign accent through phrasing without altering the spelling or a single word.

Corey often uses phrasing that is both vivid and childlike: The mother's speech is described as "puffy and low"; her eyes are "like faded jeans"; Eddie's "blue eyes are storm clouds," and after Bucky's near suffocation she feels "jerky" on the inside." It would be possible to use some of those phrases if the story had been in the third person, but too often the author would have had to introduce them with "to her it seemed like . . ." or "to her it looked like...." Although the story is not fully "as-if-spoken" with a listener identified, the fact that it is in the first person allows the author to use colloquial phrasing in her narration.

The first person is also useful when the primary point of the story is to ridicule or satirize the narrator. You can achieve an effective irony when characters try to justify or defend themselves in ways that actually damn them in the reader's eyes.

Oddly, the first person may *not* be the right choice for a story based on an event that is recent and still has highly charged feelings. To put this more positively, the third person is an excellent way of holding material at arm's length. If you have just broken up with someone who was important to you or are trying to deal with a loss through death, try transforming the event by selecting the third person. And if doing that doesn't work, shift the protagonist to someone else.

The greatest advantage of the third person is flexibility. The writer can use the protagonist as the primary means of perception, using *he* or *she*, while occasionally drawing on a more objective view for incidental or background information.

The popular notion that the first person provides a sense of immediacy or realism that cannot be achieved in the third person is not justified. Readers enter a story using *he* or *she* just as easily as they do one that begins with *I*. But the decision of which to use should not be made carelessly. Your first inclination may be entirely justified, but do consider the alternative. If in doubt, convert a sample paragraph from first person to third or the reverse fairly early in the writing.

The Focus of the Story

The **focus** of a story refers to the character who is the central concern. Don't confuse focus with **viewpoint**. In many cases, the character through whose eyes you are seeing the events is also the focus of the story, but not always.

"Three Hearts" is an excellent example of a story in which the character who is means of perception is *not* the true focus of the story. Sissy is our only means of seeing the action, so she clearly is the viewpoint character. But if you look at the story thematically, you will see that it is primarily about a dysfunctional mother, an invalid both physically and emotionally, who in spite of her disabilities responds to an emergency with astonishing energy and courage. The daughter is the narrator, but the mother is the true subject of the story.

How is this focus established when so much of the story has to do with Sissy and her brother? The opening scene places the spotlight on the mother, and the highly dramatic climax is dominated by her heroic action. The games the children play in the igloo are significant in the way they keep returning to the subject of death and the relationship between men and women, but the true theme has to do with the competence of the mother as opposed to the incompetence of the men who for three generations have been debilitated with alcoholism.

Focus is closely tied to theme, an aspect I'll return to in Chapter 27. The important point here, however, is that the character who is the means of perception is not necessarily the one on center stage. A story can be told through the eyes of a relatively innocent observer.

Reviewing Your Options

When a story idea first comes to you, it will probably be a mix of personal experience and invention. Let it run through your head like a daydream.

Don't concern yourself at this early stage about the means of perception, person, and focus. If you analyze too much too soon, you may lose the feel of the story.

There will come a point, however, when you feel you have enough to work with. This is when some writers like to make a few notes about plot and characters so they won't lose the original concept. This is also when you should consider alternative strategies of presentation. Transforming a story by altering the point of view or the focus is a lot easier when it is still in your head than it is when a draft is down on paper.

When examining the means of perception at this early stage, try to resist the temptation to play tricks with point of view: The first-person account of a disaster at sea in which all are drowned turns out to be a note in a bottle; the third-person story picturing the terrible life of an oversupervised little girl turns out to be about a happy little dog; a brother–sister story turns out in the last sentence to have concerned two robots. All these have been done, but they and stories like them all depend on a simple twist in the means of perception. Any story that relies on a one-shot trick will be forgotten as quickly as a standup comedian's joke. Viewpoint is an important aspect of sophisticated fiction, but when it is used as the whole point of a story, the result becomes trivial entertainment.

Shifting a story from third person to first or the reverse is not as radical a transformation as changing the means of perception. But as we have seen, it involves more than changing *I* to *he* or *she*. Although it is technically a matter of style, its significance really has more to do with the relationship between the writer and her or his material. If you have any doubts about which approach is most appropriate for a particular story, try a half page each way and see which feels right. To a large degree, this is an intuitive choice.

Focus, on the other hand, is fundamental. It involves the theme or central concern of the story. Make every effort to get this right at the start. Have you turned the spotlight on the right character? Do you really know what the story is suggesting? Sometimes you may be inclined to forge ahead with the first draft without being sure, and there are writers who recommend doing this. But hiking without maps or compass has its risks. Whatever you do, develop a clear focus before you ask others to spend valuable time reading the draft. Claiming that it should mean whatever readers want it to mean is simply asking them to do your work.

One final note of sympathetic caution: There will be times when in spite of your most careful efforts you will discover late in the development of a story that the means of perception really should be changed. Or, worse, you may realize that the character you had thought was the focus of a developing story is not the true subject. All your efforts may seem to crumble. It's panic time!

If this happens to you, here are four first-aid steps that may make the difference of life or death for the story: (1) Don't tear up the draft. Hollywood movies show frustrated writers ripping pages from the typewriter and crumpling them. Don't. The draft may look better in the morning. (2) With regard to the means of perception, simply rewrite the first page with the viewpoint changed. You can tell far better from writing an actual sample than you can by trying to analyze the situation in the abstract. See if your sample page *feels* better. Trust your instinct. (3) If changing from first to third person is what is bothering you, write a sample page each way. Again, trust your instinct. This is a nonproblem. (4) Focus, on the other hand, can be a real problem. If you have doubts in this area, look carefully at the first and last pages. Sometimes you can successfully change the focus of a story without staying up all night simply by rewriting the opening and the closing. Try setting the manuscript aside and writing the first and last pages from memory. A new opening and closing may be just the transformation you need. Review once again how neatly focus is established in the first half page and the conclusion of "Three Hearts."

When you start writing fiction, finding the right subject matter seems like the primary challenge. As you gain experience, however, you will find that questions of viewpoint are even more important.

19

STRUCTURE

From Scenes to Plot

Clock time distinguished from psychological time. Scene construction in two stories. Varieties of plot patterns: chronological, flashbacks, frame stories. Critical paragraphs: openings and closings. Controlling the pace. Scene awareness.

Clocks move at a steady rate. And in one sense, so do our lives. Awake or asleep, our allotted time flows from birth to death at a steady pace.

Psychological time, however, does not. Take a moment to review what you did yesterday from the time you got up to the end of the day. Notice how naturally that chronology turns into a list of events or episodes: getting dressed, eating breakfast, and, for students, attending classes, a coffee break with friends in the cafeteria, a conversation in the hall, and lunch. For non-students, the events would be different, but the rhythm from one unit of activity to the next is essentially the same. The point is that while the *clock* moves perfectly regularly, our *life* as we look back is recalled as a sequence of episodes.

These episodes have certain characteristics that every writer of fiction should consider. First, we often identify them by where they occurred—the setting. Second, we recall who was there—the characters. Third, such episodes remain clear long after we have forgotten what came just before and just afterward. Those unstructured periods of time that merely link one episode with the next (walking, waiting, driving, watching television, sleeping) tend to blend together and blur quickly.

Finally, we don't always remember these events in the order in which they occurred. Students complaining about bad teachers they have had are not necessarily going to start with kindergarten; football fans recounting dramatic games they have watched are not going to begin with the first one they attended; and a man recalling his love for a woman is not necessarily going to begin with the day he met her.

Fiction tends to imitate these patterns. What we call *episodes* in life become **scenes** in fiction. These are the basic units. And their arrangement is what we call **plot.**

Scene Construction in Two Stories

If you recall the plot of "Sausage and Beer" without looking back, you will probably think of it as taking the form of three major blocks: the trip to the hospital, the actual visit, and the bar scene. They stand out because each has a distinctly different setting.

But if you examine that story with a writer's analytical eye, you will see that there are more divisions than that. Although scenes in fiction are not as clearly defined as they are in drama, we sense a transition whenever the author changes the setting or has a character arrive or leave. There are six such divisions in "Sausage and Beer."

1. The narrator is being driven by his father to see the boy's uncle on a cold January day. (Includes a **flashback**—a scene within a scene—in which the father invites his son to visit his Uncle Theodore.)
2. A short scene outside the hospital building. This is set off by a description of the hospital and grounds.
3. The waiting room. Father and son wait for Uncle Theodore to appear.
4. The visit with Uncle Theodore. This begins with Theodore's arrival and ends with the conclusion of visiting hours. Notice that the setting hasn't changed, but there is a psychological break when Uncle Theodore appears.
5. A short scene in the car.
6. The important scene in the bar. Notice that this is not only a different setting, it is a different climate as well. The bar is warm and friendly.

Why six scenes? When the story was blocked out, this is what emerged. Initially, the number of scenes should probably be determined by the way in which the story comes to you. But once the first draft is down on paper, you should take a close look at the number and length of your scenes. Occasionally you will have to add a new scene. But more often you will find that you can cut. As I described earlier, a two-page flashback was cut from what I hoped would be the final draft before this story was published, and another page was cut from the second edition version in this textbook.

When a story appears to be too long, there is sometimes a tendency to try nibbling away at it word by word. After an hour of such work, you may find that you have cut less than a paragraph. It is far more effective to look at the scenes and weigh the possibility of eliminating one entirely.

There comes a point, of course, when a story cannot be cut further without doing damage. In terms of plot alone, this story could be reduced to a single scene—the one at the hopsital. But too much would be lost. The earlier scenes establish the relationship between father and son while also providing suspense, and the concluding scenes shift the story from a simple initiation (the boy introduced to the disturbing reality of mental illness) to a kind of first communion in which a young man is welcomed into the fellowship of adult life with all its distressing ironies.

The answer to the question of why the story is in six scenes is not a simple matter of rules. It is judgment. My sense is that more scenes would weigh the story down and fewer would begin to make it too sketchy, too simple. It is very helpful to have a rough idea of the scene pattern in advance—even a tentative outline. But it is equally important to be willing to make adjustments at any stage.

The scene construction in "Three Hearts" is slightly more diffuse. If you rely on your memory, you may recall it as essentially two major blocks: the first in the house with the mother and the other outside in the snow. But of course it has to be more complicated than that since Sissy is not with her brother when he is buried in the snow. If you look closer, you can find seven scenes. Although the divisions are sometimes fuzzy, here is one way to describe it:

1. The kitchen: Narrator, Bucky, and their mother listen to the radio. (Includes a flashback with dialogue between the parents.)
2. The hallway: Eddie comes home.
3. Outside in the yard: Sissy and Bucky play in the snow.
4. They dig a tunnel in the snowbank and play house in what they call their "igloo."
5. Back yard again: Bucky has ordered his sister to get more "firewood," which requires gathering icicles. When she returns she can't find the tunnel.
6. Back to the house: Tries to wake Eddie. Can't. Tells her mother what has happened.
7. The yard again: The mother saves Bucky. Sissy lingers there.

There doesn't appear to be any unnecessary scene here. It's important to have at least a quick glimpse of Eddie. Playing in the snow provides several references to death, and playing house in the igloo subtly reveals early attitudes toward sexual roles ("Eskimo women do all the stuff like that"). It is essential to get Sissy out of the igloo when it is knocked down (significantly by the father). And the high-drama scene is the one in which we see that this is really a story about the mother.

The end of the final scene, when Sissy is alone, may seem at first reading to be expendable. The symbol of Eddie's mitten which is "full of holes" is poignant, however, and gives the story a depth of suggestion that it would not have had if it had ended with action alone, like another Disney adventure tale.

Varieties of Plot Patterns

The two stories you have read so far both move **chronologically** from scene to scene. A majority of stories do—particularly those that are relatively short. But even in those cases, the writer is not bound to move relentlessly forward in time. The author, like the scriptwriter, is free to include glimpses of past action.

The **flashback** is a simple method of inserting an episode that occurred before the main flow (or **base time**) of the plot. The term *flashback*, first used by film writers, describes more than a simple reference to the past seen through a character's thoughts or dialogue. A true flashback consists of a whole scene that took place before the main action of the story and is presented with setting and often with dialogue.

Take, for example, the flashback that occurs in the opening scene of "Sausage and Beer." The father and son, you remember, are driving in silence, and the earlier incident is dropped in almost as if in brackets:

> The whole business of visiting Uncle Theodore had come up in the most unconvincingly offhand manner.
> "Thought I'd visit your Uncle Theodore," he had said that day after Sunday dinner. "Wondered if you'd like to meet him."
> He spoke with his eyes on a crack in the ceiling as if the idea had just popped into his head, but that didn't fool me.

Notice that the reader is informed of the fact that the story is moving back to an earlier time by the brief use of the past perfect: "*had* come up" and "he *had* said that day." This is a standard method of entering a flashback in past-tense stories, even though many readers are not consciously aware that they are being signaled by a shift in tense. In fact, many *writers* have used the technique without knowing that the *had* form is called the past perfect. Never mind the terminology; *had* is the cue for your reader. After one or two sentences, shift back to the simple past.

How do you come out of a flashback? The most obvious way is to identify the transition directly: "But that was hours ago" or "But that was when he was much younger." More often, authors simply make sure that the new paragraph starts with a bit of action or a line of dialogue that clearly indicates to the reader that the story has returned to *base time*, the events and setting of the primary plot line. In this particular flashback the reader should be set straight by the paragraph that begins: "We were well out in the New England countryside now."

The same kind of cues are used when you are writing in the present tense. The shift in these cases is from the present to the simple past tense. There is a good example in the opening scene of "Three Hearts":

> The last time I saw my Daddy drunk, his lip was broken wide open and purple.
> "Who did that to you?" Mama said.
> "My old man."

We know that we are out of the flashback as soon as the author returns to the present tense: "Mama blames herself for everything."

In many cases, you can make the return to base time clear simply by starting a new paragraph and shifting the tense. But be sure that the setting is clearly different. If your flashback takes place in, say, a restaurant, be careful not to have your characters in another restaurant when you return to base time. There's no point in needlessly confusing your reader.

Oddly, even careless readers follow cues like these without having the slightest idea of how they work. Writers, on the other hand, have to be acutely aware of the technique.

Flash-forwards are rare, but they do have a particular use. There is an excellent example in Sharon Solwitz's story "Obst Vw" which appears in Chapter 23. In a daring stylistic tactic, she opens the story with an event that will not occur until a year after the story that follows:

> Next year, writing his personal experience essay to convince admissions at Penn he's Ivy League material despite uneven grades, he'll describe in amusing detail the one baseball game his father took him to, and get in on a scholarship despite his father's explicit pessimism.

She closes the flash-forward within the same paragraph:

> But now on Rachel's bed, unraveling a hole in the knee of her jeans while her parents yell at each other downstairs, he cannot join in her raillery. "Let's go," he says.

The effect of a flash-forward is almost invariably a **distancing.** That is, the reader rises above the story, viewing the characters a bit more objectively. For those who feel that immediacy and emotional impact should be primary goals in fiction, this may seem like a poor tactic. But remember that when the emotional element is pushed too far in fiction it becomes sentimentality or melodrama. When you read this story, notice how that flash-forward helps us to keep those characters and their very real distress in perspective. Their suffering is genuine, but it is not tragic.

Multiple flashbacks are sometimes used when the author wants to suggest a complicated set of clues leading to a symbolic or a literal trial. Joseph Conrad's *Lord Jim* is in this form; so is William Faulkner's well-known "A Rose for Emily." Such an approach tends to fragment the story line, of course, and it may be for this reason that it is usually found in longer works and those that have a type of mystery or trial to maintain the story's unity and the reader's interest.

The **frame story** traditionally refers to a tale told by a character appearing in a larger work, such as the separate narrations within Chaucer's *The Canterbury Tales*. But by common usage it also refers to any story in which the bulk of the material is presented as a single, long flashback. It is possible to do this in the third person; but often a frame is achieved through the device of a narrator who recalls an incident that happened some time in the past.

"Sausage and Beer," for example, could have opened with the narrator looking back like this:

> As I stood with my wife waiting for the funeral to begin, I realized how little I had really seen of my father. It was as if he were a stranger until I was twelve. The turning point came one day when he took me to visit my Uncle Theodore.
>
> As I remember it, I had kept quiet for most of the trip. It was too cold for talk.

Notice the traditional use of the past perfect for a single sentence and then the simple past. And if the story were to have a complete frame, the ending might be rounded out with a return to the opening scene.

> Sitting there in the chapel, listening to the service intended to honor my father, I couldn't help feeling that he and I had experienced a more meaningful ritual there in that most secular bar years ago.

Such an ending seems wooden to me—a bit too obvious. But it does indicate how any story can be surrounded in a frame. Or, as an alternative, the frame can be left incomplete simply to avoid the danger of a needless summing up.

The use of the frame is well justified if there is a good reason for contrasting the attitude of the narrator at the time of the narration with that back when the event took place.

Critical Paragraphs: Openings and Closings

When you have finished your first draft, take a close, critical look at your opening and closing paragraphs. Stories with long, rambling introductions or character descriptions in the nineteenth-century manner seem dated today mainly because such passages are generally from the author's point of view. The unusual flash-forward at the opening of "Obst Vw" (Chapter 23) is in some ways an exception to this, but it is brief and factual.

One way to judge how quickly your story starts is to ask this key question: At what point do we enter the mind of the character who will be the means of perception? This is the moment when the reader is able to identify with a character. This is when the story really begins. If an entire paragraph precedes this point, consider cutting it. That material can be folded into the story later. Sometimes an entire page has to go; but again, the background information can be broken up and inserted at various points later.

Endings sometimes present problems of their own. At some point before the final paragraph you may want to develop what James Joyce called an **epiphany.** Although he used the term in a somewhat more limited sense, it has come to mean an important moment of recognition or discovery. It can take one of two forms: either the reader and the central character learn something significant from the events of the story, or the reader alone makes such a discovery. Even stories that appear at first reading to be highly unstructured usually provide this important element.

In "Sausage and Beer" there are, I think, two such moments—one recognized by the boy and the other perceived only by the reader. The first is given through the fat man at the bar who, in a serious moment almost at the end of the story, poses the question of why one of two brothers should live a normal life and the other should end up in a mental hospital. His answer is that it is just chance. We all run that risk. The boy and the reader come to realize this simultaneously.

The final sentence, however, offers an insight too complex for the boy to understand at this stage in his life. Father and son, having shared a difficult experience, are now sharing something like a communion—not a religious experience but a partaking of life itself.

Whatever your approach, resist the temptation to step in as author at the very end and explain the story. If you do, you may be explaining what the story has already shown successfully through action and dialogue. This is a form of redundancy. Cut the explanation. If, on the other hand, you are explaining themes that were not shown in the story, you need to go back and suggest those aspects through action and dialogue. If you do this successfully, no concluding explanation will be necessary.

Effective endings often consist of some small, apparently insignificant piece of action that may highlight the theme or possibly even reveal it. Occasionally a line of dialogue may serve the same purpose. In "Sausage and Beer," the father and son "ate and drank quietly, lost in a kind of communion." In "Three Hearts," Sissy fixes the holes in Eddie's mitten and stuffs it "inside of Bucky's." Without knowing it (and also without the author telling us), she has tried—perhaps ineffectually—to mend the terrible gaps in that family.

One way to study openings intensively is to go through an anthology reading nothing but first paragraphs. Which draw you and which do not? Which open up a world you wish to enter? Take some notes. Then do the same for final paragraphs. Obviously you will not be able to interpret their meaning, but study the kinds of significant action or in some cases dialogue used in each case.

Controlling the Pace of Plot

Every reader is aware that some sections in a story move slowly or drag, while others move quickly. A writer, however, has to know *why* this has happened.

In part, the **pace** of fiction is controlled by the style—particularly the length and complexity of the sentence structure. This is discussed in Chapter 28. By far the greatest factor, however, is the **rate of revelation.** That is, a story seems to move rapidly when a great deal is being revealed to the reader; conversely, it slows down when the author turns to digression, speculation, description, or any type of exposition.

A writer can, of course, maintain a high rate of revelation simply by concentrating on what reviewers like to call an "action-packed plot." This is one of the recurring characteristics of many best-sellers, adventure stories, and stories of "true romance." Extreme examples are seen in television drama series and the comics. What these stories sacrifice is richness of suggestion and subtleties of characterization.

When you write sophisticated fiction, you have to be on guard against two dangers: If you maintain a consistently high rate of revelation, entertaining your readers with a lively plot, you may bore them for lack of significance. They will find your work superficial. But if you become philosophically discursive or heavily symbolic, you may also bore your readers by lack of drama. Therefore most successfully sophisticated stories shift the pace throughout the work.

Openings are frequently given a high rate of relevation. It helps to plunge into an ongoing situation that will arouse the reader's interest. "Sausage and Beer," for example, begins with the narrator driving with his father and wondering what his Uncle Theodore will be like. The question in the mind of the boy becomes the reader's concern too. In the case of "Three Hearts," the rate of revelation is even higher. The first paragraph presents a mother apparently too sick to care for children. In the very next paragraph we are introduced to Sissy's father and Eddie with his drinking problems. With a dysfunctional family like that, anything can happen.

Both of these stories jump into a situation that arouses the curiosity of the reader. Once you as writer have overcome the reader's reluctance to get started, you can afford to fill in the setting and provide background.

As a story develops, it is a good idea to continue alternating between the vitality of fresh plot development and the richness of description and exposition. In this way the pace of fiction often resembles that of a skater in that the forward thrust is followed by a glide. It's wise, of course, not to glide too long or the story, like the skater, will lose momentum.

As you read over your first draft, try to feel where the story slows its pace. If it is only a slight pause, you have no problem. The forward moton of the narration should carry the reader. But if not enough happens for too long, the story will sag and you need to revise.

On the other hand, too much emphasis on plot may make a story superficial or melodramatic—what we have been calling *simple* fiction. In those cases you may wish to moderate the dramatic action to the point where it can be handled in the relatively delicate form of the short-short story. A story ending with a fatal automobile accident, for example, may seem less like a routine television scene if you cut the death; a story capped by a suicide (often a too-easy ending) may be more convincing if the protagonist shows his or her despair in a more subtle way.

When determining the pace of a story, consider the length. A short-short of three to six manuscript pages, for example, may be based on a single scene and may move at essentially the same pace from beginning to end. The longer a story, the more natural it is to have multiple scenes; and as soon as you do, the pacing becomes important. "Three Hearts," for example, seems like a relatively short story when printed, but it would come to slightly more than 14 double-spaced pages in manuscript. A story of this length can afford the relatively slow-paced scenes of the children playing in the snow and then in their igloo. But look at the rush of activity toward the end as Sissy leaves the tunnel, goes back to the house, returns to the tunnel, discovers it collapsed, races back to the house a second time, then returns with her mother to find Bucky. That breathless quality is not caused by the emergency alone; it is enhanced by tight, action-charged scenes.

It is sometimes difficult to judge the pacing of a story you have just written because you are still so close to the material. If possible, set the manuscript aside for a day or two and then read it nonstop as if for the first time. Also try to find others to read it. Even if they are not writers, they will be able to identify scenes that seem to drag.

Scene Awareness

When you read for pleasure, you don't have to pay attention to scenes. But when you turn to writing fiction, they become a prime concern. You can increase your awareness of scenes by analyzing them in published fiction or story manuscripts. Block out the material in your own mind. From time to time, mark the scene divisions in a couple of stories. Like an architect learning from the work of others, analyze the structure.

There may be times when a story you are writing flows so effortlessly that you won't want to get analytical as you write. Go with it! But after that heady rush is over and the first draft is complete, return to your calmer, critical self and take a close look at the scene construction. Would flashbacks help? Will the opening arouse the reader's interest? Is the conclusion subtle enough? Are there scenes that are too long or too slow or both?

Scenes form the structure of a story. If they are sound, the story will also be sound.

20

A STORY

by Ursula Hegi

Acts of Violence

My mother is taking self-defense classes. When she visits us in Connecticut on weekends, bringing fresh strawberries and pesto bagels on the train, she tries to practice her latest moves with us.

"Please, choke me from behind," she tells my wife, Sylvie, while they're setting the table on the patio.

"Could you please grab me by the front of my collar?" she asks my son, Russ, who, at twelve, is a full head taller than my mother.

She takes those classes in the roughest neighborhood of the South Bronx, in the basement of a pawnshop on East 149th. Of the nine students, my mother is the oldest, only one of two women. The other woman is half her age and owns a massage parlor behind Alexander's. So far my mother has studied how to free herself from a choking hold, attack someone who comes at her with a pool cue or broken bottle, break her attacker's nose and elbow, and drive her fist into a groin as if holding an ice pick.

She has learned one blow to the throat with the edge of her hand that can kill you. "Hit hard. Then get out," her instructor has told his students. Whenever she quotes him, my mother lowers her voice and speaks in a choppy accent: "Courts give attackers more rights than you. Someone can sue you if you don't finish him. Don't leave your calling card. Go home. Read about it in the paper. So a mugger got killed.... Hmm...How about that?"

"What is that man's background?" I want to know.

"He is about thirty and came over from Norway when he was a boy. He still has a face like a boy with his blond hair and—"

"His education, I mean."

"A bit of everything."

"I bet."

"He has a black belt and teaches other classes in karate, judo, boxing, and kick boxing."

"Where did you find him?"

"The yellow pages. He had a class starting the day I called and said I could come and watch to see if I liked it. He uses the best of each form, whatever's most effective, and doesn't care how elegant a kick looks, just how hard you hit."

"His ethics worry me."

"Me too." My mother's fine white hair bobs around her face. "But I'm not going there to study ethics."

"It's street fighting."

"That's what I want to learn."

"But why?"

"I've wanted to. Since I was a girl."

"You could still sign up for a women's self-defense class in your own neighborhood," my wife suggests. "I'm sure the YWCA has very safe programs...supportive, with other women there."

"If I get mugged—" My mother pushes her shoulders back, raising herself to her full height of five feet and one inch. "It's unlikely that my attacker will be a woman. So I might as well train against men."

Sylvie and I fret about my mother during the week. Nights we keep each other awake, imagining the worst scenarios. Even at the bookstore, between customers, we fret.

"Do you think she—no, she's not getting senile or something."

"I don't think so." Sylvie shakes her head. "She's very clear, determined. Still, she's almost seventy."

"We used to talk about new writers. Concerts. Now all she talks about is that class."

"Something's changed with her," Sylvie agrees.

"She's always avoided violence. Never even spanked me. She used to embarrass me in parking lots and stores, walk up to parents who were hitting their kids and tell them there were better ways.... You know what? I wasn't even allowed to have a toy gun. She got upset if I took the attachments from our vacuum cleaner and pretended I had a gun."

Sylvie and I search the newspaper for acts of violence instead of skimming across them. Suddenly it seems there are more reports than ever before. Grainy news photos show young men with shaved heads and swastika tattoos; missing children abducted while playing in front of their houses; round-faced girl prostitutes raped and murdered; smoldering houses scorched by arsonists; shells of cars blasted with homemade bombs.

When I was a boy, my mother used to cut any pictures that had to do with violence from the paper. Until I was six, I thought newspapers came that way—holes surrounded by words.

I have started to call my mother Monday and Wednesday evenings at eight-thirty to make sure she's come home safely from her class. For over twenty years, since her divorce, she's lived alone in Co-op City in a high rise with security guards and hidden cameras. When I offer to pay for cabs to her class, she refuses and continues to take the Number 6 IRT between Pelham Bay station and East 149th.

"As far as I'm concerned, that class is the most dangerous thing in your life."

She assures me they hold vinyl bolsters between them when they team up to rehearse their kicks and punches.

"Even that could injure you. Some of them must be twice your weight. At your age—"

"The only bad incident that has happened to me so far is a rash on the soles of my feet. The carpets there...I should have worn socks."

Every morning she practices by herself in her living room: kicks, turns, punches, stretches. "I wish I could get my legs higher," she tells Sylvie. Much of the time the muscles in her calves are sore. "They'll feel better once I'm in shape." She has to remind herself to keep her fists up—"The natural reaction is to drop them when you kick."

Her instructor talks about timing, about the element of surprise, about keeping calm. As an example he mentions one of his students who was attacked by a rapist. "He broke into her house. Threatened her. She pretended to go along. Till he got his pants off. Then she grabbed him. By the balls. Wouldn't let go. Though he tried to beat on her. She held on. Till he howled for mercy. Then she dragged him to the door. Kicked him out. He ran down the street. And she got her baseball bat. Chased after him, yelling: 'I'm not through with you yet.'"

I'm furious. "Now he wants you chasing rapists?"

"That's not what he's telling us to do."

"All he's doing is giving you a false sense of security."

"There's nothing false about it," she says. "And I never want to walk without that knowledge again.

On the weekend, when she arrives on the train with raisin scones and asparagus quiche, she is into multiple attackers. After our dinner on the patio, she instructs my wife and son to hold on to her arms while I'm suppose to approach her from the front.

"Wait a second, please—" she says, when she has us in position and the three of us tower above her. "I have to think what to do first. There are six parts to this."

"Is that what you'll say if you get into that kind of situation?" I ask.

"That's why I have to rehearse with you." Her voice is patient as if she were talking to one of the third graders she used to teach. "So it becomes automatic."

She swings her right leg toward me, stopping herself before it touches my thigh. "I'd be doing this a lot harder with real attackers," she promises and pivots herself to the side, using her right leg—which is still up—to cock back, tap my wife's knee, and from there shoot forward to lightly connect with my son's leg.

"Great kick, Grandma," Russ says.

Her face is flushed. "Once I remember the sequence, I'll be much faster."

"All you would do with this is annoy a mugger," I tell her.

"No one wants to fight a wild, screaming woman. My instructor says ninety percent is attitude...how I carry myself."

"Sylvie and I, we're concerned about you. Can't you take some other kind of class? Maybe an overall kind of fitness class. Something like aerobics—low-impact or something like that."

She looks at me steadily. "I have been beaten, brutally. Many times."

I am still, cold. The sky is motionless. My wife and son are still holding my mother's arms and I stand in front of her, defenseless. The shadow of my chest lies on her face.

"I won't let that happen again," she says.

"Who—How?"

"Those years before my father died...When his drinking got worse."

I have only seen two photos of my grandfather. In both he looks thin and serious. He died from a burst appendix when my mother was fourteen. She rarely talked about him.

"God—" I whisper, "I'm sorry.... I'm so sorry." I want to hold her, but the shadow of my chest still lies on her face, and she keeps herself so straight and brittle that I don't dare touch her.

"I wished I had known self-defense. Then."

"Would you have used it?" my son asks.

"Oh yes," my mother says without hesitation.

"But why now?" I ask.

"Because one morning last month," she says, "when I got into the elevator in my building, I felt afraid—the same way I used to feel as a girl. Children and old people...It's too easy to hurt them."

This Saturday she comes to our house with red-potato salad and kiwi cheesecake. As she closes the refrigerator, I tell her "I've been thinking all week. About your father...How horrible that must have been for you."

She leans into my arm, accepts the kiss I press on her forehead.

"But all of that is over now, Mother."

"It's never over." She steps away from me. "Once you walk with that fear—"

"But pool cues, Mother? Broken bottles? Where does that man expect you to fight? In bars?"

"He used to work as a bouncer."

I groan.

"He also trains police."

"Thugs, too, I bet."

"Probably."

"Make sure none of those types follows you when you leave that neighborhood. What you're doing now is setting yourself up for danger."

"You don't get it," my mother says softly. She takes me by the arm, leads me toward the backyard. "Put both hands around my neck."

"Mother—"

She grasps my wrists, glances at my palms as if checking my lifeline, and places my fingers around her neck. Her bones feel fragile beneath my hands. Her skin is papery, loose, as if it might tear and slip off.

"Harder," she says.

I feel huge. Dangerous.

My mother—my tiny, gentle mother—raises her right arm. She points toward the cloudless sky and pivots to the left, breaking my hold. Her elbow swings toward me. But this time she doesn't stop. She lets it crash into my sternum, jab up beneath my rib cage. The smell of cut grass rises toward me, and when I look up, the sun is spinning around my mother who stands above me, both fists raised, feet planted in her fighting stance.

21
CREATING TENSION

Tension as an indispensable element. Dramatic conflict: individuals against each other and against outer forces. Inner conflicts. Arousing initial curiosity. Generating dramatic questions. How much is too much?—avoiding melodrama.

"Well, it's a pleasant little story." If you hear that about a piece you've just written, don't smile. It may sound like a compliment, but it isn't.

Creative writing classes and editors as well receive too many "pleasant little stories," and often the authors remain oblivious to what is wrong with them. A dull story is like a dull meal at a restaurant: Patrons don't complain, but they don't come back. The sad aspect is that the chef, hearing no specific complaints, never improves.

What those pleasant little stories lack is **tension.** Tension in fiction is what keeps the reader reading. No matter how subtle or carefully written, a story is hardly a success if readers are not induced to finish it. Fiction needs a sense of energy, and that energy is created through tension.

There are many different ways of creating tension, but they all consist of pitting one element against another. The most frequently used (and the most frequently overused) is conflict between characters. Closely related is conflict between an individual and a group or some force of nature. A more subtle form of tension is internal, a character struggling with two opposed impulses. In addition, an author can create tension by withholding information from the reader, generating curiosity. This curiosity can be rekindled through a series of dramatic questions.

We use many of these techniques in daily conversation—especially when reporting some dramatic incident. When writing fiction, however, using tension effectively is a more deliberate act. If we don't provide enough tension, the story goes flat or seems lifeless. At the other extreme, if we use it with too heavy a hand, the work becomes melodramatic. When writing the first draft you may wish to rely on your natural story-telling ability, but it is essential that you examine the type and degree of tension before you launch your second draft.

Dramatic Conflict

Conflict is found in all types of narrative, including plays, films, and some poetry. We call it **dramatic conflict** partly because it is associated with plays like Shakespeare's *Henry V* and *Julius Caesar* but mainly in the general sense of being vivid or striking.

On its simplest level, dramatic conflict is the mainspring of simple fiction and drama. Adventure stories like Edgar Rice Burroughs' *Tarzan* series and, on a slightly higher level, Alexandre Dumas' *The Count of Monte Cristo*, as well as most television thrillers pit characters against each other with great regularity. Occasionally an individual faces a group such as a gang or posse. In other cases the opponent is some aspect of nature—the sea, a typhoon, a mountain. The conflict in such work is rarely complicated by inner doubts. Often conflict in simple fiction becomes an end in itself, dominating the plot and blunting subtlety of characterization and theme.

With associations like these, it is no wonder that some beginning writers unconsciously avoid all forms of conflict and keep their characters passive or isolated. But there is no need to avoid conflict in even the most sensitive fiction. It will add essential vitality to your fiction as long as you make sure that it doesn't take over, becoming the dominant effect.

The best method of keeping conflict from taking over is to develop several different instances at different points. By having more than one conflict, you generate vitality without having the work turn into a simple adventure story. Multiple conflicts are possible even in a relatively short work like "Acts of Violence."

The title itself prepares the reader for conflict, and from the very first line we see that the mother is preparing herself for possible attack from muggers: the individual against a hostile environment.

Soon, however, a new conflict takes over and begins to dominate the story: The son and also his wife oppose the mother's classes. They are concerned about the instructor's dubious background and his aggressive philosophy. "As far as I'm concerned," the son says, "that class is the most dangerous thing in your life." This starts as a friendly argument but reaches the point where the son is "furious" at his mother. She resists with quiet determination. The conflict is now between mother and son.

Finally a third conflict bursts on the scene: The mother confesses that as a child she as "been beaten, brutally. Many times." This violence at the hands of her father has caused her lifelong anxiety. It is the first of two **epiphanies**—moments of sudden awareness on the part of both reader and the narrator.

The son tries to assure her: "But all of that is over now." But the mother knows better: "It's never over." At the very end of the story we come to understand how right she is. She has her son pose as a threat, "But this time she doesn't stop." The terrible conflict from her childhood resurfaces in the form of combat with her son, and he is thrown to the ground. Our realization of how deeply embedded fear and hostility can be is dramatized in that final action. It is the second and final epiphany.

In spite of the brevity of that story, then, it is energized by four examples of conflict in succession: mother against potential muggers; mother against son in argument; mother against her alcoholic father years before. The final act of violence against the son is psychologically a lashing out against a long-dead father.

The lines of tension in "Three Hearts" are also multiple and they also span more than one generation. The father and *his* father were in conflict to the point of physical fighting. Eddie is in conflict with the entire family. In the dramatic climax, the mother digs frantically in the snow to save her son—an individual struggling against nature. Different as these conflicts appear to be, they are all connected. The collapse of the tunnel was caused unwittingly by the absent father, and the reason the mother was forced into action was that Eddie was too drunk or drugged to respond.

The males in this story are all in conflict with each other. The mother's major conflict is, significantly, not with other members of the family but with an aspect of nature.

When conflict with nature becomes more dominant than it is in either of these stories, it can present a problem that often arises in sports stories as well. In both cases you may find that the story is offering the reader a choice of two endings: Either the protagonist (or home team) wins or it loses. That's enough for another Disney adventure film, but it's hardly enough for sophisticated fiction.

If "Three Hearts" were simply an adventure story about how a boy got buried in snow and was finally rescued, the mother's role would be reduced to that of a heroic family dog. ("Oh Lassie, you found him!") Her success would provide the reader with a quick but entirely forgettable rush of pleasure. In Corey's sophisticated treatment, however, the mother digging in the snow is not an end in itself; it is a means to developing a far more insightful theme. Through her actions we come to see how a sickly, emotionally drained, and tranquilized mother can still find inner strength when a member of her family is threatened.

The general rule is this: Don't make winning or losing a battle with nature or with an opposing team the primary concern. We can read the *National Geographic* or *Sports Illustrated* for that. If your goal is to create sophisticated fiction with some depth, make sure the struggle reveals some fresh insight about a specific character or human nature generally.

Remember too that conflict with nature or society should be appropriate to the length of your story. We are all familiar with epic films and dramatic novels dealing with mountain climbing, survival at sea, floods, and fires.

Trying to force these grand topics into a short story is like sending 400 volts through a thin wire.

As writer you have the power to downsize any aspect of nature. Destructive floods can become four days of rain and its effect on a vactioning couple who are doing their best to hold a marriage together. Assaults on Mount Everest can be downsized to a grandfather who agrees to go hiking with his grandson and is determined not to show his age.

The same applies to conflict with aspects of society. Mob violence is hard to capture in four to six pages, but it can be downsized to a gang of four. Prejudice in its blunt and all-too-common form can dominate the theme, making the fiction seem like an essay in disguise, but prejudging can take many subtle forms: a child of poor parents excluded from a party; an immigrant trying to find work in a small, provincial town; a woman attending an all-male police academy. And any character who is forced to battle an insensitive bureaucracy—be it a hospital, a large corporation, or a governmental agency—faces a maze of prejudices.

Inner Conflict

One of the characteristics of simple fiction is that conflict is rarely muddied by inner conflict. Superman does not question his almost neurotic fascination with crime; Dick Tracy is never seriously tempted to take a bribe. But look at the inner uncertainties of the mother in "Three Hearts": She would clearly like to retreat from responsibilities and stay in bed, wrapped in that red robe, "rolling her head from side to side, sighing." Yet she is the one who plunges into the snow to save her son. She is clearly being pulled in two directions, but ultimately it is her mature and loving side that wins.

In "Acts of Violence" we are shown a woman who was so opposed to the very thought of brutality that she refused to spank her son, spoke sharply to strangers who hit their children in public, and even cut violent pictures out of the newspaper. Yet she is taking a particularly rough self-defense course in a dangerous neighborhood and speaks approvingly of a woman who chased her attacker with a baseball bat. These two attitudes appear at first to be a contradiction, but at the end of the story we see that they are a heightened version of an inner conflict shared by many: a desire to avoid the whole issue opposed by a determination to meet violence with violence.

As for the son, he is both fond of his mother and increasingly angry at her stubborn insistence on continuing the course. This ambivalence, a mix of opposed emotions, may be hard to recognize and translate into fiction if you are still too close to the model on whom the character is based. If you are single-minded in your love or dislike of a person, it will be hard to portray him or her as having inner conflicts. In such cases, you may have to try another source.

Going back to "Sausage and Beer," recall the way the father is torn between his sense of obligation to visit his brother in the mental hospital and an understandable wish to get out of there as soon as he can. Like the characters in the other stories, he is of two minds, struggling with inner debate.

An analysis like this is necessary to show how different types of tension can be developed, but don't get the impression that this is a good way to find new story subjects. It is not generally profitable to sit down with a determination to write a story about "a mother in conflict with her daughter." As I have pointed out, good stories are more likely to begin with people, not ideas. For example, a situation involving, say, Susan, your best friend, and Carol, her rebellious 15-year-old, may strike you as having fictional potential based on two specific evenings in which you saw them act out certain conflicts. You will probably have to sharpen or refine the lines of conflict in that initial stage of blocking out the story, and you will have to revise their relationship in later stages, but your story will have been grounded in real people and will as a result have a sense of authenticity.

One final suggestion regarding internal conflict: Be careful not to rely too heavily on your protagonist's thoughts. Long passages in which characters debate with themselves begin to sound like explanatory essays. Even too much analytical dialogue may sound like author intrusion. As much as possible, reveal conflicting attitudes through the way your character acts and talks. The mother's inner conflict in "Acts of Violence," for example, is only hinted at through what she and her son say. Even the revelation about his childhood is brief. It is not until her final dramatic act that we understand how powerful her inner conflict has been.

Inner conflict is even less articulated in "Three Hearts." Imagine the story told from the mother's point of view with her thoughts spelled out bluntly:

> Oh, if I could only stay here on my comfortable couch, warm and dreamy. But no, I must rouse myself to save Bucky. I must find inner strength. I must!

Far better to *show* those thoughts through her actions, letting us contrast her behavior with the picture we had of her in the opening scene.

Arousing Initial Curiosity

Reader curiosity, like conflict, pits two elements against each other. In this case, however, these are the *reader's desire* to find out something blocked by the *writer's refusal* to reveal it until later. Curiosity is particularly important at the very beginning because major conflicts have not yet been developed.

In commercial writing, the technique of grabbing the reader's attention at the outset is called the **hook.** Often it takes the form of rather obvious appeals: "She was the third showgirl to be murdered that week"; "'In precisely seven minutes,' the Captain announced calmly, 'we'll be blown sky high'"; "When the plague was finally over, Dr. Nighthawk found he was the last surviving human on the planet Esto." For some, a hook like these is a lure; for others, it is a good reason to stop right there.

The opening of sophisticated stories more often promises something interesting about character and situation rather than pure plot. Take a close look at the type of curiosity generated at the start of the three stories you have read:

1. "Sausage and Beer": We are driving somewhere. Where are we going and who is this Uncle Theodore?
2. "Three Hearts": We are listening to the radio after a big snowstorm. Why is the mother's voice weak? Why is she "rolling her head from side to side, sighing"?
3. "Acts of Violence": Why is this elderly woman taking an apparently rough self-defense course? Why is she willing to go to the "roughest neighborhood of the South Bronx" for her classes?

Not one of these stories starts with the narrator waking up, yawning, wondering what the day will bring. Not one starts with a lengthy physical description or character sketch. Not one gives a paragraph of explanation as to what let up to that opening scene. All three begin **in medias res**—in the middle of things.

Clearly you don't have to have a body slump to the floor or a bridge collapse into raging water; what draws the reader may be as mild as the appearance of a perfect stranger standing at the front door with his suitcase, a six-year-old child getting off the bus in a small town with no one to meet her, a loving wife and mother of three quietly announcing that the family can get its own supper because she is taking the next bus to El Paso. Situations like that are openings waiting for a story.

Generating Dramatic Questions

Important as arousing initial curiosity is, the need for stimulation doesn't stop there. That stranger at the door isn't going to hold the reader very long if he turns out to be dull Uncle Harry, who would like to stay over one night on his way to Omaha. As soon as the opening situation has been established, there have to be more questions to hold the reader's interest.

Think of these as **dramatic questions.** As soon as the stranger's identity is clarified (a notorious Uncle Harry from Australia, for example), we could raise another: Is he *really* an uncle? Or, can we trust him? Or, will he ask for money? And overlapping that: How long will he stay? As you can see from the stories you have read so far, there is usually a succession of dramatic questions. As soon as one is answered, another is introduced.

In "Sausage and Beer," for example, once the identity of Uncle Theodore is established, we wonder what he will be like in person. How irrational will he be? After that scene there is the anxiety about the bar. Doubt and uncertainty continue until the final moment of harmony. The other two stories develop similar sequences, although "Acts of Violence" ends not with tranquility but with a sudden revelation.

How often one needs dramatic questions brings us back to the matter of pacing described in Chapter 19. Judging how long a story can sustain a sense of forward movement without a compelling dramatic question (as in the igloo scene in "Three Hearts") is a matter for you to judge. The more intense these questions are and the closer they are spaced, the more rapid the pace.

Suspense is created simply by increasing the frequency or the intensity of dramatic questions. What keeps us on the edge of our seats is a heightened form of curiosity. Since it takes time to build suspense convincingly, it is not often found in short-short stories, those under 2,000 words. Even in longer stories and novels, suspense is frequently limited to specific scenes rather than becoming the primary energizing force as it is in so-called suspense thrillers.

How Much Is Too Much?

When tension is pushed beyond effectiveness, when suspense begins to obliterate thematic insights, depth of characterization, and originality, your work has spilled over into melodrama.

Melodrama is drama pushed to excess. Just what is "excess" depends first on what kind of fiction you are writing and then on the length of your work. Commercial fiction in the James Bond tradition, for example, is made intentionally melodramatic by stressing action to the point where it blots out credible characterization and thematic subtlety. Melodrama is avoided in literary fiction, however, because characterization and thematic suggestion are exactly what the writer is trying to achieve.

Length is the other factor. Strong conflicts leading to violence such as bloody fights, rape, or murder can sometimes be handled in 20 pages, but they are apt to sound unconvincing or even unintentionally comic in half that length. Even then, they are generally avoided in short fiction. Fights can be made less lengthy and less bloody, symbolic rape can be suggested by use of other acts of sexual hostility, and murder can be downsized to injury. Keep in mind the metaphor I referred to earlier: Tension is an electrical charge and the short story is a fine wire. Too much voltage will burn it out.

This is not, of course, a recommendation for blandness—only for moderation. Each of the stories you have read develops a variety of conflicts, but none is pushed into melodrama. Uncle Theodore does not attack his brother and nephew with a knife; Bucky does not die in the arms of a sobbing mother; the son in "Acts of Violence" is not killed.

Reducing the level of conflict is one way to avoid the risk of melodrama. A little wit or humor is another. It is extraordinary how something as slight as having two children play husband and wife in an igloo can disguise the fact that they are talking about serious matters such as sexual roles and death. More about that in the chapter on tone.

The essential point to remember is that while tension is necessary to keep your work energized, it should not be pushed to the point where it becomes the only memorable aspect of your work.

22

SETTING

Where Are We?

Where am I?—creating a setting. Where in the world?—borrowing or inventing place names. The uses of clock time: hour and season. Historical periods. Revising place and time.

When readers plunge into a new story, the first thing they want to identify is the **means of perception.** The second is where they are. **Setting** or **orientation** is what fixes a work of fiction not only in place but in time as well. There is a strangely abstract tone to stories that do not establish the setting fairly early. If you delay (and some stories do), it should be for a good reason.

We naturally think of setting in terms of place, but it also involves time— the hour of the day or night, the season, and occasionally the historical period.

Some stories, of course, make scant use of setting, but even the most dreamlike fantasies, like dreams themselves, usually provide details that help readers to imagine themselves in a specific place. As writers, we have to judge which aspect of the setting is important for a particular story and how we can present it convincingly.

Where Am I?—Creating a Setting

"Where am I?" is the stereotyped cry of those regaining consciousness. It is also the instinctive question of readers who have just begun a new story or novel. This is why most stories establish the immediate setting early. Like a stage set, the surroundings help to place readers in the story. A particular house, a room in that house, a field, a beach, a factory assembly line—these and countless other settings not only help to start a story and make the opening scene come alive, but they may contribute to characterization and theme as well.

Watch out, however, for the opening paragraph that is a solid block of descriptive exposition. Get your situation launched; give your protagonist a brief thought or line of dialogue to establish the viewpoint first. *Then* work in where this is taking place. In most stories the setting is established at least briefly within the first page. This is the case in the three stories you have read so far:

1. "Sausage and Beer": First comes the fact that we are in a car that is cold (brief setting) and are on a trip (the situation). Not until the second page are there more details about where they are:

   > We were well out in the New England countryside now, passing dark, snow-patched farm fields and scrubby woodlands where saplings choked and stunted each other.

2. "Three Hearts": First comes the fact that there has been a big snowstorm and that "Mama is real sick" (situation). Then within the same paragraph comes the setting:

   > Bucky and I sit at the wooden table.... Mama is lying on the kitchen couch, wrapped in a red robe....

   There is more attention paid to the mother's appearance and sickly state than to the setting, but by the end of that paragraph you know that they are all sitting in the kitchen and that the season is winter.

3. "Acts of Violence": Setting is less important in this story than in the other two, but it is established briefly in the second sentence:

   > When she visits us in Connecticut on weekends, bringing fresh strawberries and pesto bagels on the train, she tries to practice her latest moves with us.

Three short paragraphs later we learn that she "takes those classes in the roughest neighborhood of the South Bronx, in the basement of a pawnshop on East 149th." Still later we learn that she lives in Co-op City, New York, "a high rise with security guards and hidden cameras." These details are fragmentary, but they establish an important contrast between the relatively safe, suburban life in Connecticut where the son and his wife live and the mother's potentially dangerous life in the city.

The emphasis on setting varies with each story, but no matter how much you plan to use it, avoid the too-familiar "sitcom living room" that appears regularly on television: couch in the middle, coffee table centered, upholstered chairs on either side, front door to the left and stairs to the right. Everything is neat, new, and middle class. That visual pattern has been etched into the retinas of an entire generation. If you use it in fiction, you will invite the glazed inattention of television audiences everywhere.

Instead, work hard to find vivid and convincing details that will be remembered. The qualities to keep in mind are summed up in two words: *distinctive* and *specific*. Just as poems depend on the freshness of images, fictional settings depend on precise, carefully selected visual details.

Compare the following two descriptive passages

> A. It was a large, sparsely furnished room. A number of poeple wandered about, but it was hard to tell whether they were patients or visitors.

> B. The room was large, and it seemed even larger for the lack of furniture. There were benches around all four walls, and in the middle there was a long table flanked with two more benches. The rest was space. And through that space old men shuffled, younger men wheeled carts of linen, a woman visitor walked slowly up and down with her restless husband…. Or was *she* the patient?

Passage A is brief and provides few details. There would be nothing wrong with such a description if the setting—a room—were not going to be used extensively. But the story "Sausage and Beer" does make prolonged use of that room, so the version actually used (passage B) includes specific details that amplify each aspect.

In passage B, "large" is amplified with a phrase designed to help the reader feel it. The word "space" is repeated for effect. "Sparsely furnished" is made visual with specific examples. And the simple assertion that it was hard to tell which were the patients is dramatized by describing a particular couple. This is not merely a matter of adding words; it is a careful selection of those visual details that will most successfully draw the reader into that room.

Although this passage was written in a block for impact, many descriptions are spaced out in fragments so as to make them less obtrusive. The kitchen in "Three Hearts," for example, comes to us in a series of separate details scattered through the first page: The room has a "radio that sits on top of the fridge" and a "wooden table that wobbles on the crooked floor." The table is covered with a "plastic tablecloth." There is also a "kitchen couch" on which the mother lies; and when Sissy wants to fan her mother, she uses "one of Daddy's newspapers from under the couch."

One way to intensify the setting and provide visual variety is to move the action outdoors on occasion. It would have been quite possible for the author of that story to have the children play in the living room while the mother dozed in the kitchen. They could still "play house" and go through the husband–wife games that are important to the theme. Some kind of accident could occur there leaving Bucky bleeding and unconscious to provide a similar crisis. But the author has given the story visual impact by moving the children outside and having them build an igloo in the snowbank. In addition to the fact that this chilly make-believe house is an effective symbol for the actual home they live in, the setting alone impresses itself on the reader as distinctive and specific.

How much description should you provide? That depends on pacing and need. Remember that while a block of description places more emphasis on a setting, it also slows the pace. Weigh carefully whether the story can afford to lose momentum at that point. I felt I could afford a paragraph describing that room in the hospital in "Sausage and Beer" because I had just completed a scene with dialogue and action and, in addition, could rely on the anticipation of meeting Theodore to sustain interest. But starting a story with that much static description would have been a poor tactic.

Each of the two settings in "Three Hearts" contributes directly to the mood and theme of the story. It is hard to imagine the story without that somewhat shabby kitchen and the children's igloo in the snowbank. "Acts of Violence," is different in that very little is made of the setting. But that implied contrast between life in Connecticut and survival in the more hostile environment of New York contributes to the theme of the story.

When you select details that will make a setting vivid, it is natural to think of the visual aspect first, but don't forget smells and sounds. Many places have distinctive smells: a musty waiting room, a kitchen in which liver and onions are being fried, an oily-smelling filling station, a car owned by a cigar smoker. As for sounds, some houses are dominated by the roar of traffic while others are located near a jetport. Characters have to yell in an auto-body shop or a disco, reducing dialogue to short phrases. Desert winds can dominate one environment and pounding surf another. All these can help to intensify and individualize your setting.

Where in the World?

Some stories are set in a particular geographic region or a specific city. This type of orientiation is not at all necessary, but it can add a valuable dimension to fiction. If you do decide to take advantage of this approach, your first question will be one of tactics—whether to identify an actual state or city or to create your own from imagination.

In some respects, there is a fallacy in the question. Since all fiction is only an illusion, you don't have a choice between a "real" location and one of your own creation. All fictional settings are imaginary, and everyone's use of, say, New York or Los Angeles is going to be a product of imagination.

Your true choice, then, is not, "Shall I set this story in a real city?" but "Shall I use the name and certain characteristics of a real city in the exercise of my imagination? Will doing so help my readers to see what I want them to see?"

There are two good reasons for drawing on a known city and naming it. First, it can serve as a geographic shorthand for the reader. There are features of our larger cities like New York, San Francisco, and Chicago that are known even by those who do not live there. In addition, using a real city can be a convenience for you as a writer *if* you know the area well. It will save you the trouble of making up your own map.

But there are a couple of dangers as well. Unless you are really familiar with the city you are using, you may begin to depend on scenes and details you have unconsciously absorbed from other stories and from television. Students who have never been to New York, for example, are apt to fall back on such standard conventions as a rainy night on Forty-Second Street, poodles on Park Avenue, high style on Madison Avenue, rumbles on either the Lower East Side or the South Bronx, and general perversion in the Village.

The same is true for Paris. If in blind ignorance the author spices a story with shots of the Eiffel Tower, cancan dancers, and prostitutes with hearts of gold, the fiction is bound to reflect the television programs and musical comedies from which this material was taken.

To avoid this, make sure you know the city well if you are going to name it, and try to focus your attention not on the most obvious aspects of the city but on districts and details that will seem authentic to your readers without being reminders of hackneyed stories and films.

Another problem with using a specific place is that you may find transformation difficult in the early stages, and you may even find yourself limited in the kinds of revisions you want to make. Sometimes this is a mechanical problem: moving your characters around in an environment that cannot be altered. But more frequently it is a psychological limitation. You may feel wedded to a particular neighborhood, say, when a different one would lend itself better to your story. This is a particularly common problem when the plot has been adapted from recent or intense experience.

Perhaps for this reason, fictitious place names are frequently used even when the setting is closely tied to an actual place. Such names give the author flexibility while still preserving the sense of authenticity that one can achieve with details from an actual place. John Updike describes this relationship between a real place and fictional settings in his foreword to *Olinger Stories:*

> The name Olinger is audibly a shadow of "Shillington," the real name of my home town, yet the two towns, however similar, are not at all the same. Shillington is a place on the map and belongs to the world; Olinger is a state of mind, of my mind, and belongs entirely to me.

In this spirit, John Updike has used Olinger, Pennsylvania, in eleven short stories. The names and ages of the protagonists vary, but essentially they are the same boy. The approach is similar to that of Sherwood Anderson in *Winesburg, Ohio*. On a broader scale, William Faulkner blended historical and fictional elements in this way in his stories and novels set in his imaginary Yoknapatawpha County, Mississippi.

Each of the three stories you have read so far handles the matter of geography differently. "Acts of Violence" is the most specific, naming both a state and a city, but the story does not develop details from either place. "Sausage and Beer" is more general, referring to "the New England countryside." The original version had a description of their large but shabby house in Dorchester, Massachusetts, one which I had seen but never lived in. That description, however, went out with the cuts made at the time of publication. There is only one remaining reference to Dorchester in the present draft and none to Danvers, Massachusetts, where the actual hospital was and still is located. The only geographic aspect that is important in that story is New England, partly because I am familiar with it but also because it seems appropriate to the father's reserved personality.

"Three Hearts" does not provide even a passing reference to an actual place, though clearly it is northern. This is not at all an unusual pattern.

There is a long tradition of fiction that makes much more direct use of specific regions than any of these stories. Known as **regionalism,** or, formerly, **local color** writing, it became particularly popular toward the end of the last century. Mark Twain, Bret Harte, and Sarah Orne Jewett were the best-known practitioners. A number of less-well-known writers, however, gave the term a bad reputation by concentrating on regional dialects and customs in a patronizing manner.

Regionalism in the best sense is flourishing today. Every area of the country is producing short fiction that draws heavily on local attitudes, values, and culture, and there are several anthologies of short fiction that reflect these concerns. Writers with distinctly regional or ethnic backgrounds should consider drawing on those traditions.

Some excellent writers, however, are reluctant to become overly identified with a specific area. Such is the case of Annie Proulx, one of the best writers of regionally oriented fiction. Her collection of nine stories titled *Heart Songs and Other Stories* (Scribner's) are rooted in Vermont. The beginning of her first novel, *Postcards*, is set there also, but in an interview she explained that she felt obliged to move the action out of New England altogether to avoid being identified as a regional writer. Perhaps for the same reason, she set the next novel, *Shipping News*, in Newfoundland, but her use of vivid, accurate detail gives the impression that she had been born there. In addition to meticulous research, she maintains a tone of compassion for her characters. She offers an excellent example of how to enrich fiction through setting.

Good regional writing depends on two elements: personal familiarity and respect. You really have to know what you are writing about if you are going to do justice to the people of a specific region or culture. It is important to write from the inside, not as an outside observer. And even though you may see their weaknesses and vulnerabilities, you have to have a basic respect for them if you are going to avoid a patronizing tone. This is the true distinction between local color writing in its worst sense, and genuine regionalism. If you spend some time in New Mexico as a tourist, for example, you may gather some excellent material for a story about tourists in New Mexico, and you certainly will be able to draw on the physical characteristics of the area, but that doesn't mean that you are equipped to depict the life of a Navaho living on the reservation. As Annie Proulx has shown, there is no substitute for actually living in the area you plan to use.

The Uses of Clock Time: Hour and Season

The time of day or night is often important in a story. When a character is hurrying to catch a plane or get to a wedding, you can add to the suspense by identifying the time precisely, sometimes more than once. Whether it is morning (as in "Three Hearts") or afternoon approaching supper time (as in "Sausage and Beer"), specifying the time may help to give shape to specific scenes.

Watch out, however, for a pattern that has become so common it has turned into a kind of cliché: the wake-up opening. It takes many forms, such as a ringing alarm clock, the flicker of a fading dream, the smell of coffee, a pounding headache. But they all draw on the too-neat link between the start of the day and the start of a story.

Fewer, but still too many, conclude with a version of the old film ending: Watching the sun go down and "looking forward to another day." Try something new.

Even if you are not making specific use of the time of day, keep track of it in your own mind. Doing this will help you to avoid careless errors such as having a character refer to the morning coffee break one moment and quitting time after two lines of dialogue.

Carelessness in time sense can also lead to an error that is subtler but almost as damaging: A character goes to his friend's apartment to see if he can borrow her car for the weekend. She lets him in and they sit down. He says, "Can I borrow your car?" and she says "Sure." He leaves. The plot has advanced, but credibility is lost. People don't sit down as if for a conversation and then say one sentence. What's missing is some reference to the rest of what went on. It doesn't have to be in dialogue form; exposition can be used to allow for the requisite small talk and the passage of time. Often a sentence will do: "He explained how his car had broken down again" or "She was reluctant but finally agreed."

The time of year is another aspect of time that may prove to be helpful. If the season has no real significance in a story, you can ignore it without the reader's even noticing. Such is the case in "Acts of Violence." But often indicating the time of year can help to set the tone or even contribute to the theme, as it does in the other two stories.

"Sausage and Beer" starts with the fact that "It was too cold for talk." The heater does not work. And at the hospital Uncle Theodore tells about his nightmarish theory that some night the hopsital will shut off the heat and freeze the patients to death. It is not until the end of the story that this pattern of cold is broken. When father and son enter the bar together, the boy discovers "a warm, humming, soothing, smoky world" with the "sound of music blended with voices and laughter." Nonsmokers will wince at "smoky" being used in a positive way, but there was a day, sadly, in which young people viewed this as an aspect of being "adult." And of course the cold of a New England winter in the earlier scenes serves as a contrast with the warmth of friendship and particularly the newfound relationship between father and son.

The winter scene in "Three Hearts" is equally important, creating not only the igloo as a chilly make-believe home for the children but also an opportunity for them to make angel patterns in the snow, looking to Sissy like "an angel graveyard." I will return to these symbolic details in Chapter 27.

Transforming the season in the early stages of planning a story can be a valuable way of converting a highly personal experience into something manageable. An episode that occurred in the heat of midsummer can sometimes be shifted to January merely to remove it from the confines of experience. Or an event that happened to take place in autumn might lend itself to spring and at the same time give you some sense of freshness and objectivity over your material. You must, of course, be on guard against the clichés of season. A first love that ends with a paragraph about the spring buds on the apple tree is as hackneyed as the story about an old couple that ends with the fallen leaves of November. Seasons can be enormously valuable—but only when they are used with subtlety and originality.

Historical Periods

Most short stories are set in the same historical period as the one in which they are written. This is so partly because it takes time to establish the atmosphere of an earlier period, time that one can't easily spare in so short a form. In addition, if you move back to the nineteenth century, it is difficult to avoid having your stories resemble historical romances and so-called costume gothics with their standard plots and stereotyped characters.

There are, however, two ways of using an earlier historical period effectively without running the risk of echoing formulaic fiction. In both approaches the writer maintains some personal link with the earlier time. First, it is sometimes possible to develop good fiction from extensive conversations with elderly people such as grandparents or others in an older generation. Thanks in part to portable tape recorders, there has been a growing interest in oral history of the immediate past. If your subject is willing, material gathered in this manner can provide the basis of fiction that has the true ring of authenticity.

You do have to pick your subject carefully, of course. Some people are more articulate than others. Some enjoy recalling their past, but others do not—occasionally for good reason. If your informant is agreeable, however, let him or her do plenty of talking. Occasionally you will have to ask questions in order to clarify certain facts, but try not to be too directive. Let your informant determine the direction of the conversation.

The most effective interviews are with those whose childhoods were significantly different from our lives today—those who came from Europe or Asia, those who endured the hardships of farming or factory work. Be very careful, however, not to sound patronizing or, even with the best intentions, sentimentally admiring. Since you are using borrowed material, your safest route is to maintain a fairly neutral tone. Let the story and its characters speak for themselves.

Be careful, too, not to turn your story into a simple **anecdote.** Anecdotes depend primarily on a turn of events, a clever little plot. This may be entertaining in conversation, but if you use it as the basis of a story you run the risk of trivializing your subject. To guard against this, concentrate on characterization. If you focus on the ambivalences of your protagonist, you will add depth that anecdotes normally lack.

The other use of the past applies only to those writers who are themselves old enough to remember when life was different. The accumulation of memory is one of the compensating benefits of age, and that layering of experience is an excellent source for fiction. One word of caution, however: Be careful not to lay undue emphasis on the differences between the period being described and the present day. If you draw too much attention to how inexpensive things were, for example, the reader may begin to view the material as quaint. Try instead to draw readers into that period; help them to share it.

Revising Place and Time

Revising aspects of place and time usually comes early in the writing of a story. These revisions may, as I pointed out, take the form of fundamental transformations of the original experience. As the story develops, however, such sweeping changes become more and more difficult. A basic sense of geographic and seasonal setting tends to permeate a story so that revising it becomes a much more difficult matter than, say, changing a Nebraska farmhouse into a Chicago apartment or replacing the references to a winter scene with details about summer. If one has used place and season prominently, they become a part of the "feel" of the story. For this reason, it is best to make sure that the place and the season of a story are right before one has invested many hours of work.

Still, minor revisions of these details often go on through successive drafts. Heightening often is the result of chance. One selects a season, perhaps, because that is when the experience took place; and then various implications and suggestions come from the material and demand development. The use of cold as a vehicle to suggest separation and isolation in "Sausage and Beer" evolved in just this way.

In other cases, sharpening the visual details of a story is demanded because the action has gone on in a nonplace. A surprising number of unsuccessful stories are placed in some ill-defined urban area, conveniently allowing the protagonist to dodge city traffic one minute and, when the plot demands it, to wander "in the outskirts of town" the next. If you find yourself shifting in this way, change the story to a specific town or city that you know even if you do not use the name.

Muting aspects of setting may be necessary if you feel your use of place or season has become hackneyed. The kinds of clichés that damage fiction have already been described, but I should stress here that it is easy even for experienced writers to borrow from overworked conventions. Sometimes this happens because the experience has, infuriatingly, echoed a fictional cliché. There is no cosmic law that forbids life from imitating the worst in fiction. Occasionally a beautiful woman and a handsome man really do fall in love while strolling by the Eiffel Tower in Paris on a lovely June day. They may even live happily ever after. But who is going to believe it? Leave that plot to the musical comedy writers. If you really have had such a marvelous experience, find aspects of it that are further from the conventional pattern. Doing so may require moving the story to another setting or another season or both.

Occasionally the setting has to be revised because it has begun to resemble a literary convention. Stories about migrant workers tend to sound like John Steinbeck; hitchhiking stories often pick up the smells and sounds of Jack Kerouac's *On the Road* or motorcycle films; scenes involving city gangs frequently use standard details, including switchblades and leather jackets. One often has to mute these details and stress elements that the reader will see as if for the first time. Once again, be careful not to assume that details from your own life will necessarily be convincing as fiction. If you present a setting that your reader is likely to associate with another author or with a film, song lyric, television commercial, or musical comedy, your story will be damaged by the association. Muting those details and highlighting other elements will be necessary, and usually you can do this without losing your original conception.

Finally, take a hard look at those details that don't seem to serve a purpose. They may be nothing more than fragments from your memory. The fact that they are vivid in your mind doesn't mean that they necessarily belong in the story. A novel can afford a few nonessential details, but a short story doesn't have that momentum; it is easily brought to a standstill by excess baggage. In some cases you can amend those details so that they contribute to the theme or at least to the mood of your story. If that doesn't work, they probably should be cut.

Always keep in mind this essential fact: Place and time are not adornments to a story. They are a part of what you see and feel as you write; they are also the primary means by which your readers are going to enter your story and experience it as if they were physically present. It is this sense of being there that makes fiction an "as-if-real" experience.

23

A STORY

by Sharon Solwitz

Obst Vw

Next year, writing his personal experience essay to convince admissions at Penn he's Ivy League material despite uneven grades, he'll describe in amusing detail the one baseball game his father took him to, and get in on a scholarship despite his father's explicit pessimism. And he'll do well, though he's not as brilliant as his father, just a pretty smart kid who's used to working hard. But now on Rachel's bed, unraveling a hole in the knee of her jeans while her parents yell at each other downstairs, he cannot join in her raillery. "Let's go," he says.

"Wait. This is the part about who was the first unfaithful one!"

"Let's go!" he says. He has a curfew, a job to get up for tomorrow. Then there's the air outside the house, the smell of new grass mixing with the smell of Rachel when she lets him touch her under her T-shirt.

"Dame, please. It's funny, really. It's high comedy."

But she doesn't protest as he takes her hand and leads her down and outside.

Rachel is seventeen, a year older than Demian, though in the same grade. She lost a year when she went, as she says, loony, and spent several months in the bin getting her spirit broken to the point where she'd attend school and respond, numbly, to teacher and test questions. Still, her grades are better than his. Sometimes it seems to him he can't stand her, half an inch taller than he is, the way when she's not thinking about it she arcs down into herself like a long-necked bird, the way tall girls aren't supposed to. He used to love to play baseball, it was all he wanted to do—if not on the field then in a symbolic version with cards and dice in his room—and when this feeling of loathing comes over him, it brings on a desire for baseball, for playing shortstop, to be specific, standing between second and third with his knees bent, whispering in the direction of the batter—hit it to me, I dare you. He remembers his two best friends from then, brothers a year apart, Tom and John Frank, the clean, sharp edge of the way they bad-mouthed each other after the game. And then the queasiness comes, because something he has done with Rachel or is about to do has rendered him unfit for baseball.

He walks quickly now, a step ahead of her, over to the playground behind the local preschool, where they've gone the past months to talk and kiss and perform all but the final technical act of sexual intercourse. The ground is laid in gravel through which sharp, hard weeds poke up, but the chain-link fence is low enough to climb over, the large wooden sandbox lies half in the shadow of the building, the sand is cool and dry and molds after a while to one or the other's back.

Tonight, though, they do not embrace. Rachel sits down on the dark side of the sandbox. At first she seems to have disappeared. Then he sees in the dark the lesser darkness of her face, the pale stretch of her shoulders, too wide for a girl. She smells sour and sweet like strawberries. He is moved by something in Rachel, her craziness, her cynicism, facets of personality he dimly perceives he may have to own some day. He remembers a school assembly where she danced on center stage with the other dancers weaving around her, her turns and leaps bolder than theirs, more complete. "Rachel," he says, "I really like you."

She doesn't respond, but the prickle of the skin of his arms tells him he said the wrong thing. He tries again. "You're a really good dancer." He elaborates on the performance he saw, comparing her dancing to the way he used to feel about baseball. Still feels sometimes. She doesn't help him out. Her silence is a hole he walks around and around.

"Rachel," he says in despair, "I feel bad for you." He doesn't mention her parents. Really, he doesn't want to talk about them. Their dads by some fluke knew each other in college, and Rachel's sometimes asks him how his father's doing, a show of interest or courtesy his father doesn't return. Demian himself can barely manage to speak to her father, who makes more money than his father and calls him the Old Hippie. "Ask him about Woodstock," Mr. Geller once said, and Demian said, "Why don't you ask him yourself," knowing his father hadn't gone to Woodstock, as Mr. Geller also knew. Mr. Geller is soft-looking and bottom-heavy like an old pear. Demian can't stand Mr. Geller, has only broached the subject as a gift for Rachel.

She says, "They're not my real parents."

He laughs, though she has said that before.

"I'm going to divorce them," she says. "There's a new law, in Vermont."

"In Massachusetts, I think."

She shrugs, irritated with his quibble. He talks quickly to assuage her. "Then you can marry *my* parents."

"Who wants your parents?"

"What's wrong with my parents?"

"Your father has a mean streak."

"No he doesn't!"

His eyes have adjusted to the light. He can see the parts of her face that jut out, eyebrows, cheekbones, slope of nose. She seems too sharply constructed, a witch woman, though she's sitting cross-legged like a child, pouring handfuls of dry sand over her thighs. "He won't let you do stuff for no reason," she says. "For spite."

Demian knows that in similar words he has complained to her about his father, who gave him a curfew earlier than that of his friends' younger brothers, frequently refused him permission to attend parties, and who wasn't planning—he'd warned him—to let him get his driver's license till he was eighteen years old. Teenagers have glop for brains, he'd said. Though as a teenager himself—his mother had told him—he'd dropped out of college and done a lot of the drugs teenagers were supposed to say no to these days. Demian hasn't really spoken to this father since the day he refused to sign the learner's permit. But now Demian says, "He has his own ideas. He does what he thinks is right and not what everybody else does!"

She claps her hands.

"What is that supposed to mean?"

"You are so *canned.*"

He's about to stand up, leave, maybe. But she takes his arm. "Demian, I love you."

"So you can say anything you want to me?"

She puts her arms around him, thrusts her tongue into his mouth. He keeps up his end of the bargain. Soon he is urgent, panting. She is, too. His fingers are wet with her. As usual he tries to pull off her shorts. As usual she pushes away from him. Once he questioned her, learned that her noncompliance had to do with something apologetic she detected in his attitude toward sex. Since then, his efforts have been mild, ritualized. She is his first real girlfriend. He is pleased to be kissing and touching her even at the level of intimacy she has ordained. She hurls herself at his hand, trembling.

He has to be home by 10:30 and it's 11:35 by the oven clock as he tiptoes across the kitchen. He has never missed curfew before, but the evening is still warm on his skin, he fells invulnerable. And his father is surely asleep.

He takes his shoes off in the living room. His father is *inactive,* his mother says. The understatement of the year, Demian thinks. Tired from working in the bookstore, which doesn't bring in enough for him to hire a manager, his father often falls asleep on the couch in the front of the ten o'clock news, and Demian and his mother have to prod him up to bed.

But he's up now, standing in his PJs at the top of the stairs. His long, thin, still young-looking face is blank; not even his lips seem to move as he says, "You're grounded." His lips are pressed close together, a tuck in the long swatch of his face, but the words linger in the air well after his lanky body has vanished behind the master bedroom door.

In bed Demian is stiff with fury. There is no recourse; the only question is how long. And even worse than not seeing Rachel is seeing her with the weight of his father's edict on his shoulders, making him smaller than he is, unworthy of her.

Four years from now Demian will fly home from school in time to watch his father breathe in comatose sleep, then cease breathing—feeling nothing, because from now on nothing he does for good or ill will have any impact on his father. Later he'll rage at his father for dying before he was ready for him to die, and later still he may decide that if his father wasn't ideal he did the best he could. But now Demian has hopes for what he can be to his father and what his father can be to him.

Demian is up early, hours before he has to leave for Bi-Rite's, rehearsing the speech he'll give his father at the breakfast table. He has it outlined in his head like a five-paragraph essay, and now with the sun turning the sky pink, then blue, he sits at the kitchen table while his mother, who has to leave soon to teach summer school, performs five or six brisk cleaning and cooking acts. His father sips coffee. His father butters a piece of rye toast, as slowly as an old man, though his hair is still thick, his face unlined; people sometimes think he's Demian's older brother. Demian says casually into the space between bites, "I want you to reconsider."

His father looks to the left, the right, all around the room. "Who's talking? Is somebody talking to me?"

Demian's ears feel hot. This is the first direct statement he's made to his father in several months. "Dad, I'm never late. I shouldn't be punished the first time I mess up. Give me a second chance."

"Look, you." His father's voice is quiet, but it takes up the room. "If some dude walks into my store with a gun, and I say hey now just wait a minute, do I get a second chance?"

Demian sees the illogic of his father's argument, but his father stands up, learning forward as if about to fall on him. "If you get sick, kiddo. If your heart hurts, air sticks in your throat, you say with your last feeble breath, God, Jesus, Krishna, whoever—please, what did I do, could you please, please give me a second change, what's He going to say to you? Tell me, Demian."

Demian wants to ask his father what makes him think he's God, but the air or something is stuck in his throat.

"Let's say you get your girlfriend pregnant, Demian. Let's say for the sake of argument you knock up your young lady. But you aren't ready to be

Papa yet. You want to walk across Turkey in your stocking feet. You want to climb Mt. Tamalpais and keep on going."

His father has just said more, it seems, than he has ever said to Demian before. His hands are waving, his face is white, and Demian's mother pats his back, leads him back to the table. She gets him more coffee, hovers over him, though she's running late, till his face warms up. He kisses her good-bye a beat longer than he has to. Says nothing to Demian. Demian feels sick, choking on the words he can't speak to his father. "Mom," he whispers after door is shut, "is he mean, or what?"

"Demian," she says, "you've got to give him some slack. The business isn't going well."

"Who cares?" Demian's voice rises. Every once in a while he's allowed to sneer in front of his mother. It's his one respite, acting like his father in front of his mother. "Mine isn't going well, either." He watches her face, prepared to shut down at the first sign of her disapproval.

"Demian," she says, "he may have to declare bankruptcy. Don't say anything to him, please. Eat your breakfast."

Her lips look blue, like the lips of little kids who have been in the water too long. Demian eats his cereal, a piece of toast, then, absentmindedly, the rest of his father's toast. It's not even eight o'clock, he has plenty of time. He eats while his mother says nice things about his father. How good he is to her. How well his friends like him, even the rich, much-respected ones. Demian is aware that people listen when his father speaks. Demian would like his own friends to treat him as his father's friends treat his father. Sometimes he quiets his voice, thins it out a little, to see if that's the trick.

"He's way too smart for what he does," His mother is saying. "He did well in college without studying. He could remember everything he'd ever read. He was a great talker, there was nothing he couldn't have done if he'd wanted to—do you know how high his IQ is?"

"Higher than mine," Demian says.

His mother doesn't protest, just shakes her head as if in wonder. "He never got time to sit and figure things out. He was too young to have a child."

"Mom," Demian says, "he was twenty-six when I was born. He's forty-two."

"He was too young," she says firmly, gathering up her books. "But he loves you like crazy, you ought to know that."

Pedaling to work Demian thinks about his father's IQ, how many points it might be higher than this own, and tries to see him as the Disappointed Man in his mother's fiction. He says *bankrupt* under his breath, trying to diminish his father enough to forgive him. It doesn't work. He tries to feel his father's love for him, remembering a ballgame his father took him to on his tenth birthday—him and his best friend, John Frank, and John Frank's father. He remembers sitting next to John in the back of their old Rabbit with his baseball glove in his lap for catching foul balls. Remembers listening to his father up front talking with John's father, John's father laughing at his father's jokes, though John's father drove a Volvo and everyone called him Dr. Frank. Demian was proud of his father. It was clear even then that although his father talked less than his friend's father, it was his father's words that thickened in the air. His father had given him and John their own tickets to hold, and jouncing along on the back seat, they squinted at the blue and white cardboard oblongs, discussing the numbers and letters that stood for what they were about to experience. SAT AUG 1:20 PM. AISLE 518 ROW 5 SEAT 242. GAME #52 CHICAGO CUBS VS. NEW YORK METS. ADMIT ONE SUBJECT TO CONDITIONS ON BACK NO REFUND NO EXCHANGE. There was one set of letters he couldn't fathom: OBST VW. He showed the ticket to John. "Obstetrician?" John asks.

"Its a beer ad. Obst Blue Ribbon!"

"That's *Pabst* Blue Ribbon!"

"I know, fart head."

Only when they got to the park and sat down in seats behind a pillar that let him see half the field if he craned to the right, did he realize the letters stood for Obstructed View. At first he didn't mind. He'd never been to a major-leagued game before. The smell of hot dogs and popcorn filled his mouth and nose, the stands were cool and dim like a naptime bedroom, the playing field bright green under the sun. He put his glove on, waiting for his father to sit down next to him, not necessarily to talk to him, since of course he had more to say to Dr. Frank, but just to be there so Demian could ask him questions or maybe just sit quietly beside him, watching him watch the game. But when Demian had finished taking in the brightness and darkness, and located his favorite Cub, Shawon Dunston, who could hurl the ball like the end of a whip, his father was still standing in the aisle. "We'll get you guys after the game," he called to them, holding out a five-dollar bill. "Don't eat too much." Demian took the bill, folded and folded it again as his father and Dr. Frank descended the steep steps, vanishing toward seats Demian knew had an unencumbered view of the field. Still, he wasn't sure what to make of the turnaround. It wasn't exactly what he'd pictured when he'd asked on his tenth, his double-digit birthday, not for something to ride or look at or hold in his hand, but for an event to experience with his father. The man who took his father's seat told him stories about the ballplayers' personal lives. It was lots of fun sitting with John, leaning hard one way around the pillar to watch the ball come off the bat, then the other way to see where the ball ended up. Shawon Dunston threw the ball into the dugout, and the Cubs still won. But although he and John wore their gloves all nine innings, the foul balls went to seats below them in the sun. And although he and John kept good track of the game, marking the P.O.'s, F.O.'s, K's, H's on their scorecards with their short yellow ballpark pencils, some of the balls fell where neither of them could see. The man in his father's seat said Shawon Dunston would never learn to take a walk because he was mentally retarded. When Demian's father returned for them after the game, the skin of his arms looked dark gold in the sun, and it was clear to Demian that the game he'd seen was not as good a game.

Demian leans back in his chair at the Geller breakfast table, puts his feet on a second chair, takes the cup of coffee Rachel has poured him. He's never had coffee before, and he gulps it like milk, burns his throat, swallows his grimace. Rachel doesn't ask him why he isn't at Bi-Rite's this morning. She talks rapidly, of nothing he has to respond to. She's barefoot, in a long, wrinkled shirt she must have slept in. He imagines what's under the shirt; his face burns. Her brown hair looks white blond on the side where the sun hits.

She runs into the kitchen, returns with a plate of kiwi and nectarines, and two dark blue cloth napkins. But on the gray tile of the kitchen floor she has left patches of red. She is limping. He watches, frozen, as blood wells out of her foot. She sits down, crosses her leg over her knee, eats a nectarine, while her blood drip-drips onto the gray tile. He thinks, Why doesn't she wipe it up? Should he wipe it up? Someone should wipe it up. It gives him the creeps, these bright red splashes, but the cloth napkin she presents him seems too fine for this use. He's looking around for paper when she throws a piece of broken china onto the table in front of him. "Parental carnage," she says.

It's the source of her injury, picked up from the kitchen floor—a white shard, triangular in shape, a thin gold line around the part that had been rim. The broken edge is red. "Car*nage*," she says, accenting and softening the last syllable like a French word. This morning her father had relieved some of his anger by throwing a cup at the refrigerator. Her mother relieved hers by refusing to sweep. "They need to *see* this," she says, placing the broken piece of china on the blue cloth napkin in the middle of the breakfast table. She seems thrilled almost, as if the bloody shard is the final piece of the puzzle of her life. She arranges a kiwi on the napkin, a bud vase alongside. "It's our new centerpiece! A still life! What'll we call it, *Terror at Teatime?*" She speaks with a British accent, biting off her words with her teeth. "No, something simple: *Daddy*. That's it—*Daddy!*"

He starts laughing. "That's terrific. It's really funny." He laughs more, in loud bursts. He has never laughed like this before. He tells her the story of the one baseball game his father took him to, exaggerating his hopes so that their obstruction by the pillar seems purely comic. She take his hand, squeezing hard, and he elaborates, this time stressing his naïve reverence for his father, his father's indifference. What had his father called out, descending the stairs? Demian doesn't remember now, makes it up: "Try and have fun, kiddo!" "We'll be thinking of you, suckers!" "Look, you—you're lucky you weren't offed in utero!" It doesn't sound like his father but makes him laugh hysterically.

She starts laughing, too. "He slapped me this morning. I told him what I thought of people who can't control themselves, and he held me by the hair and slapped my face. Like this." She grabs a hunk of her hair, yanks her head to one side, giggles. "He said, `I'll show you how I control myself.'"

He smooths her hair where she yanked. He has begun shaking a little, though he doesn't feel sad or scared. "Sometimes in the room with him I feel like I don't exist. I don't have a body. I don't know how to talk, even." He's shaking harder, down to the soles of his feet. He has never spoken like this. "He'd slap me, too, if he thought I was important enough. The truth is, I bore him. Poor Dad, bored by his son." He replays what he said, awed by what seems to be the utter truth of it. It seems reckless and marvelous saying these things about his father. He's an explorer, charting ground never before seen by mortal eyes. "I really don't need him. If he died tomorrow it wouldn't make the least difference in my life. It might improve things."

Later, with his father's blood leaking into his brain, he'll remember what he said, and even though over the years his father had grown no more interested in him, he'll think for a moment of all the things his father wanted to do that he couldn't do, couldn't ever do now, and he'll sit down in a chair by the bed, for a moment unable to breathe.

But now he's on his knees before Rachel's chair. She puts her arms around his shoulders, presses her face to the top of his head. He hears her heart beating through her T-shirt. His teeth are chattering, and to stop them he starts kissing her through her shirt—her shoulder, the two round bones at the top of her chest, the long swell of breast. In the past he has treated this part of her body reverently, but now he sucks as if he were drinking, wetting the cloth of her shirt till it feels to his lips like rough, wet skin. He has stopped trembling. "I hate him," he murmurs, almost lovingly.

"Has he ever knocked your mother down? Called her a slut? Said he could smell it on her? I'm in the same room, here at this very table eating my cantaloupe."

He can't tell if she likes what his mouth is doing, but she has made no objection. He raises her shirt, observes her body in the daylight; thinks, *There is so much of her.* He says, "He made me sit behind a pole. He traded in his ticket and sat with a buddy. The only baseball game he ever took me to."

It doesn't sound quite awful enough. He looks at her for confirmation, but she seems not to have heard him. "Has he ever come home drunk and gotten in bed with you? And when you screamed he put his hand over your mouth? And when you bit his hand he told lies to your mother? Who still thinks you're a slut though she doesn't say so?"

"Is that true, Rachel?"

She shakes her head no. "Another example of my sick imagination."

Her voice is light but he can't shake off the terrible picture. "If it were true I'd kill him."

"Me, too."

Her last comment comes without inflection. He tries to read her face, but it doesn't help. He hugs her hard. She returns it with a slight time lag, mechanically stroking the back of his head. She seems uncharacteristically passive. He feels sure that if he were to take off his pants, she'd sigh once, then let him have her. The thought terrifies him. "Rachel, where are you?"

She looks at him, smiling with the corners of her mouth only. He wants to be gone from here, to be riding back to Bi-Rite's, whose manager is a friend of his dad's and might not question the excuse he'll make up on the way. But Rachel is sitting so still in her chair, she seems to take up no space. He imagines that if he left her, he'd never find her again. When he called, her mother would say, *She's traveling in Europe.* Her mother would say, *There's no one here by that name.*

"Rachel," he whispers. He touches her face, the curves of her arm, side of her knee, arch of her wounded foot, softly so as not to miss her faintest whispered response. Her foot feels cold, and he warms it between his hand and his face. Then he puts his lips to the injured spot, cleaning off the dried blood with his tongue, smoothing down the flap of the torn skin.

24

CHARACTERIZATION

The Art of Creating People

How we learn about others. How we learn about fictional characters. Getting to know Demian. Revealing character through action. Using dialogue and thoughts. Three goals of effective characterization: consistency, complexity, and individuality.

No, writers don't actually create people. They create fictional characters. But art is an illusion, and in this case the illusion is one of actually getting to know people. If they are fully drawn so we can see different facets, we call them "**round**" characters. If they are not developed and serve merely to advance the plot, they are "**flat**." These terms were suggested by the novelist E. M. Forster not as precise categories but as useful generalizations. A fully developed fictional character will remain in the memory of a reader as vividly as an old friend.

How We Learn About Others

Before we turn to the art of creating as-if-real characters in fiction, consider for a moment how we get to know people in daily life. We meet strangers every day. Some we will never see again, but with others we make an effort to find out what they are really like. Rightly or wrongly, we often start with a quick visual assessment. We all know how risky and unreliable this process is but still we do it. We form quick and notoriously unreliable classifications as "wimpy looking" or "assertive" or "cheap" or "elegant" on the basis of physical characteristics, dress, makeup, and the like.

Next, we start the conversation ritual. Talking with strangers is a form of exploration: What do they do for a living, what are their interests, how do they spend their nonworking hours? What do they take seriously and what bores them? Deeper questions such as political loyalties and religious beliefs are usually postponed until later meetings, although the process of apparently aimless conversation is the same then. This is why we spend so much time talking.

Talk alone, however, is not enough. In order to get to know someone really well, we need to see him or her in action. Activities such as dancing, bicycling, hiking, or participation in some social club give us a chance to see whether their behavior matches what we thought we learned from conversation. No one likes running into a thunderstorm while on a long hike or staying up all night in rehearsals for an amateur dramatic performance, but we do learn more about people when they are under stress.

These various stages in the process of getting to know someone well have one aspect in common: They provide a great clutter of specific details from which we draw certain conclusions. Many of these details are so insignificant that we are not even consciously aware that they are helping us to form our opinion. The more details we have, however, the more we come to understand the complexity of that individual.

How We Learn About Fictional Characters

Getting to know someone in daily life is a slow, inefficient process. Fiction—especially the short story—does not permit so much time. Your task as writer, then, is to create the *illusion* of getting to know someone in a casual way. The process appears to be the same as in life, but in fact it is intensified and accelerated. The writer of fiction has to supply a series of little hints, and they have to be slipped in stealthily in order to maintain the reader's sense of discovery.

There will be times when you as a writer will tire of all this indirection and will be tempted to bypass it with a solid block of character description. After all, such descriptions were popular in eighteenth- and nineteenth-century novels. But they are rarely used today because readers like the sense of getting to know characters on their own. Fiction in our own age is, as I have already pointed out, more often designed to simulate direct experience than to create the illusion of a storyteller narrating a tale. To achieve a sense of immediacy, most contemporary stories are presented almost entirely through the eyes of a single character, limiting the author's voice to occasional fragments of background information.

Another disadvantage of describing a character's personality at length is that it slows the pace. The same is true of extended physical descriptions. Like all exposition, such passages are static. The reader must wait for the story to get moving again. As much as possible, rely on dialogue, action, and thoughts.

This is not to say that you can never comment on a character. In "Three

Hearts," for example, we are told through the narrator that "Mama and Daddy can't manage Eddie." That says a lot about the character of Eddie and is close to exposition, but the comment is presented through a narrator and deals with a secondary character. Even more direct, in the very first paragraph of "Obst Vw" Solwitz as author comments that her protagonist is "not as brilliant as his father, just a pretty smart kid who's used to working hard." This may seem to reveal a lot, but as you know from reading the story, it is only a superficial generalization, a kind of first impression a college admissions officer might be able to make.

Generally speaking, contemporary fiction tends to avoid author's intrusion, adhering to the mantra of every writing class: "show, don't tell." This principle is not as restrictive as it may seem. You can create a full and revealing portrait through what a character says, does, and thinks.

Getting to Know Demian

The title "Obst Vw," pronounced "obst view," refers not only to the obstructed-view seats the boys were given at the baseball game, but also to the obstructed vision each of the characters has of the others. Not only do the parents misunderstand their spouses, neither the parents nor their children have a clear view of each other. It is a story charged with tragic misunderstandings and hostilities. But the reader's view is in no way restricted. We are given countless ways of perceiving the inner life of the protagonist and his friend. Although there are three unusual examples of author's intrusion in the form of flash-forwards, they do not comment directly on character. What we learn about the two principle characters we discover through their dialogue, action, and thoughts. Of the three modes, dialogue is dominant.

Here is a partial list of what we learn about Demian, along with a description of how the author has informed us.

1. *He loves Rachel. Through dialogue*: Awkwardly trying to avoid clichéd expressions of love, he tries, "I really like you" and "I feel bad for you." *Through actions*: We see both his strong physical attraction for her and his respect for her as well. At the end of the story we see him symbolically trying ease her psychological injuries by treating her physical wound, putting "his lips to the injured spot . . . smoothing down the flap of torn skin."

2. *He has mixed feelings about Rachel and about sex. Through thoughts*: As they sit in the sandbox she seems to him "too sharply constructed, a witch woman . . . ." Toward the end it seems to him that she would "let him have her," but "the thought terrifies him."

3. *A part of him hates his father. Though action*: He doesn't speak to his father "for several months" after his father refused to sign the learner's per-

mit for driving. *Through thoughts*: When his father grounds him for returning home late, he feels "stiff with rage." He tries to feel sympathy when his mother tells him that his father is facing possible bankruptcy, but "it doesn't work." *Through dialogue*: Later he is able to tell Rachel, "If he died tomorrow it wouldn't make the least difference in my life. It might improve things."

4. *Another part of him admires and even loves his father. Through thoughts*: When they are driving to the baseball game and he hears his father talking with Dr. Frank, Demian feels "proud of his father." At the game he wishes his father would stay with him "just to be there so Demian could ask him questions or just sit there quietly beside him, watching him watch the game." *Through dialogue*: When Rachel says his father "has a mean streak," he denies it. And years later (*thoughts* again) when his father is dying, "he'll think for a moment of all the things his father wanted to do that he couldn't do . . . and he'll sit down in a chair by the bed, for a moment unable to breathe."

5. *Love and hate for his father are not just alternating moods; they are true ambivalence. Through action* by implication but more directly through one revealing line of *dialogue*: "'I hate him,' he murmurs, almost lovingly."

6. *He is conscientious. Through action*: He conscientiously holds the after-school job, and he honors his fathers strict curfew on all but that one occasion.

7. *He is also rebellious. Through thoughts*: He feels like "an explorer" charting new ground when he (*dialogue* again) is able to say out loud to Rachel that his father's death would mean nothing to him.

8. *He is unconsciously competing with Rachel for the title of who has been the most damaged by their parents. Through dialogue and thoughts*: He tells her the story of his father taking him to the baseball game and then thinks, "It doesn't sound quite awful enough" in comparison with her situation.

9. *Although he has been damaged by his father's treatment, he will survive.* Through a rare sample of *author's intrusion*, we learn in that most unusual flash-forward which opens the story that in a year's time he will win a scholarship and will "do well." The reader is assured in this statement that the story is not going to be another melodramatic case history about a young man driven to suicide by insensitive parents.

We come to know Demian extraordinarily well—far better than if we had met and talked with a real person for a half hour. As readers, we have the feeling that we learned all this naturally, just as we might in life. Actually, we have responded to a series of carefully placed clues.

This close analysis of characterization in one story may seem intimidating, but it is intended merely to reveal what ended up in a final draft. It is not a description of how one goes about writing a story. The creative process is far less mechanical. You write a first draft with a rough outline of a plot and an idea of what your characters are like. It is not until later drafts that you decide to add more dialogue here or a fresh bit of action there or a flashback to show, say, a character's immaturity or courage or kindness. If you stay flexible, you will discover more about your characters with each new draft.

Revealing Character Through Action

Characterization in simple fiction like adventure stories tends to be revealed largely through action. Because characterization in sophisticated fiction is subtler, action is often muted to keep it from dominating. In spite of this, action is enormously important, not just to add vitality but also to reveal aspects of character.

The action in "Three Hearts" is a good example. Almost everything we learn about the mother is revealed through action. In our first view of her she is "lying on the kitchen couch . . . rolling her head from side to side, sighing." This is obviously not just a case of lethargy. She is ill and, we suspect, over-medicated. From the bit of evidence, we think of her as incapable of managing this largely dysfunctional family. But at the end of the story we see her digging in the snow in a frenzy. She, not her husband or her dissolute son, is the one who saves Bucky. Without crossing over into melodrama, the story reveals her hidden strength through action.

"Acts of Violence" relies much more heavily on dialogue. It is used extensively to reveal the mother's fears and her determination to defend herself. But in the climax of the story the mother throws her son to the ground, striking out against the very one who was most concerned about her. It is action, not words, that demonstrates the intensity of her fears and, more subtly, a growing irritation at her son's protective attitude.

Dramatic as that use of action is, it is restrained enough to keep the story from spilling over into melodrama. Picture that story with a mother committed to target practice rather than martial arts. In the final scene the mother accidentally shoots her son dead rather than throwing him to the ground. The level of action in this version would increase, but the story would be dominated by plot and a too-obvious message. Characterization would be lost in a cloud of gun smoke. It is important to remember that the intensity of action can be adjusted so that it aids rather than obliterates characterization.

"Obst Vw" is similar in that it also relies heavily on dialogue, but instead of one significant bit of action, there are two. They provide major insights into the emotional state of the two central characters. For Demian it is that baseball game in which his father leaves him in the seat with obstructed vision rather than sitting with him. It's far from child abuse in the traditional sense, but we can see by the way he keeps returning to that event how deeply it affected him. Representing an accumulation of disappointments, it becomes a kind of emblem of his relationship with his father.

As for Rachel, she is revealed in significant ways by the incident in which she cuts her foot on a cup and refuses to bandage the injury. She lets the blood drip on the floor, trying to make a joke out of it. Her self-pity is mixed with her rage against her parents. "They need to *see* this," she says.

The breaking of the mug also gives us a vista into the daily life of her parents: the father venting his anger by throwing the cup against the refrigerator and the mother making her statement by refusing to sweep it up.

Using Dialogue and Thoughts

Much of what you learn about a person in daily life is through dialogue. Even if people don't tell you exactly what is going on in their heads, they reveal themselves indirectly through what they say. The same is true in fiction.

In "Obst Vw," for example, it is clear that Demian's mother has an overriding sense of loyalty to her husband despite his dark moods and occasional irascibility. How do we come to know this? Not by the author telling us but through this exchange:

> "He's way too smart for what he does," his mother is saying. "He did well in college without studying . . . . He never got time to sit and figure things out. He was too young to have a child."
> "Mom," Demain says, "he was twenty-six when I was born. He's forty-two."
> "He was too young," she says firmly, gathering up her books."

This dialogue contributes to our understanding of her by revealing not only her unquestioning defense of her husband but a certain stubbornness even in the face of contrary evidence. In addition, it gives us a further insight into Demian's inner torment. The father's failures can't logically be blamed on having had a child at twenty-six, but if that excuse has become a family myth, the accusation is the sort that can lay a heavy guilt trip on a son.

The father also reveals a good deal about himself in an angry outburst that is so illogical it is almost funny. Demian has been grounded and has asked his father for a second chance. The father scoffs, asking if God would give him "a second chance" if he were dying. Then, groping for still another wild analogy, he says:

> "Let's say you get your girlfriend pregnant . . . . But you aren't ready to be Papa yet. You want to walk across Turkey in your stocking feet. You want to climb Mt. Tamalpais and keep on going."

Absurd as this statement is, it reveals more about the father than he realizes. At forty-two he still has the longing for freedom and adventure that many of us experience at thirteen or fourteen. Through this outburst we see in the father an instable mix of authoritarian rigidity and childish romanticism. This is a fairly complex insight considering that he is only a secondary character.

As you can see from examples like these, dialogue is a particularly effective device for revealing two different aspects of a character. We see this frequently in Rachel's dialogue as well. The most dramatic example is when toward the end she seems to be describing a sexual assault on the part of her father. Horrified, Demian asks if that is really true.

> She shakes her head no. "Another example of my sick imagination."

On the one hand she is stoic about her parents' violent antagonism against each other, occasionally making a joke of their fights. But on the other hand, she is able to exaggerate the extent of their depravity, describing her father in melodramatic terms. And then she switches back, making a joke about herself. What we see in Rachel is someone desperately trying to cope with an impossible home life, vacillating from one approach to another.

One reason dialogue is such an effective method of delineating character is that it gives readers the illusion of hearing it directly. But to achieve this illusion, the author has to present dialogue in ways readers are used to. The dialogue itself has to be fresh and true to character, but the mechanical form should be so familiar that it is not noticed. This is one of those cases where art must conceal art. That is, the creative aspect of your work should conceal the mechanical aspects.

To achieve this seamless quality in your dialogue, keep in mind certain **conventions** which you and all readers are used to but which you may not have noticed consciously. Conventions in writing are not rules, but they are patterns that are widely followed. If you decide to ignore them, make sure you have a good reason.

First, most stories use quotation marks around words spoken out loud and none around thoughts. Single quotation marks (like apostrophes) are used to set off quotations within quotations. Here is an example of all three types of presentation:

> If only, she thought, the rest of the committee had heard how enthusiastic her client had been over her proposal.
> "He really liked the design," she said. "'It's the best we've seen so far,' he told me. Those were his exact words."

If one speaker's words are more than one paragraph, use quotation marks at the beginning but not at the end of all but the last paragraph.

Second, most writers indent the first line of speech of each new speaker. Doing this may appear to waste paper, but readers are used to it both in fiction and in drama. One advantage of regular indentation is that in lengthy exchanges between two characters, the reader does not have to be told each time which one spoke.

Third, "she said," "he said," and "I said" are used more like punctuation marks than phrases, and for this reason they are repeated frequently. They are called **dialogue tags** or simply **tags.** The prohibition against redundancy just doesn't apply to them. In fact, it sounds amateurish to keep using substitutions like "she retorted," "he sneered," "she questioned," "he hissed." These become obtrusive.

In this connection, guard against adding modifiers to "said." There is usually no reason to write "said angrily" or "said shyly," since almost always the tone is clear from the dialogue itself. If you really have to reverse the reader's first assumption, it may be more effective to use a separate phrase as in,

> "Boy, are you dumb!" she said, rolling her eyes, but her tone was still loving.

Fourth, as I have suggested earlier, dialogue is rarely aided by phonetic spelling. There are some successful exceptions, but in most cases it is possible to catch the flavor of an accent or **dialect** with appropriate phrasing rather than tinkering with conventional spelling. If you are giving the impression of a foreign language being spoken, consider the value of translating a few foreign idioms directly into English as Hemingway occasionally did with his Spanish-speaking characters.

Finally, one way to compress dialogue and yet still provide a general sense of what is being said is to use **indirect discourse.** For example:

> She said that she had missed the flight, that she would be there as soon as she could make another reservation.

This is an excellent way to eliminate a paragraph of unnecessary dialogue. Indirect discourse can also be more extended and use actual phrasing from the conversation without quoting directly and without using quotation marks:

> He greeted his sister warmly, remarking on how tall she had grown, how sophisticated she had become. How long, he asked, had it been since they had seen each other?

Thoughts are equally valuable as a method of revealing character and attitude. Thoughts can be presented in a way that sounds almost like dialogue without quotation marks or, at the other end of the spectrum, they can seem closer to indirect discourse or even exposition.

One word of warning: Be careful not to use dialogue or thoughts unrealistically to present facts to the reader. It is not at all convincing to have a character think, "I am 23 years old, tall, handsome, and was born in Omaha." People don't think that way, so the reader senses that this is the writer intruding—which is exactly the case. Both dialogue and thoughts have to be motivated by the situation, not merely by the author's need to get the facts across.

Generally speaking, if dialogue is merely filling space and not contributing to the reader's understanding of character, skip over it with a sentence or two of exposition. Whole blocks of trivial conversation can be condensed with a brief statement of fact like: "They greeted her warmly," "They talked of other matters for over an hour," or "They lingered at the door, saying their goodbyes." Far better to use summaries like these than to weigh your story down with conversation that is only padding.

Those are mechanical aspects that, if followed, will help the reader to ignore the mechanical aspects. On a nonmechanical level, try to make every line of dialogue echo the character you are portraying. Keep reading it over aloud. (Those with acting experience have an advantage here.) Dialogue that merely advances the plot is not doing enough. It should echo the character of the speaker and periodically provide real insights.

Three Goals of Effective Characterization

If you look closely at fully developed characters in published fiction, you will notice that most fulfill these three characteristics: they are consistent in what they say and do, they are complex, and they are highly individualized. These are goals to aim for.

Consistency is the dominant characteristic of minor characters. The heavyset owner of the bar in "Sausage and Beer" has some important lines, but he is a "flat" character, one who is there merely to serve a function and so is not developed. In "Acts of Violence" the narrator is entirely consistent. He is concerned for the welfare of his mother throughout the story. We assume that he has learned something by his mother's single act of violence, but within the story itself he is entirely consistent.

But even complex, "round" characters have a basic consistency. The father in "Sausage and Beer" is consistently reserved. The mothers in "Three Hearts" and "Acts of Violence" both act in ways that are surprising, but their behavior is by the end of each story explained, the former motivated by a strong maternal drive and the latter responding understandably to years of childhood abuse. Demian and Rachel react in different ways to different types of parental insensitivity, but each is consistent.

Not one of these characters acts in a way that is left inexplicable at the end of the story, and that is the key to consistency. What he or she does should be clearly motivated.

Complexity is what differentiates secondary or "flat" characters from those that are fully formed. And as we have seen, it also differentiates characterization in simple fiction from that in sophisticated work.

To achieve complex characterization, you have to develop more than one aspect of a character. You can do this by establishing a pattern, countering it in some way, and showing how both elements are a part of the whole character. The mother in "Acts of Violence" is developed this way. It seems puzzling to us (and to her son) that an older and kindly woman should take a self-defense course that is so dedicated to a violent response. But at the end we see that her behavior is clearly motivated in ways we (and the son) could not have seen before.

Or you may choose to highlight some aspect of character briefly introduced before. We know that Rachel in "Obst Vw" has had a nervous breakdown earlier, but only through the course of the story do we understand the terrible stress she is experiencing in that dysfunctional family.

To achieve complexity in characterization, provide some type of fresh insight, something not revealed early in the story. This may be an aspect that the reader shares with the character, as in the stories already discussed, or something only the reader fully appreciates, as you will see in the story that appears as the next chapter. If the change is too subtle or obscure, readers will feel that the story lacks *closure*, that sense of being fully completed. "I'm not sure what the point is," they are apt to say. If the change is too great or unconvincing, on the other hand, readers will feel that the character lacks consistency. "I just don't believe she would behave like that," they might say, and the story has failed. Your job is to establish a delicate balance.

Complexity alone is not enough to hold the reader's interest and make a character memorable. A character has to be interesting in some way, and it helps if he or she is presented in an interesting environment. *Individuality* is what makes a character memorable.

A story about Dick and Jane who attend a typical university and spend the afternoon in a typical college cafeteria complaining to each other about their typically awful parents is not going to hold the attention of even your most admiring reader.

Distinctive characters in relatively unusual settings hold interest. An uncle in a mental hospital is more memorable than an eccentric but sane one who joins the family for dinner. A mother who lives in a twilight zone of pain-killers and tranquilizers who draws on inner strength to save her son in a snowbank is far more striking than a competent mother who faces the same crisis. What individualizes Demian and Rachel and makes them memorable is partly the subtle differences in their approach: Rachel with her caustic, bitter wit and Demian with his earnest appeal to reason. They are also made more memorable by being placed in distinctive settings: the sexually charged scene in the preschool sandbox, the ballpark scene in which

Demian has an obscured view of the players, and Rachel's family kitchen with shards of a broken cup on the floor.

Be careful, however, not to overdo the attempt to be different. There comes a point when distinctiveness turns artificial and unconvincing. An inconsequential tale about two bickering college roommates is not going to be improved by being transformed into an inconsequential tale about two bickering hunchbacks living in a burned-out funhouse amid the rubble of World War III. Individuality for its own sake becomes a **gimmick,** a contrived and superficial attention-getter.

As you can see from the stories you have read, well-developed characters should be consistent enough so that at least by the end of the story we understand why they said and did what they did; they have to be complex enough to seem real, not just types; and they have to have enough individuality to make them interesting and memorable. If this seems like a tall order, remember that these qualities do not snap into place in the first draft. They are the goals you keep in mind as you move through successive versions.

25

A STORY

by Marian Ury

The Cat That Had the Power of Speech

A cat came to the home of a couple in Piedmont, California, and said, "I want." It was a pretty cat, with round bright eyes and orange fur, a bushy tail, a snub nose, and the short legs and sturdy frame that when the body was properly fleshed out, would entitle it to be described as "cobby," an aristocratic term. It was raining; the cat was shivering, and even if it had been an ugly cat the couple, who were kind-hearted, would surely have brought out something for it to eat. As it was they let it in and conducted it to the kitchen, the husband preceding and the wife following behind with a towel to wipe the muddy paw-prints from the floor. "I want", said the cat. "Nice kitty", said the wife pouring a saucer of milk. "Do you suppose it's all right?" said the husband. He was a lawyer and by this utterance was referring simultaneously to the health of the cat considered from the cat's point-of-view, the inconvenience to themselves in the likelihood that it should die—for its meager belly was quaking violently—and the Law of Found Property. It had occurred to him that the cat might be claimed as his if no other owner came forward—but suppose someone did? He felt uneasy. "I want," repeated the cat, which had polished off the milk and now shook droplets from its whiskers onto the kitchen wall. "Nice kitty," said the woman and opened a can of tuna. "Let me," said her husband, spooning it onto a plate. The cat polished that off too, said "I want"—or perhaps it said "I love you" (which is the same thing)—wiped its face, pillowed its head on a paw and suddenly fell asleep.

Husband and wife both had always longed for a cat, though neither had ever spoken of it, and now that they had one that was handsome, that despite the husband's fears was in no immediate danger of death, and that moreover had the power of speech, they were thrilled. The next afternoon the husband felt himself growing vague while instructing a client on a delicate point of law. Pleading a sore throat he hurried home and found the cat curled up, nose to tail in what is known as the "contented cat position," on a cushion. True, it was that of his favorite chair. "It said, `I want,'" said his wife apologetically. "Nice kitty," said the husband. Already the cat looked fatter, its fur glossier, its whiskers longer and whiter. It seemed, in fact, likely to become quite a proper cat. Husband and wife watched with pride as it slept, its paw-tips twitching.

The woman, childless despite many years of marriage, thought the cat would be company as she did her chores, and she set herself to train it to follow her around the house. "Now kitty," she would say, "I'm going to dust the sofa legs and give the cushions a good shaking," or "Now kitty, I'm going to sort the silver and stack the napkins." The cat was not attentive, preferring to eat and sleep at its leisure, stalk birds in the garden, investigate closets, the undersides of chairs, and the tops of tables. But perhaps the reason was that her tasks were not that interesting. Still she tried. Once, too vigorous, she grazed its tail with the vacuum cleaner. "Ouch," it cried, "it hurts, it hurts!" and turned and sank a fang into her knee. "I'm sorry, kitty," she said, trembling. "I want," said the cat. She fed it, and after a while it went to sleep.

Despite this failure the woman thought she should train the cat. If only it could be made to expand its vocabulary: then it could expeditiously be told the difference between a bench—meant to be sat on—and a table-top—forbidden. She tried to show it her reasons. "Now kitty," she would say, "it's all right to sharpen your claws on the doormat, but the rug you absolutely mustn't." Or, "Now kitty, you may bite on the knitting yarn, but the lamp cord—no!" But the cat did not seem to understand and only repeated "I want" until it was fed more tuna, or let out of doors, or allowed to jump onto her husband's favorite chair. The man, too, tried to instruct it; he came home early these days, often feeling unwell. In his office his thoughts turned to the furry creature at home and he grew vague; once he found himself mumbling nonsense to an important client. "I want," said the cat, ensconced at that moment on their bed; extending a paw it snagged a corner of the bedspread. "No kitty, nice kitty," the man said. He was feeling unwell indeed, with a headache and a scratchy throat. "I want, I want," screamed the cat, seized the fringe and began to gnaw. "Kitty, mustn't!" said the woman. "I want, I want," it shouted, ripping a swathe from the fringe, wrapping it around its hind legs and hurling itself convulsively onto the rug. Husband and wife looked at each other. "It's been awfully bad-tempered lately," she said timidly. "Do you suppose it's all right?" he asked, and they rushed it to the vet.

The vet had a bristling beard and a manly manner. He poked and prodded the cat, squeezed its belly, took its temperature, gave it for good measure a rabies shot and one against feline enteritis. The cat said nothing but squirmed and whimpered. "There's nothing wrong with it," said the vet. "It's a perfectly normal cat." "I really don't care about the bedspread," said the wife, though she did. "Nor do I," said her husband patting her hand, though he did. The effort of comforting each other, greater than they had made in years, exhausted them, and they drove home without further speech.

The woman fed the cat kidney, to apologize for the insult. The man fed it tuna, because it had whimpered. It took some bites of each, leaped on the table, attacked the rug, chewed the lamp-cord, and leaped onto the favorite chair, where it went to sleep. The husband stayed home the next day; he lay in bed with a high fever. The cat ate and slept at its leisure, stalked and caught a bird, disarranged a closet, clawed the underside of the sofa, gnawed the curtains, and left paw-prints on the dining-room table. Only once did the wife venture to reproach it. It had just leaped onto her husband's favorite chair and was sharpening its claws on the back before settling down to sleep. "Oh kitty," she said, "sometimes I think you're just not trying to communicate." "Are you out of your mind?" cried the cat in a loud, clear, and remarkably ungracious voice. It never spoke again.

26

LIBERATING THE IMAGINATION

Exploring the What-if. Where did that cat come from? Varieties of nonrealistic fiction. Three basic misconceptions. Telling good from bad.

In Chapter 14, "The Sources of Fiction," I stressed the fact that personal experience is a rich source of material for new fiction. If you have been writing stories, you probably have been transforming episodes from your own life by altering the point of view, rearranging events, and changing the setting. You are beginning to create new and credible characters partially based on people you have known or briefly met. These procedures are all essential to the process of creating a carefully developed, realistic story.

But what about those flights of fancy that suddenly sweep in on us like a sudden squall? They may spring from some absurd and unrealistic notion. Some may be dreamlike in their lack of structure. They may lack "essential" elements such as well-developed characters or a setting. Like the tornado in *The Wizard of Oz*, they have the power to propel us into a fantasy world. How can we draw on such explosions of imagination, and if we manage to get them down on paper, how are we to judge whether they are merely personal flights or are worth developing into a story designed to be read by others?

Exploring the What-If

You can't train yourself to be creatively innovative any more than you can will yourself to be funny. But you can explore fanciful notions and impressions in a free manner and see what develops. If your imagination is quirky, it may come up with twenty ideas that will never make a story and then by chance hit one that really has potential.

Some writers strongly recommend keeping a journal of some sort—

handwritten, typed in a loose-leaf notebook, or recorded as a special file on a computer. Late-night writing in short bursts is best for many. It's one thing you can do when the mind is tired at the end of the day. As with dreams, anything goes. This does not mean that very much of what you write this way should go beyond your journal. Have pity on your readers! But occasionally something might develop.

One approach is to play the "What-if" game. What if your sister developed the ability to fly? What if all the dogs of the world rebelled against their masters on the same day? What if a blind man had the ability to hear the thoughts of those around him? What if an accomplished flutist found that he could not play without attracting swarms of monarch butterflies?

Another technique is to turn "it's like" into "it is." This is essentially a matter of converting similes to literal statements. If a good friend's laugh is like a sheep bleating, what if he became a sheep at awkward moments? How would his friends and associates deal with that? Could he maintain old friendships? What about his marriage? If a sleepless night is like a video of all the day's problems, what if a character goes to the movies and finds the film is about himself?

This literal treatment of similes is the pattern in several stories by Franz Kafka: Adolescents sometimes feel like an insect and are treated as such, but in Kafka's "The Metamorphosis" a young man actually becomes a six-foot cockroach. When we suffer from a sense of guilt and worthlessness, we may feel that life is like a trial, but in Kafka's novel *The Trial* the protagonist finds himself actually immersed in a dreamlike, unending court case. If you take this route, be careful not to rewrite Kafka.

A third route to innovation is to capture an actual dream or a daydream on paper and continue with the same setting and characters to see what comes next.

A more literary approach is to allow a contemporary figure to slip into one of the thousands of fairy tales that have been collected and see what happens to him or her. If John Gardner can write a serious book about the life of a dragon, you can do the same with a unicorn or the giant who has a grudge against boys named Jack.

Where Did That Cat Come From?

With all this in mind, how might "The Cat That Had the Power of Speech" have occurred to the author Marian Ury? We can only guess what actually launched that story, but in speculating about the source, we are also exploring a variety of ways to read that story.

• The author is disgusted with a married couple who completely spoil an only child, a child who is allowed to rule their lives. The author's final reaction to them: "They're out of their minds." In this case, the cat in the story becomes an effective symbol for the actual child.

• The author is appalled by a couple whose lives are dominated by an actual cat. It's almost *as if* the wretched thing talked. Here the cat is no symbol. The situation is simply an exaggeration of something that could really happen. It's *as if* the cat could talk. The cat speaks the author's view in its concluding line.

• The author is disgusted at a couple that is so polite and so passive that they let a guest disrupt their lives. Here too the story is an exaggeration of what might have actually happened, the cat serving as a symbol for the surly and demanding guest, and for domineering people generally.

• The author is fed up with the notion that all social ills are just problems in communication. This final possibility focuses on the wife's cry, "sometimes I think you're just not trying to communicate." Clearly the cat has communicated its arrogance and hostility from the very beginning. It's the "sweet" husband and wife who are not listening and not communicating their true feelings.

What do these readings share? They all agree that the story is a satire primarily of individuals who, though kind and generous, do not have the power to direct their own lives. They are victims of their own debilitating sense of politeness.

Varieties of Nonrealistic Fiction

Are we expected to believe that cats really talk? Wrong question. Anyone who asks that will have trouble with King Midas, whose touch turned objects to gold, with Alice in Wonderland, who grew eight feet tall in a matter of minutes, with Kafka's Gregor, who woke up to find himself transformed into a six-foot cockroach. This suggests an important distinction: **Realism** implies fidelity to the world as we know it, a world in which cats don't talk. **Verisimilitude** on the other hand, gives the *appearance* of truth. It's the *illusion* of truth. We accept unnatural events as natural within the context of a story.

Often such stories are based on a single premise: that a cat can talk, in this case; or that an adolescent can find himself transformed into a large insect, that a girl can be blown into a mythical world by a tornado. Such stories can be called **premise fiction** because the as-if element is clearly defined. Science fiction and futuristic work often make use of certain specific premises.

In other cases, the departure from realism is more diffuse. *Fantasy* and *dream fiction* are terms that describe this approach. These are not complex literary distinctions. As children we accepted fantasy stories as easily as we did those that reflected the real world about us.

In addition, there are other forms of nonrealistic fiction, some of them as old as literature itself. A **fable,** for example, is a short tale in which the characters are usually animals and the theme often suggests a moral. Aesop lived more than 2,500 years ago, but his fables are still a part of our culture. When the fable form is extended to make each character precisely symbolic, the result is an **allegory** such as George Orwell's *Animal Farm.*

Another approach is called **creative nonfiction.** This is writing that blurs the distinction between fiction and factual writing to produce partially fictionalized biography, autobiography, or historical accounts. It is occasionally called *nonfiction fiction.*

Metafiction is a relatively recent term for works that are less committed to realism than to commenting on the genre itself. In John Barth's highly readable story "Lost in the Funhouse," for example, the boy is also the author in the process of writing. He stops the action periodically to comment on how the story is progressing. The funhouse becomes fiction with all its tricks and special effects.

If you are drawn to nonrealistic fiction, don't feel you have to reinvent the form. Read some of these literary works and you will find approaches that can be adapted for fresh and innovative treatment.

Three Basic Misconceptions

One serious misconception about nonrealistic fiction is that what was fun to write must necessarily be fun to read. True, liberating your imagination and letting it take you in any direction provides a real sense of relief from the demands of crafted fiction. You can set aside questions of viewpoint, structure, tension, setting, and convincing characterization. But the joy you feel in producing this blizzard of words is not necessarily going to bring joy or even pleasure to your reader. Nineteen times out of twenty these flights should remain in your journal. The one that does have literary potential will probably require some basic transformations and careful revisions.

A second and closely related misconception is the hidden-meaning theory. It holds that an aimless work written from the heart must necessarily have some hidden meaning which, though unknown to the author, can be ferreted out by a conscientious reader. Overworked writing instructors and editors waste countless hours trying to interpret works that do not contain anything to interpret.

Some beginning writers submit essentially meaningless work not out of malice but because they have heard teachers provide explanations of published works that seemed unintelligible on first reading. They conclude that if Samuel Becket, James Joyce, and Thomas Pynchon can, on occasion, write that way, why can't anyone? Before you fall into that trap, study some of these more difficult novelists. You will find that they were not writing aimlessly with blind abandon.

The most serious misconception is the claim that a work of fiction should mean all things to all people. True, a group of readers will see and respond to different aspects of any work. But there is almost always a core of agreement. Earlier in this chapter I suggested four different ways of reading "The Cat," but they are closely related. We may differ in matters of emphasis, but no one is going to propose that the story is a satire of militarism, a criticism of the medical profession, or a protest against illegal drugs. It obviously does not mean all things to all people, and works that have to be defended with that claim should remain in the privacy of the writer's journal.

Telling Good from Bad

If some works should remain in one's journal and only a few should be presented for discussion and possible publication, how can we tell the difference? How can we identify what has literary potential?

The question is important, because dumping obscure, dreamlike sequences on editors is an imposition and presenting them to writing classes can spoil an entire afternoon. It is also in some ways a difficult question because we can't judge such work in the same way we evaluate a realistic story.

Is "Cat," for example, a "sophisticated story" in the sense we have been using? The characters are "flat" in that we see only one side of their personalities. They are not even named. The setting is never developed. What is left?

Plot, for one. It is structured in a series of scenes that build toward a climax. But that is also true of very simple fiction. The real distinction is that this work has a cluster of fairly sophisticated themes. Through these themes we see a literary intent. We can agree at least in general terms about what is being satirized. The themes here, unlike those in simple work, can stimulate thought and generate discussion. They provide insights into human behavior. They even provoke ethical questions: How long should civility be sustained when one is dealing with arrogant and demanding people? As for the wit, it is subtle and entertaining. Although we see only one aspect of these two characters, they represent attitudes we recognize. So does that awful cat. The story is relatively sophisticated in that it makes up in complexity of theme and satiric criticism what it does not offer in other aspects.

There are two ways of testing whether a fanciful sequence is a story that is ready for the reading public or whether it is merely a private journal entry. The first is to share it with two or three individuals who are familiar with experimental fiction. Don't be content with those initial kindly comments friends feel obliged to give; ask them to describe exactly what they drew from your work. If their answers become evasive ("Well, I don't really know what you're doing, but I liked reading it"), ask yourself what you hoped they would see. You may be able to meet your readers halfway. If, however, you were just writing off the top of your head, stick the effort back in your journal. Only small children have the right to report at length on their dreams, and they have the good sense not to ask for a literary discussion.

The second test is more analytical. Ask yourself this: What exactly am I offering to my reader? What is my aim? If it is humor, do I really have something more complex than an **anecdotal** joke? If it is satire—with or without humor—make sure you know what you are satirizing. Is it insight into something the reader has not fully recognized? If you have eliminated the pleasures of plot (as one does in the fictional essay), what is left to hold the reader? If you have simplified your characters to a cartoon level (as in most fables), have you supplied a thematic suggestion that is both fresh and complex enough to go beyond a mere truism? Finally, ask yourself whether what you have written has qualities that will draw at least some readers back for a second reading.

Take "The Cat," for example. I suggested above a number of harmonious but slightly different ways to read that story. Those characters, both human and feline, are as "flat" as cartoon figures, and the plot is certainly simple, yet the story as a whole has reverberations that go beyond the immediate plot. It generates interest and for some a haunting familiarity. Those miserable characters suggest flaws in character that we have seen in some of our friends—or perhaps even in ourselves.

Nonrealistic fiction provides many possibilities, but, like free verse, it is not anarchy. It is not scribbling. A piece may begin spontaneously with little or no plan, but before it is ready for others to read it has to be shaped and given purpose. There are many different traditions that you can draw on and learn from. It is important to familiarize yourself with them so you can distinguish an informal journal entry from a story with literary merit.

27

HEIGHTENED MEANING

Metaphor, Symbol, and Theme

Converting abstractions into images. How similes and metaphors work. Vehicles and tenors. Symbols defined. Theme: the portion of a story that comments on the human condition. When themes need revision.

Which of these two statements is stronger? (a) "Sometimes she is self-conscious about her height." (b) "She arcs down into herself like a long-neck bird."

Which of the following two has more power? (a) "He feels excited at being able to say things he has never said before." (b) "He's an explorer, charting ground never seen by mortal eyes."

Which of these two is more memorable? (a) An analytical statement about how domestic disputes between parents often do damage to their children or (b) a description of a cup smashed in anger by a father and not swept up by a mother which cuts a daughter badly enough so we can see her blood dripping on the tile floor.

The second choice in each pair is more vivid, but why? What do they have in common? Each of them has converted an abstract statement into a strong visual impression.

Similar as they are in this respect, each one represents a slightly different technique. The first is a simile, the second is a metaphor, and the third is a symbol. Casual readers don't have to know the difference; a general sense of vitality is enough. But practicing writers can't always rely on impressions. It is hard to discuss any work of fiction, our own or someone else's, unless we use words like simile, metaphor, and symbol precisely.

How Similes and Metaphors Work

First, some quick definitions. A **simile** is a comparison in which we state that one item (often an abstraction) is *like* something concrete. Often this is a visual image, but it can be anything we can respond to with one of the five senses. Thus "She fought like a lion" implies strength and courage. Notice, however, that it is not a simple comparison, as in "Lemons are like oranges." We are not suggesting that this woman used claws or bit her opponent. We are saying only that the way she fought brings to mind the ferocity of a lion. It's impossible to see abstractions like ferocity, determination, or courage, but we can easily visualize a lion in action.

A **metaphor** serves the same function, but it makes the comparison without *like* or *as.* This distinction is more significant than one might think, since a metaphorical statement is literally untrue. It is only *figuratively* true. In this case we might have, "She is a lion when fighting for civil rights." *Is* a lion? Well, is *like* a lion. When we explain metaphors, it is natural to convert them back into similes.

Similes and metaphors are both called **figurative language** or **figures of speech** because they use words in a nonliteral way. These terms do not apply to symbols, however, for reasons I will explain shortly. Some authors use figurative language more than do others. In this collection, "Obst Vw" and "Three Hearts" contain some of the best examples.

In some cases similes and metaphors are used together so naturally that one hardly notices the difference. In "Obst Vw," for example, Demian makes this statement about his relationship with his father:

> "Sometimes in the room with him I feel like I don't exist. I don't have a body."

This is such a familiar feeling that we hardly think of it as figurative language. But to feel "like I don't exist" is a simile, since he does in fact exist, while "I don't have a body" is a metaphor since it is literally untrue. Notice how much more impact it has than it would have as a simile: *"as if* I don't have a body."

Figurative language is not a literary embellishment added to make one's style sound elegant. It is natural to common speech. Many of the examples we hear in daily life are so common that they have become **clichés**—similes and metaphors that have lost all impact from overuse. Stockbrokers aren't visualizing an animal when they refer to a "bull market," parents have no picture in mind when they ask their children to make their rooms "neat as a pin," and none of us is sure why a whip is "smart." But when fresh similes and metaphors are used in fiction, they create an **image**—a mental picture—because they are original. And if they are harmonious with the vocabulary and speech patterns of a character, they will blend in to dialogue or narration just as naturally as into exposition.

Deborah Corey's "Three Hearts" is a good example. It is written in the first person from the point of view of a young girl, Sissy, yet it contains many similes and metaphors that echo the way she might talk. She describes her mother's eyes, for example, as being "like faded jeans." This suggests more than just the color; there are overtones of being worn out as well. The author is more aware of the overtones than a girl Sissy's age would be, but the phrase blends in as a natural part of her narration.

In the same way, she describes Eddie as having "an angry streak like steel running through his heart." The phrase *angry streak* alone is technically a metaphor, but it is so familiar that we don't picture the streak. Having a "streak like steel running through his heart" is both visually arresting and at the same time natural to a young girl's language. In another simile, Sissy describes not only an action but an attitude behind the action. Eddie, returning after a night on the town, "steps over us as if we are stones." The frequency and vividness of these metaphors don't make the narrator sound precocious because they are the sort we often hear from children.

When figurative language is used as a part of dialogue or, as in this case, narration, they must be harmonious with that character's natural vocabulary and speech pattern. But even if they are presented in the form of exposition, they should blend in. When they are exaggerated for effect or to seem clever, they make a work of fiction seem affected or "literary" in the worst sense. Their function is to enrich the story without being conspicuous.

Vehicles and Tenors

The terms **vehicle** and **tenor** were originally suggested by the critic I. A. Richards, and they are used frequently by writers and poets because there is no better way to analyze precisely why one figure of speech is effective and another fails. As in poetry, the terms are also essential for an understanding of how similes and metaphors differ fundamentally from symbols.

The **vehicle** of a simile or metaphor is the image itself—usually a concrete object, something we can see or at least hear or feel. The **tenor** is the implied subject. Since most (though not all) figures of speech provide a visual image suggesting the qualities of an abstract notion, you can think of the vehicle as the transporter, *carrying* a message to the reader.

In the example from "Three Hearts" in which the brother "steps over us as if we were stones," the vehicle is the picture of someone stepping over stones in a field. The tenor is the total indifference with which Eddie treats his younger brother and sister. It might take a paragraph to spell out Eddie's attitude in exposition, but the vehicle gives us a metal picture in a single phrase.

The same is true of Demian's mix of exhilaration and anxiety when he begins to express hostile feelings about his father. For one who has longed for his father's respect and companionship, it is a terrible thing to be saying "If he died tomorrow it wouldn't make the least difference in my life." How is the author to describe his emotions? She beings with a sentence of exposition: "It seems reckless and marvelous saying these things about his father." But then she shifts to the metaphor I quoted above: "He's an explorer, charting ground never before seen by mortal eyes." The explorer is the vehicle, but it would take a paragraph to describe the tenor in detail. Briefly, there are overtones of adventure, risk, pride in his courage, even bravado, fear. The best metaphors have tenors that are complex and often charged with mixed emotions.

The Impact of a Symbol

We are all familiar with symbols when they appear in political cartoons. The American flag, the cross, the Star of David, the Russian bear are all built into the culture as representing abstractions such as a country or a religion.

Simple fiction has its fairly obvious and often-used symbolic images: The drinking of a toast by two evil plotters in which the wine spills assures us that they will fail; howling dogs on the moors in a gothic novel assure us that someone is in torment. These are sometimes referred to as **public symbols** because they are widely known.

Sophisticated fiction uses fresh images. The term **private symbol** is occasionally used but is rather misleading. *Original* symbol would be a far more accurate term. Such symbols have been devised by the particular author rather than borrowed from the pool of well-known symbols. The meaning of an original symbol is revealed through the context of the story or novel. As a result, those who have not read extensively sometimes have difficulty in identifying them.

To see how a symbol differs from a metaphor, let's go back to our original example of a metaphor: "She was a lion in battle." The image of the lion is introduced simply for the purpose of comparison. There is no actual lion in the story. That's why we call it a figure of speech. Contrast this, however, with a story set in Africa that deals with a real lion. If the story is intended to contrast the cowardice of a hunter with true courage, it might be possible to describe the lion in ways that suggest the quality of courage. If this is done carefully, the lion would become a *symbol* for those qualities.

The difference between this symbolic use of the lion and the figurative use is clear once you see that in the case of a metaphor the vehicle (the lion) is not a literal part of the fiction. With a symbol, on the other hand, the vehicle is physically present in the story—all 400 pounds of him. The symbolic meaning, the tenor, is suggested through implication.

The difference between metaphors and symbols is made clear when they are used together in the same scene. At the end of "Sausage and Beer," for example, the waiter brings the order and then leaves "with a quick, benedictory smile." Translating that back to a simile: "with a smile *as if* it were the expression of a clergyman at the conclusion of a service." Father and son are then "lost in a kind of communion"—not a literal one. They are not, after all, in a church. In contrast, the sausage and beer that the waiter brings is real, not a figure of speech, and a careful reader will see that they serve as a symbol for the bread and wine of certain religious services. How can we be sure? Not just because the author says so but because the reader has been prepared by those two metaphors. In addition, the significance of the image is highlighted by its use as the title.

Sometimes complex symbols are found in stories that appear to be relatively straightforward. "Three Hearts," for example, ends with a symbolic detail that the narrator herself does not perceive. Bucky, the narrator's brother, has almost died because Eddie would not get out of bed to help. Bucky has survived only because the sickly mother has dug into the snow, found him, and performed mouth-to-mouth resuscitation. After their mother takes Bucky inside, the narrator picks up Bucky's mitten and the one that belongs to Eddie. (This action was prepared for early in the story when Mama tells Bucky, "Double up on your mittens. . . ." It is attention to details like this that require a great deal of rewriting.)

Eddie's mitten is "grey and full of holes." She pulls on the yarn "but the hole puckers together in a kiss." She then does this with every hole and the mitten finally "rumples itself into a little ball."

The story, you remember, informs us in the third paragraph that Eddie has been a continual problem, a dropout who stays out drinking all night and sleeps during the day. The family members, especially the mother, treat him gently, even with love. In exactly the same way, Sissy ineffectively tries to mend Eddie's mitten, the hole puckers "in a kiss" and eventually "rumples itself into a little ball" just as Eddie himself sleeps inside, as useless as the little ball of yarn.

That kiss, by the way, is a vehicle used to describe the puckering of the yarn, the tenor of the metaphor. The mitten, however, is real—not a figure of speech—and so becomes a symbol for Eddie's damaged and hopeless state. The question to ask when distinguishing a metaphor from a symbol is simply this: Is the vehicle a figure of speech (like that metaphorical kiss) or does it, like the mitten, exist in the story?

"Obst Vw" is a highly symmetrical story dealing with two characters almost equally. Their problems are revealed through two separate symbols, both of which are given a prominent emphasis and become central to the story.

When Demian, you remember, is taken to his first baseball game at ten by his father, his father leaves him in a seat with obstructed vision. That ticket with the abbreviation "obst vw" is highlighted by its use as title (as was the central image in "Sausage and Beer"). It suggests the obstructed vision Demian has of his father as well as his father's view of him. In addition, it comments on the relationships Rachel's parents have with each other and that Rachel has with them. In a minor but significant way, it also applies to the absurdly inaccurate view Rachel's father has of Demian's father, calling him "the Old Hippie" for no reason. In fact, every relationship in that story with the possible exception of Demian and Rachel is damaged by an obscured or distorted view.

The central symbol characterizing Rachel's emotional state is appropriately more dramatic. It is a broken cup. The father has thrown it against the refrigerator in his rage, and the mother has shown her disdain by refusing to sweep it up. It is the daughter who is injured—a rather basic symbol reaffirming the well-known fact that children are damaged when parents fight.

The real subtlety of that broken cup and the injury lies in her attitude toward it. Instead of bandaging the cut, she flaunts it, sitting there "while her blood drip-drips onto the gray tile." It's her statement to them. "They should *see* this," she says. The gesture is partly a longing for sympathy and part hostility. It may also be an unconscious appeal for Demian's sympathy. At the end of that story, you remember, Demian kisses the injured spot, "smoothing down the flap of torn skin," a sincere but possibly futile attempt to heal her wounds, both physical and emotional.

Notice that the vehicles of these two symbols—the scene at the ball park and the cut-foot episode—are not just objects. They are incidents involving action as well as visual details. Notice too that they are not just dropped into the story like meteors from outer space, they are planned for and used extensively. They are, to use a slightly shop-worn metaphor, woven into the fabric of the story.

For some readers, picking out figurative language and symbols may seem like a literary exercise that detracts from the pleasure of a story—echoes, perhaps, from unhappy English classes. As a result, some student writers avoid any symbolic suggestion for fear of sounding artificial or self-consciously literary. Caution is wise, but avoidance is limiting.

A few reassurances may help. First, symbols are not a necessary ingredient in fiction. Excellent stories and novels—sophisticated in the best sense—are written without even the hint of a symbolic detail.

Second, neither figures of speech nor symbols are the invention of teachers. They are a part of common speech. We use figurative language without much conscious thought just as the narrator does in "Three Hearts." We dream in symbols. Fantasies tend to be symbolic. They have been a special concern of writers in every age because they allow us to imply so much more than we can when using straightforward, literal language.

Finally, very few stories are ruined for a reader if he or she does not see symbolic elements at first. This may have been true for you after your first reading of "Obst Vw." Few works depend on them utterly. Nevertheless, a story becomes more meaningful if one can respond to the added dimension.

Turning now to your own work, here is a cardinal rule to remember: keep it subtle. When readers recognize an unmistakable symbol, the illusion of reality breaks and the story seems contrived. Watch out for *public symbols,* those that are so widely known that they appear in song lyrics and political cartoons. Those bearded, Christlike characters named Chris, the Adam and Eve characters living on a Pacific isle, and senior citizens walking through autumn leaves—leave those to the hack writers! The intelligent reader will spot any well-used symbol looming like a cartoon and will have difficulty taking your work seriously.

In the interest of subtlety, think twice before you let a story depend utterly on a symbol. Such works often end up sacrificing credible characterization for the sake of that central abstract idea. The best approach is to move cautiously and let the story suggest to you what might be made symbolic. Whenever possible, develop your symbolic material from the events, the setting, and the characters of the story itself. The goal is to have symbolic details serve the story, not dominate it.

The Importance of Theme

Journal entries don't usually have a theme. They record events or describe personal feelings often without any unifying concern. Sophisticated fiction, on the other hand, almost always does. Readers expect it. If you don't provide some kind of theme, readers are apt to respond with questions like, "What's the point?" or "What are you getting at?"

There are many ways to define **theme,** but I have found that this is the most useful for writers: *Theme is the portion of a work of fiction that comments on the human condition.* If we think of theme in this way, we will never confuse it with **plot.** Plot is what happens. When we talk about plot, we name characters and describe events. When we talk about theme, we are making a statement about something that applies to us all. And since it is a statement, it should be expressed as a sentence, not just a word. "Anxiety" is not a theme, it is a topic. Even "Fear of violence" is too vague. You need a full sentence, such as "Anxiety caused by childhood violence can last a lifetime."

The theme is usually implied rather than stated, so it's not always easy to agree on a single sentence. In any group of sincere readers there will always be variations based on what each person feels is most important. But discussing these different ways of describing the theme helps us to identify aspects of the story that passive readers often miss. Equally important, such discussions can clarify our thinking about own work.

Put in simplest terms, the *plot* of "Three Hearts" can be described this way: "A boy is saved from suffocating by a mother who in spite of disabilities summons inner strength." The *theme*, on the other hand, might be described as "The weakest member of a family occasionally turns out to be the strongest in a real emergency." Or if we wish to emphasize the role of women, "No matter how debilitated a mother may be, she can call on inner strength when her children are threatened." There may be readers who will want to highlight Eddie as described in that final image of the balled-up mitten: "No matter how sympathetic a family is toward a dysfunctional member, he or she may end up beyond repair." The first two descriptions of theme are like describing a glass as being half full and the third describes it as half empty, but each applies to the same story. Each describes an aspect of the human condition.

All thematic statements are necessarily simplifications. They are abstract distillations of meaning. As you can see, most sophisticated stories have a cluster of related themes. Often there is a dominant concern that provides thematic focus and then a cluster of related themes. For this reason, some critics and writers prefer the phrase **central concern** rather than *theme*. The two terms are used in the same way.

Turning to "Obst Vw," there is a range of how we might describe the central concern, but they all deal with the relationship between children and their parents. One statement would stress what the two young people shared: "Parental indifference can be as damaging to a child as actual violence." Or one might want to focus on how they were different: "Parents who act out their rage against children do more serious and lasting damage than those who are merely distant and insensitive." Or if you want to stress a more positive aspect: "When young people feel cut off from parental affection, they sometimes can find solace with someone their own age."

As you analyze the themes in published stories, it may seem as if authors somehow hold all those threads in their heads from the start. Not so. What you read in print is a final draft, and it is very unlikely that the author had all those intellectual concerns in mind when beginning the story.

Here, then, is an important aspect of the creative process that can't be taught: A complex story speaks to its author through successive drafts. The story itself develops certain characters, highlights certain scenes. Most important, it often informs the writer about new thematic possibilities. Each suggestion, of course, requires more rewriting. The author who quits after the first draft can never hear the story suggesting new implications to be developed. Although the notion of a dialogue between the story and the author is a metaphor, it is often a fundamental part of the creative process.

When Themes Need Revision

If you come to the conclusion that there is something wrong with the theme of the story you are working on, you may be tempted to abandon the work. The situation is indeed serious, but it may not be fatal. Here are some correctable problems:

A recurring weakness in student fiction is settling for a theme that is a **truism**. That is, the theme is nothing more than a widely accepted and obvious assertion. Who wants to read a story that does little but remind us that you should say "no" to drugs, that you shouldn't drink and drive, that people who don't express their emotions get into trouble. These are all reasonable statements, and they may serve as a *part* of a theme, but if that is all a story suggests, it is going to seem as dull as one of those uninspired editorials you don't finish reading.

At the beginning of the fiction section I warned against seven "deadly sins," plot patterns that have become clichés. Thematic clichés are subtler because they can be disguised, but they are equally serious. If you take the time to compose a thematic statement that describes your story and all you can come up with is one of those trite slogans, you know you're in trouble.

But all is not lost. Often you can salvage such a story. One way is to look closer at the characters you are working with. A banal theme is usually a sign that you have started with an idea rather than a character or a situation. You may not have to scrap the whole story if you can develop greater subtlety in characterization. "Obst Vw," for example, could be described as having a simple theme like: "Bad marriages produce unhappy children," but as we have seen from composing various thematic statements for that story, it has a far greater range of concerns.

A second weakness is excessive reiteration of a theme. That is, every scene bluntly repeats, say, the macho quality of the protagonist or the dishonesty of a corrupt businessman or some fundamental contrast in character between a husband and a wife. The reader soon feels battered with the repetition. The author's intent becomes so obvious that the story loses credibility. Again, the solution is to look more closely at the characters. If they were conceived as a type—a typical homeless man, a typical lawyer, a typical firefighter—replace him or her with a disguised version of a character you know. Then explore that person's individuality. Look for ironic contrasts, mixed feelings. Remember that materialists aren't *always* grasping, spiritual types aren't always motivated by good thoughts, dishonest people are occasionally capable of kindness and even love. Don't be afraid to develop the odd twists in human relationships.

Obscurity is a third problem that calls for careful revision. I've already warned against a plot that is baffling, but a clear plot with an obscure theme can be just as unsatisfying. In some cases you may find that you can't describe the theme of your own story in a single sentence. That should tell you something. Or the theme may be obvious to you but not to others. If three or more readers are puzzled, don't assume they are all dumb. Having this kind of input available is the advantage of working in a writing class or with a group of fellow writers.

If the theme needs clarification, resist the temptation to add a line of exposition explaining the story. See if you can find ways of dramatizing the theme through action, dialogue, or thoughts earlier in the story. You might also consider a concluding action that will bring the story into focus. If you review the endings of a number of stories you have read, you will see how many ways there are to highlight a theme in the final paragraph without explaining everything to the reader in the form of an analytical statement.

Theme is only one aspect of a story. The freshest and most insightful theme won't make a story succeed if the characters are not convincing and the action plausible. But without originality and complexity of theme, a story becomes nothing more than a simple piece of passing entertainment. A truly sophisticated work of fiction appeals to the mind as well as to the emotions.

28

STYLE AND TONE

Style defined. Elaborate versus sparse styles. Elements of style: diction, syntax, density, the balance of narrative modes, and tense. Varieties of tone, irony and satire.

Style is the manner in which a work is written. All fiction has style. You can't compose without it any more than you can write your name without revealing your handwriting. It is important to examine just what your style is and then to judge whether it is the best possible approach for a particular story.

More than half the stories and novels you read maintain what can be described as a **neutral style.** That is, while the writing may have particular characteristics, the average reader is not aware of them. Some fiction, however, is presented in a highly distinctive manner. And some authors maintain such an individualized style in all their work that you can identify an isolated passage just as easily as you can recognize the voice of a friend on the telephone.

Should you adopt a distinctive style when you are just beginning to write fiction? The advantage is that your work will gain a certain visibility, standing out from the rest; the disadvantage is that you will limit your options when turning to new work and eventually may appear to be repetitious.

Style is placed last in this section on fiction because it doesn't usually become a conscious concern until one has had a good deal of experience. At first, we make stylistic choices intuitively. We write in the manner that feels appropriate. A complex, highly sophisticated story may encourage us to use lengthier sentences and longer words; a story with a tough, inarticulate protagonist may call for a sparse syntax and limited vocabulary even in the exposition.

But you can't always rely on your literary intuition. As you write more, you will want to able to adopt different styles knowingly. You will also want to be able to revise the style in first drafts. Such adjustments can make a radical difference in the tone of your work. Eventually you may find yourself adopting a characteristic stylistic pattern in all your work, but try not to restrict yourself until you have explored a variety of approaches.

Elaborate versus Sparse Styles

"Acts of Violence" is written in a neutral style. The reader is not made aware of a stylistic effect. Here, to remind you, is the opening as the author wrote it:

> My mother is taking self-defense classes. When she visits us in Connecticut on weekends, bringing fresh strawberries and pesto bagels on the train, she tries to practice her latest moves with us.

The same passage, however, could be written in an elegant style. The content would be essentially the same, but by altering the **diction** (word choice) and the **syntax** (sentence structure), we radically alter the effect. The result is not too far from how Henry James might have presented it.

> My aging but agile mother, a woman who has for as long as I can remember been deeply and earnestly opposed to violence and physical force in all forms, has, for reasons that totally baffle my wife and me, taken it upon herself to enroll in a particularly combative course in self-defense. When she travels from her home in New York to spend a weekend with us in the quiet and calm of suburban Connecticut, bringing with her a rare treat of fresh strawberries from her neighborhood fruit and vegetable stand as well as our favorite pesto bagels which we are unable to obtain anywhere in this otherwise ideal state, she is ceaselessly active, rejecting tea on the patio, preferring instead to practice her latest moves with us like some young athlete no matter how we may protest.

At the other extreme, here is a sparse treatment, cutting the passage to its bare bones:

> Mother is taking self-defense classes. When she visits, she practices on us.

Or, by selecting diction that is much more informal and by using the broken syntax (incomplete sentences) we associate with casual conversation, we can convert the passage to one that is has the feel of as-if-spoken narration.

> What next? My mom and her kooky ideas. Now it's self-defense! O.K., so she still brings us fresh strawberries and pesto bagels from the city. That's fine with us. But with these classes, she's wired. All she wants is to practice these crazy moves with us.

These three versions refer to the same characters and the same situation, but if developed each would become a radically different story. Clearly, style isn't just a matter of external appearance like a coat of paint. It is an integral part of fiction which, when emphasized, becomes a part of the meaning.

There is an infinite variety of stylistic effects. Surprisingly, however, style is primarily determined by only five factors. These are **diction** (choice of words), **syntax** (sentence structure), **density** (presence or absence of figurative and symbolic language), the balance of **narrative modes** (dialogue, thoughts, action, and the like), and to a small degree **tense** (past or present). Each of these deserves a close look.

Diction

Your choice of words is a more significant factor in English than in most other languages because there is such a radical difference in sound and tone between those words that came to us from the Norse and Anglo-Saxon and those that came from the Greek or Latin through French. To cite an extreme example, contrast your reaction to these two samples:

> Edgar got in the boat and gripped the seat, sweating like an ox. He hated the sea.

> Julius entered the vessel and embraced the cushions, perspiring profusely. He detested the ocean.

In the first, the nouns and verbs are without exception of Anglo-Saxon or Old Norse origin. In the second, every noun and verb is of Latin origin. Except for the articles and the conjunctions, these could be two different languages, each with its distinctive sound, and each with its own tone. Past generations were taught that words of Latin and Greek derivation were "elegant" and "refined," and some of that prejudice remains. You should feel free to use whatever the language has to offer, but remember that your choices will affect your style.

None of us has the time to look up the derivation of every word we use, but we all have a built-in awareness of the distinction between these two verbal heritages. One is dominated by short, abrupt sounds that imply simplicity, roughness, and in some cases obscenity; the other is characterized by longer words, smoother sounds, and a sense of elegance or even pomposity.

Aside from the derivations, there are the subtle distinctions between short words and long ones, harsh ones and smooth ones, crude ones and those that sound elegant. As with nonfiction writing, you will want to choose an appropriate *level of usage*. If the story is being narrated by a city dweller who is streetwise, your choice of words is going to be dramatically different than it would be if you were writing a third-person story in a neutral style. And of course the diction of each line of dialogue should be appropriate to the character who is speaking.

Fiction is not written word by word, however. When the writing is going well, let it flow. The time to take a close look at your diction is when you read over the completed first draft. Decide what effect you want to achieve, and revise accordingly.

Syntax

Syntax means sentence structure, and it has as much to do with the stylistic effect as diction. If you count the words in the three alternative openings to "Acts of Violence," you will discover that the long-winded version uses 139 words while the terse version says essentially the same thing in 13 words! Since both of these use the same number of sentences, the difference lies in the type of syntax. The long version is filled with clauses and parenthetical phrases that keep going off in different directions. True, it gives a few more peripheral details, but none is essential to the plot. When used excessively, this style is called **overwriting** or **purple prose.** The real difference is in what is called the **voice.** The narration of these two passages appears to be coming from two quite different speakers. When you look at it that way, you can see that style, and particularly syntax, can be used as a way of defining the character of the narrator.

The same is true in the colloquial version, the one that sounds like someone speaking out loud. The character seems to be more informal, perhaps younger than the one who speaks in such a leisurely, ornate style.

Syntax also affects the pace. As we saw in the section on pacing in Chapter 19, long, complex sentences slow the reader down. This slower pace can have advantages as well as disadvantages. It may add a certain elegance and sophistication which in some stories could be entirely appropriate. Even when you are using the third person, those long sentences may serve as an echo of your protagonist's character.

Be careful, however, not to overdo it. If you extend this style beyond what you might hear from someone you know, you may inadvertently make the character seem like a satire of a pompous fool. My example, exaggerated for illustration, comes close to that. If you *intend* to satirize a wordy, slow-speaking character, fine. But it is not a happy experience to find that a story you wrote in a serious style is being read as a satire.

At the other extreme, short, simple sentences can add energy and vitality to your writing. They help when you want to provide dramatic impact. But they too can prove to be a disadvantage if pushed too far or used too unrelentingly. Pages of short, extremely simple sentences can become as monotonous as the relentless pounding of windshield wipers on a long drive.

The third version avoids that pitfall by having sentences and sentence fragments that vary in length. He sounds like a lively narrator. But when you write an entire story in an as-if-spoken style like that, be sure that the voice you are adopting accurately reflects the character you have in mind.

There are a few authors whose distinctive use of syntax is sustained in all their work. Henry James is a good example of a writer who fairly consistently uses long, complex sentences and does it with effective variations. William Faulkner varies his syntax, but he occasionally indulges in prodigiously long sentences. So does Thomas Wolfe. At the other end of the scale, Ernest Hemingway is known for his sparse, unadorned syntax, a style that has been widely imitated.

The length of sentences is only one of several variables in syntax. Internal structure can be quite different. Faulkner's lengthy sentences tend to be loose, occasionally rambling, even grammatically confused, while those of Thomas Wolfe are often rhythmic. Punctuation is another factor. Although most authors are fairly conventional, those who echo the spoken language may use more incomplete sentences and in some cases a greater use of dashes.

There is absolutely no need to adopt a distinctive pattern of syntax, but it is important to remember this: The best way to avoid stylistic monotony in both fiction and nonfiction, is to vary your sentence length.

Density

Density means compression. High density means that a great deal is implied about characterization and theme in a relatively compressed manner. Fiction can be fairly sophisticated and still lack density. "The Cat That Had the Power of Speech," for example, is fairly sophisticated because of its range of thematic suggestions, but it is a low-density story. It does not use a figurative language, and with the exception of the cat itself there is nothing symbolic. One can read it rapidly. "Obst Vw," on the other hand, is fairly dense. There are many important figures of speech and those two major symbols, the ball game and the broken cup, carry many overtones. You have to read that story more slowly and possibly more than once to draw the most from it.

Figurative language and symbolic details are commonly used to achieve density. Another way is to develop **ambivalences** and apparent contradictions. Remember that honest feelings of love can be mixed with resentment and that hostility is often fused with fascination.

A third approach is to deal with a cluster of related themes rather than a single concern. "Acts of Violence," for example, focuses almost entirely on the mother and so has less density than, say, "Sausage and Beer" and "Obst Vw," both of which deal with two major characters and touch significantly on the lives of others.

The degree of density is essentially a matter of subject matter and length. Some story ideas will come to you easily and don't merit being charged with real density or extended into a longer story. Others may develop complexities in characterization and thematic suggestion which require both density and greater length.

Occasionally, you may find that you have taken on too many threads so that the story begins to seem cluttered and confused. In such cases, you may want to back off and focus on a single aspect. The level of density may be reduced for the sake of clarity. In short, lack of density makes fiction seem slight; excessive density can make it turgid or, worse, confusing. Determine the level of density that is appropriate to your material.

The Balance of Narrative Modes

The third method of influencing your style in fiction is the balance of **narrative modes.** I am using *mode* in the special sense introduced at the beginning of the fiction section: dialogue, thoughts, action, description, and exposition.

A particular sentence may contain two or more modes, but usually one will dominate. Occasionally a scene or a whole story is presented almost entirely in one mode. This is not necessarily bad—it may produce just the style you want—but be aware of how you are affecting your style.

Depending heavily on *dialogue*, for example, may be entirely appropriate if that mode is used effectively to develop theme and characterization. If you glance quickly at any page of "Acts of Violence," you will see how much that story depends on dialogue. Dialogue not only tells us a great deal about the mother and her son, it moves the plot. "The Cat," on the other hand, has very little. This story is told more like an anecdote or a fable—from the outside. If you find yourself relying heavily on dialogue, be careful not to let the work become "talky." That usually means that you have used dialogue to reveal trivial information that could be more effectively covered in exposition.

When fiction is dominated by *thoughts*, the style may become heavy and slow. This occurs because there is a significant difference between thoughts and dialogue: When characters talk, they interact with others, but when they think, they are in isolation. An extended passage of thinking is an **interior monologue.** All too easily it begins to sound like exposition—an author's analysis. When a character thinks to himself, "I've been too selfish about this whole thing," the reader may have the feeling that what is being presented as thoughts is really just a poorly disguised form of exposition. Often you can correct this problem by presenting those thoughts through a more active mode like dialogue or action. It's far more effective to have a mother, say, digging desperately in a snowbank with her bare hands than to have her think, "Yes, when it comes to an emergency I guess I really do have more strength than the men in this pathetic family."

Action tends to enliven your style, but too much may make the story superficial. If the bulk of a story is given over to reporting what happened, there may be scant attention to characterization and theme. The opposite is true of *description* and *exposition*. They can provide valuable information, but they slow the action and add heaviness to your style.

The balance of modes is, like other aspects of style, something that comes naturally in first-draft writing. The time to examine it is when you have your first draft on paper. There is no inherent harm in favoring one mode over the others in a particular story, but try to judge as objectively as you can how this approach has affected your style. A few revisions at this early stage may make a major difference in the overall effect.

Tense

The matter of **tense** has become a controversy of sorts in the past decade. Traditionally, most short stories and novels were written in the past tense. Starting in the early 1980s, however, an increasing number of authors began using the present tense. Some people take this trend very seriously. An article in the *New York Times Book Review* attacked the practice on principle, and at least one editor still refuses to print present-tense stories regardless of worth. Still, the number of present-tense stories in print continues to increase.

The effect of the present tense on style is highly subjective and difficult to judge. For some, it seems illogical and therefore disruptive to imply that events are occurring at the time of the telling. The counterargument is that readers really don't respond to stories like these as if they were diary entries. Readers lose themselves in the action, and after the first paragraph the matter of tense is largely forgotten. Can you, for example, recall which two of the five stories in this volume are written in the past tense?

Present-tense enthusiasts often claim that fiction is livelier and more immediate in that tense. If this were so, however, past-tense fiction would not have dominated fiction for over a century.

There is one good technical reason for adopting the present tense. If a story in the past tense contains a number of flashbacks, the author must cue the reader with the past perfect each time: "She had been an excellent lawyer in her 30s," for example. Then the flashback itself, you remember, reverts to simple past tense. If the main part of the story is written in the present tense, however, the author can signal the start of those flashbacks simply by shifting to the past tense and staying there. Sharon Solwitz, for example, one of the three in this book writing in the present tense, is able to slide into that flashback about going to the ball game simply by shifting from the present tense to the past.

As you remember, that story is unusual for its use of the future tense to indicate flash-forwards. This technique is extremely rare because it breaks the reader's connection with the ongoing action and places him or her outside the story. As I pointed out, it is justified in this particular case as a device to keep the story from becoming melodramatic, but used carelessly it can spoil the illusion of reality.

It is odd that while the overall choice of present versus past tense is often highly debated, its effect on fiction is almost negligible. If you are uncertain which to use with a particular story, try an opening half page first in past tense and then in present. One will seem better than the other, and you can invent a good explanation later.

Varieties of Tone

While style has to do with the manner in which a work is written, a distinctly literary element, **tone** deals with the emotional element. In general usage, it can refer either to the emotion within the work itself or to the author's attitude toward that work.

The tone of a work itself can be described with adjectives like "exciting," "sad," "merry," "eerie," or "depressing." The tone adopted by the author might be "serious," "flippant," "ironic," "satiric," "sardonic." To see the difference, imagine an apparently sad story about a young man who is in despair over losing his girl written in a satiric way to suggest that he is taking it entirely too seriously. The *character* is downcast but the *reader* is amused. It is important when discussing tone to make it clear whether you are talking about the events in the story or the author's attitude toward the material.

What tone should you adopt? Your first inclination may be the best, but not always. If you are writing a story that is at least partially based on personal experience, it will seem natural to present it with the emotional response you still feel. Remember, though, that what you are writing is fiction, not a diary entry. If the episode you are using will seem a bit melodramatic or sentimental to readers, it may be wise to lighten up a bit.

This is exactly what Solwitz does from time to time in "Obst Vw." Her protagonist is seriously alienated from his father, but the author is careful not to let the story sound like a soap opera in which the son is driven to suicide by an insensitive father. The incident at the ball park is sad but amusing too—as he himself will later see when he writes an account of it in his college application. And when he and Rachel are alone at night, they do not fall into each other's arms like a couple in a grade-B movie, they discuss their respective problems in "the large wooden sandbox" behind the local preschool. Even in that agonizing scene when she has cut herself on the broken cup, there is something wryly comic about her act of letting the blood drip on the floor—a sad, futile, but offbeat attempt to make contact with her parents.

Irony and Satire

There are several types of irony, but they all involve a reversal of either meaning or of expectations.

Verbal irony is achieved when characters or authors say something that is intentionally different from what they really mean. In casual conversation we sometimes call this **sarcasm,** although sarcasm is generally hostile and critical. Irony can take the form of simple understatement, as when someone describes a hurricane as "quite a blow." Stronger irony can be a full reversal of meaning, as when the same character, while watching his house being washed away in the storm, says "Great day for a sail." We don't call him a crazy, because we know he is speaking ironically rather than literally.

Verbal irony in fiction occurs most often in dialogue. It suggests a character who is wry and given to understatement. As such, it is one more way dialogue can help define character. We see it in Rachel's dialogue as the two teenagers are listening to her parents shout at each other at the beginning of "Obst Vw":

> "Wait. This is the part about who was the first unfaithful one!…It's funny, really. It's high comedy."

It is also possible to use verbal irony in passages of exposition. As I have already pointed out, author's intrusion is not widely used in contemporary writing, but it is always possible to adopt a wry tone when one does step into a story.

Dramatic irony is similar except that the character making the statement does not understand that it is ironic. It's called "dramatic" because it is often associated with plays. The classic example is in Sophocles' play *Oedipus Rex.* When the messenger comes on stage saying "Good news!" those in the audience who know the story wince with the realization that the news will actually be catastrophic. For the others, the impact of the irony will be delayed until later in the play.

Dramatic irony could also be called *unconscious irony* in that the characters are not aware of it. We see it most often in comedy when characters say things that have a significance they don't yet understand. Another effective use is in first-person stories in which the narrators are not fully aware of how much they are revealing about themselves.

There is a good example of dramatic irony in "Three Hearts." While the two children are playing in the igloo, Bucky tells her sister to get some icicles. Sissy, the narrator, comments:

> The icicles are always my job. Bucky says Eskimo women do all the stuff like that. "Anything they can do without their husband's help, they do. They're brave," he told me once.

Neither of them, or course, is aware that this description of Eskimo women will apply to their mother. The statement turns out be ironic because it is prophetic without their awareness.

You can sustain an ironic tone by writing an entire story with a tone that is consistently different or even the opposite of your actual attitude. If doing that seems difficult, take another look at "The Cat That Had the Power of Speech." From the very first sentence the tone suggests that a talking cat is a perfectly ordinary occurrence.

> A cat came to the home of a couple in Piedmont, California, and said, "I want." It was a pretty cat, with round bright eyes and orange fur....

The author makes no special point or explanation about the cat's speaking ability but moves directly to a description. Even the characters behave as if this were a normal event. This total irony is similar to those jokes that start off with a dog ordering a drink at a bar.

Cosmic irony or *irony of fate* also involves a reversal, but in this case the reversal is in events rather than words. It refers to any outcome that is the opposite of normal expectations. One often hears it used in a careless way to describe anything that is unexpected. True irony, however, is stronger than that. It is ironic for a composer like Beethoven to lose his hearing or for an Olympic swimmer to drown in his own bathtub. Life occasionally provides ironic twists that are too blatant for fiction. Bad enough that America's first major toxic-waste disaster should occur in a place called the Love Canal, but what story writer would have dared call the culprit the Hooker Chemical Corporation?

Ironic reversals in fiction tend to be muted so that they don't become obtrusive. One occurs in "Sausage and Beer" in the visit with Uncle Theodore. Although one might expect that bizarre behavior would be the most disturbing aspect of such an experience, it is actually Theodore's one moment of lucidity that jolts the boy.

In "Three Hearts" it is ironic that while the mother appears at first to be the weakest and least functional of all the characters, she ends up to be the only strong one.

Satire is almost always rooted in irony. Essentially satire is exaggeration for the purpose of ridicule. The writer usually adopts a solemn or serious tone when in fact she or he is making fun of the topic at hand. Occasionally the technique is reversed and a serious subject is treated as if it were high comedy. Either way, there is always a tension established between the apparent tone and the true intent.

Many readers are introduced to simple satire through magazines such as *Mad* and *National Lampoon*. Neither these nor the satiric sketches one often sees on television are very subtle. In fiction there is a greater range and greater subtlety.

"The Cat That Had the Power of Speech" is satiric. In the previous chapter we considered various thematic statements that would apply to that story, and they were all forms of satire.

Satire is often the voice of protest. As such, it tends to sacrifice subtlety of character in order to stress the theme or message. You can see this in "The Cat." In a sense, strong satiric pieces are to mainstream literature what the political poster is to a painting.

If this approach interests you, keep in mind that there are two dangers in the writing of satire. The first is lack of focus. Decide in advance just what kind of person, institution, or tradition you wish to ridicule. Keep your satiric attack precise and detailed.

The other danger is a matter of excess. If your exaggeration becomes extreme, you will find the piece turning into slapstick. Such work may, like cartoons, be very funny, but also like cartoons quickly forgotten. If you want to study (and enjoy) some examples of light but durable satire, read some of the novels by J. P. Marquand or Peter DeVries. For heavier, more biting satire, try George Orwell's *Animal Farm*, a comic but ultimately savage attack on Soviet communism of the 1930s, or Joseph Heller's *Catch-22*, a funny yet bitter view of war.

Style and tone are enormously important, but don't let them distract you when you are starting a new work. You can suffer a serious case of writer's block if you stare at a blank piece of paper or computer screen worrying about your options. As I have urged before, let the story develop. Have faith in your original vision. Once you have a rough draft safely down on paper, then turn critic and examine these literary aspects.

Remember, too, that this chapter is largely a distillation of abstract concepts. For a real appreciation of what you can do with style and tone, you have to read a lot of fiction. This chapter will help you identify and evaluate those literary elements, but your growth and development over the years will come from fiction itself.

29

READING, WRITING, AND REVISING

Reading: why writers read regularly and how they read. Writing: estab-lishing a regimen. Revising: making it your major commitment. Seven crit-ical questions for writers and serious readers.

Studying a textbook gives you a language for discussing fiction in ways that are precise and helpful. It also helps you to start asking the right kinds of questions about fiction, both your own and that of others. And taking a course develops your critical skills as well as the all-important capacity to accept criticism with an open mind. Important as all that is, it's only the beginning. If you plan to develop your abilities, you will have to follow a three-part program on your own. It consists of reading, writing, and revising.

Why Writers Read

Here is a humbling question for all those who take creative writing courses, for those who teach them, and for those who write textbooks as well: How did literature flourish in all those centuries before creative writing courses were introduced in the 1940s? The answer is simple: Writers spent more time reading than writing. They learned from studying other writers. And they still do.

Courses and textbooks speed up the process, but they are no substitute for reading a lot of good fiction. Student writers who have read extensively before attending college have a distinct advantage. And graduates who con-tinue the reading habit in spite of other demands will continue to have an edge over those who don't.

The key to developing as a writer is as simple as it is important: Spend at least as much time reading as you do writing. Preferably more. Surprising as it may seem, there are many who do not. As a result, they don't expand their abilities, because they have cut themselves off from the greatest resource a writer has: published fiction.

Keep in mind, however, that the word *reading* refers to two quite different activities. Passive or recreational reading is the sort we do when we want to turn off and be entertained. It is a relatively inexpensive, legal pastime and has no dangerous side effects. We all need to do it from time to time, but we learn almost nothing from it. Active reading, on the other hand, is what writers do. It is analytical reading. When we read actively, we are not only making value judgments ("terrible character development," "slow pacing," "skillful irony," and the like), we are examining the work for interesting techniques ("a flashback within a flashback—interesting," "that house is taking on the significance of a character!"). We are also responding competitively ("I could do that scene better," "could I ever match that?").

Active reading may require finishing works you do not enjoy. You can't judge them accurately until you do. In such cases, the pleasure you derive stems from a writer's curiosity and a sense of personal growth rather than from the immediate experience.

For some, active reading means keeping a pencil and paper handy for notes—not just on plot development and names of characters but on interesting techniques. Many find it helpful to keep a literary journal. Written comments about what you have read will bring the work back into focus just as a photo album helps you recall past experiences. In the case of stories in literary journals, be sure to note where the stories were published so that you can refer to them later.

At first you may have a problem knowing where to find good fiction. Anthologies provide a good initial step. They will introduce you to new authors. Some anthologies cover the past few decades. Recent short stories can be found in two annual collections, *The Best American Short Stories* and *Prize Stories, the O. Henry Awards*. These are in almost every library and can be ordered through a bookstore. It is decidedly preferable to own your own copy so you can make marginal comments.

As for magazines, there are two large-circulation publications that include fiction in every issue: *The New Yorker* (usually one story every week) and *The Atlantic*, a monthly. There are also about 100 little magazines, many of them quarterlies, which publish stories along with poems, articles, and reviews. Some, like *The North American Review* and *Story*, specialize in fiction. More titles are listed in Appendix B.

How do you find these publications? Start by reading whichever magazines are available in your library. Then select one or two and subscribe. A subscription costs less than many compact discs. When you have your own copy of the magazine, you will be sure to read it, will feel free to mark it up, and will have it for future reference.

Writers of fiction are even more isolated than poets. They do not give readings as often, and they have difficulty finding individuals who are willing to read and criticize their work. Quarterlies and little magazines provide the best way for writers to stay in touch with others in their field.

If you decide to invest time and energy in writing fiction, make sure you invest at least as much time in reading what others have written. If you value fiction, you will not find the cost of books and subscriptions excessive. Your development as a writer will depend in large measure on how active and perceptive you are as a reader.

A Regimen for Writing

One great advantage of taking a creative writing course is that it provides a regimen of regular deadlines. We may hate them at the time, but they serve their purpose. The writing gets done. Sometimes the work is good, sometimes it is rushed and not so good, and always we feel harried; but that kind of pressure is surprisingly effective in improving abilities.

It is almost impossible to maintain a sufficient pace of writing at college if you are not taking a writing course. Some students rise early and try to put time in before turning to regular assignments; others reserve the late-night hours for creative work. Still, it takes considerable effort to keep the writing time from getting squeezed—particularly toward the end of the semester.

One way to counter this problem is to form your own support group. If you meet with three or four other writers, you can give each other encouragement as well as deadlines.

Once you graduate, you face an even greater challenge. Everyone knows that when it comes to weight loss or body building a regular program is necessary, but some forget that the same applies to writing. Those who wait for the perfect fictional idea to spring from the heavens forget that much of our progress as writers of fiction is a matter of trial and error. To put it bluntly, we learn nothing when we write nothing. Busy people can't wait for spare time to develop; they have to create it.

Under these circumstances it is all the more important to join a writers' group or start one of your own. All it takes is three individuals who are serious about their work. Five is ideal, and eight is about maximum. There is solid benefit from receiving criticism of your own work, and the deadlines serve as great motivation.

Be careful, however, to consider whether the other members are working with material that is like yours in intent if not in style. Some so-called writers' clubs are more social than literary. Or they may have more commercial writers than you find helpful. The best way to judge is to attend one or two meetings on a provisional basis before committing yourself.

If you can't find or form a group, you may have to impose a schedule on yourself, such as a completed story every two weeks. Those who are at the stage of submitting work for publication often use contest dates to prod them into intense activity. Due dates are listed in *Poets and Writers*, a highly useful publication. The addresses of this and other helpful journals are listed in Appendix B, "Resources for Writers."

Rewriting and More Rewriting

As I have pointed out, those who have just started to write fiction usually spend very little time on revisions. It is not that they are so sure of themselves, it is simply a matter of not knowing how to evaluate what they have done. What is there on the page seems fine.

One of the functions of this textbook is to make such writers less satisfied with their first or even second draft. As one develops, the time one spends on revisions usually becomes greater and greater. Unfortunately, doing so is not always possible when one is taking a course. An academic term is relatively short, and the effectiveness of a course requires a high output of new material. Revision work cannot in most cases be given as much credit as new writing.

When you are finished with your writing courses, however, you can and should double the time you spend revising. You may get the feeling that writing fiction is like eating the dessert first, the initial draft being the fun part. Most professional writers spend from four to five times as much time on the revisions than on the first draft.

A new draft is not just tinkering. First read your manuscript through to the end with as much objectivity as you can. Those who work with a computer sometimes prefer to do this review on a printed copy to avoid spending time making one-word changes at this stage. Mark in the margins which paragraphs need expanding or cutting. Decide where you need new material. Then follow though on all the notations. The result constitutes a "new draft." It may take several such drafts spaced out over a period of days or even weeks before a story is ready for fine tuning. Those little revisions in phrasing should be postponed until you have what you consider the best possible draft.

Seven Critical Questions

The following seven critical questions can be used after you have reread a draft of your own story or work by someone else. They can also be used to stimulate discussion in a class or informal writers' group. Although they echo the topics raised in the fiction section of this textbook, they are arranged in an order that is most conducive to group discussion. Characterization is a good starting point, and more abstract concerns like theme and style are best reserved until later.

Not every question will be appropriate for every story, but as a whole these seven represent the kind of concerns every writer should consider about a work in progress. If you review the major headings often, they will become internalized. You will find yourself reading critically rather than passively.

Feel free to reproduce this list without written permission as long as credit is given and copies are not sold for profit.

1. *Are the primary characters convincing or, in the case of satire, effective?* If the story develops characters fully, do you have the sense of having actually met them? How much do you know about them? If the story is satiric, the characters are probably not intended to be realistic in the same way, but are they effective? It's essential that the reader knows what they represent.

When discussing a fictional character in a class or an informal group, be careful not to go off into personal preferences as if this were a real person. Keep the focus on characterization—the ways in which character is presented in the story. How much do you find out about this character and how are you informed?

2. *Is the viewpoint effective?* Is it consistent? Would the work be improved if it were presented through the eyes of a different character?

3. *Is the structure effective?* Just how many scenes does it have? Are additional scenes needed? Or is it cluttered? If so, can certain scenes be cut or combined? Are the transitions effective? If there are flashbacks, is it clear where they begin and end? Is there a scene that seems to drag?

4. *Is there enough tension to keep the story moving?* If not, is it because there is not enough interaction between characters? Does it need more action? If, on the other hand, it is "action-packed," does all that drama bury subtlety of theme and characterization?

5. *Is the setting effective?* Is it interesting? Does it contribute to the theme of the story? If there is only one setting, would a second one help to provide variety and contrast?

6. *Is the theme fresh and insightful?* What exactly is the story suggesting? How would you sum it up in a single, complete sentence? Is it a truism or some insight you hadn't considered in quite this way before?

7. *Are the style and tone effective?* Is the style too elaborate or formal for the material? Or is it so sparse that it is tiresome to read? Would variation in sentence length help? Is there an effective balance of modes? Is it too talky or too

packed with action? Or does too much exposition or description slow it down? Is it melodramatic or sentimental? If so, is poor characterization at fault? If it is a satire, is it clear as to what is being satirized?

I have stressed the fact that writers should be regular readers of published work and tireless rewriters of their own work. This list of seven key questions should serve as a guide in both areas.

Part Three

The Writing of Drama

30

THEATER

A Dramatic Art

The appeal of live performance. The unique aspects of drama: its dramatic impact, visual appeal, auditory aspects, physical production, continuous action, a spectator art. Getting started: selecting a concept, primary characters, a plot outline.

The transition from writing fiction to writing plays is not as great as one might think. Both depend heavily on plot. Both reveal character through action and dialogue. Both are presented with a distinctive tone and are unified with some kind of central concern or theme.

The primary difference, however, is that a play is a live performance. It is produced physically in front of an audience and is performed by actors. This is theater's greatest asset and explains why it is flourishing today in spite of competition with film and television.

Ever since the first "talking movie," critics have predicted the end of legitimate theater. But not even the competition of television and then video have stopped the constant growth of new theaters. Many middle-sized cities have resident companies, and these are augmented with university theater programs of high quality.

Legitimate theater—live performance on a stage—continues to be popular in part *because* of television, not in spite of it. The economics of mass-audience television drama requires all but a few specially funded programs to reach for the widest possible audience. As a result, there is a certain uniformity in sitcom and action-drama scripts. Plotting, characterization, and theme are reduced to the simplest level and repeated with ritualistic regularity. Those who prefer subtlety and originality remain hungry for legitimate theater.

Every **genre** has its special attributes—qualities that distinguish it fundamentally from other forms of writing. It is a mistake to think of a play as fiction acted out on the stage or as a poem performed or as a low-budget version of film. It is none of these things. Before you begin writing your first play script, consider carefully what the special characteristics of the genre are.

The Unique Aspects of Drama

There are six aspects of drama that are unique to this genre. You will be able to find plays that do not contain all six just as you can find some poems that make little use of rhythm and some stories without dialogue. But they are rare. Most playwrights value all six as the prime assets of the genre.

• First, **drama** is by definition a *dramatic art.* That is, it generally has an emotional impact or force. In the case of comedy, we call it vitality. This is not just a tradition; it is a natural aspect of an art form that requires an audience to give its undivided attention for two-and-a-half to three hours.

This impact is often established early in a play with a **dramatic question** that seizes the attention of the audience long before the theme becomes evident. Dramatic questions are usually blunt and simple: Is this stranger a threat? Whom are they waiting for? Why do these characters hate each other? In most cases, these initial questions develop into specific conflicts. Although the need for tension like this is not as strong in very short plays and in comedies, it is usually greater in drama than in either fiction or poetry.

As in fiction, **irony** and **satire** often add to the dramatic aspect of a play. Still another device is the use of *shock.* Unusual or violent situations can explode when the audience least expects them.

Dramatic impact is hard to sustain, however. For this reason, most plays work up to a series of peaks, allowing the emotions of the audience to rest in between. This system of rising and falling action does not follow any prescribed pattern and is often intuitive on the part of the playwright, just as it is in the writing of short stories. But the need for such structure tends to make drama more sharply divided into scenes and acts—divisions that help to control the dramatic impact.

• Second, drama is a *visual art.* Action on the stage is usually a significant and organic part of the whole production. In most cases, the movement of characters on the stage is as important as the lines themselves.

The visual concern extends beyond the characters. The set itself is often an important part of the production. Sophisticated lighting boards can convert the set from a static backdrop to a dynamic factor in developing the modes of each scene. The addition of projected images and even movie sequences—experiments in mixed media—offers one more appeal to the visual aspect of theater.

• Third, drama is an *auditory art.* It appeals to the ear. Except for stage directions, every word is **dialogue** and is intended to be spoken out loud. The sound of those lines becomes very important. In some respects, this element brings playwrights closer to poets than to writers of fiction. Playwrights often read their lines out loud or have others read them, listening to the composition rather than studying it on the page.

This special attention to the sound of language applies as much to plays that are in the tradition of realism as to those that create the dreamlike distortions of nonrealistic drama. Not only are the sounds important, but the space between the lines can be utilized. In theater, silence can have as much dramatic impact as a shout.

- Fourth, drama is a *physically produced art*. This is sometimes difficult to remember for those who have been writing fiction. Since sets have to be constructed with wood and nails, there is not the freedom to shift from scene to scene the way one can in a short story. Scriptwriters should keep in mind just what kinds of demands they are placing on set designers and stage crews.

At first this requirement may seem like a limitation, but there are compensating assets. Playwrights have an intense, almost personal contact with their audiences that is entirely different from the detached connection fiction writers have with their readers. Also the constraints of the stage often stimulate the imagination. For many playwrights these aspects outweigh any disadvantage.

- Fifth, drama is a *continuous art*. Members of the audience, unlike readers of fiction or poetry, must receive the play at whatever pace the playwright sets. They cannot linger on a sage observation or a moving episode. They cannot turn back a page or review an earlier scene. If you are shifting from writing fiction to drama, you can be more blatant with your themes and can, as we will see, make use of refrains to highlight key phrases.

As you become involved in play writing, you will find that the flow of drama is an aspect you can utilize. There is a momentum to a play that you can control. With practice you can make one portion of a scene move rapidly and another more slowly. Fiction writers can't maintain quite this kind of control over their readers.

- Finally, and closely connected, is the fact that drama is a *spectator art*. Even more than with spectator sports, audience reaction is important. Poets are relatively far removed from such concerns. It is rare indeed for poets to change lines of their verse because of critical review or poor public response. Novelists are slightly more susceptible to "audience" reaction. Their circle of readers is potentially larger than a poet's, and authors tend to be aware of this. Many novelists will make fairly extensive revisions on the basis of their editors' suggestions. Usually, however, the publication of the work marks the end of the revision process.

Not so with plays. Playwrights often revise when their work is in rehearsal and after the opening-night reviews, and even later if changes seem necessary. They frequently base their revisions on audience reaction—those awful moments when it laughs at the wrong moment or squirms with boredom.

This does not mean that dramatists are slaves to the reactions of audiences and critics. In most cases playwrights have a basic conception of the work which remains unalterable. But there is a direct and dynamic relationship between playwrights and their audiences. For many, this is one of the real pleasures in writing for the legitimate stage.

Getting Started

Poems frequently begin with an image; stories usually begin with a character in a situation. Plays more often begin with what is called a **concept.**

A dramatic concept includes a basic situation, some type of conflict or struggle, and an outcome, all in capsule form. You can, of course, start a play as tentatively as you might begin a story, hoping to shape and develop the plot as you work through the first draft. But such an approach is generally not as successful in play writing because so much depends on the whole dramatic structure.

Plays, like stories, often evolve from personal experience, but the need to create a dramatic situation with conflict or struggle between two or more people often requires transformation of the original episode from the start. Although this is a risky generalization, it is probably fair to say that plays tend to be less closely tied to direct personal experience than are stories. In any case, you should feel free to explore newspaper stories and accounts told to you about individuals you have not met, as long as the situation is familiar enough for you to make it appear authentic.

If you keep a literary journal, jot down a number of possible concepts. If one seems to take shape in your mind, add the names and a brief description of one or two characters. Actually giving these characters names at the outset will help stimulate your imagination.

Next, try some sample dialogue. It helps if you can begin to hear two characters interact. See if you can create a little scene that at least roughly contributes to the concept you have in mind. Read the lines out loud. Imagine actors (male or female) saying those lines. Close your eyes and visualize the scene.

If you have done all this and you still feel that the concept has potential, begin to block out the action. That is, develop an outline in which each brief sequence of events is described in a telegraphic phrase or sentence. Such an outline might start this way:

1. Morning: Tammy and Max are in a frenzy to clean up the apartment, urging each other to hurry. Tension in the air.
2. Doorbell rings. Mrs. Colton enters. Looks around, disapproving. Tammy and Max apologize for remaining mess.
3. Tammy excuses herself. She must get to work. Exits.

4. Mrs. Colton launches a tirade against Tammy. Max continues to pick up the place, defending Tammy as best he can.

Since this is for your own benefit, adopt whatever form seems natural to you. Most playwrights, however, find some kind of outline helpful because drama, much more than fiction, is constructed in specific **scenes.**

Even if you are writing a one-act play with a single set—a good pattern to start with—you will want to think in terms of scenes. I will have more to say about this in the chapter on plot (Chapter 32), but from a playwright's point of view a **scene** is not one of those major divisions of an act that may be printed in the script; it is a far shorter unit marked by a character entering or leaving the stage. The little outline above, for example, contains three distinct scenes.

Some short plays have been written without these subtle yet important divisions, but they are rare. *Hello Out There*, which is presented as the next chapter, uses eight such scenes. After your initial reading, go over the script and mark these divisions. You will see how they provide structure for the play.

As for the form of the script, follow the pattern used by the plays included in this volume. At first it may seem monotonous to repeat the name of each speaker, but it is the customary practice, one that actors depend on in rehearsal. If you are working with a computer, you may be able to program the name of each major character as a macro so that it will appear on the left margin with a simple two-stroke command.

Stage directions are written in italics. Italics in manuscript are still indicated by underlining even if your computer is capable of producing special type. Underlining is a traditional signal to the printer. Place directions in parentheses when they are short. It is helpful to include names of characters after the title, listing them in order of appearance.

There are three complete plays in this section. The first is serious, **realistic,** and highly dramatic. The second is dreamlike, initially comic, but serious in theme. The third is a **farcical, satiric** fantasy. These three short works are markedly different in tone and treatment and are a good indication of what an enormous latitude you have in tone and treatment.

To get started, then, begin with a good concept—not just an idea, but a situation with potential conflict between two or more characters. It may take several complete sentences to describe. Then develop your characters, fleshing them out with notes about their backgrounds and personalities. These are for your own benefit. Next, block out the action by outlining a plot scene by scene.

As you write, keep in mind that your script is more than something to be read on the page. You are creating a live performance for a live audience. Make their experience a memorable one.

31

A PLAY

by William Saroyan

Hello Out There

for George Bernard Shaw

Characters

A YOUNG MAN
A GIRL
A MAN
TWO OTHER MEN
A WOMAN

Scene

There is a fellow in a small-town prison cell, tapping slowly on the floor with a spoon. After tapping a minute, as if he were trying to telegraph words, he gets up and begins walking around the cell. At last he stops, stands at the center of the cell, and doesn't move for a long time. He feels his head, as if it were wounded. Then he looks around. Then he calls out dramatically, kidding the world.

YOUNG MAN: Hello—out there! (*Pause.*) Hello—out there! Hello—out there! (*Long pause.*) Nobody out there. (*Still more dramatically, but more comically, too.*) Hello—out there! Hello—out there!

A GIRL'S VOICE is heard, very sweet and soft.

THE VOICE: Hello.
YOUNG MAN: Hello—out there.
THE VOICE: Hello.
YOUNG MAN: Is that you, Katey?

THE VOICE: No—this here is Emily.

YOUNG MAN: Who? (*Swiftly.*) Hello out there.

THE VOICE: Emily.

YOUNG MAN: Emily who? I don't know anybody named Emily. Are you that girl I met at Sam's in Salinas about three years ago?

THE VOICE: No—I'm the girl who cooks here. I'm the cook. I've never been in Salinas. I don't even know where it is.

YOUNG MAN: Hello out there. You say you cook here?

THE VOICE: Yes.

YOUNG MAN: Well, why don't you study up and learn to cook? How come I don't get no jello or anything good?

THE VOICE: I just cook what they tell me to. (*Pause.*) You lonesome?

YOUNG MAN: Lonesome as a coyote. Hear me hollering? Hello out there!

THE VOICE: Who you hollering to?

YOUNG MAN: Well—nobody, I guess. I been trying to think of somebody to write a letter to, but I can't think of anybody.

THE VOICE: What about Katey?

YOUNG MAN: I don't know anybody named Katey.

THE VOICE: Then why did you say, Is that you Katey?

YOUNG MAN: Katey's a good name. I always did like a name like Katey. I never *knew* anybody named Katey, though.

THE VOICE: *I* did.

YOUNG MAN: Yeah? What was she like? Tall girl, or little one?

THE VOICE: Kind of medium.

YOUNG MAN: Hello out there. What sort of a looking girl are *you*?

THE VOICE: Oh, I don't know.

YOUNG MAN: Didn't anybody ever tell you? Didn't anybody ever talk to you that way?

THE VOICE: What way?

YOUNG MAN: You know. Didn't they?

THE VOICE: No, they didn't.

YOUNG MAN: Ah, the fools—they should have. I can tell from your voice you're O.K.

THE VOICE: Maybe I am and maybe I ain't.

YOUNG MAN: I never missed yet.

THE VOICE: Yeah, I know. That's why you're in jail.

YOUNG MAN: The whole thing was a mistake.

THE VOICE: They claim it was rape.

YOUNG MAN: No—it wasn't.

THE VOICE: That's what they claim it was.

YOUNG MAN: They're a lot of fools.

THE VOICE: Well, you sure are in trouble. Are you scared?

YOUNG MAN: Scared to death. (*Suddenly.*) Hello out there!

THE VOICE: What do you keep saying that for all the time?

YOUNG MAN: I'm lonesome. I'm as lonesome as a coyote. (*A long one.*) Hello—out there!

THE GIRL appears, over to one side. She is a plain girl in plain clothes.

THE GIRL: I'm kind of lonesome, too.

YOUNG MAN (*turning and looking at her*): Hey—No fooling? Are you?

THE GIRL: Yeah—I'm almost as lonesome as a coyote myself.

YOUNG MAN: Who *you* lonesome for?

THE GIRL: I don't know.

YOUNG MAN: It's the same with me. The minute they put you in a place like this you remember all the girls you ever knew, and all the girls you didn't get to know, and it sure gets lonesome.

THE GIRL: I bet it does.

YOUNG MAN: Ah, it's awful. (*Pause.*) You're a pretty kid, you know that?

THE GIRL: You're just talking.

YOUNG MAN: No, I'm not just talking—you *are* pretty. Any fool could see that. You're just about the prettiest kid in the whole world.

THE GIRL: I'm not—and you know it.

YOUNG MAN: No—you are. I never saw anyone prettier in all my born days, in all my travels. I knew Texas would bring me luck.

THE GIRL: Luck? You're in jail, aren't you? You've got a whole gang of people all worked up, haven't you?

YOUNG MAN: Ah, that's nothing. I'll get out of this.

THE GIRL: Maybe.

YOUNG MAN: No, I'll be all right—*now.*

THE GIRL: What do you mean—now?

YOUNG MAN: I mean after seeing you. I got something now. You know for a while there I didn't care one way or another. Tired. (*Pause.*) Tired of trying for the best all the time and never getting it. (*Suddenly.*) Hello out there!

THE GIRL: Who you calling now?

YOUNG MAN: You.

THE GIRL: Why, I'm right here.

YOUNG MAN: I know. (*Calling.*) Hello out there!

THE GIRL: Hello.

YOUNG MAN: Ah, you're sweet. (*Pause.*) I'm going to marry *you.* I'm going away with *you.* I'm going to take you to San Francisco or some place like that. I *am*, now. I'm going to win myself some real money, too. I'm going to study 'em real careful and pick myself some winners, and we're going to have a lot of money.

THE GIRL: Yeah?

YOUNG MAN: Yeah. Tell me your name and all that stuff.

THE GIRL: Emily.

YOUNG MAN: I know that. What's the rest of it? Where were you born? Come on, tell me the whole thing.

THE GIRL: Emily Smith.

YOUNG MAN: Honest to God?

THE GIRL: Honest. That's my name—Emily Smith.

YOUNG MAN: Ah, you're the sweetest girl in the whole world.

THE GIRL: Why?

YOUNG MAN: I don't know why, but you are, that's all. Where were you born?

THE GIRL: Matador, Texas.

YOUNG MAN: Where's that?

THE GIRL: Right here.

YOUNG MAN: Is this Matador, Texas?

THE GIRL: Yeah, it's Matador. They brought you here from Wheeling.

YOUNG MAN: Is that where I was—Wheeling?

THE GIRL: Didn't you even know what town you were in?

YOUNG MAN: All towns are alike. You don't go up and ask somebody what town you're in. It doesn't make any difference. How far away is Wheeling?

THE GIRL: Sixteen or seventeen miles. Didn't you know they moved you?

YOUNG MAN: How could I know, when I was out—cold? Somebody hit me over the head with a lead pipe or something. What'd they hit me for?

THE GIRL: Rape—that's what they *said*.

YOUNG MAN: Ah, that's a lie. (*Amazed, almost to himself.*) She wanted me to give her money.

THE GIRL: Money?

YOUNG MAN: Yeah, if I'd have known she was a woman like that—well, by God, I'd have gone on down the street and stretched out in a park somewhere and gone to sleep.

THE GIRL: Is that what she wanted—money?

YOUNG MAN: Yeah. A fellow like me hopping freights all over the country, trying to break his bad luck, going from one poor little town to another, trying to get in on something good somewhere, and she asks for money. I thought she was lonesome. She *said* she was.

THE GIRL: Maybe she was.

YOUNG MAN: She was *something*.

THE GIRL: I guess I'd never see you, if it didn't happen, though.

YOUNG MAN: Oh, I don't know—maybe I'd just mosey along this way and see you in this town somewhere. I'd recognize you, too.

THE GIRL: Recognize me?

YOUNG MAN: Sure, I'd recognize you the minute I laid eyes on you.

THE GIRL: Well, who would I be?

YOUNG MAN: Mine, that's who.

THE GIRL: Honest?

YOUNG MAN: Honest to God.

THE GIRL: You just say that because you're in jail.

YOUNG MAN: No, I mean it. You just pack up and wait for me. We'll high-roll the hell out of here to Frisco.

THE GIRL: You're just lonesome.

YOUNG MAN: I been lonesome all my life—there's no cure for that—but you and me—we can have a lot of fun hanging around together. You'll bring me luck. I know it.

THE GIRL: What are you looking for luck for all the time?

YOUNG MAN: I'm a gambler. I don't work. I've *got* to have luck, or I'm a bum. I haven't had any decent luck in years. Two whole years now—one place to another. Bad luck all the time. That's why I got in trouble back there in Wheeling too. That was no accident. That was my bad luck following me around. So here I am, with my head half busted. I guess it was her old man that did it.

THE GIRL: You mean her father?

YOUNG MAN: No, her husband. If I had an old lady like that, I'd throw her out.

THE GIRL: Do you think you'll have better luck, if I go with you?

YOUNG MAN: It's a cinch. I'm a good handicapper. All I need is somebody good like you with me. It's no good always walking around in the streets for anything that might be there at the time. You got to have somebody staying with you all the time—through winters when it's cold, and springtime when it's pretty, and summertime when it's nice and hot and you can go swimming—through *all* the times—rain and snow and all the different kinds of weather a man's got to go through before he dies. You got to have somebody who's right. Somebody who knows you, from away back. You got to have somebody who even knows you're wrong but likes you just the same. I know I'm wrong, but I just don't want anything the hard way, working like a dog, or the *easy* way, working like a dog—working's the hard way and the easy way both. All I got to do is beat the price, always—and then, I don't feel lousy and don't hate anybody. If you go along with me, I'll be the finest guy anybody ever saw. I won't be wrong any more. You know when you get enough of that money, you *can't* be wrong any more—you're right because the money says so. I'll have a lot of money and you'll be just about the prettiest, most wonderful kid in the whole world. I'll be proud walking around Frisco with you on my arm and people turning around to look at us.

THE GIRL: Do you think they will?

YOUNG MAN: Sure they will. When I get back in some decent clothes, and you're on my arm—well, Katey, they'll turn around and look, and they'll see something, too.

THE GIRL: Katey?

YOUNG MAN: Yeah—that's your name from now on. You're the first girl I ever called Katey. I've been saving it for you O.K.?

THE GIRL: O.K.

YOUNG MAN: How long have I been here?

THE GIRL: Since last night. You didn't wake up until late this morning, though.

YOUNG MAN: What time is it now? About nine?

THE GIRL: About ten.

YOUNG MAN: Have you got the key to this lousy cell?

THE GIRL: No. They don't let me fool with any keys.

YOUNG MAN: Well, can you get it?

THE GIRL: No.

YOUNG MAN: Can you *try*?

THE GIRL: They wouldn't let me get near any keys. I cook for this jail, when they've got somebody in it. I clean up and things like that.

YOUNG MAN: Well, I want to get out of here. Don't you know the guy that runs this joint?

THE GIRL: I know him, but he wouldn't let you out. They were talking of taking you to another jail in another town.

YOUNG MAN: Yeah? Why?

THE GIRL: Because they're afraid.

YOUNG MAN: What are they afraid of?

THE GIRL: They're afraid these people from Wheeling will come over in the middle of the night and break in.

YOUNG MAN: Yeah? What do they want to do that for?

THE GIRL: Don't *you* know what they want to do it for?

YOUNG MAN: Yeah, I know all right.

THE GIRL: Are you scared?

YOUNG MAN: Sure I'm scared. Nothing scares a man more than ignorance. You can argue with people who ain't fools, but you can't argue with fools— they just go to work and do what they're set on doing. Get me out of here.

THE GIRL: How?

YOUNG MAN: Well, go get the guy with the key, and let me talk to him.

THE GIRL: He's gone home. Everybody's gone home.

YOUNG MAN: You mean I'm in this little jail all alone?

THE GIRL: Well—yeah—except me.

YOUNG MAN: Well, what's the big idea—doesn't anybody stay here all the time?

THE GIRL: No, they go home every night. I clean up and then I go, too. I hung around tonight.

YOUNG MAN: What made you do that?

THE GIRL: I wanted to talk to you.

YOUNG MAN: Honest? What did you want to talk about?

THE GIRL: Oh, I don't know. I took care of you last night. You were talking in your sleep. You liked me, too. I didn't think you'd like me when you woke up, though.

YOUNG MAN: Yeah? Why not?

THE GIRL: I don't know.

YOUNG MAN: Yeah? Well, you're wonderful, see?

THE GIRL: Nobody ever talked to me that way. All the fellows in town—
    (*Pause.*)

YOUNG MAN: What about 'em? (*Pause.*) Well, what about 'em? Come on—tell
    me.

THE GIRL: They laugh at me.

YOUNG MAN: Laugh at *you*? They're fools. What do they know about any-
    thing? You go get your things and come back here. I'll take you with me
    to Frisco. How old are you?

THE GIRL: Oh, I'm of age.

YOUNG MAN: How old are you?—Don't lie to me! Sixteen?

THE GIRL: I'm seventeen.

YOUNG MAN: Well, bring your father and mother. We'll get married before we
    go.

THE GIRL: They wouldn't let me go.

YOUNG MAN: Why not?

THE GIRL: I don't know, but they wouldn't. I know they wouldn't.

YOUNG MAN: You go tell your father not to be a fool, see? What is he, a farmer?

THE GIRL: No—nothing. He gets a little relief from the government because
    he's supposed to be hurt or something—his side hurts, he says. I don't
    know what it is.

YOUNG MAN: Ah, he's a liar. Well, I'm taking you with me, see?

THE GIRL: He takes the money I earn, too.

YOUNG MAN: He's got no right to do that.

THE GIRL: I know it, but he does it.

YOUNG MAN (*almost to himself*): This world stinks. You shouldn't have been
    born in this town, anyway, and you shouldn't have had a man like that
    for a father, either.

THE GIRL: Sometimes I feel sorry for him.

YOUNG MAN: Never mind feeling sorry for him. (*Pointing a finger.*) I'm going
    to talk to your father some day. I've got a few things to tell that guy.

THE GIRL: I know you have.

YOUNG MAN (*suddenly*): Hello—out there! See if you can get that fellow with
    the keys to come down and let me out.

THE GIRL: Oh, I couldn't.

YOUNG MAN: Why not?

THE GIRL: I'm nobody here—they give me fifty cents every day I work.

YOUNG MAN: How much?

THE GIRL: Fifty cents.

YOUNG MAN (*to the world*): You see? They ought to pay money to *look* at you.
    To breathe the *air* you breathe. I don't know. Sometimes I figure it never
    is going to make sense. Hello—out there! I'm scared. You try to get me
    out of here. I'm scared them fools are going to come here from Wheeling
    and go crazy, thinking they're heroes. Get me out of here, Katey.

THE GIRL: I don't know what to do. Maybe I could break the door down.

YOUNG MAN: No, you couldn't do that. Is there a hammer out there or anything?

THE GIRL: Only a broom. Maybe they've locked the broom up, too.

YOUNG MAN: Go see if you can find anything.

THE GIRL: All right. (*She goes.*)

YOUNG MAN: Hello—out there! Hello—out there! (*Pause.*) Hello—out there! Hello—out there! (*Pause.*) Putting me in jail. (*With contempt.*) Rape! Rape? *They* rape everything good that was ever born. His side hurts. They laugh at her. Fifty cents a day. Little punk people. Hurting the only good thing that ever came their way. (*Suddenly.*) Hello—out there!

THE GIRL (*returning*): There isn't a thing out there. They've locked everything up for the night.

YOUNG MAN: Any cigarettes?

THE GIRL: Everything's locked up—all the drawers of the desk, all the closet doors—everything.

YOUNG MAN: I ought to have a cigarette.

THE GIRL: I could get you a package maybe, somewhere. I guess the drug store's open. It's about a mile.

YOUNG MAN: A mile? I don't want to be alone that long.

THE GIRL: I could run all the way, and all the way back.

YOUNG MAN: You're the sweetest girl that ever lived.

THE GIRL: What kind do you want?

YOUNG MAN: Oh, any kind—Chesterfields or Camels or Lucky Strikes—any kind at all.

THE GIRL: I'll go get a package. (*She turns to go.*)

YOUNG MAN: What about the money?

THE GIRL: I've got some money. I've got a quarter I been saving. I'll run all the way. (*She is about to go.*)

YOUNG MAN: Come here.

THE GIRL (*going to him*): What?

YOUNG MAN: Give me your hand. (*He takes her hand and looks at it, smiling. He lifts it and kisses it.*) I'm scared to death.

THE GIRL: I am, too.

YOUNG MAN: I'm not lying—I don't care what happens to me, but I'm scared nobody will ever come out here to this Godforsaken broken-down town and find you. I'm scared you'll get used to it and not mind. I'm scared you'll never get to Frisco and have 'em all turning around to look at you. Listen—go get me a gun, because if they come, I'll kill 'em! They don't understand. Get me a gun!

THE GIRL: I could get my father's gun. I know where he hides it.

YOUNG MAN: Go get it. Never mind the cigarettes. Run all the way. (*Pause, smiling but seriously.*) Hello, Katey.

THE GIRL: Hello. What's *your* name?

YOUNG MAN: Photo-Finish is what they *call* me. My races are always photo-finish races. You don't know what that means, but it means they're very close. So close the only way they can tell which horse wins is to look at a photograph after the race is over. Well, every race I bet turns out to be a photo-finish race, and my horse never wins. It's my bad luck, all the time. That's why they call me Photo-Finish. Say it before you go.

THE GIRL: Photo-Finish.

YOUNG MAN: Come here. (THE GIRL *moves close and he kisses her.*) Now, hurry. Run all the way.

THE GIRL: I'll run. (THE GIRL *turns and runs. The* YOUNG MAN *stands at the center of the cell a long time.* THE GIRL *comes running back in. Almost crying.*) I'm afraid. I'm afraid I won't see you again. If I come back and you're not here, I—

YOUNG MAN: Hello—out there!

THE GIRL: It's so lonely in this town. Nothing here but the lonesome wind all the time, lifting the dirt and blowing out to the prairie. I'll stay *here*. I won't *let* them take you away.

YOUNG MAN: Listen, Katey. Do what I tell you. Go get that gun and come back. Maybe they won't come tonight. Maybe they won't come at all. I'll hide the gun. When they let me out you can take it back and put it where you found it. And then we'll go away. But if they come, I'll kill 'em! Now, hurry—

THE GIRL: All right. (*Pause.*) I want to tell you something.

YOUNG MAN: O.K.

THE GIRL (*very softly*): If you're not here when I come back, well, I'll have the gun and I'll know what to do with it.

YOUNG MAN: You know how to handle a gun?

THE GIRL: I know how.

YOUNG MAN: Don't be a fool. (*Takes off his shoe, brings out some currency.*) Don't be a fool, see? Here's some money. Eighty dollars. Take it and go to Frisco. Look around and find somebody. Find somebody alive and halfway human, see? Promise me—if I'm not here when you come back, just throw the gun away and get the hell to Frisco. Look around and find somebody.

THE GIRL: I don't *want* to find anybody.

YOUNG MAN (*swiftly, desperately*): Listen, if I'm not here when you come back, how do you know I haven't gotten away? Now, do what I tell you. I'll meet you in Frisco. I've got a couple of dollars in my other shoe. I'll see you in San Francisco.

THE GIRL (*with wonder*): San Francisco?

YOUNG MAN: That's right—San Francisco. That's where you and me belong.

THE GIRL: I've always wanted to go to *some* place like San Francisco—but how could I go alone?

YOUNG MAN: Well, you're not alone any more, see?

THE GIRL: Tell me a little what it's like.

YOUNG MAN (*very swiftly, almost impatiently at first, but gradually slower and with remembrance, smiling, and* THE GIRL *moving closer to him as he speaks*): Well, it's on the Pacific to begin with—ocean water all around. Cool fog and seagulls. Ships from all over the world. It's got seven hills. The little streets go up and down, around and all over. Every night the foghorns bawl. But they won't be bawling for you and me.

THE GIRL: What else?

YOUNG MAN: That's about all, I guess.

THE GIRL: Are people different in San Francisco?

YOUNG MAN: People are the same everywhere. They're different only when they love somebody. That's the only thing that makes 'em different. More people in Frisco love somebody, that's all.

THE GIRL: Nobody anywhere loves anybody as much as I love you.

YOUNG MAN (*shouting, as if to the world*): You see? Hearing you say that, a man could die and still be ahead of the game. Now, hurry. And don't forget, if I'm not here when you come back, get the hell to San Francisco where you'll have a chance. Do you hear me?

> THE GIRL *stands a moment looking at him, then backs away, turns and runs. The* YOUNG MAN *stares after her, troubled and smiling. Then he turns away from the image of her and walks about like a lion in a cage. After a while he sits down suddenly and buries his head in his hands. From a distance the sound of several automobiles approaching is heard. He listens a moment, then ignores the implications of the sound, whatever they may be. Several automobile doors are slammed. He ignores this also. A wooden door is opened with a key and closed, and footsteps are heard in a hall. Walking easily, almost casually and yet arrogantly, a MAN comes in.*

YOUNG MAN (*jumps up suddenly and shouts at* THE MAN, *almost scaring him*): What the hell kind of jailkeeper are you, anyway? Why don't you attend to your business? You get paid for it, don't you? Now, get me out of here.

THE MAN: But I'm not the jailkeeper.

YOUNG MAN: Yeah? Well, who are you, then?

THE MAN: I'm the husband.

YOUNG MAN: What husband you talking about?

THE MAN: You know what husband.

YOUNG MAN: Hey! (*Pause, looking at* THE MAN.) Are you the guy that hit me over the head last night?

THE MAN: I am.

YOUNG MAN (*with righteous indignation*): What do you mean going around hitting people over the head?

THE MAN: Oh, I don't know. What do you *mean* going around—the way you do?

YOUNG MAN (*rubbing his head*): You hurt my head. You got no right to hit anybody over the head.

THE MAN (*suddenly angry, shouting*): Answer my question! What do you mean?

YOUNG MAN: Listen, you—don't be hollering at me just because I'm locked up.

THE MAN (*with contempt, slowly*): You're a dog!

YOUNG MAN: Yeah, well let me tell you something. You *think* you're the husband. You're the husband of nothing. (*Slowly.*) What's more, your wife—if you want to call her that—is a tramp. Why don't you throw her out in the street where she belongs?

THE MAN (*draws a pistol*): Shut up!

YOUNG MAN: Yeah? Go ahead, shoot—(*Softly.*) and spoil the fun. What'll your pals think? They'll be disappointed, won't they. What's the fun hanging a man who's already dead? (THE MAN *puts the gun away*). That's right, because now you can have some fun yourself, telling me what you're going to do. That's what you came here for, isn't it? Well, you don't need to tell me. I *know* what you're going to do. I've read the papers and I know. They have fun. A mob of 'em fall on one man and beat him, don't they? They tear off his clothes and kick him, don't they? And women and little children stand around watching, don't they? Well, before you go on *this* picnic, I'm going to tell you a few things. Not that that's going to send you home with your pals—the other heroes. No. You've been outraged. A stranger has come to town and violated your women. Your pure, innocent, virtuous women. You fellows have got to set this thing right. You're men, not mice. You're homemakers, and you beat your children. (*Suddenly.*) Listen, you—I didn't know she was your wife. I didn't know she was anybody's wife.

THE MAN: You're a liar!

YOUNG MAN: Sometimes—when it'll do somebody some good—but not this time. Do you want to hear about it? (THE MAN *doesn't answer.*) All right, I'll tell you. I met her at a lunch counter. She came in and sat next to me. There was plenty of room, but she sat next to me. Somebody had put a nickel in the phonograph and a fellow was singing *New San Antonio Rose*. Well, she got to talking about the song. I thought she was talking to the waiter, but *he* didn't answer her, so after a while *I* answered her. That's how I met her. I didn't think anything of it. We left the place together and started walking. The first thing I knew she said, This is where I live.

THE MAN: You're a dirty liar!

YOUNG MAN: Do you want to hear it? Or not? (THE MAN *does not answer.*) O.K. She asked me to come in. Maybe she had something in mind, maybe she didn't. Didn't make any difference to me, one way or the other. If she was lonely, all right. If not, all right.

THE MAN: You're telling a lot of dirty lies!

YOUNG MAN: I'm telling the truth. Maybe your wife's out there with your pals. Well, call her in. I got nothing against her, or you—or any of you. Call her in, and ask her a few questions. Are you in love with her? (THE MAN *doesn't answer.*) Well, that's too bad.

THE MAN: What do you mean, too bad?

YOUNG MAN: I mean this may not be the first time something like this has happened.

THE MAN (*swiftly*): Shut up!

YOUNG MAN: Oh, you know it. You've always known it. You're afraid of your pals, that's all. She asked me for money. That's all she wanted. I wouldn't be here now if I had given her the money.

THE MAN (*slowly*): How much did she ask for?

YOUNG MAN: I didn't ask her how much. I told her I'd made a mistake. She said she would make trouble if I didn't give her money. Well, I don't like bargaining, and I don't like being threatened, either. I told her to get the hell away from me. The next thing I knew she'd run out of the house and was hollering. (*Pause.*) Now, why don't you go out there and tell 'em they took me to another jail—go home and pack up and leave her. You're a pretty good guy, you're just afraid of your pals.

THE MAN draws his gun again. He is very frightened. He moves a step toward the YOUNG MAN, then fires three times. The YOUNG MAN falls to his knees. THE MAN turns and runs, horrified.

YOUNG MAN: Hello—out there! (*He is bent forward.*)

THE GIRL comes running in, and halts suddenly, looking at him.

THE GIRL: There were some people in the street, men and women and kids— so I came in through the back, through a window. I couldn't find the gun. I looked all over but I couldn't find it. What's the matter?

YOUNG MAN: Nothing—nothing. Everything's all right. Listen. Listen, kid. Get the hell out of here. Go out the same way you came in and run—run like hell—run all night. Get to another town and get on a train. Do you hear me?

THE GIRL: What's happened?

YOUNG MAN: Get away—just get away from here. Take any train that's going—you can get to Frisco later.

THE GIRL (*almost sobbing*): I don't want to go any place without you.

YOUNG MAN: I can't go. Something's happened. (*He looks at her.*) But I'll be with you always—God damn it. Always!

He falls forward. THE GIRL stands near him, then begins to sob softly, walking away. She stands over to one side, stops sobbing, and stares out. The excitement of the mob outside increases. THE MAN, with two of his pals, comes running in. THE GIRL watches, unseen.

THE MAN: Here's the son of a bitch!

ANOTHER MAN: O.K. Open the cell, Harry.

The THIRD MAN *goes to the cell door, unlocks it, and swings it open. A* WOMAN *comes running in*

THE WOMAN: Where is he? I want to see him. Is he dead? (*Looking down at him, as the* MEN *pick him up.*) There he is. (*Pause.*) Yeah, that's him.

Her husband looks at her with contempt, then at the dead man.

THE MAN (*trying to laugh*): All right—let's get it over with.
THIRD MAN: Right you are, George. Give me a hand, Harry.

They lift the body.

THE GIRL (*suddenly, fiercely*): Put him down!
THE MAN: What's this?
SECOND MAN: What are you doing here? Why aren't you out in the street?
THE GIRL: Put him down and go away.

She runs toward the MEN.
THE WOMAN *grabs her.*

THE WOMAN: Here—where do you think *you're* going?
THE GIRL: Let me go. You've no right to take him away.
THE WOMAN: Well, listen to her, will you? (*She slaps* THE GIRL *and pushes her to the floor.*) Listen to the little slut, will you?

They all go, carrying the YOUNG MAN's *body.* THE GIRL *gets up slowly, no longer sobbing. She looks around at everything, then looks straight out, and whispers.*

THE GIRL: Hello—out—there! Hello—out there!

CURTAIN

32

THE DRAMATIC PLOT

The importance of concept. The scene as the basic unit of drama. Providing dramatic questions throughout the play. Controlling the pace through rising and falling action. The value of subplots.

A good dramatic plot starts with a good concept. As I explained in Chapter 30, a **concept** is a very brief description that includes a basic situation, some type of conflict or struggle, and an outcome.

A concept is not the same as a theme. The **theme,** which we will examine in Chapter 39, is that portion of a play that comments on the human condition. It is far more abstract. The *theme* of Shakespeare's *Othello*, for example, suggests that when blind trust in another person is combined with a poor ability to judge character, the result can be total disaster. The *concept*, on the other hand, is more specific: A kind-hearted nobleman places his trust in a scheming and evil underling and is driven to murder the woman he loves.

Think of a concept as a complete sentence that will convince anyone that your play is well worth reading or seeing. Here are some concepts that are distinctly unpromising, and ways they could be improved:

- "It's a play about jealousy."

    Who is jealous of whom? Why? And what is the outcome? Contrast that statement with "Because Estelle could never forget her unfaithful father, she couldn't trust her husband until she confronted her past."
- "War is hell."

    This is a truism that has been repeated so often it no longer has impact. To become meaningful, it would have to be presented through specific characters. Here is one possibility: "For years the family revered the memory of Frank, who had been killed in the Vietnam War, but only belatedly did they realize how seriously his younger brother had been psychologically damaged in the same war."
- "A play about a college student getting a summer job."

    Yawn! We need specifics and some assurance that this is going to be a fresh treatment of a frequently used situation. For example: "Kathline is delighted to be hired as a mechanic at an auto repair shop but faces a moral dilemma when she discovers that her new friends are reconditioning stolen cars."

These concepts briefly describe who is involved and what happens. They don't, of course, do justice to the complexities and insights that a good play would provide, but composing a statement like this is a good way to test whether you have a situation that is dramatic enough to keep your audience in the theater. The concept is the starting point, whereas themes, the intellectual component of a play, often take shape in the writing and are highlighted in subsequent drafts.

We can be fairly certain, for example, that the starting point of William Saroyan's *Hello Out There* was not an abstract theme about dangers of hypocrisy in society and the fundamental need for individuals to make genuine contact with one another. More likely he began with a vision of a well-meaning drifter held in a small-town jail on a false rape charge and a young woman trapped in the same town, a prisoner in a different way. These two join forces, trying to break free, only to be overwhelmed in the end. With a concept like that, the playwright is ready to block out a plot.

The Scene as Basic Unit

As I explained earlier, the word *scene* is often used to describe subdivisions of acts in longer plays. They may be written into the program notes and involve a lapse of time or even a change of setting. In some cases they replace acts altogether.

For dramatists and actors, however, the word *scene* also refers to each unit of action that begins with an entrance or an exit and ends with the next shift of characters on the stage. To avoid confusion, think of these as *secondary scenes*. They are the essential and basic units of action for the playwright, the actors, and the director as well.

Occasionally, a secondary scene may have a dramatic unity in itself. That is, it may build to a **climax** and then be punctuated by the departure of one or more characters. More often, the unity is subtler. It establishes the almost unnoticed rise and fall of action that distinguishes the play that is "dramatic" from one that seems "flat" or "dull."

Hello Out There is an excellent example of careful scene construction. It is a one-act play presented in one primary scene. There is one stage set and one apparently uninterrupted flow of action. But from a playwright's point of view, the work is divided into eight secondary scenes. Each of these is marked by an exit or entrance, and each has an influence on the rise and fall of dramatic impact.

Here are the scenes listed in the kind of outline some playwrights find helpful when planning a new play. The word *girl* is used rather than the more contemporary phrase *young woman* simply to conform with Saroyan's script.

1. Man alone on stage; talks to girl offstage
2. Girl enters; they get to know each other
3. Girl exists; man gives brief monologue
4. Girl returns; they make pact
5. Girl exits; husband enters, argues, shoots
6. Husband exits, girl returns
7. Husband and pals return, drag body out
8. Girl alone on stage; repeats refrain

This sparse outline demonstrates how many separate units will be involved, but it doesn't indicate which are major scenes and which are minor, which are highly dramatic and which merely develop relationships. Each of these secondary scenes deserves a closer look.

Although the opening scene has only one actor on the stage, it is far from static. Notice that the man is not musing philosophically to himself or addressing the audience. His first lines call out for contact with someone else, and then almost at once he is interacting with the young woman even before she is on stage. This is no prologue. Psychologically, the play begins as soon as these two characters are in voice contact.

The second scene begins when the young woman actually appears. If one merely reads the script on the page as if it were fiction, her entrance may not seem significant. But a playwright always keeps the visual aspect in mind, imagining the action from the audience's point of view. In production, her arrival on stage is the psychological start of a new scene.

This second scene is the longest in the play. Saroyan has to fill in a great deal of background and, in addition, draw these two strangers together convincingly. It would have been possible to have Emily on stage from the start, but postponing her entrance helps to keep that long second scene from becoming even longer.

The third scene is very brief. She goes out to look for tools, and he is left on the stage alone. But it is important because it allows him to lash out vehemently against what he sees as injustice. The fact that he is alone on the stage indicates to the audience that he is speaking his inner conviction. Were it not for this little scene, we might feel that he was cynically lying to the girl simply to save himself.

The fourth scene is one in which Emily and Photo-Finish make the pact to meet in San Francisco. Notice that their relationship has grown with surprising speed. In a story, one might be tempted to spread the action out over the course of a day or more; but Saroyan's dramatic sense leads him to keep the action continuous.

Emily leaves, ending the fourth scene, and there is only a moment of sound effects before a new character suddenly appears on the stage. The tension mounts as we learn that this is the angered husband. An argument pushes the dramatic impact to new levels, and the husband draws his gun. The scene culminates with three shots.

In the sixth scene the husband has fled and Emily returns. The dying **hero** and heroine are alone on the stage. If this were opera, it would be the point where the final duet is sung. As realistic drama, it is a brief, terse, yet tender moment.

But a problem arises here. How is the playwright going to maintain dramatic interest in that brief yet important section which follows the death of the protagonist? Once again, a new secondary scene is prepared for—the seventh. First the audience hears activity building offstage. Saroyan is careful to include this in his stage directions: "The excitement of the mob outside increases." The husband, two friends, and then the wife all burst on the stage. Emily demands that they put the body down—in what we can assume is the first dramatically assertive act of her life. She is slapped and pushed to the floor.

The last of these secondary scenes is so brief that it consists of only one line. But to understand just how powerful the device is, imagine the girl delivering that last line with the other characters still on stage, struggling to drag the body off. Emily would be literally upstaged. In addition, her line would be a mere continuation of the preceding dialogue. Having her alone on the stage, probably with a single beam of light on her, isolates the final words. Her plight—now matching that of Photo-Finish at the very beginning of the play—becomes the focal point of the play.

When one first reads a play like this, it is easy to assume that it is one continual flow of action. Such an approach would, of course, be possible. But it would be far more difficult to hold the audience's emotional involvement for that length of time. Exits and entrances in this play provide the basic organizational structure with which the dramatic impact is heightened and lowered and then heightened again in regular succession, holding the audience from beginning to end.

Because most of us have seen more films than plays, it is easy to be influenced by the rapid pace of their scenes. The camera not only can blend extremely brief units of action into an apparently smooth flow, it can shift setting without a break. Changing the set on the stage is time-consuming and tends to break the illusion of reality. For this reason, many full-length plays and almost all one-act plays maintain a single set. In addition, very short scenes such as the ones Saroyan uses to reveal Photo-Finish alone on the stage are kept to a minimum.

In judging the length of your secondary scenes, keep imagining the effect on your audience. Too many short scenes will make the action seem choppy; lengthy scenes may create monotony and slow the pace. You can make these decisions more easily if you have a chance to hear your script read aloud or, best of all, to see it in production.

Providing Dramatic Questions

How are you going to hold your audience in their seats? When you write fiction, this is less of a problem. A story or novel can be read in installments. But when you produce a play, you are asking an audience to give it their uninterrupted attention—often while sitting on uncomfortable seats.

Because of this, most plays are energized with a series of **dramatic questions.** These are like lures to hold the interest of the audience. We have already seen how fiction also makes use of dramatic questions (Where are we going? What will this stranger be like?), but plays depend on them to a far greater degree.

Looking at the full range of drama from Sophocles to our own decade, there are certain dramatic questions that recur frequently. This recurrence does not make the plays redundant; one hardly notices the similarity. But their widespread use does suggest just how important the dramatic question is.

1. *Will he come?* Shakespeare charged the first act of *Hamlet* with this question, applying it to the ghost. More recently, it has been broadened to cover the full length of plays. Clifford Odets' *Waiting for Lefty*, written in the thirties, Samuel Beckett's *Waiting for Godot*, and Harold Pinter's *The Dumb Waiter* all rely heavily on anticipation of a character who never appears. And to some degree, the question is a factor in *Hello Out There* as soon as the threat of a lynching is raised.

2. *Who did it?* This is, of course, the literary version of "Whodunit?" We find it running the full length of drama from *Oedipus Rex* to Tennessee Williams' *Suddenly Last Summer*. The trial scenes in *The Caine Mutiny Court Martial* and, in a loose sense, *Tea and Sympathy* and *The Crucible* are simply variations of this question. In many cases the audience knows who is guilty; the dramatic question arises out of the attempt on the part of the *characters* to determine guilt. It is a highly variable device, though the trial scene has become overused.

3. *Will he or she succeed?* This is by far the most used of all dramatic questions. It has been applied to noble and evil characters alike.

4. *Will he or she discover what we know?* The classic example is *Oedipus Rex*, in which the audience is held by the drama of a character gradually discovering terrible truths about himself. It is also a factor in *Othello*. And it has been adapted in plays of psychological self-discovery such as Arthur Miller's *Death of a Salesman*.

5. *Will a compromise be found?* This question has held audiences in such var-

ied plays as Sophocles' *Antigone,* John Galsworthy's *Strife,* and more subtly in Tennessee Williams' *A Streetcar Named Desire.* In all three of these examples, by the way, the dramatic question is merged with the theme itself—a connection none of the other questions has.

6. *Will this episode end in violence?* This is frequently used in contemporary drama. In fact, it is one of the final questions in *Hello Out There.* Even though almost every indication points to a tragic ending, we are still deeply concerned.

7. *What's happening?* This is the question most frequently asked of plays in the **absurdist** tradition. Like dream fiction, these works plunge the audience into a confusing, often inexplicable environment. Playwrights like Pinter, Beckett, Ionesco, and occasionally Albee utilize ambiguity as a dramatic question. This is, however, a risky device for the novice. Like free verse, it seems easy at first but often slides into meaninglessness. It requires wit or ingenuity of thematic suggestion to keep the play alive. In short, a dull play is not improved by being made an obscurely dull play.

The opening dramatic question is often referred to as the **hook.** It arouses interest from the start. But most plays move from one dramatic question to the next so that the audience is kept wondering about immediate outcomes as well as about what the ultimate resolution will be. *Hello Out There* is a good example of how the playwright can create a new question just as an old one has been resolved.

The play begins with a man in jail, and the audience immediately wonders why he is there. What did he do? Should we sympathize with him? Through the girl we begin to get answers to these questions, but at the same time a new cluster of dramatic questions is forming: Will she help him? And if she does, will they succeed? Toward the end of the play, we have a sense of foreboding: It is not likely that the outcome will be happy. But as in all tragedies, we still concern ourselves with the survival of the protagonist. There is for most members of the audience a lingering hope that he will live up to his nickname and win by a photo-finish.

Don't confuse these questions with the theme. Saroyan's thematic concern is with the loneliness of individuals; he is comparing life in a small and hostile town with being in jail. I will return to various aspects of theme in later chapters. My concern here is for the basic technique of generating dramatic questions. They are truly theatrical devices and are essential if a play is to hold the attention of the audience.

Controlling the Pace

Pace is all-important in a play. Scenes that appear to drag continue to be revised well into production. Although one rarely hears about a play in which the pace is too rapid, it is possible to race too quickly through scenes that should unfold character or clarify aspects of the plot. And too much dramatic voltage at the beginning of a play can create a slump later on.

Traditional terms are helpful if we remember that they apply mainly to the plots of traditional plays. **Rising action,** for example, accurately describes the mounting complications with which many plays from all historical periods are begun. In full-length dramas, problems may be compounded with subplots involving secondary characters acting as **foils** to highlight or set off the major characters. The **crisis** is not the very end but the turning point at which the protagonist's fortunes begin to fail. From there on we have **falling action,** which in tragedies results in a **catastrophe** or **denouement**—often the death of the hero.

Sound old-fashioned? True, Aristotle described drama in those terms. True, they apply to Greek and Elizabethan tragedies. But they also apply to many modern works by such playwrights as Eugene O'Neill, Arthur Miller, and Tennessee Williams. In condensed form, they can be seen in William Saroyan's *Hello Out There* as well.

The rising action involves the young man meeting an ally and planning an escape. The crisis occurs when the enraged husband returns. From there on it is falling action through to the death of the protagonist. Although the play is brief and in one act, the plot structure is similar to that of a traditional three-act play or an Elizabethan tragedy of five acts.

This plot form continues to be popular not because playwrights who use it are imitative but because it is good theater. It lends itself to a variety of situations and it holds audiences.

This is, however, only one way to handle the pacing of a dramatic plot. Another method focuses on characterization and is sometime referred to as the *onion approach*: A series of scenes exposes the inner life of a character or a couple like peeling the layers of an onion. Eugene O'Neill's *The Iceman Cometh* reveals a single character this way; Edward Albee's *Who's Afraid of Virginia Woolf?* exposes the illusions of a couple with equal intensity.

Another type of loose plotting is sometimes called the *Grand Hotel* pattern, though the title refers to a novel by Vicki Baum, not a play. The novel brings together a number of different characters to portray European society in the 1920s. This approach weaves together many parallel plots and lends itself to longer plays. A good contemporary example is *The Hot l Baltimore* by Lanford Wilson. Once again a hotel (this one not so grand) is used to link characters, and the plot is episodic. Arthur Miller's relatively short *A Memory of Two Mondays* deals with the men who work in the shipping room of an auto-parts warehouse. It is concerned almost equally with all the characters. The pace in plays like this is controlled not by the rise and fall of a protagonist, but by a series of dramatic questions arising from the problems faced by a number of different characters.

In the case of **comedy** and **farce,** which I will examine in more detail in

Chapter 40, pace is often controlled by an increase in the intensity. In satire, this means increasing the degree of exaggeration. The opening scenes are presented as relatively mild satire; but as the play builds, so does the intensity of the satire.

Clearly there are no firm rules about how to construct a good plot. You are free to draw on certain traditional patterns or experiment with new approaches. This is not to say that anything will work, however. You must maintain forward movement in some way. If you don't create dramatic questions and don't make use of rising and falling action, you will have to find some other method of keeping your production alive. A series of surprising revelations about a character, for example, will generate dramatic interest. A continuing exposé of an initially harmonious or apparently moral group will also serve. In any case, low-key scenes must be alternated with dramatic ones effectively enough to maintain interest. If you ignore pacing and let your play go slack, your audience will be quick to let you know.

The Resonance of Subplots

A **subplot,** as the name implies, is a sequence of actions involving secondary characters that runs parallel to the main plot. It is difficult to use in short plays because of the time required to introduce secondary characters in any detail, but as soon as you start working with a longer play, the technique is well worth considering.

A subplot usually echoes or contrasts the action of the main plot. If, for example, the main plot deals with a couple's serious marital conflict, the subplot might introduce another couple with similar but less serious problems. Or the subplot might contrast the challenges faced by a woman as single parent with those faced by a man in similar circumstances.

Often the subplot is lighter than the primary plot, thereby establishing a tonal contrast, a kind of counterpoint. It can even provide comic relief, a technique of easing tension which I will discuss in more detail in Chapter 40.

The problems generated in the subplot are usually resolved before the conclusion of the main plot so as not to interfere. Be careful not to allow the subplot to dominate the play. If it begins to compete with equal intensity the play will seem to lack a focus. The only exception to this principle is what we have been calling the Grand Hotel pattern, in which there are many equally important plots. These are not, however, true subplots since there is no central and dominant story line.

After you have written several short plays, you will want to expand your horizons with a full-length work. At that point, consider the value of a subplot. It often generates true resonance and range of suggestion to a play that would have seemed thin without it.

Plot exists in narrative poetry; it is important in fiction; but it is central in most dramas. Although there are plays that take the form of an extended monologue, those few that succeed depend on highly sophisticated wit and verbal ingenuity. They are risky models. The long history of drama is dominated by visual activity and the lure of an unfolding plot. A story can afford to suspend the flow of action for passages of reflection or description, but a play is much less forgiving. It must hold everyone's full attention without interruption for the length of the performance.

Accomplishing this is a challenge, but it has its positive side. A dramatic plot gives you as playwright an opportunity to seize and hold the attention of an audience with a sustained intensity rarely given the written page. This direct and charged contact between artist and viewer is one of the special rewards for the playwright.

33

CONFLICT

The Driving Force of Drama

Conflict as the prime energizing force. Person against person. Triangular conflicts. The individual against society. Inner conflicts and how to reveal them. Creating a network of conflicts.

Simple dramas have simple conflicts. Such plays are usually based on a blatant struggle between good and bad. The loyalty of the audience is fixed from start to finish. It's our team versus theirs. If the tension is intense, the result is **melodrama,** an exaggeration of suspense at the expense of characterization. We see this pattern so often in popular film and television dramas that it is easy to underrate the real potential of conflict in sophisticated drama as well.

But conflict does not have to obliterate characterization and subtlety of theme. In fact, conflict is the primary energizing force in most sophisticated dramas. When we say that a work is "dramatic" or "powerful," we are implying that conflict has been used convincingly. Dramatic questions, described in the previous chapter, arouse curiosity. Conflict evokes fear, excitement, anger, commitment. It pumps adrenaline.

Person Against Person

At the heart of many plays, one individual is pitted against another in some way. The **protagonist,** the prime character, contends with an **antagonist,** the opponent. You can make good use of this basic pattern without turning your play into a melodramatic slugfest if you are careful to develop two essentials: subtle characterization and insightful themes.

Hello Out There is a good example. As we will see, there are many conflicts in the play, but the primary one is between the protagonist, Photo-Finish, and the outraged husband. In a melodrama the hero would be blameless and the villain pure evil. While Saroyan is far from impartial, he is careful to develop Photo-Finish's weaknesses—his perilous lifestyle and his habit of taking risks, relying on luck for survival. As for the antagonist, the husband is not a cold-blooded murderer. He is frightened, unsure about his wife, and intimidated by his pals.

The other essential for avoiding melodrama is generating complexity of theme. We have all seen dramatic works in which the only theme is simply good against bad. I will review the full range of themes in Saroyan's play in Chapter 39, but it is worth pointing out here that one theme suggests a parallel between being a prisoner in a cell and being trapped in a small, mean-spirited community. Another theme focuses on the degree to which violence is motivated by attempts to "save face." A third theme develops the way loneliness can affect both men and women. The primary conflict in this play is a means of developing a number of related themes rather than being an end in itself.

Melodrama is sometimes thought of as simply an excess of violence. Not so. It is excess violence in the absence of convincing characterization and insightful themes. The playwright has to weigh the degree of violence in a conflict against how fully the characters have been developed and how complex the theme. Clearly, length has a good deal to do with it.

Novice playwrights are sometimes tempted to push conflict to the point of murder or suicide simply to keep a lackluster script lively. Before you go to this extreme, make sure that your characters and themes are strong enough to keep from being overpowered by the action. The shorter the play, the more difficult this is to do.

Fortunately you have the ability as playwright to adjust the level of conflict almost as easily as you turn the volume up or down on a radio. And you can do this without changing the structure of the play. Murder can be moderated to a fight, and a fight downgraded to a verbal attack. Suicide can, as we will see in *Hello Out There*, be downsized to poignant expressions of despair.

Your judgment as to how much intensity is appropriate to dramatize a conflict depends on your ability to spot at what point you have pushed your drama into melodrama. Review for a moment that final scene in *Hello Out There* in which Emily, alone on the stage, repeats that plaintive cry, "Hello—out—there!" Now picture a revised ending in which Emily stabs herself in the heart, letting her lifeless body drop on top of her newfound friend, fake blood trickling across the stage. That's true melodrama. Why? Because the play has already been charged with as much violence as the situation can absorb. One step further and the audience will no longer take the scene seriously. What the playwright had hoped would be moving might well produce only snickers.

Triangular Conflicts

Three-way conflicts have certain advantages over those limited to two opponents. Triangles add more than just an additional character. They compound the possibilities of character development.

The first pattern that comes to mind is the love triangle, the relationship of two individuals threatened by a third. It has an venerable history. Medea's betrayal by her husband Jason, who fell in love with another woman, has been told and retold from Euripides' tragedy around 440 B.C. to Robinson Jeffers' modern verse play. The same pattern of betrayal and revenge is repeated endlessly in contemporary play and film scripts on both serious and comic levels.

If you plan to use a love triangle as the basis of conflict in a one-act play, you will have to work hard to achieve originality. The sexy baby-sitter and the obliging secretary are **stereotypes.** But triangles do continue to exist in life, and in some cases the unique circumstances of an actual case will suggest a fresh dramatic situation.

Triangles don't necessarily have to involve love relationships. Three individuals vying for a job, a promotion, or an award become a triangle. Two parents and a child too often become a triangle in conflict. Two senior workers who find themselves having to take orders from a newly promoted younger associate can be an explosive triangle.

The third member of a triangle doesn't even have to be a person. In contemporary dramas, both husbands and wives have been seduced by professional commitments that become the third member of a triangle. A married person's involvement with a political cause or a new religious faith can also have the impact of an infidelity. Watch out, once again, for versions that have been overdone. The marriage that is threatened by a husband's preoccupation with his business can, if not done in a fresh manner, become as hackneyed in drama as in fiction. Merely reversing the sexes doesn't add much if the characters are still cardboard. And there should be a moratorium on drama plots based on painters and writers who wreck their marriages for the sake of art. But even setting these aside, there are enough triangulations left to serve future dramatists for some time to come.

The Individual Against Society

Society or some aspect of it can serve as a highly dramatic opponent for an individual. A part of *Hello Out There* is a familiar conflict between an individual and a portion of a community that is out to lynch him. Sadly familiar as that is, it gives the playwright an opportunity to comment on society as a whole. Saroyan unmistakably takes sides. On the one hand, all the characters are treated with some compassion—even the worst of them. Society, on the other hand, is pictured as the real culprit. Photo-Finish, musing to himself, says "This world stinks." Later, outraged at the charge of rape and also at how the town has treated Emily, he says, "Rape? *They* rape everything good that was ever born." When there is still hope of escape, she asks, "Are people different in San Francisco?" "People are the same everywhere," he says. "They're different only when they love somebody. More people in Frisco love somebody, that's all." In the conflict between the individual and society as a whole, Saroyan clearly sides with the individual.

Society for Saroyan is a fairly general concept, but others have portrayed it in much more specific terms. Some playwrights see society as the rich and powerful. Their work takes a political stance. For many black playwrights, society is the white world. I will have more to say about socially conscious drama and themes of protest in Chapter 39, "Dramatic Themes." What concerns us here is the way in which society can be seen as the opposing force, creating a conflict that is almost always repeated in the form of individual against individual.

The dramatic impact that can be generated by a writer's pitting the individual against society is enormous. If you take that route, however, be careful not to let your play turn into a sermon. Sermons have their place, but they make poor drama—except for those who already agree. The most successful plays dealing with society are the ones that can translate those relatively abstract convictions into person-to-person conflict. Even when social statement is the primary concern of the playwright, it is personal conflict between credible characters that has immediate impact.

Inner Conflicts and How to Reveal Them

Presenting inner conflicts is one of the best ways to achieve subtlety in characterization. The very phrases with which we describe such indecision suggest dramatic tension: a character is "of two minds," "struggling with himself," or even "at war with herself." Such individuals are torn between love and fear, courage and timidity, anger and affection. Or they may be attracted to two different people, two opposing ethical positions, two sexual identities. Inner conflict is a part of the human condition.

But how is one to reveal what goes on in the mind of a character in a genre that depends almost entirely on dialogue and actions? If you have been writing fiction, your first inclination may be to consider **monologues.** After all, Shakespeare used them. The soliloquies of Hamlet and Lady Macbeth are among the most quoted dramatic lines in the language. But remember that those monologues were imbedded in five-act plays. If we hadn't heard those monologues so often and studied them so carefully out of context, they would blend into the work as a whole. In addition, Elizabethan drama accepted the convention of major characters expressing their inner conflicts eloquently in blank verse. In a contemporary, realistic play that is intended to reflect more closely the behavior and speech of daily life, the inner debate expressed through a monologue often seems artificial.

When monologues are used in realistic drama today, they are usually brief. Saroyan's first scene begins with a short sequence, and he repeats the device by having Photo-Finish alone on the stage in that abbreviated third scene. This second monologue is particularly important because it is the only hard evidence the audience has that Photo-Finish really is fond of Emily and is not just using her for escape. Although Emily's two lines at the very end of the play take only a moment, they effectively reveal her inner lament.

During the 1960s and 1970s there was a certain vogue for long monologues among playwrights in the **absurdist** school. Their plays were often dreamlike, philosophical, and talky. The best of them maintained interest through flashes of insight and wit, but the approach was short-lived. It takes remarkable skill on the part of both playwright and actor to hold the attention of an audience with thought alone.

A far more effective way to reveal inner conflict is to provide your protagonist with a *confidant*, a personal friend who is not quite central to the action. If you are working with two couples, the wives or the husbands can sometime reveal inner conflicts with each other that they are reluctant to share with their partners. In longer plays, the confidant may be a **foil,** a minor character who serves primarily to set off a primary character by contrast. The foil is often a relatively comic character in an otherwise serious play.

Another approach is to use action. People often reveal their inner conflicts through the way they behave, often quite unconsciously. It is not difficult to have your characters do the same. There is a small example in *Hello Out There* which, though easily missed, represents a well-used device. Emily is torn between the desire to do whatever Photo-Finish asks and her fear of leaving him for a minute. When he asks her to go and look for cigarettes, she does leave, but almost at once she comes running back. Alternating behavior like this can be used in more significant scenes as well. A character starts to do one thing, then abruptly does another. Often no lines are needed to spell out the inner conflict.

Sometimes inner conflict takes the form of indecision; in other cases it is true **ambivalence,** two opposing desires that exist simultaneously. In either case, it is an excellent way to humanize a character and make him or her credible.

As you examine these different types of conflict, keep in mind that although they are enormously important, they don't make a good starting point for a play. You don't begin by deciding to write about a triangle or a battle with society and then filling in the blanks. Plays begin with a concept—specific characters in a dramatic situation. Once you have that in place, you will be able to see where the major conflicts lie and start revising the script so as to make the best use of them.

Creating a Network of Conflicts

Until now, we have been examining various types of conflict as if they were separate and distinct. A well-developed drama, however, contains a network of conflicts that reinforce each other.

One of the reasons *Hello Out There* serves as such a good model for short, realistic plays is that it generates just such a network of conflicts. Essentially, of course, it is a struggle between Photo-Finish and his antagonist, the outraged husband. In a simple melodrama, that conflict would stand alone as the prime and perhaps only concern of the work. Saroyan has made sure, however, that it is only one of many interrelated conflicts.

When the play opens, no antagonist is in sight. The first major conflict to be introduced is a prisoner against a hostile town. The enemy is "them," a vague notion of forces outside that jail. This conflict of man against society is highlighted when we learn that the name of the town is Matador. If the town is the bullfighter, he is the bull in the pen, waiting for the deadly sport to begin.

Next we learn that Emily is also pitted against this town. Her life is not threatened, but her spirit is. She is not just lonesome, she is alienated. The men in town, she reports, laugh at her. Her father takes what little money she earns. She is willing to take great risks to escape.

Their conflict with this oppressive town is soon overshadowed by the direct confrontation between Photo-Finish and the husband. But the man is not acting alone. The town remains an antagonist right through to the end of the play.

Although the husband is the enemy, he has his own conflicts. First, it is clear that he and his wife are antagonists. He actually puts his gun away when Photo-Finish starts revealing the truth. The man keeps calling Photo-Finish a liar, but he continues to listen. And when he is asked whether he is in love with his wife, he doesn't answer. Pathetically, when he is told that his wife asked for money, he responds with "How much did she ask for?" Clearly this is a tormented relationship.

We see still more conflicts when it is revealed that he is being driven by pressures from his wife and friends. As Photo-Finish puts it, "You're a pretty good guy, you're just afraid of your pals." Saroyan has him repeat this line for emphasis. As with so many acts of violence, the perpetrator is motivated in part by fear of his own peer group. This doesn't excuse his actions, but it does humanize him.

When you look closely at what drives these characters, it is clear that this play is far from the simple television plot of man against the mob. The tragic killing is a result of a network of conflicts. In the end, Emily is the ultimate victim, herself isolated and in conflict with the town of Metador.

At first, it may seem almost impossible to generate so many different conflicts in the limited time frame of a short one-act play. But if you get to know your characters well, you will see that none of them is purely good or purely bad. They are all driven by different and conflicting forces and needs. Once you understand this, developing and dramatizing a variety of conflicts will become a natural part of the revision process through successive drafts. The network of conflicts you build into your play will serve as its driving force.

34

DRAMATIC CHARACTERIZATION

The need for vividness. The importance of first impressions. Creating depth of character. Characters in flux: "character change" and shifts in audience perception. Using minor characters effectively.

On a literal level, the title of this chapter refers to the special ways characters in plays are developed. It also suggests quite correctly that such characters are often more *dramatic* than those in fiction in the sense of being vivid and slightly exaggerated. What we think of as being **realism** on the stage is almost always an intensification of what we might expect in life.

This special vividness of characters on the stage is due partly to the nature of the genre. As I pointed out earlier, drama is a continuous art. Unlike fiction, it is presented at a single sitting and at a regular rate. There is no going back to review a passage that introduced a character or to fill in some missing detail. Imagine novelists insisting that their work be read non-stop from cover to cover in a public place miles from home in the company of total strangers. It's no wonder playwrights tend to paint in bold colors!

There is a second factor that tends to make characters on the stage just a bit stagy. Writers of fiction have at their disposal a whole array of techniques with which they can develop characters. They can quote thoughts naturally and frequently without slowing the action, they can thrust a reader into a flashback at any moment, they can even comment on a character in their own voice if they wish. Not so for playwrights. Essentially they are limited to what a character says and does. True, there are ways of extending these limitations—techniques I will turn to shortly—but the basic restriction is there. Because playwrights rely so heavily on the two devices of action and dialogue, they tend to use the more boldly.

The Importance of First Impressions

When the protagonist of a play enters for the first time, what he or she does and says provides an initial impression that will linger for the length of the play. Those first few lines have a crucial influence on the audience's judgment of a character.

In the case of *Hello Out There*, Saroyan is faced with a particularly difficult challenge. How can he induce an audience to look favorably and sympathetically at a small-time gambler and drifter who has been jailed for rape? With this question in mind, take a close look at the way Saroyan handles those very first lines:

> YOUNG MAN: Hello—out there! (*Pause.*) Hello—out there! (*Long pause.*) Nobody out there. (*Still more dramatically, but more comically, too.*) Hello—out there! Hello—out there!

Normally, playwrights don't provide so many stage directions since both directors and actors like to have leeway. But in this case Saroyan is clearly concerned with creating just the right initial impression. He keeps his protagonist alone on the stage and gives him lines that establish his mood and character before revealing the actual situation.

Those very first lines are hesitant, nonthreatening, appealing. They focus on loneliness and reach out for sympathy as much as for companionship. His tone is insistent—we are encouraged to take him seriously—yet it is also comic. And those same qualities dominate that entire initial scene. Why is this so important? Because if the audience is not won over in the first few minutes, it will not believe him when he claims that the charge of rape is false. Deciding whether to accept as true what strangers say is based entirely on a quick judgment of character. The fact that the audiences of this play trust Photo-Finish's claim of innocence just as quickly as Emily does is a dramatic illustration of how rapidly a good playwright can establish character.

For some, there are lingering doubts about his actual feelings toward Emily. He is, after all, a street-wise character in a life-and-death situation, and Emily is no beauty. Does he really feel love for her? Or does he see her as the last chance of escape? If we read the play script as if it were a story, his sudden protestations of love seem preposterously rapid, far too quick to be taken seriously. But the play insists that you believe it. As I pointed out before, we know that he is presenting his inner thoughts honestly in the little monologue that forms the third scene because he is speaking to himself. He refers to her as "the only good thing that ever came their way." And later when he realizes that there is practically no chance of escape, he gives her his last eighty dollars to escape her own imprisonment in that town and get to San Francisco. There can be no ulterior motive in this offer. So both in lines of dialogue and in action we are assured that his love for her is genuine.

How can an aspect of character that would be hard to believe in fiction somehow work in drama? The answer lies in one of the subtler distinctions between the two genres. As I have mentioned, characters tend to be slightly exaggerated in drama and their emotions are allowed to develop and shift at a faster rate. Certain aspects of character and especially changes in attitude that would be unconvincing if read on the page become credible when viewed in production.

When you read a script, you are not reading a play; you are reading lines of dialogue and a few stage directions that are merely two ingredients which go into a full production. The rest is provided by the actors, the director, the set designer, costume designer—an entire team. How, then, can a writer learn how to create effective dramatic characterization in a script when what appears in production is influenced by so many others? Mainly by seeing as many plays as possible in production and studying the scripts. With experience, one begins to judge what is possible and how to go about creating it. Saroyan, for example, knew that he could convince an audience that a man like Photo-Finish could sincerely fall in love in what by real-life standards is only minutes because the playwright had a sense of what works on the stage. And the continuing popularity of this play (it has become a kind of classic) demonstrates that he was right.

Important as your protagonist's first lines are, don't spend hours getting that introduction just right in your first draft. Once you have your opening scene in mind, plunge in and get it down on paper. After you have completed the first draft, however, take a second look at that opening. Has it done all it can to give an audience a "handle" on your protagonist? Read the first two minutes of dialogue and ask yourself whether they individualize that character. With your first draft safely down on paper, you will have a clear idea of how that character is developed later, and you can then make sure that the audience has started off with just the right impression.

Creating Depth of Character

The central characters in serious, realistic drama are usually well rounded and carefully delineated. Achieving this effect in a short one-act play is a challenge, but it can be done. Saroyan manages to give us a good deal about Photo-Finish in only a few minutes of playing time. He is lonely but not a whiner. He has a whimsical sense of humor yet can be serious not only about practical things but about broader concerns like what makes people so mean. There is a merry quality to the way he treats Emily, but we know almost from the start that he is genuinely scared about his position. These contrasts provide a range of characteristics and attitudes, and it is this range that gives us a sense of knowing him as an individual.

Characterization in this play is particularly important because so much depends on the audience feeling sympathy for this unsuccessful gambler and born loser. Only if we take him seriously will we respond to one of the major themes of the play: the capacity of love to transform "little punk people" to something fine.

Achieving depth of character in a play is somewhat similar to the technique in fiction except that it has to be presented more rapidly. The goal is to balance consistency with variation. Consistency requires that the character never behave in a way that seems implausible. A line of dialogue or a particular action may seem surprising to the audience at first, but in realistic drama it must ultimately be explained.

On the other hand, excessive consistency makes the character overly predictable. In drama, predictable means dull. So every major character should have a variety of characteristics. Photo-Finish, for example, is not a naive college sophomore on spring vacation. He is a small-time hustler who has been living precariously on the fringes of the racetrack world. His ability to see the good qualities in a young woman like Emily and even to appreciate the conflicts in the outraged husband are in sharp contrast to what we might expect. That contrast is important, but equally important is the fact that for most viewers it is credible. If he were a convicted mass murderer on the run and ended up marrying Emily and going to medical school, the audience would tiptoe to the exits.

Notice, too, that there is nothing in the play to suggest that Emily is tall, beautiful, or sophisticated. Even her name, Emily Smith, suggests the ordinary. Yet she is elevated in stature at the very end, and we take her concluding cry of "Hello out there!" seriously.

One way to achieve both consistency and some measure of contrast is to take the time to write out a character sketch. Put down more than you will ever need: what their parents were like, whether they had sisters or brothers, where they went to school, what they were good at, and what their weaknesses are. Determine some aspects that suggest consistency ("gentle temperament; almost never loses her temper") and some contrasting trait ("can't stand messy people or a disorderly house").

You will end up with far more material than you will ever use, especially in a short play. But like packing for a trip to a strange country, you never know what you will need More important, just taking 30 minutes to write out a full background sketch will assure you that you are working with a fully formed character, not just a cardboard cutout.

If you have trouble writing more than a few sentences, try basing your description on a friend or member of your family. But be inventive. Don't lock yourself into that particular individual. Make a point of transforming some aspects so you will begin to deal with a newly formed stage character. Alter a basic element such as age, sex, or appearance so that you don't lose friends or, worse, become inhibited out of respect for the person who served as model. Keep in mind that the process of creating a dramatic character is almost never pure invention; it is a transformation of what is familiar to you. The goal is to create a new and interesting character who is generally consistent in outlook and nature and yet who occasionally demonstrates certain contrasting traits as well.

Major Characters in Flux

Drama by definition cannot be static, and this rule applies to the characters as well as the plot. Major characters in realistic drama usually go through some type of significant development, for good or for bad. They are not the same at the end of the play as they were at the beginning. This process is often referred to as *character change*.

Another way to achieve that all-important sense of change and discovery is to reverse the process: Allow the character to remain the same but provide information that will dramatically shift the audience's perception of him or her. Oddly, this approach can generate just as much impact.

The phrase *character change* is often used informally to describe both patterns, but it is a bit misleading. Characters in plays rarely go through a fundamental personality change any more than people do in life. Only in comedies do villains finally see the light, go through a complete character transformation, and undo the damage they have done. Still, there is nothing wrong with using the term *character change* as long as we remember that what we are really talking about is a shift either in the character's attitude or in the audience's perceptions of that character.

Such shifts can be highly dramatic. In plays, as in life, characters are shaped by dramatic events and end up stricken with remorse, given new hope, shattered by a crisis, or strengthened by it. Friendships form between unlikely pairs, and "ideal" couples become alienated. Quite often a naive character is suddenly made aware of some harsh aspect of life; occasionally a sophisticated character is taught how to appreciate some simple truth. The impact of these shifts is similar to when an apparently trustworthy character turns out to be dishonest or one we had assumed was incompetent has actually been in control. These are all the stuff of powerful drama.

Where does one find characters who have gone through such a shift in outlook? Start with your own life. Even if you feel that your development has been uneventful, it has in fact moved in stages, each one introduced by some fresh view of yourself or the world about you. Always keep in mind that you can transform a relatively mild personal experience so that it has dramatic impact.

In addition, consider what you have heard about other members of your family, present and past. Almost every family has stories with dramatic potential. There is also "cold material"—reports you have read in the newspaper or history texts, stories about individuals not connected with you personally. If you take this route, consider grafting the events on to someone you have known. This association will help to make your characterization more convincing.

The further you get from your own life and experiences, the greater the danger that you will begin to borrow from something you have seen on television or in a movie. Sometimes this happens entirely unconsciously. Remember that in the back of your unconscious memory is a great, musty storehouse of stock characters from fiction and film. If you put them in your play, they will be no more convincing than mannequins. You are on safer ground when you develop characters who are at least indirectly linked to people you know.

The other type of character change focuses on audience perception. As writer, you have to pay attention to what you withhold and what you reveal at every stage. You have probably seen this technique in murder mysteries in which the character who seems least likely to be the killer is revealed in the end to be just that. In such scripts characterization is often relatively simple, but the same approach lends itself to more sophisticated dramas.

One of the best-known examples of this technique in full-length plays is in *The Country Girl* by Clifford Odets. It concerns the efforts of an older actor to make a comeback. For much of the play the audience is convinced that he is doing his best to cope with a very difficult wife. But it turns out that he is an alcoholic and she has been heroically trying to cover for him. The audience has been as misled, as have the other characters, and the revelation has genuine dramatic impact.

There are all kinds of deceits that can be used in this manner. Some are the result of conscious scheming as in the Odets play, but others develop from self-deception. If you are working with this type of reversal, be careful to drop small hints along the way so that when the correct view is revealed the audience will have that special sense of, "Oh, I should have seen it."

The diagram on the following page illustrates these various ways you can develop your central characters or shift audience perception of them.

Using Minor Characters Effectively

E. M. Forster's distinction between "round" and "flat" characters in fiction applies just as well to drama. Although "flat" characters are seen in only one dimension, like cardboard cutouts, and they rarely change or develop, they can be essential elements of a play. In comedy, for example, all of the characters are relatively "flat." Yet as you will see in *Coulda, Woulda, Shoulda*, which appears as the next chapter, the two parents, "flat" as they are,

Patterns in Character Development

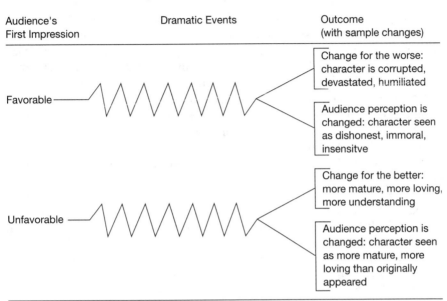

Audience's First Impression	Dramatic Events	Outcome (with sample changes)
Favorable		Change for the worse: character is corrupted, devastated, humiliated
		Audience perception is changed: character seen as dishonest, immoral, insensitve
Unfavorable		Change for the better: more mature, more loving, more understanding
		Audience perception is changed: character seen as more mature, more loving than originally appeared

become essential to our understanding of the protagonist and the theme itself.

In satiric plays, secondary characters are like cartoon figures, exaggerating human foibles. In highly didactic plays committed to a particular political or social thesis, characters are also drawn in bold, exaggerated manner without depth. Their function is to illustrate ideas, not to portray an as-if-real person.

Even in realistic plays that develop the major characters fully, the minor characters are usually "flat." They may serve as **catalysts**—necessary elements for the advancement of plot or for the development of a major character without themselves changing.

The two men who accompany the husband in *Hello Out There*, for example, are extremely important since their presence just outside the jail room drives the husband to the point of murder. In that aspect, they are far from "minor." They are essential elements. But as individuals, they are faceless, even interchangeable, and completely unchanging.

There is a tendency to become careless with minor characters, creating them to perform trivial tasks that are not truly essential—delivering pizza or mail. Anyone who has been active in professional theater companies can tell you that production costs place a premium on plays that can be presented with a minimum number of actors. And entirely aside from those practical considerations, there is an aesthetic value to economy. A play is apt to have more power if a lot is suggested by a few carefully developed characters as opposed to a more diffuse theme cluttered by too many characters.

There are two questions to ask about any minor character: What significant function does this character serve, and exactly what would happen if we removed him or her? If we apply those questions to the pair of unnamed men in the Saroyan play, we can see why they are so important. The men serve the function of a mob; without them, the play would suggest that the husband was driven to murder by an unquestioning sense of revenge rather than by being driven in part by trying to look good in the eyes of other men.

Minor characters are generally as static as stage props, but they can serve significant functions. Don't add them the way you add a couch or a chair to the set. Use them as essential elements or drop them from your script.

Characterization in a realistic play is a continuing concern at every stage of writing. It takes time and many revisions to make major characters both vivid and credible. You have to consider both consistency and variation. Realistic drama is, among other things, the illusion of getting to know total strangers surprisingly well in a very short period of time.

The play that follows is, in sharp contrast, **nonrealistic.** It creates its own world. Read it through once for pleasure; then read it for analysis. You will see that while characterization takes a different form and has different goals, it is still a crucial aspect of drama.

35

A PLAY

by Glenn Alterman

Coulda, Woulda, Shoulda

Characters

CY
YETTA
MARTY

Scene

A small, simply decorated kitchen. It is about 11:30 A.M. Yetta is seated at the kitchen table finishing her coffee. Cy is rushing around, getting dressed.

CY: You're kidding? He said that?
YETTA: That's what he said.
CY: When?
YETTA: This morning when I gave him his bath.
CY: What a kid.
YETTA: Could you bust?
CY (*looking around*): Where's my belt?
YETTA: On the chair. (*He gets it, puts it on.*) Stood up in the tub, put his hand on my shoulder and said, "Ma, I want to be a rabbi."
CY: A rabbi? You're kidding? Every morning it's something else.
YETTA: At first, first, I thought he said "a rabbit."

CY (*stops for a moment*): What?

YETTA: Yeah, thought he said "I want to be a rabbit, Ma." Almost dropped the sponge I laughed so hard. I mean can you imagine? But then he looked at me, seemed so serious. You know those eyes of his. Said it again, loud and clear, black and white. Looked like a little Moses in the tub waiting for the waters to part. (*Slowly, very strong.*) "Ma, I want to be a rabbi. A rabbi, you understand?" I stopped, smiled, what could I...? Said, "Sure, okay honey, if that's what you want." Washed the soap off, towel-dried him, baby powder, kissed him on the head and gave him a big hug. Well he gave me a look, got upset, started to cry.

CY: Cry? Why?

YETTA: I don't know. I asked him, wouldn't answer. Looked at me like I was the worst mother in the world. Like I'd just stabbed him in the heart or something. Ran to his room, slammed the door, locked it shut. Wouldn't let me in. Couldn't get him out. Been in there all morning.

CY: All morning?

YETTA: All morning long!

CY: You're kidding? Where's my shoes?

YETTA: By the sink. (*He gets the shoes, starts putting them on.*) I've been sitting here, waiting for you to get up. We've got a problem, Cy.

CY: I'll say, our son—Marty! I'm taking that lock off his door first thing when I get home tonight. Enough of this shit!

YETTA: What are you talking about? You've got to go talk to him.

CY: Me? About what? I didn't have no fight with him.

YETTA: What fight? Who fought? A misunderstanding, that's all.

CY: I don't got time for this now. He'll come out when he's good and ready. And stop giving him so many baths for Christ's sake!

YETTA: Talk to him.

CY: Didn't you hear me?

YETTA: He's your son!

CY: I'm late. I'll talk to my son—later.

YETTA: When, at four in the morning when you get home?

CY (*grabbing his coat, starting to go*): Whenever!

YETTA (*blocking the door*): The drunks of the world can wait!

CY: Hey, the drunks of the world put food on this table and don't you forget it. You should thank God we got that bar. (*Then, looking through his coat pocket.*) Where's my keys?

YETTA (*ignoring him, looking toward the bedroom, calling sweetly*): Marty, come on out. Daddy's leaving for work, come say good bye.

CY (*looking around*): Where the hell's...?

YETTA (*sweetly, calling to the bedroom*): Marty.

CY: Where the hell are they?

YETTA: On the bureau, where you left them!

CY (*as he storms off, calling to the bedroom*): Marty, come on out. I don't got all day. (*Yetta looks anxiously toward the bedroom. Loud banging.*) Martin get out of there! You hear me? Out!

(*It's quiet for a moment. Then returning, carrying the keys, under his breath*):

He doesn't want to come out.

YETTA: So you're just gonna leave?

CY: What do you want me to do, break the door down?

YETTA (*turning away, upset*): Go 'head, go. GO!

CY (*He starts to leave, but then returning, upset*): Why's it always gotta be this way? Huh, why? Why do I got to leave here almost every day with you crying and me with a knot in my stomach? Why, huh, I'm asking you?

YETTA (*tensely, looking straight at him*): I am not crying!

CY: Can't I leave here just once, JUST ONCE YETTA, a pleasant goodbye, kiss on the cheek? Why's it always got to be Marty's been bad, or Marty's...? Always something!

YETTA (*furiously*): The drunks of the world are waiting. Go ahead, go!

MARTY (*from the bedroom, yelling*): Stop it! Stop it already, both of you!

(*A light change. They both turn toward the bedroom. A door slams. Marty enters. He's in his forties, wearing large children's pajamas, a pair of glasses and a black hat. He's carrying a pen and pad.*)

YETTA: What? What's wrong?

MARTY: I can't concentrate! This constant arguing, bickering back and forth!

YETTA: You don't have to yell.

MARTY: Why, did anybody ever just talk here?

CY: Told you he'd come out when he was good and ready.

YETTA: Marty, take your hat off in the house.

MARTY: Ma, I'm trying to finish this scene, please!

YETTA: So what's stopping you? We were just . . .

MARTY: Please, I've got a whole play ahead of me.

YETTA (*very cool*): Sorry, Mister Playwright.

MARTY: Alright, let's just go back a bit. You were standing here, Ma, I'm still in the bedroom, and he's about to leave.

YETTA: But you're here now, just say goodbye. What's the big...?

MARTY: Ma, please, don't tell me how to write my play. I'm still a kid in this scene. There's a scene later on when he leaves us that's the big goodbye scene.

YETTA: He leaves us?

MARTY: Yeah, but it's not for years. There's still five scenes before . . .

YETTA: What happens then?

MARTY: Ma!

YETTA: What? After he leaves, what happens then? Tell me.

MARTY: You divorce. He runs around, starts drinking, becomes a drunk. Finally, burnt out, broke, he has to move back in with his mother, gets diabetes, loses both his legs. There's a big father-son hospital scene. And then when I leave, he dies.

CY: I die? Alone?

MARTY: Yeah, but it's not till late in the second act.

YETTA: What happens to me?

MARTY: You…never remarry, Ma. End up bitter, alone, miserable in Miami.

YETTA: That's it?

CY: This is a comedy?

YETTA: Was that all true? Is that what really happens?

MARTY: It's a play, Ma, make-believe.

CY: So you made all that up, right? It's not really…?

MARTY: Let's see, where were we? Ma, you were just about to cry. Dad . . .

YETTA: Does he really leave us?

MARTY: How do I know? I'm not God.

CY: Of course not Yetta! I'd never leave, I swear!

MARTY: You liar! You leave when I'm eleven years old.

CY: But you just said…!

MARTY: I make it up as I go along.

CY: What are you tryin' to pull here, huh?

MARTY: Nothing.

CY: Got to start trouble again, don't you?

MARTY: What?

CY: Some things never change!

MARTY: What are you talking about?

CY: You, Mister Playwright! It's just like when you were a kid, little mister in-between.

YETTA: Why are you blaming him?

CY: How she cooed and pampered you—her little Lord Fauntleroy.

MARTY: I hated…That's why I always ran to my room. Dad, you've got it all wrong!

CY: Yeah, wrong, right! You sucked up all her…! Nothing left for me. No room left at the inn!

MARTY (*throwing his pad and pen down*): That's bullshit!

YETTA: What's going on here?

MARTY: You were too busy fooling around with all your girlfriends! Never home with us. Couldn't wait to…!

YETTA: What's all this blame? Blaming!

CY: Only reason I fooled around was because your mother wouldn't…!

YETTA: The play, Marty! Your play! WHAT THE HELL'S GOING ON HERE?

(*Marty and Cy look at her. It's quiet in the room for a moment, then*)

MARTY: Nothing, Ma, nothing. This is part of the play. A dramatic moment. Dad and me were rehearsing the big father-son confrontation scene, top of the second act.

YETTA: So much anger, hostility? Can't you fix it? Make it funny?

MARTY: Ma, this isn't "It's a Wonderful Life." You can't always make things better. Now let's see, where were we?

CY (*putting his arm around Marty's shoulders*): Marty, you gotta change that ending. Please, me dying all alone like that, it's just too sad.

MARTY: Everybody's a critic.

CY: Please?! Couldn't you just…?

MARTY (*walking away from him*): I'm sorry, I can't.

YETTA: You've made me the villain here, you realize that?

MARTY: No I didn't.

YETTA: Couldn't you just . . .

MARTY: Coulda-woulda-shoulda! What happened, happens. It all stays in the play!

CY (*upset, starting to leave, going toward the bedroom*): Well then it happens without me!

MARTY: Dad, you don't leave yet! We've still got . . .

CY (*as he leaves*): No? Just watch me! (*He leaves, goes to the bedroom, slams the door.*)

MARTY (*calling to him*): Dad, that's my room! (*Marty turns to Yetta. She looks at him for a moment, then starts to leave.*)

MARTY: Where are you going?

YETTA: I'm sorry, Marty.

MARTY: But Ma, you don't leave.

YETTA: No? You still haven't finished the play yet, remember? And what happens, happens. (*She leaves, goes to Marty's bedroom.*)

MARTY (*calling to her*): Ma. Ma!

(We hear the bedroom door slam and lock. A light change. Marty slowly looks around the kitchen. He picks up the pen and pad off the floor, writes something.)

"Marty slowly looks around the kitchen. He picks up the pen and pad off the floor, writes something."

(*He sits down, takes his hat off and puts it on the table.*)

"He sits down, takes his hat off and puts it on the table."

(*Suddenly he turns toward his bedroom.*)

"Suddenly he turns toward his bedroom and calls out . . ."

(*Just as Marty opens his mouth . . .*
                                        Blackout)

CURTAIN

36

THE NONREALISTIC PLAY

Realistic and nonrealistic drama distinguished. Distortion of time.
Distortions of character. Dreamscape settings. Risks in the nonrealistic
approach. Learning from nonrealistic plays. Making choices.

Until now, we have been dealing with **realistic drama.** It creates an illusion
that reflects and conforms with the world about us. Events may be surprising, but they are believable. It avoids the **deus ex machina,** the improbable
event used to solve a problem. The passage of time is generally chronological. If the plot skips ahead a week or a year, the jump is made clear. There is
no imprecise blurring of past and present or of different centuries. Settings
are clearly defined (a living room, a jail cell, a forest), borrowed from the
world as we know it. Characters are mortal and limited in the same way we
are. They can't fly like birds or turn into frogs.

The term "realism" also applies to a period in literary history, but I will
use the term in its nonhistorical, purely descriptive sense. These plays mimic
life.

Nonrealistic drama, on the other hand, is an illusion that in some ways
resembles a dream. Such plays often *seem* real just as dreams usually do, but
the plot may be an illogical sequence of events in which time is distorted or
ignored, characters may behave in ways that lack motivation, and the setting
may be strange or a satiric exaggeration.

Nonrealistic drama is a broad term that covers a variety of approaches,
all of which depart from what we think of as the natural order. It includes
fantasies, dream plays, cartoon-like satires, and premise plays. Like free
verse, these plays don't abandon all form; they merely replace the familiar
conventions of realism with a set designed for that particular play.

At first glance, these two approaches appear to be entirely different.
Actually they have much in common and frequently borrow techniques
from each other. I will begin by describing their differences, but keep in
mind that there is no sharp line between them.

Distortions of Time

Realistic drama keeps track of time. If there is a gap, it is often made clear in the program notes: "Next week," the audience is told, or "A year later." Nonrealistic plays tend to ignore or twist it.

Samuel Beckett's *Waiting for Godot* has become a popular prototype for **theater-of-the-absurd** plays and illustrates the way time can be ignored. There is nothing in the script that indicates a historical period. You can think of it as a contemporary or a medieval drama—take your pick. And while there are references to times of the day, there is also a sense that this has been going forever. The play is like a long and rather hazy dream with no distinct beginning or end. This indifference to both historical time and clock time is common in nonrealistic plays.

Another approach to time is to warp it. Time warps are popular in science fiction, but they are often given some kind of rational explanation. In nonrealistic drama, time frequently slides without explanation.

Time in *Coulda, Woulda, Shoulda* is particularly inventive. As the play opens, we see a young married couple with a child of about four or five. The familiar kitchen setting and the two parents seem to suggest that this is going to be a realistic play. Our assumption, however, is shattered when Marty the son enters. The stage directions tell us that he is "in his forties, wearing large children's pajamas, a pair of glasses and a black hat. He's carrying a pen and pad."

What's going on? In one sense, the time has leaped forward 35 years. Marty has grown up. You could show this in a realistic play by starting a new scene without the parents or with them grown old, thereby accounting for the passage of time "logically." But in this play the parents remain just as they were, and Marty appears as an adult—a blend of the 40-year-old playwright and the child he was, still in his pajamas.

Later he confirms this fusing of time periods by saying, "I'm still a kid in this scene." On one level he is referring to the script he is writing in which the character based on himself is still a child, but in another sense the line refers to the scene in the play we are watching. He is *both* the 40-year-old playwright and the child in the same scene. Is this logical? Not literally. But think for a moment what it would be like to be writing a play that includes a character based on yourself at four or five. As you write, aren't you both the playwright and the child? The distortion of time then becomes a metaphor: The situation is *like* being a writer and a child at the same moment.

Alterman doesn't stop there, however, with his time tricks. Marty as playwright begins to tell his parents what will become of them in the future. His father will become a drunk, go broke, get diabetes, lose both his legs. As for his mother, she will end up "bitter, alone, miserable in Miami."

Is the playwright, Glenn Alterman, saying that this is what will really happen to the mother named Yetta, or is the playwright in the play named Marty making this up? We laugh, but to Cy this is no joke.

The distortion of time becomes a commentary on the illusion of theater in this exchange:

YETTA: Was that all true? Is that what really happens?
MARTY: It's a play, Ma, make-believe.

She has believed his story enough to be alarmed at the future that seems to be in store for her and her husband. We smile at how quickly she has been taken in by something that is "only a play." But what about us in the audience? Aren't we accepting the illusion that these people on the stage are going through a real crisis?

Toward the end of the play, there is one more time shift. First Marty's father leaves and then his mother. But notice that they don't go outside. Instead, they go into Marty's room and slam the door. Where are they really? In Marty the playwright's mind. The bedroom, after all, is the room for memory and for dreams.

If you look closely at what this play does with time, you will see that there are three scenes. The first, with the parents alone, is unmistakably the past. It is Marty's childhood. The second is a dreamlike blend with the parents as they once were and the son grown, an "unrealistic" mix of two periods. We accept the absurdity of it just as we accept similar distortions in dreams. The final scene begins as soon as both parents are offstage. Marty, alone, is writing a play about what is happening to him. And what will happens when he calls out to them after the last line of the play? We can't say for sure, but isn't it logical that the three of them will go through this again? Anyone who has written about people who were once close to them will remember how often one goes through these confrontations.

The distortion of time in that play occurs within the life of the protagonist. We can call this type *biographical time warps*. Another way to bend time is to slide historical periods together, creating *historical time warps*. Characters from history can appear in contemporary time periods; characters from the present can slide back. When those shifts are made in fairly simple drama and films designed for mass audiences, they are usually introduced with a so-called scientific explanation involving some kind of time machine. The concept was not entirely new even when H. G. Wells popularized it in *The Time Machine* in 1895, and it has been repeated in plays, films, and novels regularly ever since. When historical time warps are used in more sophisticated contemporary works, however, that half-hearted attempt to provide a mechanical explanation is usually dropped. The result is looser, more dreamlike.

The play by David LeMaster which appears as the next chapter is a wild, flamboyant use of historical time warping. I won't spoil it by analysis in advance, but picture Abraham Lincoln as fugitive, an Uzi in hand, holing up in a cheap motel room. That's just the start.

I have focused on time here because it is one of the most visible distortions in many (though not all) nonrealistic dramas. In a broader sense, however, it constitutes a different approach to plot itself. The realistic plot is a sequence of actions that is considered logical in the sense that it is similar to our daily lives. The nonrealistic plot can be called logical in that it makes sense symbolically, though not literally. If you find this premise difficult to imagine, contrast the sense of reality we have in daily living with our equally vivid sense of reality when we are in the middle of a dream. Both have the power to evoke pleasure, fear, laughter, and tears, as do both realistic and nonrealistic plays.

Distortion of Character

Characters in realistic drama, you remember, are a mix of consistency and variation. The variations are what give a character individually, but they have to be explained at some point. If a normally kind father strikes his child apparently without cause, the audience expects to find out what drove him to it before the play ends.

Characterization in nonrealistic drama may be confusing in literal terms, but usually there is a symbolic explanation. Marty in *Coulda* is a good example. In the central portion of the play he is both a child in pajamas and an adult "in his 40s." His parents treat him as a child ("Marty, take your hat off in the house") and also as an adult playwright ("Sorry, Mister Playwright"). He also has a third role, that of a seer or oracle who can literally see into the future. His mother asks, "After he leaves, what happens then?" And when Cy learns what is in store for him, he says, "I die? Alone?" They're not talking about a play being written, they've come to believe that this is their future.

So in one character we have a child, an adult playwright, and an oracle of future events. Alterman the playwright is doing in dramatic terms what Pablo Picasso did in art when he drew figures portraying simultaneously both frontal and profile views. There is a logic there, but it is a symbolic logic, not a literal representation.

The parents are less obviously symbolic, but they too are handled symbolically. In the opening scene they appear to be highly realistic. They are fond and concerned parents. The father's growing irascibility in no way violates what we would expect in a realistic play. But as soon as their son appears as a grown man, their role changes. They become credulous individuals, prepared to believe that their son can see into the future. At the end of the play, their role changes once again. By entering Marty's room, they become mere memories rather than flesh-and-blood characters. The implication is that they may be recalled by Marty as playwright at any time.

Coulda is an inventive mix of realistic and nonrealistic elements. In other plays, we are in a nonrealistic dream world from start to finish. In a bitter and brutal play called *The Lesson* by Eugene Ionesco, a raving professor berates his young students in a manner that by realistic standards we would classify as child abuse. Eventually he kills them for no apparent reason. If we made the mistake of viewing this play as an attempt at realism, we would find it an appalling act of violence without credible motivation. The arbitrary nature of the killing would lead us to judge the play to be a failure. "That's just not believable," we would say. But the playwright is not concerned with psychological motivation or even characterization. His theme has to do with the nature of authority and the abuses of absolute power. He has, in effect, drawn a savage cartoon to illustrate his point. Cartoons have the power to argue, even shock, but they deal with ideas, not people as people.

When characters in nonrealistic plays are satiric representations of abstractions like the professor in *The Lesson*, they are usually "flat." They don't have much background. They seem to spring fully formed from nowhere. But this doesn't mean that such characters are more easily created. You have to make sure that the audience understands your intent. If you are too obvious, the play may turn into a simple skit, but if you are not clear enough, the audience will be too baffled to applaud.

When historical figures are used in nonrealistic plays, characterization is often comically different or even the opposite from the generally accepted view of that individual. It's easy enough to do this in an adolescent way just to get laughs—as simple and forgettable as drawing a mustache on a picture of the Mona Lisa. But when it is done with skillful wit, distortion of a historical or public figure can become ingenious and insightful satire.

In the play you are about to read, the butt of the satire is not Abraham Lincoln himself but bizarre conspiracy theories and the overnight creation of celebrities. The historical figures in this case are the means to an end, not the end itself.

Dreamscape Settings

Many nonrealistic plays call for realistic **sets**. *Coulda* takes place in a realistic kitchen and the LeMaster play you are about to read is set in a cheap motel room. But in some plays the set itself is nonrealistic. Often the distortions are symbolic. Elmer Rice's *The Adding Machine* deals with a protagonist who is a cipher in a highly mechanical and stratified society in which his associates go by numbers rather than names. Appropriately, he is named Mr. Zero. His apartment is covered with numbers—on the walls, the furniture, and even the lampshades. The set amplifies the symbolic imagination that dominates the play.

Sometimes a dreamlike set is so striking and so fanciful that it remains in the memory long after the characters have been forgotten. The set in Ionesco's play *The Chairs*, for example, is a castle in the middle of the sea. The semicircular room is very sparse but has a total of ten doors—all of which are used. The script calls for the realistic sound of boats moving through the water as guests arrive, but we have no idea where they are coming from. The audience does not concern itself with questions of where this might be; it accepts this dreamlike setting just as it accepts the time warps in *Coulda*.

Risks in the Nonrealistic Approach

Since there are no clear guidelines in nonrealistic drama, it is easy to spend valuable time developing a script that doesn't have much potential. Here are three approaches that are apt to defeat your best efforts.

The first is the too-familiar **allegory.** No matter what you do with characters who resemble Adam and Eve, they will still seem like all the cartoons we have seen over the years. The same applies to Christ-like figures no matter how sincere your intent. And the last-couple-on-earth plot is as tired in drama as it is in fiction. You run against terrible odds if the audience's reaction is "Oh not another one of those" at the very outset.

Another type to guard against is the humorless sermon. It seems to be a particularly great temptation in nonrealistic plays, because they tend to be what is known as thesis-driven rather than character-driven. That is, nonrealistic plays are often dominated by an idea rather than rooted in character. But for this very reason, the thesis shows through more blatantly. Your intent may be true to your deepest convictions, but you're not going to win converts by having a character shout "Don't you realize that violence generates more violence?" or "The trouble with you rich slobs is . . ." or "Under the skin we're all the same." It doesn't matter how noble your intentions are, sermons are box-office turkeys.

This doesn't mean that your plays should be bland. Nor should they be without conviction. It does mean that you have to present your case obliquely. One of the best ways is to introduce comic elements. When Marty the playwright in *Coulda* tells his parents that his mother will "end up bitter, alone, miserable in Miami," his father says "This is a comedy?" It's a laugh line, but in an almost subliminal way it contributes to the theme as well. It asks a larger question: Just what is comedy? Where is the division between comedy and serious drama? In this case, Marty, the playwright in the play, is writing what seems like a serious and possibly humorless script, but the playwright Alterman is a witty writer with a flare for comedy. We laugh at aspects of the play we are watching, but hidden just below the surface is a serious statement about how difficult it is to write a play based on people who still have a strong emotional hold on you. That genuine and challenging concern sneaks up on you after the curtain drops.

The third danger, and the worst, will sound familiar to you because I described a version of it in the fiction section: the hopelessly obscure nonrealistic play. If your audience can't see any coherent pattern, it will simply walk out. You can't depend on novelty value alone. And you can't draw on the emotional appeal of characterization the way realistic drama often does, because your approach is necessarily idea-oriented. For these reasons you should be sure that the ideas you are working with hold together and make a statement that is both logical and compelling.

Martin Esslin puts it this way in *The Theatre of the Absurd*:

> Mere combinations of incongruities produce mere banality. Anyone attempting to work in this medium simply by writing down what comes into his mind will find that the supposed flights of spontaneous invention have never left the ground, that they consist of incoherent fragments of reality that have not been transposed into a valid imaginative whole.[1]

As often as this wise warning is repeated, obscure and confused plays continue to be the bane of drama workshops. When they get into production, they are an agony to watch. Some are unintelligible because the playwright has not read his or her script from the audience's point of view. Private references known only to the playwright, personal visions from waking or sleeping dreams, and symbols too elusive to be grasped even after a careful reading all contribute to the unintentionally obscure play.

Worse, some plays are knowingly obscure. The motive may be a misguided notion that sounding deep will win a following. Or it may be a simple disdain for the audience. It should (but doesn't) go without saying that drama is one of the most public arts. It involves not only the writer but producers, directors, actors, and ultimately audiences. It should never be treated as a private indulgence.

Learning from Nonrealistic Plays

When one first approaches nonrealistic drama, it sometimes seems like literary anarchy without limits or traditions. Actually it has a significant history from which one can learn a good deal. Although the focus of this text is on the process of writing, not literary history, a brief introduction to the two

---

[1] **The Theatre of the Absurd**, Martin Esslin, Penguin Books.

major schools of nonrealistic drama is important. Studying what has been done in this area is one of the best ways of discovering new directions for your own work.

The first of these two schools is **expressionism.** This movement encompassed painting, fiction, and poetry beginning at the turn of the century and continuing through the 1920s. Early examples in drama are seen in the plays of August Strindberg, a Swedish playwright. Plays like *The Dance of Death* and *The Dream Play* are readily available in translation and provide vivid contrasts to the realistic drama of the time by such playwrights as Henrik Ibsen. Strindberg's plots were frequently dreamlike, his characters symbolic rather than psychologically comprehensible, and his tone frequently dark and pessimistic.

Another excellent example of early expressionism is the Czech dramatist Karel Čapek. His nightmarish vision of the future, *R.U.R.*, is an early sample of science fiction complete with robots who revolt against their masters. More thematically comprehensible than many of Strindberg's more dreamlike works, *R.U.R.* has a strong element of social protest. This contemporary-sounding play was written in 1920.

For a good example of American expressionism, I would recommend Elmer Rice's *The Adding Machine*, a play I described earlier with regard to the highly symbolic and dreamlike set. Costumes, set, action, and dialogue are all distorted as they are in dreams, but also as in dreams there is an internal consistency that allows us to make sense of it all. We know what it means to be treated like a number, and most of us have on occasion been made to feel like a zero. What we see and hear in this play is distorted, but what we feel is sadly familiar and real.

In the 1950s and 1960s there was a new surge of interest in nonrealistic drama. This movement became known as **theater of the absurd** because many of the playwrights shared the existential notion that life is absurd in the sense of being without ultimate meaning. Oddly, few of them recognized the other important aspect of existential thought: that we create meaning and values by the way we act. As a result, absurdist plays tend to be pessimistic and often cynical.

This school is best represented by the works of Eugene Ionesco, whose plays *The Lesson* and *The Chairs* I have already described. Other such playwrights include Samuel Beckett, Harold Pinter, and occasionally Edward Albee.

Making Choices

As I have pointed out, there are very real risks in the nonrealistic approach. In spite of these, however, there are distinct assets as well. It is a particularly tempting approach if your theme is more important to you than your characters. You can cut through to the heart of your statement in a bold and imaginative manner without having to create credible characters or to construct a plausible plot. You are working with a medium that, like the political cartoon and the poster, lends itself to strong statements. As for form, you can let your imagination take flight. Like free verse, nonrealistic drama offers freedoms and also the obligation to find new and effective structures.

You may already have a strong preference for one approach over the other. Many playwrights do. But in deciding which basic route to take, keep an open mind. Consider the special nature of your projected play. If you are deeply concerned with the complexities of character, it may be best to work in a realistic manner. If, however, the concept you have in mind is charged with a strong idea or has come to you in a satiric vein, you may want to consider the freedom of the nonrealistic play. Your final decision will be based partly on what type of drama you enjoy reading and seeing and partly on the nature of the work you have in mind. Be sure to consider both factors.

37

A PLAY

by David J. LeMaster

The Assassination and Persecution of Abraham Lincoln

Characters

ABRAHAM LINCOLN
JOHN WILKES BOOTH
EDWIN BOOTH, aka ELVIS PRESLEY
UNION SOLDIER

Scene

Curtain up on a cheap room at the Motel 6. Abraham Lincoln bursts in, slams and bolts the door, then peers through the curtains to make sure he hasn't been followed. He is covered in blood. Lincoln pulls a suitcase out from under a double bed and rummages through its contents. Then he grabs the push-button phone and punches in a number.

LINCOLN: Mary? It's me. Did we pull it off? Good. Now listen, Booth is on his way, so skip town fast. No, go to Singapore first. You don't want the media following you. Right. I'll meet you in the Bahamas on the 20th. That's right. We don't have to worry about this Civil War thing anymore. From now on it's gonna be margaritas and sunshine.

(We hear three sharp knocks on the door. Lincoln hangs up, pulls an Uzi from his suitcase, and leaps over the bed to the door. He makes three sharp knocks in reply.)

BOOTH (*outside*): Sockdolagizing all over the place!
LINCOLN: Sic semper tyranus!

(*Enter John Wilkes Booth, a black man wearing a cheap polyester suit. Booth glances out the window as he shuts and bolts the door.*)

LINCOLN: Anybody outside, Booth?
BOOTH: We're cool.
LINCOLN: Help me get this off.

(*They peel away the bloodstained clothing to reveal a special effects jacket. Lincoln wears a Hard Rock Cafe T-shirt.*)

BOOTH (*pointing to Uzi*): What's that?
LINCOLN: Protection.
BOOTH: Protection? Come on, Abe. You don't know how to use this thing.
LINCOLN: I know good enough.
BOOTH: Put it down, you're gonna hurt someone.
LINCOLN: You telling me I don't know how to use a gun?
BOOTH: Just be careful, dude, that's all.
LINCOLN: Mind your own business, actor boy. Now how do we get out'a here?
BOOTH: Will you calm down? I'm the man with the plan.
LINCOLN: Well the man with the plan better start planning me onto the five o'clock to the Bahamas.
BOOTH: You got the money?
LINCOLN: I got the money.
BOOTH: In small, unmarked bills?
LINCOLN: In Susan B. Anthony dollars. What do you think, you muddle-headed dolt?
BOOTH: Relax. Soon as my brother Edwin gets here, we'll get this show on the road.
LINCOLN: Eddie? You said nobody else knew.
BOOTH: Chill, daddy-oh. We got it all worked straight.
LINCOLN: Chill? What kind of rhetoric is that? (*Mumbles.*) Actors. Look, you got any quarters? I want a Dr. Pepper.
BOOTH: You can't get a Dr. Pepper, you idiot! You're supposed to be dead. Now sit your ass down and relax. Here. How about some music?

(*Booth turns on a radio.*)

ANNOUNCER'S VOICE: Flash! The President of the United States has been shot! President Abraham Lincoln was announced dead at 9:00 this morning after receiving a mortal wound to the head during a performance at Ford's Theater in Washington. Vice President Johnson has assumed the Presidency and promises the American people he will stand tall in Lincoln's place.

JOHNSON'S VOICE (*Southern drawl*): Ladybird and I will do our best to serve this nation's darkest hour. . .

(*Lincoln shoots the radio with his Uzi.*)

LINCOLN: I always hated that son of a bitch!

BOOTH: Chill, man! You're gonna get the cops up here! You want the pigs blowing your cover and carting you to the pen?

LINCOLN: I haven't the slightest idea what you just said.

BOOTH: Look, why don't you lie down with Mr. Valium and take some Z's, comprende?

LINCOLN: I beg your pardon?

BOOTH: Sit your butt down, lanky boy, and shut the hell up! (*Lincoln sits.*) Now. We've got some planning to do. You sure Mrs. Lincoln knows where to go?

LINCOLN: She's going to Singapore first.

BOOTH: Good, we don't want nobody following her.

LINCOLN: Booth?

BOOTH: What?

LINCOLN: Do you really think we pulled it off?

BOOTH: What are you worried about? You heard it yourself on the radio.

LINCOLN: But the acting. Was I good?

BOOTH: You were alright.

LINCOLN: Alright?

BOOTH: Yeah. Alright. (*Quickly.*) Now look, the Union pigs are gonna be outside the hotel room waiting for me, but I'm gonna double cross them. I'm sending my brother Edwin. And they'll never suspect, because—

LINCOLN: What do you mean "alright"?

BOOTH: Huh?

LINCOLN: Are you patronizing me?

BOOTH: What are you talking about?

LINCOLN: You said my acting was alright.

BOOTH: Yeah. It was alright.

LINCOLN: That's all?

BOOTH: What do you expect me to say?

LINCOLN: I don't care—anything but alright.

BOOTH: It was fine.

LINCOLN: Fine?

BOOTH: What?

LINCOLN: I'm fine?

BOOTH: You were alright. You were fine. You were extraordinary. YOU'RE GONNA WIN THE FREAKIN' ACADEMY AWARD! WHAT THE HELL DO YOU WANT ME TO SAY?

LINCOLN (*pause*): Tell me I was good.

BOOTH (*pause*): You were good.

LINCOLN (*pause*): You're just saying that.

BOOTH: No, really. You were fine. Er...good.

LINCOLN: Will you give me some criticism?

BOOTH: What?

LINCOLN: I need some—

BOOTH: Look, we gotta finish these plans.

LINCOLN: I want to know what to work on for next time.

BOOTH: Next time?

LINCOLN: If there's a Civil War in the Bahamas.

BOOTH: There ain't gonna be no Civil War—

LINCOLN: But if there is. Tell me what to work on.

BOOTH: Well. (*Pause.*) You don't die very well.

LINCOLN: What do you mean?

BOOTH: Forget it.

LINCOLN: No. tell me!

BOOTH: It's just that you didn't die real well, that's all.

LINCOLN: That's all? But that's the only thing I did!

BOOTH: Can we do the plans now?

LINCOLN: What was wrong with it?

BOOTH: Nothing, I—look Abe, it's just that your leap from the balcony was too much, okay?

LINCOLN: Too much? But I was dying.

BOOTH: Whatever. People don't die that way.

LINCOLN: What do they do?

BOOTH: I don't know—they just die, that's all. They don't jump off the balcony. And they don't give soliloquies.

LINCOLN: They do in Shakespeare.

BOOTH: This ain't freakin' Shakespeare! And for God's sake, it didn't have to go fifteen minutes. Five minutes would've been plenty.

LINCOLN: Rubbish. Damned Method Actor.

(*There's a knock on the door. Lincoln grabs the Uzi and leaps across the bed.*)

BOOTH (*wrestling with him*): Put that thing down! What's the matter with you? Did you shoot up before we left the theater?

LINCOLN: They're not taking me back alive!

BOOTH: No one's taking you back! It ain't the Union troops—it's my brother.

(*He opens the door adn in walks Edwin Booth, aka Elvis Presley. He wears a red, white, and blue tuxedo.*)

ED: Thank you very much.

BOOTH: Mr. President, this is my brother, Ed.

LINCOLN: Say, you look familiar. Don't I know you?

ED: Well, I—

(*Lincoln accidentally fires the Uzi. Edwin drops dead.*)

LINCOLN: Oops.

BOOTH: You just shot my brother!

LINCOLN: You were right.

BOOTH: Right?

LINCOLN: People don't deliver soliloquies when they die. They just drop dead.

BOOTH: You dirty rat! You done killed my brother! What are we gonna do now?

LINCOLN: Why are you asking me? I thought you were the man with the plan.

BOOTH: Plan? I'll tell you one thing, I didn't plan on you putting the hit on my number one man.

LINCOLN: Sorry. Guess I got carried away.

BOOTH (*looks out window*): Damn! It's the Union pigs!

LINCOLN: They're not taking me alive!

BOOTH (*frantic*): Chill, man! We can detour to Mexico and meet Whitman. . .

LINCOLN: Who's Whitman?

BOOTH: Dealer friend. Writes poetry about grass.

LINCOLN: Forget it. I'm not trusting you and your hippie friends anymore.

BOOTH: Then you're on your own. I'm out'a here!

LINCOLN: Where are you going?

BOOTH: I ain't going to jail for you! I'm turning myself in.

LINCOLN: Like hell you are.

(*Lincoln shoots Booth. Pause. Now there are two dead bodies.*)

LINCOLN (*pause*): Damn.

VOICE OUTSIDE: Booth! We know you're in there! Come out with your hands up!

LINCOLN (*panicking*): Give me two minutes.

VOICE: You got about sixty seconds and we're coming in to get you!

(*Lincoln looks around room, then sees Elvis. He puts on the tux and tries imitating Elvis' walk in front of the mirror. Enter a Union soldier in a Civil War uniform.*)

SOLDIER: Alright, John Wilkes Booth, we got you surrounded and I—Oh! It's you! Edwin Booth.

LINCOLN (*as Elvis*): Hi. How you doing.

SOLDIER: Oh! I'm your biggest fan!

LINCOLN: Thank you very much.

SOLDIER (*sees bodies*): Why look at this! You've killed your own brother!

LINCOLN: Had to. He killed the President of the United States.

SOLDIER: Oh, Mr. Booth. What a great man you are.

LINCOLN: Thank you very much.

SOLDIER (*shouts out doorway*): Hey fellas! Edwin booth shot his brother and some other guy cuz they killed Mr. Lincoln!

VOICES: Hooray!

SOLDIER: Mr. Booth. May I have your autograph? It's for my daughter—

LINCOLN: Sure. No problem.

(Lincoln puts his arm around the soldier and they exit. Lights down. We hear the radio announcer's voice.)

ANNOUNCER: And now, in his new "I Killed the Man Who Assassinated Abraham Lincoln" Tour, America's greatest heartthrob—Edwin Booth!

(Spotlight on Lincoln. He has completed the transformation into Elvis and sings "A Hunk, a Hunk of Burning Love." Lights fade with the song.)
(Blackout.)

CURTAIN

38

VISUAL IMPACT

The impact of the familiar. Distortions that enhance realism. Symbolic sets. The bare stage. Lighting effects. Costumes: realistic and symbolic. Action: defining scenes, setting the pace, dramatizing conflict. Writing from the tenth row center.

A script is not a play. A script is a manuscript that describes a play. The play itself is a dramatic performance presented on a stage.

Because most of us have read more play scripts than we have seen actual productions, it's easy to forget that the actors' lines are only a portion of the total dramatic work. A good script also provides direction for set designers, lighting technicians, costume designers, and a director who will choreograph action on the stage. True, your first efforts are unlikely to end up in production, but you should always write as if they will.

There are, of course, many different things you can do on a stage. You can deliver poetry readings, recite monologues, have several actors present dialogues. But unless you have the visual component, what Aristotle called *the spectacle*, you don't have a drama.

This visual component is made up of several different elements: the physical set, the lighting, the costumes, and the all-important action of actors. Although directors, set designers, and actors all need some latitude, they also need a play that gives them the opportunity for visual impact. This chapter has one urgent message that I will repeat several times: When you write any type of play script, maintain a mental picture of what your stage looks like scene by scene, moment by moment.

The Realistic Set: The Impact of the Familiar

The term **set** includes everything the audience sees except the actors themselves. Although each set designer will approach a play slightly differently, playwrights usually specify what the locale is and which properties are essential. These general suggestions often classify the set as falling into one of three loosely defined types: realistic, symbolic, or bare.

The *realistic set* is so common today that we tend to think of it as the traditional approach. Actually it is a fairly recent development—less than 200 years out of the 2,500 year-old tradition of Western drama. Truly realistic details on the stage had to wait until the introduction of electric lights. When Ibsen's plays were first produced in England in the late nineteenth century, audiences gasped with amazement at the sight of a perfectly reproduced living-room scene complete with real books in bookcases, portraits on the walls, and doors that opened and shut. Soon the stage directions for the plays of James M. Barrie and George Bernard Shaw began to reflect this new realism by including the most minute descriptions, even to the title of a book left "carelessly" on a coffee table.

We can no longer depend on that kind of naive wonder, of course. Film and television have made realism commonplace. But when a realistic set is constructed with skill and imagination, it still can create enormous impact. Even today, highly effective sets presented on traditional stages are occasionally greeted with applause even before the first character appears on stage. The audience is applauding the illusion of the familiar.

How much detail should a script include? There is no standard policy, but the tendency now is to be brief. One reason is that there is such a variety of stages today that playwrights can no longer be sure of just how their work will be presented. The traditional stage has what is known as a *proscenium arch*, which forms a picture frame for the action, and a curtain that signals the beginning and closing of the dramatic illusion. But an increasing number of stages now have no arch and no single picture effect because they are open on three sides. This design allows more of the audience to sit close to the action. In such theaters, the curtain is replaced by a dimming of the lights. **Theater in the round** or **arena theater** extends this concept further by having the audience encircle the playing area as it does in a circus tent. The playwright's description of the set in the script should be flexible enough to allow set designers to adapt to a wide variety of stages.

In *Hello Out There*, for example, Saroyan merely states that this is to be "a small-town prison cell." On a traditional stage, this might be handled quite literally with walls and barred windows. But on a stage that is surrounded on all sides by the audience, the cell might be suggested by no more than a few bars suspended in dreamlike fashion. A good deal can be left to the imagination of the audience even in a realistic play.

Distortions that Enhance Realism

A realistic stage set always requires imagination. In fact, it is the distortions of reality that stimulate the imagination. A living room on the stage, for example, has no fourth wall. The audience imagines itself in that room even though in a literal sense we are looking at a half-dismantled house. In a play called *Period of Adjustment* by Tennessee Williams the focal object is a television set. Because it is often on, it is placed with its back to the audience upstage center. The set in the Broadway production was meticulously realistic, yet from a literal point of view the audience was impossibly wedged between the back of the television set and where the wall should be. In other plays, the audience finds itself behind fireplaces. Oddly, the mind of even the least imaginative theater-goes not only accepts this kind of distortion, it gives him or her the vivid sense of being in the room with the actors.

The significance of this impression for playwrights is that one can use a high degree of distortion to achieve a realistic effect. This is particularly helpful in plays that include both indoor and outdoors scenes. A yard may be separated from the interior of, say, a kitchen by a low board; a door may be used to suggest the division between two areas without adjoining walls. The same applies to the second story of a house suggested only by a flight of stairs. If the actors treat these divisions as real, the audience will perceive them this way too.

In Arthur Miller's *Death of a Salesman*, for example, the script calls for an upstairs room, two rooms downstairs, and a portion of the yard outside. It is realistic in that the entire set is treated as if it were a real house and yard, yet it requires an act of imagination to separate what is outside from what is inside. An actor in the kitchen can obviously see what another actor is doing outside; but it is soon made clear that a character must open the door in order to see. This setup is not as extraordinary as it seems when you recall that children at the beach can create the same sort of illusion playing house with various rooms merely marked in the sand. It's no accident that we call drama a play.

Another ingenious use of realistic design is seen in William Ritman's set for Harold Pinter's *The Collection*. Working closely with the director and the playwright, Ritman managed to present the illusion of three entirely unconnected separate settings on the relatively small stage of the Cherry Lane Theatre in New York. It has been duplicated on larger stages since then. As the action shifts from one area to the next, the lights on the other two are dimmed. The illustrations (drawn by Richard Tuttle) appear on pages 346 and 347. Turn to them now and notice how the illusion of where one is shifts in each case.

The great advantage of a set like this is that the playwright does not have to stop the action in order to change a set. As I have mentioned, dropping the curtain or even dimming the lights breaks the illusion and returns the audience to the theater itself. If in addition you ask a stage crew to scurry about in the dark and change a set, that break becomes even lengthier and more distracting. A set divided into different playing areas allows a playwright to maintain a steady flow of action.

The Collection, showing emphasis on the modern apartment, with the other areas dark.

The Collection, showing emphasis on the telephone booth, which is, in the play, some distance from either home.

Set design for Harold Printer's *The Collection* by William Ritman. Illustrations by Richard Tuttle. Reprinted by permission of William Ritman and Richard Tuttle.

The Collection, showing emphasis on the ornate apartment, with the other areas dark.

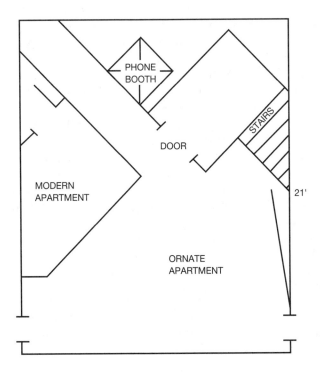

The Collection: a diagram of the stage, showing the technique of representing three entirely different scenes simply by shifts in lighting. Note how the unusual angles add both variety and depth even on a small stage.

A word of warning, however. If you, like most people, have watched more television and films than plays, you may unwittingly suggest an impossibly complex set. Remember that whatever you call for in the script will have to be built with wood and held together with nails. The set I described for *Death of a Salesman* is about as complex as you can get even on a big stage. It is a serious challenge in a small space. The three-part set for *The Collection* has the advantage of being essentially on one level, but on a small stage this is about the maximum number of playing areas that you can manage.

Fiction, film, and drama can all create the illusion of realism, but they do it in quite different ways. Fiction calls for the greatest use of imagination, translating words into as-if reality directly; film uses the least imagination, though it must convert a flat image into the illusion of reality. Drama has the advantage of live performers and three-dimensional sets, but it must use distortions creatively to develop a sense of actually being there.

The Symbolic Set

No matter how many distortions are used in a realistic set, the goal is to place the audience in an environment that is similar to the world in which we live. The goal of the *symbolic set* is in some ways just the opposite: it takes the audience out of this world. As in dreams, the surroundings may generate familiar sensations—fear, anxiety, confusion, or even childlike pleasure—but they don't resemble a familiar place.

Also like dreams, the symbolic set "makes sense" on a symbolic rather than a literal level. The undefined but dreary landscape of *Waiting for Godot* by Samuel Beckett, for example, does not bring to mind any specific place on earth, but it does seem to echo the dreary and uncertain lives of the characters who try without much success to make sense of life itself.

Other symbolic sets may be far more specific in detail. In Chapter 36 I pointed out how precise Ionesco is in describing the reception room of the castle in the middle of the sea in *The Chairs*, but you won't find that island in any atlas. Ionesco, like Elmer Rice, uses the set to suggest pictorially certain aspects of the human condition.

Some symbolic sets give delight through deception. The set of William Carlos Williams' play *Many Loves* is actually a series of tricks. As the audience enters the theater, the curtain is already raised and stagehands and electricians are still at work preparing the stage. One is on a ladder repairing a hanging lamp; another vacuums the floor. Members of the audience tend to check their watches and mumble about sloppy amateur productions. Only gradually do they realize—usually one at a time—that the play has already begun. The stage crew are in fact the characters.

Then actors begin rehearsing a play, and the audience gradually becomes absorbed in that "reality." Just as the play within a play appears to be a major concern, a director jumps up from the first row and objects. And so does the playwright—not Williams but the author of the play-within-a-play. Our attention turns to the relationship between these two men. The "many loves" of the title are as instable as the audience's perception of just what is the true setting of this play.

As I have pointed out, nonrealistic plays like the two you have read in this text can be presented with realistic settings, and essentially realistic plays like Arthur Miller's *After the Fall* can employ dreamlike shifts that are themselves highly symbolic. The choice is yours as to whether you want a stage set that suggests a real place or one that is designed to mimic a mood or suggest a theme directly.

The Bare Stage

This third approach, the *bare stage*, can be used in either realistic or nonrealistic plays. Thornton Wilder's *Our Town* is one of the most famous examples of an essentially bare-stage play. The script calls for a couple of folding chairs, two stepladders, and a plank, which in certain scenes is laid between them. The play is realistic and serious in tone, and leaving the stage almost bare in no way reduces the illusion of reality.

When *Our Town* was first produced in 1938, presenting a major production without an elaborate set was considered innovative. Yet no one was confused. Like many daring experiments in theater, it was based on an old tradition. Elizabethan audiences were required to use their imaginations to visualize the rapid succession of scenes in Shakespearean plays. If this approach interests you, examine closely how Shakespeare ingeniously identifies the setting at the beginning of each new scene.

If you plan to call for such a set, be sure that you indicate through the dialogue and stage directions where the characters are and what props we are being asked to imagine.

Here are some suggestions for making the best use of your set no matter what type:

- Don't assume that because your play is nonrealistic the set should be. And conversely, if your play is realistic, don't feel bound to call for an elaborately realistic set. Select a stage set that will be the most effective for your particular play.
- Consider ways in which the set can have an impact right from the start. Think twice before you call for the too-familiar sit-com living room—couch centered, two upholstered chairs on either side, front door to the left, kitchen door to the right, and stairs. We've been there too often.

- Be practical. Remember that some stages are small, budgets are limited, and there are limits to what one can build. You don't have to tell the set designers precisely how to proceed, but don't make impossible demands.
- Above all, use the set. Keep it in mind as you write, and give your characters a chance to move about in the space you have provided.

Lighting for Effect

Lighting is the newest of all dramatic techniques. The Greeks depended on the sun, as did the Elizabethans. And from the time of the first enclosed theaters in the late sixteenth century until 1914, lighting consisted of a glare of footlights designed simply to illuminate actors.

In 1914 the first spotlights were hung on the balcony rail of Wallack's Theater in New York. That was a radical improvement. But the progress made in the past twenty years with modern lighting boards is a quantum leap forward for drama. Although some playwrights leave lighting cues entirely to the director, others see lighting as an integral part of the whole effect and write basic instructions into the script.

The most obvious use of lighting is to suggest the time of day. It is natural enough to have the lights rise in the early morning or slowly dim as the sun sets. If the fading light also echoes an increasingly somber mood of the scene, the lighting will be additionally effective.

Much more often, lights are used simply to reflect the tone of the scene, whether inside or out. Quiet, low-key, or intimate scenes are enhanced with lowered lights; and conversely, scenes that are lively or dramatic can be charged with brighter lights. Techniques like these can be effective with any type of drama, but they are more frequently associated with nonrealistic plays.

In addition to influencing the overall tone of a scene, lights can be used to highlight a particular portion of the set while leaving other areas dark. As you can see from the illustrations of the three-part setting for *The Collection,* lighting effectively directs the audience's attention from one portion of the stage to another. In effect, selective lighting has the power to change the set.

In Arthur Miller's play *After the Fall,* a play that gives the illusion of a sequence of memories, lighting becomes essential to achieve the effect. Miller states in the script that his characters must "appear and disappear instantaneously, as in the mind; but it is not necessary that they walk off the stage." This effect is normally achieved through a complex series of lighting shifts. This technique is well worth considering if you have many scenes. It allows you to use a variety of sets without the distracting break in illusion caused by conventional scene shifts.

Lighting can also place a special emphasis on a character or highlight a key speech the way music occasionally does in film. Although Saroyan does-n't provide light cues in *Hello Out There*, it would be dramatic to isolate Emily at the very end with a single overhead spot in an otherwise darkened stage. This effect might repeat a similar one for Photo-Finish at the beginning of the play, drawing those two scenes together visually just as they are in dialogue.

Costumes: Realistic and Symbolic

Like the lighting, the costumes are a visual effect that in some cases is left to the director but in other cases is written into the stage directions. In realistic plays with a contemporary setting there usually is no mention of costumes in the script. Plays set in an earlier historical period may call for some description, though the director has the option to use contemporary dress. Nonrealistic plays, however, may make special use of costume to achieve symbolic significance. In such cases, playwrights sometimes become very specific.

The script for Alterman's *Coulda, Woulda, Shoulda* initially makes no mention of costume, so most directors would use what would be natural for a bartender and his wife. But the costume of Marty, the son, is precisely described in the script. His entrance is a dramatic turning point: the moment when an apparently realistic play suddenly becomes nonrealistic. How is this change achieved? First with a simple but significant stage direction: "A light change." This signals that something important will happen. Then the door opens and the audience is jolted by the sight of Marty as an adult "wearing large children's pajamas, a pair of glasses, and a black hat."

It is essential that the playwright be precise in the description of costume here, and it is equally essential that a director follow those directions. The fact that the character who has been described as a child is now standing there as a man "in his forties" is startling, but that alone doesn't communi-cate the symbol the playwright has in mind. Marty is not just a child grown up, he is simultaneously an adult playwright (he is carrying a pen and pad) and a child in his pajamas.

Why the black hat? Remember that as a little boy he had announced that he wanted to become a rabbi. He did not become a rabbi, but he wears the black that is frequently worn by rabbis, and in the tradition of prophets he seems to have the power to predict the future. In fact, he has to remind his mother. "I'm not God." But as any playwright knows, creating a good play is the next best thing.

In that absurd and comic costume, then, the character named Marty becomes part child, part playwright, and part prophet.

David LeMaster also uses costume for both comic and seriously thematic purposes in *The Assassination and Persecution of Abraham Lincoln*. Right from the explosive start of that play, costume is played against the dialogue to generate a wild incongruity. Lincoln's costume is one of the most familiar of any historical figure, but placing him in a Motel 6 room and having him talk like an escaped gangster on a modern phone plunges the audience into a bizarre world.

Not only is costume played against dialogue, it runs counter to action as well. Having Lincoln pull an Uzi from his suitcase and later kill first Edwin Booth, aka Elvis Presley, and then John Wilkes Booth is not exactly the Lincoln we remember from history books.

When a play begins like that with the dramatic volume on max, how can it generate still more impact for a finish? In this case, costume is used once again. Lincoln, facing death at the hands of a Union soldier, puts on Elvis Presley's costume, practices that famous strut, and passes himself off as the great American idol. It's a happy ending since, as everyone knows, Elvis never died.

In the next chapter I will return to some of the satiric themes running just under the frothy surface of this play, but our concern here is visual impact. The play makes full use of costume both for its comic effect and for its satiric statement as well.

It is not necessary to specify costuming any more than it is required to give stage directions regarding the lighting. Both will be left to the director if the script doesn't refer to them. They are valuable options, however, especially if you are reaching for special visual effects.

The Visual Impact of Action

Action gives shape to a play. As I described in the chapter on plot, most plays are divided into a number of secondary scenes. Those units are begun and ended by entrances and exits. On this basic level, then, the very structure of a play depends on action.

These entrances and exits have a significant effect on the pace and rhythm of a play. If you have too many of them, the work as a whole may seem choppy and disjointed. If you have too few—a more common weakness—the play may seem static no matter how absorbing the theme may be.

For this reason, most playwrights outline their plays by scene and think of the whole drama in terms of these relatively short units. If an individual scene goes on too long, it may have lost visual impact and appear to sag. The solution may be to revitalize it by adding more action or simply to cut unnecessary lines. In some cases it should be broken into two scenes by means of another entrance or exit.

Take a close look at the action you provide within each scene. Up to a point a good director can enliven a static scene by adding **stage business,** minor activity such as crossing the room, opening a window, pacing up and down. But there are limits to this. And occasionally you may find that you have made matters even more difficult for the director by specifying that your characters sit while they talk.

In the opening scene of *Coulda* the two parents discuss their young son. If the stage directions required those two characters to sit on a couch delivering those lines, there would not be much even good actors could do to keep the scene alive. But if you look closely, you will see that the playwright has not only allowed but has specified constant action. At the very outset Cy is described as "rushing around, getting dressed." He interrupts his wife by asking "Where's my belt?" She tells him and he puts it on. Next he asks, "Where's my shoes?" She tells him and he gets them, starts to put them on. Toward the end of that scene he grabs his coat and starts to go. His wife physically blocks the door, insisting that he talk with his son. As she continues to call to Marty, Cy discovers he doesn't have his car keys. Just before Marty's entrance, Cy finds the keys. He is constantly moving about on the stage, creating motion that echoes and dramatizes his growing agitation.

In a casual reading of the script, one would hardly notice this sequence of apparently inconsequential stage directions. But they represent the difference between an inept, static scene and one that has energy. Visually, that scene is kept alive until the dramatic appearance of Marty takes over.

The play is divided into three scenes—short, long, short. The first, as I have pointed out, is energized by minor action. The second, the relatively long one, also has action, but the dominant concern is thematic. The audience is held by questions about the creative process and the relationship between art and life. The last scene, short as it is, has the most stage directions. There is a good reason for this. The playwright is facing the difficult situation of having a character alone on the stage, so every bit of action has to be spelled out to keep that scene not only alive but vivid. If you look at that work closely, you will see that the playwright has paid close attention to the dynamics of motion on the stage.

Of the three plays you have read in this section, *The Assassination and Persecution of Abraham Lincoln* is by far the most charged with action. This is so partly because it is a satiric farce. In contrast, *Hello Out There* is a miniature tragedy that builds in stages to a crisis and ends in catastrophe, and *Coulda* is a comedy with a serious set of themes.

Satire always ridicules through some type of comic exaggeration, but a satiric farce like *Lincoln* achieves its comic effect by extreme exaggeration and often with the most unlikely situations.

A **farce** cannot wait for the gradually rising tension of a realistic tragedy like *Hello Out There*, nor can it take the time to unfold a humorous treatment of a serious subject as *Coulda* does. It plunges abruptly into the most unlikely situation from the very start, and each scene must cap or outdo the previous one. For this reason, *Lincoln* leaps from one bizarre scene to the next, never dwelling on any one long enough to lose the audience.

There are seven scenes in this play, compared with three in *Coulda*, and each is supercharged with action. Two, in fact, end with murder. If this were presented in a serious tone, it would be the worst sort of melodrama, but comedy deflates melodrama by intentionally making it absurd, so we laugh at it.

Notice that the death in *Hello Out There* is carefully prepared for and convincingly presented. It is entirely different from the two murders in *Lincoln*, which are not taken seriously by either Lincoln himself or the audience. Tonally they are on the level of Saturday-morning cartoons, though they have a satiric function that is far more sophisticated than what is aimed at children. This is a dramatic demonstration of the fact that the same type of action can create entirely different responses in the audience depending on how it is presented.

How does all this apply to your own work? In practice, the most common problem with early drafts of both serious and comic plays is that there is simply not enough action to keep the play moving. Neither profound nor witty language recited by static characters on the stage is enough to gather an audience larger than the playwright's closest and most loyal friends. One way to test whether your script is static and potentially dull is to write a description of each scene without quoting any of the dialogue. If you can summarize certain scenes with bland statements like "They sit on the couch and blame each other for the state of their marriage," you may have some serious rewriting to do.

Writing from the Tenth Row Center

When you write fiction, you tend to see each scene through the eyes of a chosen character. You are emotionally in the scene. When you write drama, however, a good portion of you must remain outside the action. You should be seeing your work, scene by scene, as if you were in the reputed best seat of the house—tenth row center.

If you have been writing fiction and are turning to drama for the first time, it may take a while to imagine yourself in the audience. It's important, though, because drama is a performance-oriented genre. Far more happens on the stage than appears on the page.

Out there in the tenth row looking at your own work you will never confuse the script and the play. Scripts don't portray fully the visual aspects like the set, the lighting, and costuming. As for pacing, scripts can be read at five times the speed of a play in performance. They allow you to skim over dreary, static scenes and get to the good part. Out there in the tenth row, however, you are picturing what your play would look like and hearing what it would sound like to the audience. You can judge for yourself whether a character has been rendered immobile or talks too long. You can identify whether a scene drags. From that vantage point you can make judgments about the set, the lighting, the costumes, and most of all about action. When you revise, you will have your eyes on the play, not just the script.

39
DRAMATIC THEMES

Theme and plot defined. Presenting themes through tragedy. Sliding themes into comedy. Hiding themes in farce. The thesis play: social and political issues in black theater and plays by women. Finding your own themes.

The **theme** in drama is that portion of the work which comments on the human condition. It is similar to a theme in fiction except that in drama it is frequently presented in bolder and more vivid ways—that is, more dramatically.

Be careful not to confuse theme with plot. **Plot** is a description of what happens. In describing plot, we refer to specific characters and events. In describing the theme, we refer only to the concepts or suggestion being made by the play. For example, the *plot* of Shakespeare's *Hamlet* might be described in highly condensed form like this: "A Danish prince named Hamlet has been urged by the ghost of his murdered father to avenge the father's death, but Hamlet, by nature an introspective and cautious individual, delays taking action and eventually is killed along with his mother and his stepfather."

Here, in contrast, is one of a number of different ways we could describe the *theme:* "The agonizing conflict between our instinct for vengeance and our ethical code of civilized restraint can lead an individual to disaster." Notice that the thematic statement does not name a particular character or identify exactly what happened. It focuses on the idea behind the play, not the events or characters.

For the sake of clarity and accuracy, a theme should be described in a complete sentence. Referring to the theme of that play simply as "revenge" or "indecision" is too vague to be helpful. Taking the time to describe in complete sentences one or two themes in your own work often helps to clarify your intent. If you find it impossible to do so, it may mean that your work is shallow or insubstantial.

As in fiction, what appears at first to be a single theme is often made up of a number of different but closely related concerns. The longer and more intricate a play, the more thematic suggestions it may contain. But as we will see, even short plays can contain a variety of related concerns. For this reason, the phrase **central concern** is in some ways more accurate than *theme*. I will use the two terms synonymously as I did in the fiction section.

Themes do not generally provide answers to the questions a play raises. *Hamlet* doesn't tell you precisely how to deal with unruly stepfathers, and *Hello Out There* is hardly good advice on how to handle a lynch mob. Although there are plays that do take very specific positions on political and social issues, these are said to present **theses** rather than dealing with themes. A thesis is a specific argument. The function of a play with a thesis is to persuade or convert, not to explore, I will return to that approach later in this chapter.

The three plays in this volume are quite different in treatment: a tragedy, a comedy, and a farce. Yet each has a cluster of related themes. The plays are helpful models for your own work because they manage to suggest a good deal in a very short space. As we examine them, however, keep in mind that the complexity of thematic suggestion that you see in a published play is not usually what came to the playwright in the first draft. Themes often develop slowly as the writer moves through successive drafts.

Presenting Themes Through Tragedy

Hello Out There is remembered by theatergoers mainly for its dramatic impact, but if it had nothing more to offer than that, it would be a melodrama. The terror of an individual facing a lynch mob has been repeated frequently in film and television dramas. The elevation of the play above the level of a simple thriller is achieved partly through characterization; but the real complexity lies in its thematic suggestion.

The play has several themes woven together. Your selection of which one you feel is *the* theme depends on which aspects of the play you found the most compelling. This is not to say that the play means whatever you want it to mean. It has been written with certain concerns clearly and intentionally stressed. Which one seems the most important, however, will vary with each individual.

Here are three thematic statements, each of which is suggested in the play through dialogue and action:

1. The world is full of genuinely lonely people whose efforts to make contact with others are frustrated at every turn.
2. Being poor and young in a small, mean-spirited town is very much like being a prisoner in a jail.

3. If you depend on luck to survive, the time will come when you may lose out—perhaps disastrously.

This is not an exhaustive list. Probably you could add others. But these represent a core, and we can support each not just with conjecture but from hard evidence from the play.

I put the one about lonely people first because Saroyan places such a heavy emphasis on it. His main technique is repetition. "Hello out there" is clearly the cry of a lonely person. It is not only used in the title, it appears as the opening and closing lines. In between, it is repeated twenty-five times!

In addition, Saroyan repeats the word "lonesome" twelve times, six of them just before and just after Emily appears for the first time.

How does Saroyan get away with so much redundancy? He has, after all, violated a basic "rule" that is still generally honored in the writing of exposition and most fiction. But drama has different rules. Remember that it is a continuous art form. A dramatic performance flows by the audience nonstop. Repetition is necessary to highlight themes. This intentional use of redundancy is, incidentally, one of several ways in which drama is more like poetry than fiction.

Photo-Finish is not the only character who is lonely and reaching out for contact with someone else. Emily is equally isolated. She tells Photo-Finish that the men in town laugh at her, and her father takes what little she earns. She has hung around the jail just to be able to talk with him. She describes her feelings directly:

> It's so lonely in this town. Nothing here but the lonesome wind all the time, lifting the dirt and blowing out to the prairie.

Even the woman who has accused him of rape is given the benefit of the doubt. She is pictured as a sad and lonely woman alienated from her husband.

As in many tragedies, there is a moment when it seems as if this yearning for companionship will be fulfilled by Photo-Finish and Emily, but his luck runs out and she ends up being in the same position he was in at the beginning of the play.

The second thematic statement shifts the emphasis to the parallel between Emily's life trapped in an isolated prairie town and someone held in jail. Those who have identified with her might see this as a primary theme. Clearly it is *a* theme even if it isn't the dominant one. The fact that the playwright has so carefully placed her in exactly the same position as Photo-Finish was at the beginning of the play and given her the very same lines is ample evidence that this was one of his concerns.

The third thematic statement, the one suggesting that those who depend fully on luck will eventually fail, is supported partly through the action of the play but also from the young man's nickname. In explaining it to Emily, he tells her that he has earned that reputation because the horses he bets on always lose by a nose. The fact that he is a gambler stresses the theme of luck, and his bad track record is a forewarning of his ultimate disaster.

As a writer you have to be careful about significant names like Photo-Finish. If you are too blatant, you undermine the sense of realism. If Saroyan had named his protagonist *Hy Risk*, it would seem contrived. But *Photo-Finish* is explained as a nickname and so seems plausible—though hardly subtle.

As you may have noticed, Saroyan also uses names of towns to highlight certain thematic aspects. The town where the protagonist is about to meet his death like a bull in the arena is called "Matador." And the town from which the freewheeling, irresponsible men come is "Wheeling." Saroyan makes sure that the audience does not miss these names by repeating each one twice—a recognition of the fact that in drama every significant detail has to be repeated.

The various themes or concerns in *Hello Out There* are presented fairly directly, and if you work with the script closely they may seem too obvious. But remember that the audience watching a play in performance cannot dwell on technique. If they respond to details like the name "Matador," they will do so almost subliminally. It is possible to find names that are thematically suggestive without hammering the audience with the implication. Many people have read or seen Miller's *Death of a Salesman* without noticing that the protagonist, a man who is low in the social order, is appropriately named Willy Loman.

Sliding Themes into Comedy

Technically *Coulda, Woulda, Shoulda* is a comedy because the complications that arise early in the play are more or less resolved at the end. There is no catastrophe as there is in most tragedies. Also there are many details that are satiric and just plain funny.

But it is not written merely to produce laughter. It is a play which, unlike most sitcoms, has themes worth examining and intricacies that call for a second look. In short, it has **resonance.**

Again, there is no one "correct" statement of the theme, but here are four that are clearly supported by evidence from the script:

1. Writing a play is like playing God—but not quite.
2. Writing a play about one's parents brings up old hostilities and frustrations.
3. Parents (and nonwriters generally) rarely understand what goes into writing a play.

4. Writing a play forces the playwright to look back to childhood and forward into the future at the same time.

The first goes to the heart of what is called the creative process. There *is* something godlike in creating people and places on the stage. Indeed, Quakers until fairly recently felt that the writing of both fiction and drama was too presumptuous to be encouraged in school. But as the play clearly demonstrates, the process is far too difficult to be compared with divine creation. We mortals work at it. "I'm not God," Marty tells his mother.

The second—the emotional difficulties encountered when one is writing about parents—is one that will be recognized by anyone who has tried it. There is something sadly comic about Marty's harsh dramatic treatment of his parents. He pictures his father getting a divorce, running around, turning to drink, getting diabetes, losing his legs, and then dying. What a revenge! As for his mother, she ends up "bitter, alone, miserable in Miami." That takes care of her!

This is the point at which the father asks, "This is a comedy?" We in the audience can see that this play that Marty is writing is, like so many therapeutic scripts, a sadly humorless failure, and that fact is partly what makes what we are watching a comedy. The hostility we are apt to reveal unconsciously in the dramatic scripts we write is a serious theme, but rather than present it directly, this play develops it through gentle satire.

The third thematic statement—that others don't understand what goes into a creative work—will also be familiar to those who write drama or fiction. Nonwriters tend to assume that what they see happen on the stage is what actually occurred in the playwright's life. And in this case the parents extend that misapprehension into the future, treating their son as some type of seer or prophet. "It's a play, Ma, make-believe," Marty tells her, but she doesn't believe him. The tradition of dumping on one's parents (especially celebrity parents) in drama and also in fiction is an old one, and the general public will never believe that much of such works may be "make-believe."

The fourth thematic statement turns the spotlight away from the audience and back to the playwright. In the act of writing, one must look back to childhood—often to unpleasant episodes—but such writing also requires speculating about the future. What might become of this character? Where will he or she end up? The implications are not always rosy.

There is another theme which, although not a major one, does add a depth to the characterization of father and son. The play touches on the fact that there is often a conflict between one whose first loyalty is to earning a living even at the expense of being a caring, considerate parent and one who is willing to risk financial insecurity to express himself through art. This theme is not developed at length, but it provides dramatic tension and adds to our understanding of both characters.

These are all serious themes, but rather than being thrust at the reader through repetition of key words and phrases as they are in *Hello Out There*, they are slid in almost unnoticed midst the laughter. That moment when Marty enters is a perfect example. There he is, a man in his forties in kids' pajamas. The audience, having expected a child, laughs. When we look at the script, stopping the action long enough to see what is being suggested thematically, it seems clear that the play is showing us the writer as he is (the adult man with his pen and pad) and the child that is within him. But the audience watching the play in production isn't analyzing. It's laughing. The themes will be communicated almost unconsciously, and of course they will become clearer after the performance is over. Comedies can have just as many serious themes as tragedies, but they tend to be presented less directly, woven into the laughter.

Hiding Themes in Farce

Farce is so exaggerated, so bizarre, so close to slapstick that if there *are* themes, they are often buried even more than they are in a comedy. Watching or reading *The Assassination and Persecution of Abraham Lincoln* for the first time, one may have the feeling that it is a bad-dream version of the Three Stooges. There are, however, several serious thematic concerns which probably register subliminally on first viewing and which appear more distinctly when one reads the script. Here are four, though here too you probably can add to the list:

1. Conspiracy theories about the death of famous people can reach absurd limits.
2. The current mania for destroying the reputations of formerly respected leaders is getting out of hand.
3. When it comes to believing that famous people like James Dean and Elvis Presley are really not dead, the public will buy anything.
4. If you are a famous leader or a popular celebrity, you seem to be able to get away with murder.

All of these themes are presented satirically. That is, each is exaggerated for the purpose of ridicule. And because the level of exaggeration is extreme and outlandish, the play is also a farce. The themes themselves, however, are quite serious, even biting commentaries on our society.

The first theme, alleged conspiracies, has its roots in the plethora of theories about the assassination of President Kennedy. If you push those to the point of absurdity (just a gentle nudge is enough in some cases), you come out with something like the theory that President Lincoln was involved in a secret plot with his alleged assassin, John Wilkes Booth.

The second theme is based on our sense of shock at seeing such a well-respected president ridiculed not only as a fraud but also as a rather vain actor who is concerned over how well he portrayed his death scene. This brings to mind all the historical biographies that have been published in the past decade designed to reveal the weaknesses, foibles, and in some cases the immorality of famous people. Some of these may be well founded, but others are clearly sensationalized. This "secret story" of Lincoln is the ultimate in sensational accounts.

Third, the play is also a satire of those ever-popular rumors that James Dean, Adolf Hitler, Elvis Presley, and others have been sighted alive in unlikely places. All LeMaster has to do to satirize this phenomenon is to render Lincoln immortal in the form of Elvis singing "A Hunk, a Hunk of Burning Love."

The fourth theme is based on the widely held suspicion that if you are famous enough it is unlikely that you will be held accountable even for murder. Lincoln in this play commits two murders without a flicker of remorse. Unpunished, he ends up a show-biz personality.

Which of these four is the *central* concern? That depends on which aspect you want to stress. They are closely related social commentaries on our society. Our fascination with conspiracy theories, exposés of famous people, rumors of immortality, and the occasional failure of the justice system are very much a part of the current scene.

LeMaster and Saroyan are both concerned with social issues in spite of the fact that their plays are fundamentally different in approach. Alterman's themes, on the other hand, focus on the creative process and the relationship between life and art.

In reviewing the way these three playwrights present their themes, you can see how crucial it is to present your themes through implication in ways that are neither too subtle for an audience to grasp in a single viewing nor so obvious as to appear forced and artificial. In serious, realistic drama, you depend on the credibility of characterization and the dramatic power of the plot to keep the themes from being too obvious. In comedy, themes are disguised by being a part of the humor. In highly exaggerated satire, the themes are so well buried under the farcical surface that some viewers may even miss them. But they are there and will be picked up by those who are familiar with social satire.

The Thesis Play: Social and Political Issues

Drama has always been associated with social statement and political protest. Medieval miracle plays were originally intended to teach Biblical stories to illiterate peasants, but some became vehicles for satire. Vehement political protests were made through plays during the depression years of the 1930s; and later, opposition to the Vietnam War became an equally strong topics.

Today, **black theater** is a dynamic force in socially concerned drama. Some plays develop themes of black identity, sharing the black experience with the whole society. Others present a specific thesis—a demand for political or social change or a call for reform.

The development of black theatre is relatively recent. With a few rare exceptions, theater was a white art form until well into the 1960s. Black playwrights like Langston Hughes, Ossie Davis, and Lorraine Hansberry are known to most for one successful play each, but few white theatergoers can name the others they wrote. Langston Hughes alone turned out more than 20 plays. As a result, black playwrights, as well as black directors and actors, have been deprived of audiences and of the training that comes from regular production. This backlog of artistic frustration amplifies a deep sense of social injustice, to produce themes of bitter denunciation.

The harshest of these are written consciously and directly to a white audience. Plays like *The Toilet* by Amiri Baraka (LeRoi Jones) are intentionally designed to shock white, middle-class theatergoers. Rather than *themes*, these plays present *theses*—strong statements that often recommend specific social action.

Conscious appeal to a white audience is also found in plays that are thematic and less accusatory. In Charles Gordone's *No Place to Be Somebody*, for example, the plot of the play is stopped twice for lengthy monologues delivered like prose poems from the center of the stage. One of these is formally titled "There's More to Being Black than Meets the Eye." The other is a verse narrative of what it is like for a black to try living like white suburbanites, suffering the scorn of both urban blacks and white neighbors.

Other plays address themselves more specifically to black audiences. The seven plays selected originally by the Free Southern Theater group for their pilot program are good examples: *Purlie Victorious* by Ossie Davis, and *Do You Want to Be Free?* by Langston Hughes among others. Another important play of the period is Martin Duberman's *In White America*. August Wilson has also achieved wide critical acclaim.

Women have also had a significant impact on drama in the past decade. As with black drama, plays by women vary from those that explore the woman's experience to those that make strong social or political statements. One of the more innovative playwrights is Ursule Molinaro, whose works vary from brief, nonrealistic plays in the absurdist tradition to full-length works. In one, *Breakfast Past Noon*, a mother and daughter have a series of arguments without ever addressing each other directly. They refer to each other consistently in the third person. The effect is like two antagonists who refuse to make eye contact. The play is a highly effective dramatization of a hopelessly alienated relationship.

This play and others by women have been collected in an anthology called *The New Women's Theatre* edited by Honor Moore. For a retrospective collection that gives historical perspective, I would recommend *Plays by and About Women* edited by Victoria Sullivan and James Hatch.

Finding Your Own Themes

If the themes of your work do not reflect your genuine feelings, the play will probably not ring true. If you borrow conventional concerns or truisms that do not affect you directly, you will probably find yourself borrowing stock characters and settling for hackneyed situations. Plays that have vitality, whether they are serious or comic, usually have themes that are strongly felt by the dramatist.

But don't feel that to be dramatic you have to focus on a social cause. Look at *Coulda*. It doesn't deal with themes like injustice, inequality, or violence. Instead, it explores the nature of art and life. These are not trivial matters, and clearly the playwright takes them seriously in spite of the comic nature of the play. The fact that a play is comic doesn't mean that it has to be mindless.

Can you say the same about a farce? There are plenty of lively farces written for stage and screen that are designed simply for laughs, but they are simple in the literary sense—entertaining but as insubstantial as Saturday morning cartoons. LeMaster has a great sense of crazy humor, but what gives *Lincoln* resonance, what makes it worth a careful second look on the page, are the thematic concerns we have been examining.

Themes are not a good starting point for drama. Intellectual ideas themselves are apt to lead to intellectual productions—a risky route for drama. But if you start with a situation that is emotionally charged, themes will emerge. Then they can be clarified and intensified.

Where does one find supercharged situations that might develop into a drama? One area to explore is your own roots. If you have a distinctive racial or national background, there will be tensions and perhaps successes and defeats associated with it. If your own life has been relatively secure, what about your parents' lives?

Even if you feel that your life has been in the mainstream and essentially uneventful, it hasn't been entirely smooth. No one's is. Seek out those situations that made you mad or frustrated or challenged, and transform them until they are large enough and significant enough for the stage.

In some ways, finding good thematic material for a play is similar to the process in fiction. But there are these three differences:

First, you need a situation or an incident that has genuine conflict. Fiction also thrives on conflict, but it can be subtle. Drama calls for something with real impact. Look for those moments in your life or in the lives of those close to you when individuals or groups of individuals were pitted against each other. Ask yourself exactly what were the themes behind the conflict. A play in which two individuals compete for a job may have action with no thematic element. But a play in which a young woman is about to be fired from her job in an appliance store for a theft which in fact her father has committed—there is a play concept with a cluster of potential themes about ethics, family loyalty, love, and the status of women.

Second, you need a theme that can be handled on a physical stage in a limited period of time. Never mind dramatizing *War and Peace*. Focus your theme on one manageable incident. If your concern is racial justice, for example, let one specific situation stand for the general problem. If the events you have in mind include several different settings or occurred over a span of several years, see if you can transform them into a plot that can be handled with a single set and a single time period. Unity of place and time are far more important in drama than they are in fiction, especially if your play is short. Your themes will be easily lost if the plot is fragmented.

Finally, consider ways to reiterate your theme. Remember how all these thematic repetitions in *Hello Out There* seemed so blatant when examined on the page? They blend together in an actual performance just the way brush strokes in a Rembrandt portrait merge when viewed from a proper distance.

Regardless of whether you are working with tragedy, comedy, or farce, fresh and significant themes will add depth and a sense of resonance to your work.

40

The Voices of Comedy

Tonal choices: humor and wit. Comedy of character versus comedy of situation. Satire: from subtle to farcical. Comic relief. Five pitfalls of comedy. Developing a comic sense

It may seem odd to analyze comedy. We think of it as springing from an intuitive ability. While it is true that a sense of humor can't be taught, almost no one is totally humorless. You don't have to be an accomplished comedian to translate what you see as a comic situation into a dramatic scene or an entire play. Doing so does, however, take more than intuition.

Before you adapt a comic situation for the stage, it is important to understand how wide a range of approaches you have at your disposal. Some differences are matters of tone; others are far more fundamental. The very intent of gentle comedy is different from, say, bitter satire. Inserting a farcical scene into a play that is otherwise built around a humorous development of character can do real damage. You can avoid a great deal of rewriting if you determine what type of comedy is appropriate for your particular play before you even outline the plot.

Tonal Choices: Humor or Wit

Although there is no sharp line between the tonal effects of humor and of wit, and both are often found in the same work, they do refer to significantly different approaches. Humor tends to be gentle and supportive. It shares with an audience foibles that we have experienced or are familiar with, such as the awkwardness of young people in love, the tensions associated with rituals like a job interview or a wedding, the anxieties, frustrations, and misunderstandings that parents face dealing with children and, conversely, that children experience dealing with parents. We tend to smile or laugh *with* such characters, not *at* them.

Humor is often based on gentle incongruities: the priest at a beer party, the gang member at an art opening, a man married to a woman half his age. Some of these situations have been overused in the endless stream of situation comedies for television, but fresh events occur in our daily lives and can be developed with greater insight than one often finds on the tube.

Wit, on the other hand, is often based less on the human condition than on verbal tricks: jokes, puns, plays on words. It often appears in the dialogue. Or it may be based on surprise: a totally unexpected turn of plot or an absurd set of misunderstandings. Tonally, wit is often sharp, clever, even jolting compared with the softer approach of humor. It can even be nasty. If you can imagine a graph that measures emotional response, humor would be shown by a gently undulating line while wit would produce spikes.

Satire is a form of wit with a specific purpose: to ridicule a person, a type, or an institution through exaggeration. As we will see, satire can be soft and humorous, but because it is always a form of criticism, it is more often sharp and biting.

Gentle humor is the dominant tone in the opening scene of *Coulda, Woulda, Shoulda*. When the mother, Yetta, reports that their son in the bath announced solemnly that he wants to be a rabbi, the audience assumes, incorrectly, that this is going to be a mildly humorous, realistic play. When Marty actually enters, revealed as an adult in a child's pajamas, the humor is more intense, but it is still humor.

The play maintains this tonal vein in spite of the serious themes. But in addition there are also some samples of wit in the lines. After Marty has announced the terrible future in store for both his parents, his father asks, "This is a comedy?" There is double meaning here, since the play we are watching is indeed a comedy, but Marty's play within a play appears to be a dismally depressing melodrama. A similar kind of double meaning occurs after Yetta complains about "so much anger, hostility" in her son's play and begs him to "fix it." Marty's response is, "This isn't `A Wonderful Life.'" The comment operates like a triple pun, applying to the play on the stage (with its serious themes), to Marty's play within a play (a depressing melodrama), and to what we see of their lives as well.

Wit, not humor, dominates *The Assassination and Persecution of Abraham Lincoln*. There's nothing gentle about the opening. The incongruity of Abraham Lincoln on the run, talking like a gangster, and handling an Uzi submachine gun is jolting. And before you can get used to that, you learn that he is in a plot with John Wilkes Booth, the man we had always thought was Lincoln's assassin. The script is peppered with little witty details: Lincoln calling Booth "actor boy" (historically he was an actor) and Booth getting his revenge by calling Lincoln "lanky boy"; Lincoln shooting the image of President Johnson on the television, neatly blending Andrew Johnson, actual successor after Lincoln's death, and Lyndon Johnson, successor after Kennedy's assassination. Even murder gets a laugh line: "You were right," Lincoln says, "people don't deliver soliloquies when they die."

The play is far from subtle, but it is an ideal example of how sharp-edged wit can be.

On a broader level, every scene has a jarring reversal. In addition to "Honest Abe" being seen as a thief and a con artist, his historical assassin is portrayed as his friend, the author of the Gettysburg address speaks contemporary street lingo, the nineteenth-century President Johnson is blurred with the twentieth-century one, Lincoln aspires to be an actor as Booth was in life, and finally Lincoln becomes transformed into a most unlikely alter ego, Elvis. None of this is gentle humor; it is all strident wit and irreverent satire.

Comedy of Character versus Comedy of Situation

The differences between humor and wit are matters of tone. Now we turn to matters of substance. Some comedies are rooted in character while others downplay characterization and depend almost entirely on the situation.

When you are in the early stages of writing a comedy, it is worth asking whether the concept you have in mind depends on building comic characters or whether your primary attention is on ingenuity of events and overall plot. That is, when you describe the work to someone in a sentence or two, do you find yourself talking about who is involved or about what happens.

Suppose, for example, you are exploring the possibility of a comedy in which an editor has hired a well-recommended journalist whom she comes to trust and admire only to find out that the newcomer is for all his charm a pathological liar with a capacity to disrupt the staff and her personal life as well. A play like this will probably be rooted in character. Plot will also be important (it always is), but your primary task will be to convince the audience that this editor deserves sympathy and the new journalist is credible as a smooth operator and a fraud.

Now imagine that you are developing a play with a young husband and wife who hope to move out of their apartment and are doing everything possible to induce the landlord to break the lease. They pretend they are keeping a dog, but the landlord loves animals; they paint the place black, but he is delighted; they pose as drug dealers, but all he wants is a cut of the profits. This is clearly a comedy in which the invention of original incidents is essential. The characters in such a play may be left reasonably undeveloped, while the focus of your efforts will be on plot. You have to keep generating fresh new incidents and end with some kind of unexpected and comic resolution.

Although these two approaches to comedy overlap, they represent an important distinction because they will determine where your primary attention must be placed right from the start. In the case of character-based comedy, you will not have to delve into character as deeply as you would in serious drama, but vividness and credibility are essential. It may help to write out a character sketch for your own use. You may find yourself satirizing certain types. Your major goal will be to make them convincing and memorable.

In situational comedy, on the other hand, you depend on plot. Not only do you have to generate lively action, you have to maintain an effective pace throughout. The sequence of events will have to move from mild to extreme, each scene topping the previous one. You may have to mute some scenes toward the beginning in order to keep them from upstaging those toward the end. More likely, you will have to devise ways of intensifying those close to the climax so that the audience will sense the development.

Of the two comedies you have read, *Coulda* relies more heavily on character. Although it is a short play, we get to know both parents as people. They are quite different from each other in temperament and values. The son also is a rounded character with hostilities running in conflict with almost childlike needs for support and approval. *Lincoln*, on the other hand, is all situation. It relies almost entirely on a wild, innovative plot and witty dialogue. The characters are so "flat" that they are almost like cartoon creations. We are not really shocked when they are shot or turn into other characters. We're focusing on the rush of bizarre events.

Satire: From Subtle to Farcical

Satire ridicules by exaggeration. Good satire defines its target carefully, aiming not just for laughs (though that's an important element) but for criticism. Because satire is funny, one hardly notices that it is almost always a moral statement. Even the silliest satire on television attacks people (usually public figures), types (particularly the pompous and hypocritical), or institutions (the bigger the better). Since stage plays have the advantage of being aimed at smaller, more selective audiences, satires tend to be more sophisticated. Often they are more challenging and provocative. It is no accident that totalitarian regimes maintain tight control of theaters and playwrights.

Satire covers a wide spectrum from the mildest sort of friendly spoof to the most vitriolic attack. In every case, however, there is some degree of exaggeration and some form of criticism.

Gentle as Alterman's humor appears to be at the beginning of that play, it soon generates some formidable satire. The short-tempered and insensitive father whose first priority seems to be getting to work, the indulgent mother who actually believes her beloved son can see into the future, and most of all the angst-ridden, humorless playwright who is blind to the fact that his script is a way of unloading a lifetime of hostilities. In our laughter, we recognize familiar types. The satire, however, is rooted in character and is softened with elements of compassion. They are all unhappy people, and to some degree we feel sorry for them.

The satire in *Lincoln*, on the other hand, is so heavily exaggerated that we call it **farce.** It is extreme in plot and pitiless in tone. No one comes off well, but we laugh.

Some farcical satires are essentially mindless and without a sharp focus, but this play is neither. As we have seen, *Lincoln* has precise targets. In fact, all the themes I suggested in the last chapter are actually presented in the form of biting satire. The play attacks people who believe in absurd conspiracy theories, books and plays that revel in undermining the reputations of historical figures, people who become convinced that certain deceased heroes are not in fact dead, and celebrities who appear to get away with criminal acts. That may seem like a diffuse set of satiric targets, but they all focus on negative attitudes that are sadly prevalent in our own decade.

Comic Relief

To this point, we have been treating comedy as if it were totally distinct from serious drama. Actually, the two are frequently blended. In fact, one of the most common weaknesses in student-written plays is a failure to employ **comic relief** in plays that are heavily dramatic. The play Marty is trying to write in *Coulda* is just such a work.

Most of us were introduced to the technique of comic relief when we first read a Shakespearean tragedy or his history plays. Shakespeare had a talent for judging just how much the audience could take and how to relieve the pressure with some kind of wit or satire.

His clowns (as in *King Lear*) specialize in wit: jokes, puns, and clever phrasing often commenting on the more serious aspects of the play in ironic terms. In the history plays such as *Henry IV: Parts I and II* and more briefly in *Henry V*, he employs satire of character in the form of Sir John Falstaff, a loudmouthed liar and reveler who almost, because of his faults, becomes engaging and memorable.

Even Shakespeare, however, had to learn the technique. An early play, *Titus Andronicus*, is unrelieved and heavy-handed drama ending with a hideous bloodbath. The lack of comic relief turns it into a melodrama that few find moving. For good reason it is rarely produced, but it serves as a most important reminder that no matter how much talent we may posses, we all go through a learning stage.

Contemporary drama almost always contains some form of comic relief. In fact, the comic sections may almost match those portions that are serious. After all these years, comic relief still takes the two forms Shakespeare found effective: a witty minor character who can comment on the action or even kid the protagonist without being centrally involved, or a more major character, a foil, who is presented in satiric form. They may appear only briefly and apparently casually, but there is nothing casual about *when* they appear. The playwright must decide when the audience will start squirming and must counter that restlessness by inserting comic relief.

Five Pitfalls of Comedy

Comedies are such fun to read and to watch that we forget they require just as much work as serious drama. No checklist is going to guard against all the potential problems, but there are five areas, in which many student plays (and some produced plays as well) founder. Consider them carefully.

• *Poor pacing.* I have already pointed out how important pacing is in situational comedies that depend on a sequence of scenes building toward a climax. But pacing is a concern in any comedy. If you open a play with the liveliest action or the strongest satire, you have nowhere to go but down. More often, problems in pacing occur in the latter half. Try to work the pace up as the play progresses. Longer plays can absorb a slow scene from time to time, but a one-act play of less than a half hour playing time is like a hundred-yard dash—it's a mistake to pause along the way.

• *Fragmentation.* Sometimes writing a satire becomes such fun that one forgets what the original aim was. Ask yourself just what the target is. As in the case of *Lincoln*, it may be a cluster of targets, but be careful not to stray too far. Drama, even satiric drama, has to have more structure than the routine of a standup comic or an evening of improvisation. Fragmented satire may receive laughs, but it is not going to be repeated unless it is organized with considerable care and given a unifying central concern.

• *Imitation:* No form of writing in any genre is more subject to being imitative than comic drama. The reason is that television writers pump an endless stream of popular and largely forgettable comic drama into the American consciousness 365 days a year. Memories of these plots and characters are apt to lie like sludge in the recesses of our memories. It is all too easy to recycle them.

Television is forever imitating television, looting last year's sitcoms shamelessly. The writers know they are not working for the ages; like managers of fast-food chains, they are meeting a commercial demand. But when one writes for the stage, one hopes to create something a little more enduring. Check to make sure that both your characters and your plot are fresh. Don't be content just to reach for laughs; give your audience some nutriment as well.

• *Slapstick* is farce with little or no thematic content. This is a vaudeville term referring to the stick designed to make a loud "whack!" when actors hit each other. Vaudeville died, but the Three Stooges maintained the tradition in every detail except for sexual innuendo.

Slapstick comedy has no goals other than obtaining laughs. It has its appeal just as comic strips do, and there is no harm in it. But as we have seen, it is possible to write comic drama with a considerable degree of sophistication. Even when comedy is pushed to the level of farce as *Lincoln* is, it will have substance if the humor is derived from precise satiric attacks on what the playwright finds reprehensible. Most sophisticated comedies have serious implications.

- *Visually static comedy* is the final pitfall. There is a fundamental difference between the performance of a standup comic, no matter how clever, and a comic play. Adding a second standup comic provides more wordplay, but unless there is a plot—a visual component—it is not drama. The very word *actor* implies action, and drama without dramatic action is a contradiction in terms. Judging by recent contest submissions, clever but plotless scripts have in the past few years become one of the most serious pitfalls for aspiring dramatists.

Developing a Comic Sense

If you are interested in writing comedy, you need to engage in two essential activities: read as many comic plays as you have time for, and see as many as you can afford. Never mind what century: You can learn from the few samples of Greek comedies just as you can from the Elizabethan period and contemporary works.

One advantage to reading plays is that you can finish one in a single setting. The more you read, the better. Granted, Elizabethan English slows you down, but start with a play you have read before and you will see how much more rewarding the second experience is. To find contemporary dramas, turn to Appendix B, "Resources for Writers," in the back of this book and follow through by spending time in the nearest library.

Naturally, you will find some works that strike you as unsuccessful. Be careful, however, not to shrug them off. Often you can learn from the mistakes of others if you take the time to analyze exactly what you would have done differently.

Scripts are, you remember, only descriptions of plays in performance. Attending actual performances, professional or amateur, will give you a richer understanding of what goes into successful comedies. Whenever possible, read the script in advance and then attend a performance while the work is still fresh in your mind. Remember that you are not concerned primarily with entertainment; you are in a learning mode. Compare your response to the script with your experience seeing the play in performance. Every evening is different, surprising even the actors on occasion. But you will get a sense of what aspects of comedy work well on the stage if you remain critically alert.

In essence, the task is to immerse yourself in comedies of all sorts. The best playwrights have learned from other playwrights. Now it's your turn.

41

ACHIEVING DRAMATIC GROWTH

Three ways to "see" your own play. Core questions that must be asked and honestly answered. Immersion in drama: reading, seeing, taking part.

You have now read three quite different plays—a tragedy, a comedy, and a farce. You have begun to see drama as a succession of interrelated scenes. You have become conscious of the need for conflict, vivid characters, and action. And you have come to expect some significant themes whether the play is serious or comic. That's a start.

Continued growth as a playwright, however, will depend on two additional factors that no textbook can give you. The first is the ability to act as your own severest critic. This is an art in itself. The second, for those who want to go still further, is to plunge yourself into theater—reading plays, seeing plays, and taking part in productions.

Three Ways to "See" Your Own Work

It is unlikely that your initial efforts will be given a full production. There are, however, ways to "see" your work in imagination. This process is fundamentally different from evaluating your own poetry or fiction because of the fact that a script is not a play. In your mind, you have to translate those words on the page into a live performance. There are three ways of doing this.

Begin with a silent reading. You naturally read and reread sections as you write and revise, but this is different. When your first draft is complete, set aside time to give it your sustained and undivided attention. Lock the door and turn off the phone. Read the play without interruption. Don't stop to make corrections or notes or get a cup of coffee. In this reading, you are your own first audience.

As you read, picture all the action. Visualize where each actor is stand-ing as she or he speaks. Supply the action in your mind's eye. Don't revise as you read; don't even analyze. Just experience it.

When you are through and the imaginary curtain drops, switch roles. You are now the director at the end of the first dress rehearsal. With clip-board in hand, write down everything that went wrong—scenes that were static, characters that sounded like alien creatures posing as humans, themes that echoed editorials you wouldn't bother to finish. Be tough, but compas-sionate. "You can do better," tell yourself.

After more revisions and a lapse of time (days, not weeks), take the sec-ond step: Read it out loud. One mechanical purpose for this is timing. The total playing time can be estimated fairly accurately if you allow for action that occurs without lines. If the play is divided into acts and scenes, it will be important to know how long each one is. You will need this information when deciding where to cut and when to expand. You will also want to record the total playing time. This information is often asked for when a play is submitted to a contest.

In addition to these mechanical concerns, the spoken reading is an effec-tive way for you to judge the quality of your revised dialogue before anyone else hears it. Lines that seemed fine on the page may sound awkward or not true to character when spoken. Long speeches that seemed effective when read silently sometimes sound ponderous when read out loud. Remember Lincoln's discovery in LeMaster's play: "People don't deliver soliloquies when they die."

Next, more rewriting. Always that. Then you may be ready for the third method of "seeing" your play: a group reading.

Your readers will do a better job if they are familiar with the script. They don't have to memorize the lines, but they need to have some sense of the character they are playing. In addition to readers, you need a few listeners. Participants are concentrating on their lines and won't have time to think critically about the work. The listeners should be encouraged to take notes. It is also helpful to tape-record the reading for your own review.

In the discussion that follows the reading, make sure that it doesn't go soft with flattery (delicious as that is) or deteriorate into general conversa-tions about the issues suggested by the play. Remind your critics that the subject is the play itself. To keep them focused, you may wish to photocopy the six "core questions" listed below (giving credit, of course) and use them as guidelines for the discussion.

While poets and writers of fiction usually turn to other writers for criti-cism, dramatists value *everyone's* reactions. Because drama is a spectator art intended for a wider, more general audience, the response of nonwriters becomes particularly valuable. The more the better. They may not be able to provide solutions, but they can pick out dull scenes, faulty characterization, the whiff of sentimentality, or the heavy hand of melodrama. In the case of comic drama, their failure to laugh will tell you a good deal.

Poets listen politely to comments from their listeners after a reading, but they rarely act on them. Playwrights, on the other hand—even highly successful ones—pay close attention to audience reaction and often make successive revisions during the run of a play.

Core Questions That Must Be Asked—and Answered

Here are six question you as playwright must ask yourself—and you must provide honest answers. These questions will also help to keep friendly critics on track.

1. *Scenes: Are there any scenes that drag?* If so, is the reason lack of action or lack of development? Are there dramatic questions that hold the attention scene by scene? Focusing on specific scenes is far more helpful than sweeping statements about the play as a whole.

2. *Conflict: Exactly what kind of conflict is there?* Who is pitted against whom? Or is a character struggling against some aspect of society? Is the conflict strong enough to hold an audience? Is it augmented by inner conflict? Is it excessive (melodramatic) or too gentle (nondramatic)?

3. *Characterization: Are the characters convincing and/or memorable?* In the case of serious realistic drama, it is essential that at least the major characters be convincing, but in the case of comedy, farce, and nonrealistic plays, vividness may be what makes a character memorable. This question has nothing to do with whether the audience *liked* a particular character; it asks only whether the characterization is *effective.*

4. *Action: Is there enough action?* Are there exits, entrances, and significant activity to keep the play visually stimulating? Does the visual aspect contribute to the total effect?

5. *Themes: What themes are being explored and how are they developed?* Just what themes reached the audience? (As playwright, don't explain your intent and ask for confirmation. Let your critics tell you what they saw.) Are the themes too blatant (preachy) or too familiar (truisms) or too obscure (fuzzy)?

6. *Tone: How would you describe the tone, and is it effective?* This is the most difficult question, because tone is an elusive concept. Major tonal problems: Is it melodramatic? Is it sentimental? Is it unjustifiably offensive? (Yes, there are thesis-driven plays that can be defended as justifiably offensive.) More

subtle tonal concerns: Is it too bland, too saccharine, emotionally unsatisfying, needlessly negative, in need of comic relief?

There is one more question that playwrights must ask of themselves: Am I listening to criticisms with an open mind, accepting those that seem justified, or am I taking a defensive attitude? Only by accepting and weighing criticism objectively can one grow and develop as a writer.

Immersion in Drama

Writing a play can be valuable even if you never do it again. You will learn a good deal about the medium, and your capacity to enjoy performances will be greatly enhanced. As with sports, those who have done it at least briefly have a special understanding. But if you want to go on from there and develop as a playwright on your own, you will have to immerse yourself in the medium.

This process must involve both reading and viewing, and if possible it should include participation in a production. The advantage of reading play scripts is that doing so enables you to cover so much ground. It gives you a broad view of the medium. If you read one play script each night five times a week, you will have read 260 plays in a year, and the chances are that not one of them was offered in production in your area during that period.

Every library has collections of "best plays" for particular years, and these will give you a wide variety. When you find a playwright whose work you admire, try to find more by the same individual. And don't limit yourself to recent work; you can learn a lot from the way Shakespeare presents a dramatic question early in his tragedies or sets the scene in a history play or balances heavy drama with comic relief. If you are interested in strong themes, the plays of George Bernard Shaw will show you ways of masking highly didactic notions with wit and satire. Reading plays from all periods will be more profitable for you than any number of "how to" books on technique.

As much as possible, supplement your reading by seeing performances. Take in whatever is available—student and amateur productions as well as those presented by professional companies. If cost is a factor, you may be able to get special rates just before opening night. Since it is the play itself that concerns you and not the level of performance, a missed line or two won't bother you.

Another excellent way to immerse yourself in drama is to take part in a production. Even if acting is not your primary concern, a bit part will help you to understand the dynamics of putting on a play. Or you might consider volunteering for the stage crew. Working with hammer and saw gives you a respect for both the limits and the opportunities of a state set. Being part of the crew also gives you a chance to see a production repeatedly. If you are not at a college or university, consider a summer stock company. The mechanics of producing a play should be a part of any playwright's education.

Poets and writers of fiction have the option of living and writing in relative isolation. Books and magazines serve as their connection with other writers. Playwrights, on the other hand, thrive on being where the action is. The actual writing of a script may be a relatively solitary act, but the production—the actual play—requires the physical and emotional cooperation of many. It is truly a collaborative art. Make an effort to experience this in some way.

Above all, however, is the need to know what other dramatists have done. You have at your disposal a host of playwrights covering a span of 2,500 years as your teachers. They have faced the same problems you will, considered some of the same options you will. Let them be your guide to the potential of the genre. Then you will be equipped to apply your own individual vision and your particular voice to a script that is uniquely yours.

A

SUBMITTING WORK FOR PUBLICATION

Myths about publishing. Judging whether one is ready to submit material. Mechanical considerations: the manuscript, keeping records, computers. What to submit. Where to submit: listings, agents, small presses, double submissions. Marketing plays. A planned approach to publication.

Some novice writers submit material long before there is any chance of publication; an equal number are reluctant to submit even though they are ready. The sad fact is that even writers who have taken creative writing courses often know very little about aspects of marketing.

First, let's clear away a number of unfounded myths about publishing. One hears, for example, that nothing is published without "pull," that neither fiction nor drama can succeed without containing sex and violence, that poetry must be obscure to gain critical approval, that agents are unreliable, that book publishers are interested only in the bottom line, and that you have to live in New York to publish a play. Equally fanciful is the claim that if a piece of writing is really good it will be published without serious effort on the part of the writer.

There are two essential facts to remember: First, publication is no more fair than life itself; there will always be good works that are not accepted and thoroughly amateurish material that is. Second, if talent, practice, and a practical system of submission are combined, one can alter the odds in one's favor.

There are two tests that will help you to decide whether you are ready to submit material. First, you should have written in that particular genre for some time. When you read that a story is an author's first publication, it doesn't mean that he or she is a novice. In most cases, the person has been writing for years. So-called "first novels" usually have been preceded by considerable practice in short stories and quite frequently by one or two unpublished novels as well.

The second test is whether you have been a regular reader. I have repeatedly stressed the need to read carefully and regularly in the genre of your choice. Writers who do not spend twice as much time reading as they do writing are at an enormous disadvantage. They risk settling into a rut, repeating themselves in style and content. Successful writers and poets are almost always perpetual students. Through reading, not only are they discovering new approaches for their own work, they are getting to know individual magazines and book publishers.

If you have been writing for some time and have been an active, conscientious reader, you may be ready for the long and sometimes frustrating process of submitting material.

Mechanical Considerations

If you are one of those dwindling few who still use a typewriter, the manuscript should be typed with a dark ribbon on a good grade of standard typewriter paper. Everything but your name and address should be double spaced. Be sure not to confuse this with the space-and-a-half available on some typewriters. Use pica type, 10 characters to the inch (standard on many typewriters), not elite or 12 cpi (characters per inch). If in doubt, check with a ruler.

Almost all writers today, however, use computers. A computer-printed manuscript should look the same as those that are typed. Simply follow the form described above. Pica type translates as 10 cpi. Resist the strong temptation to use fancy type, italics, gothic, or script. With all manuscript submissions, underline the material that is to be printed in italics. (Never use italic font unless you have been asked to submit a cassette, still a rare practice with major publishers.) And never vary your type size.

As for the printer, laser and bubble jet are equally good. Bubble jets are slightly cheaper. (There are almost no dot matrix printers left, but if you still have one, make sure it is "near letter quality.") Place your name and address on the left, about two inches down from the top, and type "Fiction" or "A Poem" on the right. Some authors add the word count and their social security number there, but these are not essential.

The title is usually centered, in capital letters (not underlined or placed in quotation marks) about a third of the way down the page. Your name and address are single-spaced, and all fiction is double-spaced. Poems are sometimes single-spaced. Here is how it looks:

```
Woody B. Grate                          Fiction
205 Main St.                            5,280 wds.
Middletown, IL 62666                    015-42-3642



                      LOOKING FORWARD
```

The story begins two double line spaces below the title. Remember to double-space it and indent the first line of each new paragraph three to five spaces. Never use separate title pages for stories or individual poems. Use them only for book-length collections of poems, novels, or plays. The pages (after the first) should be numbered in Arabic numerals along with your last name in the upper right corner: "Smith 2," "Smith 3," and so on.

Never place the manuscript in a folder or binder, and do not staple it. A simple paper clip will do. Novels should be sent loose in a box. Covering letters are not necessary with poetry or fiction unless you have something specific to say. If the editor has added a kind word to a previous rejection slip or has actually written a letter, be sure to remind him or her. In any case, be brief and factual. Defending or even explaining your work is a sure sign of an author's amateur status.

If all these instructions seem rather restrictive, remember that freshness and originality belong in what you write, not in the packaging.

If you don't know anyone on the staff, merely send the manuscript to the fiction or poetry editor at the address given in the magazine or a directory. But if you have met or corresponded with an editor or even a junior reader, send it to him or her.

For mailing, the envelope should be large enough so that the manuscript need not be folded. If you buy 9 1/2" x 12 1/2" envelopes for sending, you can enclose a 9" x 12" self-addressed, stamped envelope (SASE) for its return, or merely fold the second envelope so that it can be placed inside the first with the manuscript. In either case, be sure that your address and proper postage are on it. Failure to do this not only irritates the editor but increases your chances of never seeing your manuscript again.

Poems and stories are sent first class. Novels are wrapped or boxed and sent in padded mailers. Special Fourth Class is slightly cheaper but slow and unreliable. First class is preferred. United Parcel rates vary by zone but are often less expensive than first-class mail rates.

In awaiting a reply, allow two to three months for poetry and short stories and an agonizing six months for novels. Resist the temptation to inquire about work sent until twice the expected time has passed.

Keeping records is extremely important. It is impossible to remember what went out when and to which magazine if you do not keep a submissions notebook. In addition, it is invaluable to record not only which editors had a kind word or two, but which magazines sent specifically worded rejection slips. The lowest level of rejection slip is merely a printed statement saying that they appreciated receiving your work but were unable to use it. In addition, most magazines have one or two special slips with wording like "this was of particular interest to us" or "we hope to see more of your work." Take these seriously. Next on the scale is the penned comment on the bottom of the slip like "good dialogue" or "try us again." These are infuriatingly brief, but they are worth recording. Be careful, however, not to inundate a magazine with weekly submissions. An editor who has commented on one poem is not going to be impressed with a flood of inferior work. Treat such individuals as potential allies who deserve only your best efforts.

The highest point on this scale is the rejection *letter*. Even if brief, this is close to acceptance. If the editor suggests specific revisions that seem appropriate, revise and resubmit. If they don't, send your next really good piece. These are two situations in which you should definitely include a short covering letter.

Computers: For the Uninitiated

If you already work with a computer, skip this section. If you don't, read it carefully. Should you get one? If you spend four or more hours a week writing prose or poetry and can afford the investment, you are foolish not to buy a computer. In most undergraduate writing classes today, almost no one still uses a typewriter.

A computer will not create a good writer any more than a new car will produce a good driver, but it will certainly aid in your process of development. The ease of revision will without question improve the quality of your work. You will find yourself going through many more revisions than when each one had to be retyped. You can move blocks of fiction or lines of poetry quickly and painlessly, and you can compare two versions of the same scene or stanza instantly by flipping from one document to the other. Best of all, what you see is always a neat, clear draft. You can read it at a steady pace, judging the flow accurately.

In addition, you can keep a record of everything you have done on diskettes with backup copies stored elsewhere. This is an excellent insurance against loss.

Surprisingly, a computer probably won't reduce the time you spend revising. Many recent converts find that they spend more time revising simply because the process is so much more pleasurable than it was when it involved cutting, pasting, and retyping. But the extra time does improve the final draft.

There are three disadvantages that no computer magazine will warn you about. First, your typing accuracy will deteriorate. Corrections are so easy to make that you become permanently careless. (It is for language what a calculator is for basic math.) The spell check will lull you into false confidence. It is no substitute for proofreading since it is illiterate when it comes to spotting fifth-grade errors such as confusing *its* and *it's* or *to, two* and *too.*

Second, your computer *will* die with no warning at some point. It will plunge all your work into oblivion. I stress *will*, not *when*. Your only safeguard is to make backup copies on diskettes and update them at least daily. (I back mine up every hour.) It's hard to remember to do this until you have an entire story or even a novel simply disappear permanently and (contrary to claims) irretrievably. It will take one major disaster before you start to update your backup copy regularly. Finally, you will bore all your noncomputing friends. Conversationally, computers are as addictive as baseball.

What kind to buy? That's a big topic, but here are some basic guidelines:

- Talk with friends about their own computer experiences. In most cases they will tell you more than you really want to hear. Ask them not only what computer they recommend but what software package they prefer. The software is like a language, and you will be investing time to master it.
- If your primary need is writing, don't spend extra money for capabilities required by business firms, chemical laboratories, and computer-game freaks. Encyclopedias that talk are of use only to illiterates. There is a real temptation to be swept into more capabilities than you will ever use.
- If this is your first computer, stick to major brands that offer a full-year guarantee, and make sure it is in writing. Unlike automobiles, computers are just as likely to have major breakdowns in the first year as in the third. To be specific, I had a nationally known, highly recommended computer that had to be junked in precisely 364 days of moderate use. It was replaced but would not have been on the following Monday.
- For nonoffice work, bubble-jet printers are just as good as laser printers and somewhat cheaper.
- Beware the web! Yes, it has some educational value when used with specific goals in mind. But for some people, surfing becomes a black hole, sucking up all available free time. Serious writers are always short of time and have to be on guard against all forms of addiction.

What to Submit

The decision of what to submit must rest ultimately with you. Although the advice of other serious writers can be helpful, don't be swayed by friends who do not know what you are doing. Classmates or neighbors who never read sophisticated fiction or poetry are not going to be very helpful as critics.

This does not hold for play scripts, however. Since such work is designed to reach larger audiences, the advice of nonwriters may be of real value.

Poets should select a group of three or four poems for submission at one time. Writers of fiction should limit each submission to one story. Once the choice is made, send the work out repeatedly. A single editorial rejection means absolutely nothing. A manuscript is not "dead" until it has been turned down by at least ten magazines. The best approach is to send the work out on the very day it is returned; otherwise you are apt to lose courage. As a practical matter, just as many manuscripts are accepted after six or eight rejections as after only one. This is largely due to the fact that so many nonliterary factors go into the selection of a work for publication, such as the number and kind of manuscripts already on hand, the balance of a particular issue, and the personal preferences of the first reader. Once you make the decision to send a work out, stand by it until you have cumulative proof that the work is unpublishable.

Where to Submit

Don't submit "blind"—that is, to magazines you haven't read. Directories such as those listed in Appendix B can be helpful, but they won't tell you enough to make a judgment as to whether a particular publication is suitable for your type of work. "Blind submissions" not only waste your time and money, they are a terrible burden for the editors, who frequently work for little or no salary.

As I have suggested in earlier chapters, the place to start studying publications is your nearest library. Pick out the literary quarterlies. Since there will be a confusing array of magazines, you may want to use the list of literary journals in Appendix B as a guide. Look these magazines over and make a list of those that print work like yours. Note approximately how many poems and how many stories they print, the name of the poetry or fiction editor, and the address. Directories (including the one in Appendix B) cannot be perfectly current.

Mainstream novels—those aimed at a broad audience—should be circulated through a literary agent, a topic I will turn to shortly. You are on your own, however, with innovative or experimental novels, collections of stories, and book-length collections of poetry. Look over your own shelves and list the publishers who handle work that is somewhat similar to yours. Then do the same in a bookstore. Next, look up the addresses of the publishers in *The International Directory of Little Magazines and Small Presses*. Major presses are listed in *Literary Market Place* (known as *LMP*).

Sending out query letters will save a great deal of time, postage, and frustration. Small, independent presses are able to publish only a few titles a year, and you have to catch them the very month they are open to new submissions. A great majority of your letters will bring you a negative response, and a surprising number won't be answered at all, but this situation is far better than having your manuscript tied up for half a year. Query letters should be no longer than one page. Simply describe the work in positive (but not glowing) terms and enclose a bibliography of your previous publications, if any. You can include sample poems, a story, or a chapter, but this is not necessary unless your list of previous publications is very scant.

Once you have decided to send out a book-length manuscript, keep submitting it until you have been rejected by at least 13 or 14 publishers. This will take about three years—time enough for you to complete the next novel or collection.

Circulating novels and book-length collections of short works raises four questions that are asked at every writers' conference. First, what about **vanity presses**? A vanity press is a for-profit publishing firm that charges the author for publication costs and sometimes for revisions. Many such organizations are perfectly honest, but it is rare indeed that a vanity press with its minimal system of distribution can do much for a novel that has been rejected by major publishers. Be sure to read their proposed contract very carefully.

Cooperative presses are quite different. They are generally nonprofit and run by individuals who love books and are willing to live a marginal economic life to work with them. Such presses are used less for novels, but they are a growing outlet for collections of poems and stories. The author still has to pay, but because no one is making a profit, the investment is likely to cost less.

Another question raised by those submitting book-length manuscripts is whether it is appropriate to make use of a personal contact at a publishing house. Yes, it most certainly is. Even if your acquaintance is not in the editorial department, submit through him or her. Using such a connection probably won't get a bad manuscript published, but it may bypass that first reader who has a great many manuscripts to review. In the case of rejections, the writer is apt to receive a lengthier comment if the reader has some personal interest. I can testify to the fact that such personal contact is not a prerequisite for having stories or novels accepted; but it is neither unethical nor a waste of time to make use of any interested reader or publisher.

Third, should you submit copies of the same work to different publishers at the same time? Not unless the publisher has specifically stated "multiple submissions accepted" in one of the directories. An increasing number of magazine editors have adopted this policy and even a few small publishers, but most have not. You will read tantalizing reports about agents submitting a novel manuscript to a group of publishers simultaneously in what is called a "brokered offering," but that is only done for nationally known authors whose previous works have sold extremely well.

Generally speaking, book publishers assume that if they accept a novel, they are investing in an author. Standard contracts usually insist on a first refusal on whatever book-length manuscript you may submit next. This does not apply to individual stories or poems, but most editors assume that if they are going to spend time reading and evaluating a manuscript, they are the only ones considering it. Some authors do take a chance and double submit. But remember that the publishing world is small and closely connected. Becoming known as one who double submits is like having a bad credit rating: it's hard to correct. If in doubt, send a query letter.

Finally, what about agents? Don't even consider using an agent if you write short stories intended primarily for little magazines or if you write poetry of any sort. Placing material in literary quarterlies is an honor well worth struggling for, but they pay relatively little, and an agent's 10 or 15 percent of relatively little is hardly enough to cover postage. Agents, unlike writers, cannot afford to work for love alone.

On the other hand, you *should* consider looking for an agent if you have completed a mainstream novel or if you have a group of five or six potentially publishable stories that might be considered by quality magazines (*The Atlantic* or *The New Yorker*), the women's magazines (*Redbook, McCalls*), or the men's magazines (*Playboy, Penthouse*). Manuscripts submitted to such magazines through agencies usually receive more careful scrutiny by readers with more editorial authority.

Most reputable agents are now charging a flat 15 percent of the proceeds of all material sold through them and make no other charges whatever, regardless of how much postage or time they spend. In return, they expect to handle all your work. A few agents are now requiring a "reading fee" for unpublished writers. Don't confuse this with a "criticism fee," for which you will receive a critical report. Watch out for those who charge "overhead"— additional fees. All this may become a growing trend, but the basic 15 percent contract is still the standard.

If you are unpublished, it will be difficult but not impossible to find an agent. Some writers try to place their first book themselves and then secure an agent to handle the contract when it is offered by a publisher. Others send query letters to many different agents (addresses in *LMP*), describing the completed manuscript they hope to place. It is perfectly all right to send out many query letters at the same time. Be sure to ask the agents to recommend another one if they cannot take on your work themselves. Occasionally they will recommend a younger agent who is looking for new clients.

Marketing a play requires a somewhat different approach. There are four basic techniques that can be adopted separately or together:

- *Enter play contests.* The best listings are in the *Dramatists Sourcebook* (Theater Communications Group, 355 Lexington Ave., New York, NY 10017). This annual is fully revised each August. In addition, consider *Poets and Writers Magazine* (201 West 54th St., New York, NY 10019).

- *Submit to theaters.* Again, use the *Dramatists Sourcebook*. Another listing appears in *Writer's Market* (Writer's Digest Books), but it is much shorter. Each theater has special needs, requirements, and deadlines, so read the fine print carefully.

- *Work with a theater group.* Any theater experience will be useful. In addition, you will meet people who will guide you. Even as a volunteer you will benefit.

- *Submit to publishers of plays.* The two major publishers are Baker's Plays and Samuel French. Their addresses are in Appendix B. They accept many new plays (mostly mainstream) each year. If you are offered a contract, consider the terms carefully.

There is probably no other branch of the arts more committed to personal contact than drama. "Networking" is the polite word. More bluntly, "pull" is extraordinarily valuable. If you know a producer, director, actor, or even a stagehand, write to him or her. This situation is not merely a matter of commercial corruption. The fact is that although book publishers come to know potential writers through little magazines (which they read with professional care), producers have no such resource. They may be completely unaware of a playwright whose work has appeared in small theaters in some other state. This situation will continue until there are more little magazines willing to specialize in original play scripts and more low-budget stage companies in the smaller cities. Meanwhile, playwrights must struggle with the particularly difficult task of getting known through word of mouth.

Writers of fiction, poetry, and drama all have to adopt a realistic attitude toward publication. It is naive to assume that marketing your work is crass and demeaning. Publishers have no way of discovering you if you make no effort to circulate your work. On the other hand, a mania to publish at all costs can be damaging to the creative process. It often leads to imitative and conventional work and to feelings of hostility toward editors and publishers.

To avoid these most unrewarding extremes, begin with an honest evaluation of your own work. Then follow through with a planned, long-range program of submissions. There are, of course writers who achieve wide recognition very suddenly, but this is rare and not always a blessing. Ideally, creative work is a way of life, and the effort to publish is an important though not a central portion of that life.

B
RESOURCES FOR WRITERS

General reference books. Informative magazines. Little magazines. Poetry anthologies. Poets writing about their craft. Listening to poetry. Fiction anthologies. Books about the craft of fiction. Magazines and books for playwrights. Publishers of play scripts.

General Reference Books

The following four reference books are of particular interest to writers of fiction and poetry. They are published annually and can be found in most libraries. A specialized directory and information book for dramatists is described in the drama section of this appendix.

- *The International Directory of Little Magazines & Small Presses*, Dustbooks. This is by far the best (and most expensive) listing of little magazines, quarterlies, literary journals, and small presses. It devotes a paragraph to each magazine, describing what it publishes and listing names of editors, payment scale, and the like. It gives cross-listings by subject, genre, and region. It does not list large-circulation magazines or major publishers. Dustbooks also offers *The Directory of Poetry Publishers*, which is handy for those working only with poetry.
- *Literary Market Place*, R. R. Bowker Co. *LMP* no longer lists magazines, but it remains the most authoritative annual listing of mainstream book publishers, literary agents, writers' conferences, and addresses of those in publishing. It is entirely factual and does not contain articles on how to write or market your material. It is astonishingly expensive, but most libraries have it.
- *The Writer's Handbook*, The Writer, Inc. This annual is dominated by how-to articles on all aspects of writing, with an emphasis on commercial markets. There is also a list of magazines.
- *Writer's Market*, Writer's Digest Books. This has fewer articles than *The Writer's Handbook* but more listings. Many are commercial (science, sports, travel) or technical journals (hardware, real estate, toys), but there is a basic listing of literary journals. If you are not interested in commercial nonfiction, you will do

better with one of their more specialized publications such as *Poet's Market* and *Novel & Short Story Writer's Manual.*

Informative Magazines

These magazines provide information and advice for writers, poets, and to a lesser degree, dramatists. They do not generally publish fiction or poetry. Consult library copies for current subscription rates.

- *AWP Chronicle*, Tallwood House, Mail Stop 1E3, Fairfax, VA 22030-0079. Published by Associated Writing Programs, this is in tabloid format and is published six times a year. Articles, interviews, criticism, and news items about writers, poets, creative writing programs, contest winners, and the teaching of writing. Circulation 13,000.
- *Poets and Writers Magazine*, 72 Spring St., New York, NY 10012. This nonprofit publication is a must for anyone who writes poetry or fiction. It is published six times a year. Its articles deal with problems faced by all literary writers: how to find time to write when teaching, how to arrange readings, publishing translations, dealing with small presses. It is also the best source of contest and grant application deadlines, dates of conferences and readings, and winners of awards. Circulation 58,000.
- *Publishers Weekly*, 205 East 42nd St., New York, NY 10017. Of particular interest to those in the business end of publishing, this magazine covers which books are about to be released, who is doing what in the field, author profiles, and future trends.
- *The Writer*, 8 Arlington St., Boston, MA 02116. This monthly focuses more on mass markets than does *Poets and Writers Magazine*. Articles give advice on writing and marketing a great variety of material from gothic novels to "confessionals" and from poetry to greeting-card verse.
- *Writer's Digest*, 1507 Dana Ave., Cincinnati, OH 45207. This lists fiction and verse outlets. It is similar in emphasis to its competitor, *The Writer* (above).

Little Magazines

These magazines, also known as *quarterlies* (though they may appear from two to six times a year) and *literary journals*, publish fiction, poetry, and articles in varying proportions. The following list, a small sampling of the many fine literary journals being published today, has been selected especially for writers of fiction and poetry. They should all be available in your public or university library. (If not, urge your librarian to add the missing titles.) Most are quarterlies unless otherwise noted. Be sure to read at least one copy before submitting.

- *Agni*, Boston University, Dept. DB, 236 Bay State Rd., Boston, MA 02215. Fiction, poetry, and excerpts from novels; two issues a year.
- *American Poetry Review*, 1721 Walnut St., Philadelphia, PA 19103. Mostly poetry and articles about poetry; some fiction, art, interviews. Six times a year in tabloid form; larger circulation than most little magazines.
- *Beloit Poetry Journal*, Box 154, RFD 2, Ellsworth, ME 04605. All poetry; a quarterly established in 1950.
- *The Black Warrier Review*, P.O. Box 862936, University of Alabama, Tuscaloosa, AL 35486. A balance of fiction, poetry, art, interviews, reviews; two issues a year.
- *Field*, Rice Hall, Oberlin College, Oberlin, OH 44074. Devoted to poetry (including long poems) and essays on poetry; two issues a year.
- *The Georgia Review*, University of Georgia, Athens, GA 30602-9009. A balance of fiction, poetry, interviews, criticism, reviews. Highly competitive.
- *The Gettysburg Review*, Gettysburg College, Gettysburg, PA 17325. Fiction, poetry, articles, satire.
- *Glimmer Train Stories*, 710 SW Madison St., Suite 504, Portland, OR 97205-2900. Fiction and an occasional interview. Send **SASE** for submission guidelines.
- *The Missouri Review*, 1507 Hillcrest Hall, University of Missouri–Columbia, Columbia, MO 65211. Fiction, poetry, articles, interviews, reviews. Three issues a year.
- *New England Review*, Middlebury College, Middlebury, VT 05753. Fiction, poetry, articles, longer poems and parts of novels.
- *The North American Review*, University of Northern Iowa, Cedar Falls, IA 50614. Mostly fiction (including short-shorts); some poetry; nonfiction with an environmental focus.
- *Paris Review* 541 East 72nd St., New York, NY 10021. Fiction primarily; also poetry, articles; famous for its interviews with authors and poets. Circulation 10,000.
- *Ploughshares*, Emerson College, 100 Beacon St., Boston, MA 02116. Poetry and fiction primarily; revolving editorship with special issues often limited to one genre. Check current issue for future plans.
- *Poetry*, 60 West Walton St., Chicago, IL 60610. Poetry and reviews; informally known as "Poetry Chicago"; twelve issues a year; copyright does not revert to the author.
- *Poetry East*, Department of English, DePaul University, 802 West Belden Ave., Chicago, IL 60614. Mainly poetry; also fiction, articles, interviews, criticism; some issues limited to a particular topic.
- *The Poetry Miscellany*, English Department, University of Tennessee, Chattanooga, TN 37403. Mostly poetry with some interviews, criticism, reviews; a very impressive list of contributors.
- *Prairie Schooner*, 201 Andrews Hall, University of Nebraska, Lincoln, NE 68588-0334. Fiction, poetry, articles, interviews.
- *Sewanee Review*, University of the South, 735 University Ave., Sewanee, TN 37383-1000. Articles, fiction, poetry in about that order.

- *Stories*, P.O. Box 1467, Arlington, MA 02174-0022. Exclusively short stories; send **SASE** for guidelines before submitting.
- *Story*, 1507 Dana Ave., Cincinnati, OH 45207. Strictly fiction; four issues a year. Has become one of the foremost fiction magazines.
- *Story Quarterly*, P.O. Box 1416, Northbrook, IL 60065. Fiction primarily; also interviews, art, satire; two issues a year.
- *TriQuarterly*, Northwestern University, 2020 Ridge, Evanston, IL 60208. Fiction, poetry, criticism. Tends to be innovative or experimental. Read first; then write for contributors' guidelines.
- *The Virginia Quarterly Review*, One West Range, Charlottesville, VA 22903. Articles, poetry, fiction, reviews, in about that order.

Poetry Anthologies

Anthologies contain the works of many different writers. The following will introduce you to a wide variety of contemporary poets. *Collections*, on the other hand, are limited to the work of one author or poet. Use anthologies to browse and explore. Get to know those whose work you enjoy. Then consider collections of those writers you particularly admire. You can locate them by using the "Authors" section of the *Books in Print* catalogue in any library or bookstore. You can order copies through your bookstore. Collections are often available at poetry readings as well. Owning your own copy will allow you to study the poet's work at leisure.

- *The Best American Poetry*, Touchstone Books. An annual with different editors each year. An excellent survey of current work.
- *Contemporary American Poetry*, A. Poulin Jr., ed., Houghton Mifflin (paperback). This extensive paperback collection offers a good variety of poets. Women and black poets are well represented. It is frequently adopted for college courses.
- *The Harvard Book of Contemporary American Poetry*, Helen Vendler, ed., Harvard University Press. This is a solid collection compiled by a distinguished critic, but it is not available in paperback.
- *No More Masks! An Anthology of Poems by Women*, F. Howe and E. Bass, eds., Anchor/Doubleday. From Amy Lowell to Nikki Giovanni; full spectrum of women poets in this century. Unfortunately it is no longer in print, but it is available in most libraries.
- *Poems for the Millennium*, J. Rothenberg and P. Joris, eds., University of California Press. Highly experimental and innovative poetry from the modern and postmodern schools. No metered or rhymed poetry.
- *Strong Measures: Contemporary American Poetry in Traditional Forms*, P. Dacey and D. Jauss, eds., Harper & Row. This 492-page paperback is devoted to poetry in a great variety of metrical forms. There is no free verse. It includes a useful appendix with definitions of metrical terms. The emphasis is in sharp contrast with *Poems for the Millennium* (above).

Poets Writing About Their Craft

By far the best way to learn from poets is to read their poetry itself; but after you have done that, it is often helpful to read what they have written in prose about their craft. Here is a brief sampling:

- *Letters to a Young Poet*, Rainer Maria Rilke; paperback editions of this classic still available from both Norton and Random House.
- *On the Poet and His Craft: Selected Prose of Theodore Roethke*, Ralph J. Mills, ed., University of Washington Press.
- *Poetry and the Age*, Randall Jarrell, Echo Press.
- *The Triggering Town, Lectures and Essays on Poetry and Writing*, Richard Hugo, Norton.
- *Twentieth Century Pleasures: Prose on Poetry*, Robert Hass, Echo Press.

Listening to Poetry

There are two ways to hear poets read their own work. First, attend poetry readings. Almost every college and university offers a series of poetry readings that are open to the public. Coffee houses often have "open mike" evenings in which anyone may read. In addition, larger libraries and organizations such as the Y.M.C.A., Y.W.C.A., and Y.M.H.A. invite poets to read their works. Attending writers' conferences in the summer (listings in *LMP*; ads in *Poets and Writers*) is also a good way to hear poets read their own work.

The second approach is through recordings. Most libraries have audio and video cassette collections. Compact discs and tapes may also be ordered through good music stores. Some serious poets prefer recordings over live readings because they can locate and then follow a printed version of each poem while listening to it, and also because they can repeat a poem or a stanza as many times as they wish. In this way, listening to a recording becomes a true learning experience.

For Fiction Writers: The Big Three

In addition to the little magazines listed earlier, these three large-circulation magazines are of special interest to writers of fiction:

- *The Atlantic* (a distinguished monthly; usually one story each issue)
- *Esquire* (usually one story; published fortnightly)
- *The New Yorker* (weekly; normally one story each week. Some find the new, rather trendy policy annoying, but it is still a serious publication.)

Fiction Anthologies and Collections

There are two widely read annual anthologies of short stories published in magazines during the previous year. While no two editors will agree on the "best" stories published in any year, these volumes provide a fine overview of good contemporary fiction.

- *The Best American Short Stories*, Houghton Mifflin. This volume has been published annually since 1915. Edited for 36 years by Martha Foley, the collection is still referred to informally as "the Foley collection." The editorship is now changed each year.
- *Prize Stories: The O. Henry Awards*, William Abrahams, ed., Doubleday. Better known as "The O. Henry collection," this is another view of the best fiction published during the previous year. It serves as an excellent companion work to *The Best American Short Stories*.

In addition to these two annuals, there are many short-story anthologies designed mainly for college use. They offer an opportunity to discover authors you may not have read. Here is a listing:

- *Classic Short Fiction*, Charles H. Bohner, ed., Prentice-Hall. This large paperback gives a sampling of nineteenth-century fiction but focuses primarily on the major writers of our own period.
- *Editors Choice: New American Stories*, George E. Murphy, Jr., ed., Bantam. There are several volumes under this title, all paperback. The selections were made by magazine editors.
- *Look Who's Talking*, Bruce Webber, ed., Pocket Books. An inexpensive collection of American stories from the 1930s to the present, many with a strong sense of voice.
- *Modern Short Stories*, Arthur Mizener, ed., Norton. A good, comprehensive collection of twentieth-century work.
- *Modern Short Stories: The Fiction of Experience*, M. X. Lesser and J. N. Morris, eds., McGraw-Hill. An anthology stressing the relationship between personal experience and fiction.
- *Necessary Fictions: Selected Stories from the Georgia Review*, S. W. Lindberg and S. Corey, eds. An anthology of recent work from a distinguished quarterly.
- *New American Short Stories: The Writers Select Their Own Favorites*, Gloria Norris, ed., New American Library. There is also a second anthology with the same title followed by "2." Both volumes consist of contemporary short stories, each selected by the individual author and accompanied with a brief commentary by him or her. These commentaries are of particular interest to those who write fiction.

Like poetry anthologies, these volumes will introduce you to a variety of work. But when you find an author you admire, see if he or she has published a collection of stories. In many cases you can find such volumes in your local library. If you wish to order your own copy, turn to the "Author" section of *Books in Print* in your library or bookstore.

A number of university presses publish collections of short stories by a single author in paperback. Among the first to do this was the University of Illinois Press (Urbana, IL 61801). They published four paperback collections a year for almost 20 years until the budget of the National Endowment for the Arts was cut and it could no longer help support Illinois and many other literary publishers and magazines. Other presses following this invaluable tradition are, in modified forms, The Johns Hopkins University Press (Baltimore, MD 21218), the University of Pittsburgh Press (Pittsburg, PA 15260), among others. Write to these publishers if you wish a list of their short-story collections and prices. Outside the university, small publishers like The Permanent Press (Noyac Rd., Sag Harbor, NY 11963) and Sarabande Books (Dundee Rd., Suite 200, Louisville, KY 40205) publish new fiction and would provide you with catalogues.

Books About the Craft of Fiction

As in the case of poetry, there is no substitute for reading extensively in the genre itself, but as a supplement, here are four works on fiction writing that will be useful:

- *The Art of Fiction: Notes on Craft for Young Writers*, John Gardner, Random House.
- *Becoming a Writer*, Dorothea Brande, Tarcher.
- *Writing Down the Bones: Freeing the Writer Within*, Natalie Goldberg, Shambhala (distributed by Random House)
- *Writing Fiction: A Guide to Narrative Craft*, 4th ed., Janet Burroway, Harper Collins.

Magazines for Playwrights

- *Drama Review*, 55 Hayward, Cambridge, MA 02142. This quarterly focuses on contemporary avant-garde drama. Articles are often in depth and cover a wide range of generally innovative drama: women's theater, European trends, mixed-media productions, and so on.
- *Poets and Writers Magazine*, 72 Spring St., New York, NY 10012. Listed earlier as a resource for poets and fiction writers, this bimonthly is occasionally valuable for dramatists.
- *Theater*, 222 York St., New Haven, CT 06520. Calling itself "a critical journal of contemporary theater," this publication appears three times a year. In addition to articles, it has interviews, reviews, and some plays.

Books for Playwrights

- *Best Short Plays*, Chilton Book Co. (paperback edition, Applause Theater Book Publishers). This annual has been published for decades. Back issues can be found in many libraries.
- *Dramatists Sourcebook*, Theater Communications Group, 355 Lexington Ave., New York, NY 10017. This annual is fully revised each August. It contains a wealth of current information including submission policies of many theaters, contests, and the like. It is the basic source of information for any playwright.
- *One Act: 11 Short Plays of the Modern Theatre*, Samuel Moon, ed., Peter Smith, Publisher. A good variety of twentieth-century short plays including some innovative work, but none more recent than the 1970s. At last report, still in print.
- *Twenty-Four Favorite One-Act Plays*, Catmell and Cerf, Doubleday. This paperback collection contains a variety of fairly traditional plays, from serious to light.

Publishers of Play Scripts

These publishers buy, print, and sell play scripts, both one-act and full-length. Since they deal largely with schools and regional companies, their selections tend to be conservative and easily playable. Each publisher puts out a catalogue describing its plays briefly.

- *Walter H. Baker Co.*, 100 Chancy St., Boston, MA 02111. In business since 1845, Bakers Plays offers not only a great many rather light comedies and mysteries, but also a number of serious dramas that have had Broadway success. Their scripts are relatively inexpensive and offer a good way to study plays not found in drama anthologies. They accept unsolicited manuscripts (that is, those not sent through agents).
- *The Dramatic Publishing Co.*, P.O. Box 129, Woodstock, IL 60098. Established in 1885, this company prints from 40 to 60 titles a year.
- *Samuel French, Inc*, 45 West 25th St., New York, NY 10010. The oldest (1830) of these three venerable publishing houses, Samuel French, Inc. has branches in England and Canada and publishes about 50 titles a year.

In addition to these publishers specializing in drama, many other houses print paperback editions of plays. Copies may be difficult to find, however, because few bookstores stock more than a sampling. The best solution is the same as for poetry and fiction: Start with the computer file in your library. Try specific titles listed here. Explore the "Subjects" file. If you want to order a copy, do so through your bookstore. They can tell you whether it is still in print. Or you can check first with the "Authors" section of *Books in Print* and order directly from the publisher (addresses in *LMP*).

Remember, finally, that if your interest is in play writing, it is essential that you see as many productions as you can. Whenever, combine your study of the script with the experience of seeing the work performed. Each approach will provide insights the other cannot.

A Final Note

If you are in college, it will seem as if you have no time to do anything but complete your assignments. And if you are out of college, it may seem that you are being swept along with the demands of daily life. We all like to believe that we "have no choice." But the fact is that the allocation of time is fundamentally a matter of personal choice. Consciously or unconsciously we set priorities. Serious writers allocate time not only to write but to expand their abilities and vision through these resources as well.

INDEX OF AUTHORS AND TITLES

CREDITS

"Coulda Woulda Shoulda" by Glenn Alterman. Copyright © 1996 by Glen Alterman. Reprinted with permission of the playwright.

"A Tribute to the Founder" (fragment) by Kingsley Amis from A LOOK ROUND THE ESTATE, Harcourt, Brace. Copyright © by Kingsley Amis 1962–67. Reprinted by permission of the author.

"This Winter Day" from OH PRAY MY WINGS ARE GONNA FIT ME WELL by Maya Angelou. Copyright © 1975 by Maya Angelou. Reprinted by permission of Random House Inc.

"Coast to Coast" by Philip Appleman from LET THERE BE LIGHT published by HarperCollins. Copyright © by Philip Appleman 1991. Reprinted by permission of Philip Appleman.

"Desire" by Philip Appleman from LET THERE BE LIGHT published by HarperCollins. Copyright © by Philip Appleman 1991. Reprinted by permission of Philip Appleman.

"Ice River" copyright © 1981 by David Baker. Reprinted by permission of the author and Ahsahta Press/Boise State University.

"Lust" by Steven Bauer © 1989 by Steven Bauer, from DAYLIGHT SAVINGS, A Peregrine Smith Book, Gibbs Smith. First published in *Denver Quarterly*. Reprinted by permission of the author.

"We Real Cool" by Gwendolyn Brooks, © 1991, from BLACKS, published by Third World Press, Chicago. Reprinted by permission of Gwendolyn Brooks.

"After Spring" (Chora) and "Even with Insects" (Issa) from CHERRY BLOSSOMS, JAPANESE HAIKU, SERIES III, translated by Peter Beilenson. © 1960 by Peter Pauper Press. Reprinted by permission of the publisher.

"What the Mirror Said" Copyright © 1978 by Lucille Clifton. Poem first appeared in *American Rag*, 1978. Reprinted by permission of Curtis Brown Ltd.

"Three Hearts" by Deborah Joy Corey, © 1998 by Deborah Joy Corey. Reprinted with the author's permission, FTW Publications, and *Story*. First appeared in *Story*, 1989.

"Buffalo Bill's" from TULIPS & CHIMNEYS by E. E. Cummings, edited by George James Firmage. Reprinted by permission of Liveright Publishing

GLOSSARY-INDEX

This section can be used both for a quick review of literary terms and as an index. The definitions are limited to the aspects discussed in the text. Numbers refer to pages and *ff.* means the discussion continues on following page(s). Words in small capitals indicate cross-reference in either the same or a closely related form; for example, METERED may be found under *Meter*, RHYMING under *Rhyme*. A few literary terms not used in this text have been included.

Abstraction, 6, 58ff. A word or phrase that refers to a concept or state of being. It is at the opposite end of a scale from *concrete* words, which refer to objects we can see and touch. *Peace* is an abstraction; *dove* is a concrete word.

Absurdist, 304, 312. See THEATER OF THE ABSURD.

Allegory, 250. A work in PROSE or VERSE in which characters, setting, and other details form an all-inclusive SYMBOLIC system. *Pilgrim's Progress* and George Orwell's *Animal Farm* are good examples.

Alliteration, 70, 84. See SOUND DEVICES.

Alliterative verse, 84. A RHYTHMICAL system based on a regular pattern of stressed syllables in each line without regard to the unstressed syllables. It usually employs a CAESURA in the middle of most lines. So-called because it traditionally makes regular use of *alliteration* (see SOUND DEVICES). Example: *Beowulf.*

Allusion. A reference, usually brief, to a familiar person or thing—often a detail from literature.

Ambiguity. A THEME or IMAGE in literature that has two or more possible meanings. *Intentional ambiguity* can be used effectively to expand thematic suggestion or increase RESONANCE by suggesting that two or more meanings are equally true or that they combine to suggest a third, broader conclusion. *Unintentional ambiguity* is a weakness usually resulting in confusion of intent or uncertainty in meaning.

Ambivalence, 44, 130, 267, 312. Contrasting emotions held at the same time. It may be expressed or implied by the writer or revealed in a character's attitude. Lack of ambivalence sometimes results in SIMPLE WRITING.

Analogy. See METAPHOR AND SIMILE.

Anapestic foot, 88. See METER.

Anaphora, 107. Repetition of a word or phrase at the beginning of two or more lines, sentences, or clauses. It is a common RHYTHMICAL technique in FREE VERSE and is also found in some PROSE, especially oratory.

Anecdote, 221, 252. A clever, sometimes humorous account usually told in conversation rather than written. Anecdotal FICTION tends to be SIMPLE, depending more on a twist of events (PLOT) than on CHARACTERIZATION.

Antagonist, 308. A character who opposes the PROTAGONIST in a NARRATIVE work.

Archaic diction, 53. Words that are associated primarily with an earlier period and are no longer in general use.

Arena theater, 344. See STAGE DESIGNS.

Assonance, 71, 79. See SOUND DEVICES.

Author's intrusion, 181. Any passage in FICTION written from the author's point of view (see MEANS OF PERCEPTION).

Automatic writing, 152. See STREAM OF CONSCIOUSNESS.

Ballad, 10, 97ff. A NARRATIVE POEM often (but not always) written in *ballad meter:* quatrains (see STANZAS) of alternating iambic tetrameter and trimeter (see LINE) with a RHYME SCHEME of *abcb. Folk ballads* are often intended to be sung and are relatively SIMPLE. *Literary ballads* are a SOPHISTICATED use of the old form.

Ballad meter, 97ff. See BALLAD.

Base time, 193. See PLOT.

Black theater, 363ff. Plays written by African-Americans. Although playwrights such as Langston Hughes and Ossie Davis wrote hundreds of works in the 1930s and 1940s, the term is most frequently used to refer to those who have come into prominence since the 1960s, such as Amiri Baraka, Paul Carter Harrison, Lonne Elder III, Adrienne Kennedy, and August Wilson.

Black verse. VERSE written by African-Americans such as Lucy Smith, David Henderson, Conrad Kent Rivers, Lucille Clifton (page 23), Maya Angelou (page 25), Gwendolyn Brooks (page 34), and Nikki Giovanni (page 26).

Blank verse. Unrhyming iambic pentameter (see METER).

Breath units, 112. See RHYTHM.

Caesura, 84. A pause or complete break in the RHYTHM of a LINE of VERSE, frequently occurring in the middle. It is particularly noticeable in Old English ALLITERATIVE VERSE (also see SOUND DEVICES) such as *Beowulf.* It is also found in metered VERSE.

Catalyst, 321. A minor, often undeveloped ("flat") character or an apparently minor event in drama or fiction that nonetheless advances the plot in some significant way or reveals some important piece of information.

Catastrophe, 305. See PLOT.

Central concern, 260ff., 357. See THEME.

Characterization, 142ff., 233ff., 315ff. The illusion in FICTION or DRAMA of having actually met someone. The illusion depends on consistency of details, complexity of insight, and individuality. SIMPLE characterization stresses consistency at the expense of complexity and often results in a STOCK CHARACTER or a *stereotype,* found in SIMPLE WRITING. Fully developed characters are called "round" and those that are not are called "flat."

Chronology, 193. See PLOT.

Cinquain. A five-line STANZA, also called QUINTET.

Cliché, 50ff., 148, 254. A METAPHOR or simile that has become so familiar from overuse that the vehicle (see METAPHOR) no longer contributes any meaning whatever to the tenor. It provides neither the vividness of a fresh metaphor nor the strength of a single, unmodified word. "Good as gold" and "crystal clear" are clichés in this specific sense. The word is also used to describe overused but nonmetaphorical expressions such as "tried and true" and "each and every."

Climax, 300. See PLOT.

Comedy, 366ff. DRAMA that is light in TONE and ends happily. Such plays are usually characterized by humor, wit, and occasionally satire. When comedy is used to lighten the TONE of a play, it is called *comic relief. Farce* is comedy in which characters and PLOT are exaggerated to an extreme, unreal degree for comic effect. Humor is often based on an incongruous situation while wit is more often verbal: jokes, puns, and plays on words.

Comic relief, 370. See COMEDY.

Commercial fiction, 146. FICTION that is SIMPLE and conforms to certain rigid CONVENTIONS of PLOT and CHARACTER, usually for the sake of publication and profit. Short story forms include the "pulps" (confessionals and romance periodicals such as *Romantic Interludes* and the "slicks" (*McCalls, Redbook, Ladies' Home Journal*), though such magazines occasionally publish sophisticated fiction as well. Novel types include "gothic," "romance," and "action thrillers" designed primarily for a mass market.

Conceit. A relatively elaborate or fanciful metaphor. The term is used both in a descriptive sense (as in the conceits of John Donne) or in a negative sense implying artificial complexity.

Concept, 299. A brief, factual description of a play (or film script) that explains the basic situation, some type of conflict or struggle, and the outcome. It is not to be confused with THEME, which describes in abstract terms that portion of a work which comments on the human condition.

Concrete poetry, 107. See SHAPED POETRY.

Concrete words, 58. See ABSTRACTION.

Conflict, 206ff., 308ff. See TENSION.

Connotation, 7. An unstated suggestion implied by a word, phrase, passage, or other element in a LITERARY work. The term ranges from the emotional *overtones* or implications of a word or phrase to the symbolic significance of a character, setting, or sequence of actions. It is contrasted with *denotation*, the literal meaning.

Consonance, 71. See SOUND DEVICES.

Convention, 11, 142, 239ff. Any pattern or device in LITERATURE that is repeated in a different works by a number of different writers. It is a broad term that includes basic devices like PLOT, DIALOGUE, the division of a play into acts and SCENES, and the FIXED FORMS of POETRY such as the SONNET and BALLAD. It also refers to recurring patterns in subject matter. Such conventions can be subtle or HACKNEYED. The term includes everything that is not unique in a work of LITERATURE.

Cooperative press, 385. See VANITY PRESS.

Cosmic irony, 128, 272. See IRONY.

Couplet, 73, 95. See STANZA.

Creative nonfiction, 250. Writing that blurs the distinction between FICTION and factual writing to produce partially fictionalized biography, autobiography, or historical account. It is occasionally called *nonfiction fiction*.

Creative writing, 139. Generally used to describe college courses in the writing of FICTION, poetry (see VERSE), and DRAMA, or any combination of these. It excludes courses in expository writing, assertive writing, and (usually) COMMERCIAL WRITING. Although all forms of writing require creativity in the broad sense, *creative writing* normally applies to the three more imaginative GENRES and in varying degrees make use of LITERARY techniques.

Crisis, 305. The turning point in a play at which the PROTAGONIST'S fortunes begin to fail.

Dactylic foot, 88. See METER.

Dead metaphor, 51. A METAPHOR (or by extension a simile) that has become so familiar that it no longer provides a visual impression and has become built into the language, as in *a current of electricity* or *stereotype*. Unlike a CLICHÉ, it has the strength and impact of an unmodified word.

Denotation, 71. See CONNOTATION.

Denouement, 305. See PLOT.

Density, 6ff., 267ff. The degree of compression in a poem, play, or work of fiction. High density means that a great deal is implied about character and/or THEME. The PACE may necessarily be slower. Low density reveals less but usually increases the pace.

Deus ex machina, 328. The use of an unexpected and improbable event to solve a problem in drama or fiction. Literally "a god out of a machine," it is an unconvincing turn of events. Occasionally it is used for comic effect.

Dialect, 240. DIALOGUE that echoes a regional or ethnic speech pattern. With some exceptions, it is achieved by word choice and word order rather than the obtrusive use of phonetic spelling.

Dialogue, 143, 238ff., 282. Any word, phrase, or passage that quotes a character's speech directly. In FICTION it normally appears in quotation marks to distinguish it from thoughts. *Monologue* is reserved for relatively lengthy and uninterrupted speeches. *Interior monologues* are directly quoted thoughts (usually written without quotation marks). *Indirect dialogue* in FIC-

TION (also called *indirect discourse*) echoes the phrasing of dialogue without actually quoting. *Soliloquies* are monologues spoken in plays.

Dialogue tag, 240. The phrase that identifies the speaker in fiction, such as "he said" or "she said." In twentieth-century fiction, the repeated use of "said" is preferred to alternatives such as "responded," "complained," or "cried out."

Diction, 265ff. The choice of words in any piece of writing. Diction is a significant factor in determining STYLE.

Dimeter, 89. See LINE.

Distance, 131, 194. An aspect of TONE that appears to suggest how close an author (or narrator) is to his or her fictional material. Highly autobiographical and apparently personal work gives the illusion of very little distance. TRANSFORMING the PROTAGONIST or the setting or adding an IRONIC or humorous TONE increases the distance.

Double rhyme, 74. See RHYME.

Drama, 282ff. A narrative presented by performers speaking and acting on a stage. Drama is generally a "dramatic art" (has emotional impact or force), a visual art, and an auditory art. In contrast to the written script, drama is presented physically on a stage, moves continuously, and is designed for spectators, not readers. A *script* is a written description of a play.

Dramatic conflict, 206ff. See TENSION.

Dramatic irony, 128, 271. See IRONY.

Dramatic monologue. A poem that is presented in the first person as if it were the speech or thoughts of a particular character or PERSONA. The speaker often unwittingly reveals aspects of his or her character or attitudes.

Dramatic question, 210ff., 282, 303. The emotional element in a play or work of FICTION that holds the attention of an audience or readers. An initial dramatic question is called a *hook*. Dramatic questions are relatively SIMPLE emotional appeals based on withheld information to generate curiosity or SUSPENSE. When dramatic questions are stressed at the expense of THEME or CHARACTERIZATION, the result is usually MELODRAMA.

Elizabethan sonnet, 98ff. See SONNET.

End-stopped line, 76, 91. See ENJAMBMENT.

Enjambment, 76, 91. LINES in VERSE in which either the grammatical construction or the meaning or both are continued from the end of one line to the next. One function of this technique is to mute the rhythmical effect of METER and/or RHYME. It is contrasted with *end-stopped* LINES, which are usually terminated with a period or a semicolon.

Epic poem, 6. A long NARRATIVE poem that deals with mythic and historical events such as the *Iliad* and *Beowulf*.

Epigram, 95. A brief and pithy saying in VERSE. It may appear as a portion of a longer poem (especially as a COUPLET) or as a short poem in itself. For example, Goldsmith's warning:

> Ill fares the land, to hastening ills a prey,
> Where wealth accumulates, and men decay.

Epiphany, 196, 206. A moment of awakening or discovery on the part of a FIC-TIONAL character, the reader, or both. Originally suggested by James Joyce, this term is generally limited to FICTION.

Exposition, 144. Factual writing as in an essay or report. In fiction, it refers to passages that give background information or commentary directly, not through action or dialogue. It is one of the five NARRATIVE MODES.

Expressionism, 335ff. See REALISTIC DRAMA.

Eye rhyme, 72. See RHYME.

Fable, 250. A short tale in which the characters are usually animals and the theme often suggests a moral. Aesop's fables are still a part of our culture. When the fable form is extended to make each character a part of an over-all symbolic system, the result is a type of ALLEGORY such as George Orwell's *Animal Farm.*

Falling action, 305. See PLOT.

Falling meter, 90. See METER.

Farce, 361ff. See COMEDY.

Feminine rhyme, 72. See RHYME.

Fiction, 140ff. Writing that tells an untrue story in PROSE. It may be SIMPLE, like most COMMERCIAL WRITING, or it may be SOPHISTICATED. Fiction is also subdi-vided loosely by length: *Short-short* stories (see page 145) are usually three to six typed, double-spaced pages; *short stories* are most often about 7 to 24 pp., *novellas* tend to be 50–150 pp.; *novels* are commonly 250 pp. and up. Complexity of PLOT tends to increase with length.

Figurative language, 62ff. See IMAGE.

Figure of speech, 59ff. See IMAGE.

First-person narration, 181ff. See PERSON.

Fixed forms, 94ff. Traditional VERSE forms that follow certain CONVENTIONS in METER, RHYME scheme, or syllabics (see RHYTHM). Examples: the BALLAD, SONNET, and HAIKU.

Flashback, 193ff. See PLOT.

Flash-forward, 194. See PLOT.

Flat character, 233. See CHARACTERIZATION.

Focus, 187. The character or characters who are the primary concern of a story. When it is a single individual, he or she is also referred to as the PROTAGO-NIST. In first-person fiction, however, the focus may be on a character other than the NARRATOR.

Foil, 305, 312. A secondary character in FICTION or DRAMA who sets off a pri-mary character by contrast in attitude, in appearance, or in other ways.

Foot, 88. See METER.

Formalism, 69. See NEW FORMALISM.

Formula, 148. Popular CONVENTIONS that characterize SIMPLE FICTION and DRAMA. These conventions are usually patterns of PLOT combined with STOCK CHAR-ACTERS. Sample: The-sincere-brunette who competes with The-scheming-blonde for the attentions of The-rising-young-executive who at first is "blind to the truth" but who finally "sees the light."

Frame story, 195. See PLOT.

Free verse, 3, 102ff. VERSE that is written without METER, depending instead on RHYTHMICAL patterns derived from TYPOGRAPHY, syntactical elements, the repetition of words and phrases, syllabics (see RHYTHM), or so-called breath units (see RHYTHM). Free verse contains no regular RHYME, depending instead on SOUND DEVICES such as assonance, consonance, and alliteration.

Genre, 1ff., 281ff. Any of several types of imaginative writing. In common usage, genres refer to FICTION, POETRY, and DRAMA. Classifications like "mysteries," "westerns," and "science fiction" are often referred to as *sub-genres* or *genre writing.*

Gimmick, 150. An unusual twist of PLOT or CHARACTERIZATION. This somewhat colloquial term is generally used in a pejorative sense to describe contrived, attention-getting details.

Hackneyed language, 51ff. A broad term that includes CLICHÉ as well as non-metaphorical phrases and words that have been weakened by overuse, such as "tried and true." Such language is closely associated with SENTI-MENTALITY and with STOCK CHARACTERS.

Haiku, 85, 94. Originally a Japanese VERSE form. In English it is usually written as a three-line poem containing five syllables in the first LINE, seven in the second, and five in the third. Traditionally they draw on some aspect of nature and either state or imply a particular season.

Heptameter, 89. See LINE.

Hero, 302, 309. See PROTAGONIST.

Hexameter, 89. See LINE.

Hook, 210. See DRAMATIC QUESTION.

Horizontal rhythm, 105. See RHYTHM.

Hyperbole, 62. A figure of speech (see IMAGE) employing extreme exaggeration, usually in the form of a simile or METAPHOR.

Iambic foot, 88. The most popular type of METER in English (ta-*TUM*).

Image, 5, 59ff., 120ff., 254. An item that can be perceived by one of the five senses. The most common are visual details. Closely related images used near each other, they are called an *image cluster* (p. 65). Images may be used literally, as a SYMBOL, or in a figure of speech. A figure of speech (also called *figurative language*) uses an image in a stated or implied comparison. METAPHORS are the most common figures of speech. Other figures of speech include similes, PUNS, HYPERBOLE, and SYNECDOCHE.

Image cluster, 65ff., 120. See IMAGE.

In medias res, 210. Literally. "in the middle of things." Fiction that begins abruptly in the middle of an ongoing plot.

Indirect discourse, 240. See DIALOGUE.

Interior monologue, 268, See DIALOGUE.

Internal rhyme, 79. See RHYME.

Irony, 126ff., 271ff. A reversal in which (a) a literal statement is knowingly or unknowingly the opposite from the intended meaning or (b) an event is surprisingly or dramatically different from reasonable expectations. The first general type involves words and can take two forms. One is *verbal* or *conscious* irony, in which the author or a character makes a statement that he or she knows is the opposite of the intended meaning (like saying, "Great day for a sail" during a hurricane). It is similar to sarcasm. The second is *dramatic irony*, in which a character *unknowingly* makes a statement that is the opposite of the true situation or events to come. The second general type involves events, not words. It is called *cosmic irony* or *irony of fate*. Here an event is dramatically opposite normal expectations (like the firefighter who dies from smoking in bed).

Italian sonnet, 99. See SONNET.

Legitimate theater, 281. Plays performed by actors on a stage as contrasted with television DRAMA, cinema, and the like.

Line, 2ff., 89ff. A unit of VERSE that when printed usually appears without being broken, the length being determined by the poet alone. The inclusion of the line as a part of the art form rather than merely a printer's concern is one of the fundamental distinctions between VERSE and PROSE. In metered VERSE, all lines usually contain the same number of *feet* (see METER); in *sprung rhythm* and *alliterative* VERSE, lines are linked by having the same number of stressed syllables; and in FREE VERSE, the length of lines is more of a visual concern (see TYPOGRAPHY). The following terms represent eight types of lines used in metered verse: (1) monometer (one foot), (2) dimeter (two feet), (3) trimeter (three feet), (4) tetrameter (four feet), (5) pentameter (five feet), (6) hexameter (six feet), (7) heptameter (seven feet), (8) octometer (eight feet).

Literary, 7. Writing in PROSE or VERSE in which style, suggestion, and implication are developed with some degree of conscious care. Such work is differentiated from purely factual and utilitarian writing such as reports, news items, and scientific articles, as well as from personal writing such as diaries, letters, and journals. In this text, the term SOPHISTICATED WRITING is often used as a synonym for *literary writing* to avoid implying a value judgment.

Local color, 218. See REGIONALISM.

Lyric, 70, 88. Originally a Greek term referring to VERSE that is to be accompanied by a lyre. Today it generally refers to a relatively brief, subjective poem expressing a strongly felt emotion. Thus, poems of love, deep feeling, observation, and contemplation are *lyrics* in contrast to BALLADS and other types of NARRATIVE POETRY. *Lyrical* is often used loosely to describe poetry that sounds musical because of its SOUND DEVICES and RHYTHM.

Means of perception, 180ff. The agent through whose eyes a piece of FICTION appears to be presented. This character is also the one whose thoughts are revealed directly. The term is synonymous with *point of view* and *viewpoint*. In short fiction it is generally limited to a single character.

Melodrama, 132, 149, 211, 308. SIMPLE WRITING (usually DRAMA or FICTION) that is dominated by SUSPENSE and exaggerated forms of dramatic TENSION. It usually makes use of STOCK CHARACTERS as well. SOPHISTICATED LITERATURE also uses conflict, but melodrama does it blatantly and at the expense of other literary concerns.

Metafiction, 250. Fiction that refers to the act of writing. It tends to be less concerned with realism than with commentary on the genre itself. John Barth's story "Lost in the Funhouse" is a classic example.

Metamorphosis, 155. Same as TRANSFORMATION.

Metaphor and Simile, 59ff., 254ff. A *simile* is a figure of speech (see IMAGE) in which one item (usually an abstraction) is compared with another (usually a concrete noun) that is different in all but a few significant respects. The comparison (a type of *analogy*) uses *like* or *as*. Thus, "She fought like a lion" suggests courage but not the use of claws and teeth. The item being described (the woman) is called the *tenor*, and the one introduced merely for comparison (the lion) is the *vehicle*. A *metaphor* implies rather than states a similar comparison without using *like* or *as*. Since it is literally untrue, it often has more impact than a simile: "She was a lion when fighting for civil rights." A SYMBOL is achieved when the vehicle is an actual object or event and the tenor is implied: "Historically, lions, not lambs, have achieved social change." The sentence describes the vehicle as an actual lion; the tenor, courage and determination, is implied. Thus *lion* is used symbolically.

Meter, 86ff. See table on p. 89. A system of STRESSED and unstressed syllables that creates RHYTHM in certain types of verse. The CONVENTIONALIZED units of stressed and unstressed syllables are known as *feet*. Metered verse normally contains the same number of feet in each LINE and the same type of foot throughout the poem. The effect is usually muted by occasional substitution of other types of feet. If the pattern ends on a stressed syllable, it is called *rising meter;* if the pattern ends on an unstressed syllable, it is called *falling meter.*

Mixed metaphor, 61. A METAPHOR that is internally confusing or illogical because the two vehicles (see METAPHOR) are contradictory. Example: "The bitter taste of rejection rang in his ears."

Modes, 143, 268ff. See NARRATIVE MODES.

Monologue, 311. See DIALOGUE.

Multiple flashback, 195. See PLOT.

Narrative, 84, 96, 119ff. Any work that tells a story (see FICTION, DRAMA, NARRATIVE POETRY).

Narrative modes, 143, 268ff. The five methods by which FICTION can be presented: DIALOGUE, thoughts, action, description, and EXPOSITION. Most writers use all five in varying proportions.

Narrative poetry, 84, 96, 119ff. VERSE that tells a story. This may take the form of the BALLAD, the EPIC, or a tale in verse such as Hecht's "Lizards and Snakes" (p. 35).

Narrator, 119ff., 183, 186. A character who appears to be telling a story, novel, or narrative poem. He or she may be clearly identified as in first-person writing (see MEANS OF PERCEPTION) or implied as in most third-person writing. A narrator is often but not always the PROTAGONIST.

Neutral style, 263. See STYLE.

New formalism, 69. A recent poetic movement (starting in the 1980s) based on a renewed interest in metrical forms and, often, innovative use of such forms. Also called *neo-formalism.*

Nonrealistic drama, 328ff. See REALISTIC DRAMA.

Nonrecurrent stanzas, 105. STANZAS of unequal length often used in FREE VERSE. They serve some of the same functions as paragraphs in PROSE.

Novel, 145. See FICTION.

Novella, 145. See FICTION.

Occasional verse, 10, 75. VERSE written for a particular occasion such as an anniversary, birthday, death, or dedication. It may be simple and comic or serious.

Octave, 89ff. An eight-lined STANZA in METERED VERSE. Also the first eight lines of a SONNET.

Octometer, 89. See LINE.

Ode. A LYRIC poem, usually serious and metered, commemorating or honoring a person, place, or event.

Off rhyme, 77. See RHYME.

Omniscient point of view, 182. The MEANS OF PERCEPTION in which the author enters the mind of all major characters. *Limited omniscience* restricts the means of perception to certain characters. Most short FICTION and many novels limit the means of perception to a single character.

Onomatopoeia, 71. See SOUND DEVICES.

Orientation, 213ff. The sense in FICTION, DRAMA, or NARRATIVE POETRY of being somewhere specific. A more general term than SETTING, it includes awareness of geography, historical period, season, and time.

Overtone, 1. See CONNOTATION.

Overwriting, 266. FICTION or VERSE that is overblown, excessive in phrasing, or overly modified. Also called *purple prose.* It is the opposite of a sparse STYLE.

Oxymoron, An apparent contradiction presented either as a figure of speech (see IMAGE) as in Roethke's "I wake to sleep" or as a simple phrase such as "a silent scream" or "cruel kindness."

Pace, 197ff., 304. The reader's sense that a story or play either moves rapidly or drags. This is determined by the RATE OF REVELATION and by the STYLE.

Paradox, 127, 304. A statement that on one level is logically absurd yet on another level implies a reasonable assertion. Example from Heller's *Catch 22:* "The Texan turned out to be good-natured, generous, and likable. In three days no one could stand him."

Parody, FICTION, DRAMA, or VERSE that imitates another work, usually but not necessarily for comic effect. Often the form is similar but the characters or plot is altered.

Passive voice. Grammatical construction in which the subject is hidden: "Mistakes were made" as opposed to the active construction, "I made a mistake." Use of passive construction tends to weaken one's STYLE.

Pathos. Work that evokes a feeling of sympathy or pity. Unsuccessful, excessive, or insincere pathos produces *bathos*.

Pentameter, 89. See LINE.

Person, 185ff. Any of several methods of presenting fiction: (a) First person ("I") gives the illusion of a story being told directly by a character either in neutral style or "as-if-told." (b) Third person ("he" or "she") is equally popular. (c) The "you" form reads as if the reader is being addressed directly. It is rarely used. (d) The "they" form is used least of all. *Person* is *how* a story is presented; the MEANS OF PERCEPTION is *who* appears to present it.

Persona, 130, 140ff. Broadly, a character in a poem, story, or play. The term is frequently used to identify a fictitious NARRATOR (implied or identified) in a poem.

Personification. Attributing human characteristics to inanimate objects, as in "the merry breezes."

Petrarchan sonnet, 98. See SONNET.

Plot, 142, 193ff., 356ff. The sequence of events, often divided into SCENES, in FICTION, DRAMA, or NARRATIVE POETRY. It may be chronological, or it may be nonchronological in any of four ways: By *flashback* (inserting an earlier scene), by *multiple flashbacks*, by a *flash-forward* (rare), or by using a *frame* (beginning and ending with the same scene). *Base time* refers to the primary plot from which flashbacks and, less often, flash-forwards depart. A *subplot* is a secondary plot that echoes or amplifies the main plot or provides comic relief. In traditional drama the increasing complications are called *rising action*, the turning point is the *climax*, which is followed by *falling action*, which in turn leads to the final *catastrophe* (also called the *denouement*), often the death of the PROTAGONIST. Contemporary drama (and some fiction) often follows modified versions of this structure, frequently treating the death in a symbolic rather than literal manner.

Poetic, 2ff. In addition to being an adjective for *poetry* (see VERSE), this term is used to describe fiction or drama that makes special use of RHYTHM, SOUND DEVICES, figurative language (see IMAGE), SYMBOL, and compression of meaning and implication.

Poetry, 1ff. See VERSE.

Point of view, 181ff. See MEANS OF PERCEPTION.

Premise Fiction, 249. Nonrealistic fiction based on a single, clear, as-if element as in much science fiction.

Private symbol, 65, 256. See SYMBOL.

Prose, 2. Writing in which the length of the LINES is not determined by the author and so has nothing to do with statement or form. Prose also tends to be less concerned with RHYTHM, SOUND DEVICES, and compression of statement than is VERSE. Prose fiction usually (but not always) depends on a NARRATIVE to hold interest.

Prose poetry, 112. A hybrid literary form in which the writer maintains control over line length as in VERSE but generally ignores other poetic devices such as a regular RHYTHMICAL SYSTEM, SOUND DEVICES, and figurative language (see IMAGE).

Prose rhythm, 109. RHYTHM created in PROSE and oratory often through the use of ANAPHORA.

Prosody. The construction of a poem (see VERSE) including SCANSION (metrical scheme), stanzaic patterns (see STANZA), DICTION, phrasing, and the like.

Protagonist, 157, 308. The main character in a piece of FICTION, a play, or a NARRATIVE POEM. This character is often opposed by an *antagonist*. The term is broader than *hero*, which suggests greatness. Protagonists who are base or ignoble are sometimes referred to as *antiheroes*.

Public symbols, 65, 256. See SYMBOL.

Pun, 62. A figure of speech (see IMAGE) in which two different but significantly related meanings are attached to a single word. Most SOPHISTICATED uses of the pun are a form of METAPHOR with a vehicle (see METAPHOR) that has two meanings, as in Dylan Thomas' "some grave truth."

Purple prose, 266. A colloquial synonym for OVERWRITING.

Pyrrhic foot, 89. See METER.

Quatrain, 75, 97. See STANZA.

Quintet. See STANZA.

Rate of revelation, 197. The rate at which new information or insights are given to the reader regarding CHARACTER, THEME, or PLOT. It is one of the primary factors that determine PACE of FICTION, DRAMA, or NARRATIVE POETRY.

Realism, 249. Narrative in which characters, events, and settings are similar to those in everyday life. In fiction this is contrasted with *fantasy, science fiction*, ALLEGORICAL fiction, and most METAFICTION. To avoid the notion that a literary work should conform slavishly to daily life, some prefer the word *verisimilitude*, the *illusion* of reality. Thus, Kafka's dreamlike scenes "seem real" without being conventionally realistic.

Realistic drama, 328ff. DRAMA in which, like realistic fiction, characters, events, and settings are similar to those in everyday life. Costume, set, and PLOT conform to what we see in daily life. This is opposed to *nonrealistic drama*, which creates its own world in somewhat the same manner as a dream. *Expressionism* is sometimes used as a synonym for nonrealistic drama, but more strictly it refers to a dramatic school culminating in the 1920s and 1930s with the works of O'Neill, Rice, and others.

Refrain, 121. A phrase, LINE, or STANZA that is repeated periodically in a poem.

Regionalism, 218. FICTION and VERSE that draw on the customs, traditions, attitudes, and occasionally the DICTION of a particular geographic region. It is a more contemporary term than *local color* writing, a term that is tainted by certain nineteenth-century authors who adopted the patronizing TONE of an outsider.

Resonance, 65, 120. That aspect of TONE in SOPHISTICATED WRITING that is created by the use of SYMBOLIC and suggestive details. It is a layering of meaning and implication not found in SIMPLE WRITING. Resonance adds to the DENSITY of a work.

Rhyme, 71ff. Two or more words in poetry (see VERSE) that are linked because their final syllables sound alike. In *true rhyme* the matching sounds must be identical and the sound of the preceding accented vowels in each word must be unlike. *Slant rhyme* and *off-rhyme* use similar rather than identical vowel sounds. *Double rhyme*, also called *feminine rhyme*, is a two-syllable rhyme as in "running" and "sunning." In an *eye rhyme* (also called *sight rhyme*) the words look alike but sound different (like *have* and *grave*). *Rhyme scheme* is a pattern of rhymed endings that is repeated regularly in each STANZA of metered (see METER) VERSE. *End rhymes* are placed at the ends of lines while *internal rhyme* links two or more rhyming words within the same line.

Rhyme schemes, 69. See RHYME.

Rhythm, 4, 82ff. A systematic variation in the flow of sound. Traditional rhythms include established patterns such as METER, *alliterative verse*, and *syllabic* verse. Unique rhythms are those created uniquely for a particular poem, as in FREE VERSE. In METERED VERSE, rhythm is achieved through a repeated pattern of stressed and unstressed syllables. In *alliterative* VERSE, the pattern is determined by the number of stresses in each line without regard for the unstressed syllables. In *syllabic verse*, the number of syllables in any one line matches the number in the corresponding line of each of the other STANZAS. In FREE VERSE, rhythms are achieved by TYPOGRAPHY, repeated syntactical patterns, and breath units. Rhythms in PROSE are achieved by repetition of key words and phrases known as ANAPHORA. Variations in line length (both left and right margins) and extra spacing within the line create what are called *horizontal rhythms*. Space between lines creates *vertical rhythms*.

Rising action, 305. See PLOT.

Rising meter, 90. See METER.

Round character, 233. See CHARACTERIZATION.

Run-on line, 91. See ENJAMBMENT.

Sarcasm, 127, 271. See IRONY.

SASE, 381. "Self-addressed stamped envelope," which should accompany any submission you wish returned.

Satire, 128, 272ff., 353, 367, 369ff. A form of wit in which a distorted view of characters, places, or institutions is used for the purpose of criticism or ridicule. At least some exaggeration (if only through a biased selection of details) is necessary for satire to be effective.

Scanning, 88. The analysis of METER in metered VERSE, identifying the various feet (see METER) and the type of LINE used.

Scansion, 88, 90. The noun that refers to SCANNING.

Scene, 191ff., 300ff. In DRAMA, (a) a formal subdivision of an *act* marked in the script and indicated to the audience by lowering the curtain or dimming the lights, or (b) a more subtle subdivision of the PLOT suggested by the exit or entrance of a character. The former are here called *primary scenes* and the latter *secondary*. In FICTION, the scene is a less precise unit of action marked either by a shift in the number of characters or a shift in time or place.

Sentimentality, 132, 150. A form of SIMPLE WRITING that is dominated by a blunt appeal to the emotions of pity and love. It does so at the expense of subtlety and LITERARY SOPHISTICATION. Popular subjects are puppies, grandparents, and young lovers.

Septet. A seven-line STANZA.

Sestet, sextet, 98ff. A six-line STANZA in metered VERSE. Also the last six lines of the SONNET.

Set, 343ff. See SETTING.

Setting, 143ff., 213ff., 332. Strictly, the geographic area in which a PLOT takes place; but more generally, the time of day, the season, and the social environment as well. It is a more precise term than ORIENTATION. In DRAMA the setting is usually specified at the beginning of the script. What the audience sees on the stage (excluding the actors) is the set. Set design of *The Collection* appears on pages 346–347.

Shaped poetry, 106. VERSE in which TYPOGRAPHY is employed in an extreme fashion to make the lines, words, and word fragments suggest a shape or picture that becomes of greater importance than RHYTHM or sound. Also called *concrete poetry.*

Short-short story, 145. See FICTION.

Short story, 145. See FICTION.

Simile, 59, 254. See METAPHOR.

Simple writing, 7ff., 140ff. Writing in which the intent is made blatant, the STYLE is limited to a single effect, or the TONE is limited to a single emotion. It includes the adventure and horror story (MELODRAMA), many love stories, most greeting-card verse (SENTIMENTALITY), most patriotic VERSE and politically partisan FICTION and DRAMA (propaganda), and that which is single-mindedly sexual or sadistic (pornography). It also includes work that is so personal or so obscure that it remains unintelligible even to conscientious readers. Antonyms for *simple* are SOPHISTICATED and LITERARY.

Slant rhyme, 72, 77. See RHYME.

Sonnet, 98. A METERED and RHYMED FIXED-FORM poem of fourteen LINES, usually in iambic pentameter (see LINE). The Italian or Petrarchan sonnet is often rhymed *abba, abba; ede, ede.* The first eight lines are known as the OCTAVE and the last six as the SESTET. The Elizabethan sonnet (see Shakespeare's "Sonnet 29," page 19) is often thought of as three quatrains and a final rhyming COUPLET: *abab, eded, efef gg.*

Sophisticated writing, 7ff., 140ff. Writing in which the intent is complex with implications and ramifications, the STYLE makes rich use of the techniques available, and the TONE has a range of suggestion. A value-free synonym for LITERARY WRITING, it is the opposite of SIMPLE WRITING. Not to be confused with the popular use of *sophisticated.*

Sound devices, 4, 70ff. The technique of linking two or more words by *alliteration* (similar initial sounds), *assonance* (similar vowel sounds), *consonance* (similar consonantal sounds), *onomatopoeia* (similarity between the sound of the word and the object or action it describes), or RHYME. In addition, *sound clusters* link groups of words with related vowel sounds that are too disparate to be called true samples of assonance.

Spondaic foot, 89. See METER.

Stage business, 353. Minor action or facial expressions on the part of an actor, often not included in the script.

Stage designs, 344ff. The *conventional stage* has a raised playing area that is located behind a *proscenium arch* from which a curtain is lowered between acts and SCENES. The effect is like seeing a performance in an elaborate picture frame. *Theater in the round, theater in the square,* and *arena theater* place the action in a central arena with the audience seated on all sides. Compromise designs include a variety of apron stages with the audience on three sides.

Stanza, 73ff., 95ff. Normally, a regularly recurring group of lines in a poem that are separated by spaces and frequently (though not necessarily) unified by a metrical system and by rhyme. Common forms include the *couplet* (two lines); *tercet* or *triplet* (three lines); *quatrain* (four lines); *quintet* or *cinquain* (five lines); SESTET or *sextet* (six lines); *septet* (seven lines); OCTAVE (eight lines). The term is occasionally applied to irregular units in FREE VERSE, which are used more like paragraphs in PROSE.

Stereotype, 310. See STOCK CHARACTER.

Stock character, 148ff. Characters in FICTION or DRAMA that are SIMPLE and also conform to one of a number of types that have appeared over such a long period and in so many different works that they are familiar to readers and audiences. Their DIALOGUE is often HACKNEYED. Minor characters are often stock types, but when major characters appear so, the work as a whole may be SIMPLE as opposed to SOPHISTICATED. Also known as *stereotypes* or *"flat"* as opposed to *"round"* characters.

Stock situation. A situation in FICTION or DRAMA that is too familiar to have freshness or impact.

Stream of consciousness, 152. FICTION appearing to resemble a character's thoughts quoted directly without exposition. Although wandering and disjointed, the technique is designed to reveal character. This is in sharp contrast to *automatic writing,* in which the writer's goal is not CHARACTERIZATION (or even FICTION), but self-exploration.

Stress, 4, 83. In metered VERSE, the relative force or emphasis placed on a particular syllable. In the word "awake," for example, the second syllable is stressed. See METER.

Style, 263ff. The manner in which a work is written. It is determined by the author's decisions, both conscious and unconscious, regarding DICTION (the type of words used), SYNTAX (the type of sentences), NARRATIVE MODE (relative importance of DIALOGUE, thoughts, action, description, and EXPOSITION), and PACE (the reader's sense of progress). It is closely connected with TONE. *Neutral style* is that in which no one technique is pronounced.

Subplot, 306. See PLOT.

Substitution, 91. The technique in METERED VERSE of occasionally replacing a foot (see METER) that has become the standard in a particular poem with some other type of foot. A common form of substitution is the use of a trochee for emphasis in a poem that is generally iambic.

Suspense, 182, 211. A heightened form of curiosity that creates excitement and a sense of drama. In moderation, it provides effective TENSION. When excessive, it turns a work into MELODRAMA.

Syllabics, 84ff. See RHYTHM.

Symbol, 63ff., 256ff., 348. Any verbal detail such as an object, action, or state, that has a range of meaning beyond and usually larger than itself. *Public symbols* are those that have become a part of the general consciousness: the flag, the cross, Uncle Sam, and the like. *Private* (or *unique*) symbols are those devised by individual writers for a particular work. Usually the reader is first introduced to the *vehicle* (see METAPHOR) and then perceives the *tenor* as an additional or expanded meaning. This device is in contrast to similes and METAPHORS, in which the vehicle is introduced merely to serve as a comparison and has no other function.

Synecdoche, 62. A FIGURE OF SPEECH in which a part is used for the whole. "Many hands," for example, suggests many people; "bread for the poor" suggests food generally.

Syntactical rhythm, 107, 110. See RHYTHM.

Syntax, 110, 264, 266. Sentence structure; the arrangement of words in the sentence. It is sometimes used to create RHYTHM in FREE VERSE and a distinctive STYLE in FICTION.

Tag, 240. See DIALOGUE TAG.

Tenor, 61, 255ff. See METAPHOR.

Tense, 269ff. The verb form used in FICTION. The past tense ("She ran to the window") is traditional in fiction, but the present tense ("She runs to the window") is increasingly popular. The past perfect ("She had run to the window an hour before the explosion") is often used briefly to introduce a flashback (see PLOT).

Tension, 130, 205ff. A force and a counterforce within a work of LITERATURE. In FICTION, DRAMA, and NARRATIVE POETRY it can be created through conflict between a character and another character, a group, an aspect of nature, or an inner struggle. It can also be generated when the writer withholds information to arouse the reader's curiosity or a sense of suspense. In VERSE, tension is more often generated by a contrast or conflict in THEME, TONE, or both. It is tension that provides a sense of vitality in a work.

Tercet, 74, 96. See STANZA.

Terza rima, 75, 97. A traditional VERSE form consisting of iambic pentameter tercets (see STANZA) in which each stanza is linked to the next through a rhyme scheme of *aba bcb cdc* etc.

Tetrameter, 89. See LINE.

Theater in the round, 344. See STAGE DESIGNS.

Theater of the absurd, 304, 329, 335. A somewhat loosely defined dramatic "school" in the *expressionistic* (see REALISTIC DRAMA) tradition beginning in the 1950s. Shared convictions: that life is "absurd" in the sense of lacking ultimate meaning and that the intellect cannot determine truth. Shared techniques: the use of nonrealistic situations, SATIRE, and a tendency to develop a static quality rather than a DRAMATIC PLOT. Examples include works by Ionesco, Beckett, Pinter, and some by Albee, Genet, and Adamov.

Theme, 117, 143ff., 259ff., 299, 356ff The primary statement, suggestion, or implication of a LITERARY work. It describes that portion of a work that comments on the human condition. Same as *central concern*. It does not have the moral implications of *message* nor the didactic element of *thesis*. A thesis states or clearly implies a particular conviction or recommends a specific course of action. Theses are often propagandistic. Most SOPHISTICATED WRITING is unified loosely by a theme rather than a thesis.

Thesis, 357, 362ff. See THEME.

Third-person narration, 181. See PERSON.

Tone, 123ff., 131ff., 270ff. The emotional quality of a LITERARY work itself and of the author's implicit attitude toward the work as well. Some prefer to separate the two aspects of this definition, but most writers think of them as two forms of the same quality. Tone is described with adjectives like "exciting," "sad," "merry," " eerie," or "depressing" as well as with terms like "satiric," "sardonic," "ironic," and "dramatic."

Traditional rhythm, 82ff. See RHYTHM.

Transformation, 155ff., 168ff. Radical alteration of an experience or of an early draft of a story or play in order to create fresh LITERARY work. (Also called *metamorphosis*.) It is far more basic than *revision*. This process can be either conscious or unconscious. It is usually employed either to clarify existing patterns, to break up patterns that appear to be too neat or contrived, or to help a writer regain control over an experience that is still too personal to develop in LITERARY form.

Trimeter, 89. See LINE.

Triplet, 74, 69 See STANZA.

Trochaic foot, 88. See METER.

True rhyme, 71. See RHYME.

Truism, 117. A statement that reiterates a well-known truth; a platitude.

Typography, 103ff. The technique in VERSE (and particularly FREE VERSE) of arranging words, phrases, and lines on the printed page to create a RHYTHMICAL effect. When used to an extreme degree to create a picture, it is called SHAPED POETRY.

Unique rhythm, 83, 102ff. See RHYTHM.

Vanity press, 385. A commercial publisher who charges the author a part or all of the printing costs. Regular commercial publishers assume all costs themselves and pay the author an advance and a percentage (generally between 10% and 15%) of the sales. *Cooperative presses*, in contrast, are usually nonprofit and share the expense with the author or poet.

Vehicle, 61, 255ff. See METAPHOR.

Verbal irony, 126, 271. See IRONY.

Verisimilitude, 249. See REALISM.

Verse, 1ff. The form of LITERARY writing that uses line length as an aspect of the art form and is typically concerned with SOUND, RHYTHM, and compression of language. The word *verse* is occasionally used as a synonym for LINE, STANZA, or REFRAIN. Although *verse* is often a general synonym for *poetry*, many prefer that the term *poetry* be limited to verse that is SOPHISTICATED.

Vertical rhythm, 105. See RHYTHM.

Viewpoint, 180ff. See MEANS OF PERCEPTION.

Villanelle, 100ff. A French verse form of nineteen lines in iambic pentameter (see LINE) divided into five tercets (see STANZA) and a final four-line STANZA with only two rhymes, in this pattern: *aba aba aba aba aba abaa.* Line 1 is a REFRAIN that is repeated entirely as lines 6, 12, and 18; and line 3 is repeated to form lines 9, 15, and 19. One of the challenges of this form (other than the mechanics) is to give subtly different meanings to the repeated lines. An example: "The Waking" by Theodore Roethke, p. 31.

Visual rhythm, 103ff. See TYPOGRAPHY.

Voice, 266. A writer's implied relationship with his or her narrator. In first-person works, the range varies from autobiographical or confessional to works that appear to be presented through a PERSONA. Voice determines the DISTANCE between narrator and writer and is a major factor in determining the TONE of the work.

White space, 105. The margins of a poem, the extra spaces between words, and the extra space left between lines. These may be used as visual devices in establishing RHYTHM in poetry.